Peace Movement Directory

ALSO BY JAMES RICHARD BENNETT

*Political Prisoners and Trials: A Worldwide
Annotated Bibliography, 1900 through 1993*
(McFarland, 1995)

Peace Movement Directory

North American Organizations, Programs, Museums and Memorials

JAMES RICHARD BENNETT

McFarland & Company, Inc., Publishers
Jefferson, North Carolina, and London

Library of Congress Cataloguing-in-Publication Data

Bennett, James Richard, 1932–
Peace movement directory : North American organizations, programs, museums and memorials / James Richard Bennett.
p.   cm.
Includes bibliographical references and index.
ISBN 0-7864-1006-X (softcover : 50# alkaline paper) ∞
1. Peace movements—North America—Directories.   2. Peace—Museums—North America—Directories.   3. Peace—Societies, etc.—Directories.   I. Title.
JZ5514.B46 2001   327.1'72'0257—dc21   2001030569

British Library cataloguing data are available

Manufactured in the United States of America

*McFarland & Company, Inc., Publishers
Box 611, Jefferson, North Carolina 28640
www.mcfarlandpub.com*

ACKNOWLEDGMENTS

This directory is a collaboration between the compiler and the hundreds of people who supplied me with information—not only the officers of the organizations, programs, museums, and memorials, but the many secretaries, spouses, and friends who responded to my queries. I especially want to thank John MacLeod, who provided considerable information regarding Canadian peace gardens, and whose visit to Fayetteville, Arkansas, in January 2000 to discuss peace parks energized the project; and Cliff Hughes, who generously assisted during the final weeks with the index. Others who helped in special ways with photos, information, or personal assistance include: Jo Bristah, Rhett Baird, Martin and Ruth Tucker, Joy Fox, Bettina Lehovec, Lewis Randa, Marjorie Wunder, Elbert Hilliard, David Smead, Jo Bennett, Annabelle Patton, the Rev. Thomas Kearns, Steven Jonas, M.D., Marlene McMahon, Lucy Nichol, Bettie Lu Lancaster, Floyd Schmoe, Beverley Delong, Alva Robinson, Koozma Tarasoff, Sandra Taylor, Enid McKenzie and Anthony Hunt. To the many others unnamed who freely offered me information and photos, I thank you.

CONTENTS

PREFACE

Arrangement

Entries are listed in alphabetical order by state or province in the United States, Canada, and Mexico, then by cities in alphabetical order in each state or province, and then in each city the individual organizations, college programs, museums, journals, and memorials also in alphabetical order.

I. United States: states in alphabetical order, cities within each state, and memorials and organizations in alphabetical order in each city.

II. United States and Canadian Border: from east to west.

III. Canada: provinces in alphabetical order, and again cities and memorials and organizations.

IV. United States and Mexican Border.

V. Mexico: same arrangement.

All entries are listed according to their name in English, except for those in Québec and Mexico, where the French and Spanish names, respectively, come first, followed by the name in English. For example: Le monument des jeunes pour la paix et le désarmement/Youth Monument for Peace and Disarmament. The title/topic index gives the name of all organizations, college programs, museums, journals, and memorials included in the directory and an extensive subject listing with cross-references. This reference work contains approximately 1,400 entries, of which about 230 are memorials and about 1,170 are organizations (including museums). Thus the directory with index provides readers with an encyclopedic reference to the peace movement in North America by state or province, city, organization, and subject/activity.

The major sources consulted in the compilation of this directory include *Encyclopedia of Associations, Housmans Peace Diary 1999 with World Peace Directory, COPRED's Global Directory of Peace Studies and Conflict Resolution Programs, 2000 Edition,* numerous Internet links and directories of the affiliates of national organizations (Quakers, Fellowship of Reconciliation, Peace Action, Catholic Worker, etc.). In addition, letters requesting information were sent to all governors of states and provinces and to mayors of many cities.

How to Interpret Directory Listings

The first line contains the following: (1) Entry Number; (2) Name of Organization, College, Museum, Memorial, or Journal; (3) Year Founded or Dedicated. An accompanying question mark indicates estimated year; (4) Type: Each entry is identified on the first line as org (organization), porg (for profit organization), col (college), mus (museum), jour (journal), lib (library), or mem (memorial). Each org, porg, col, mus, jour, and lib is also starred to distinguish it from memorials.

On the second line the following information is provided: (1) Address; (2) Phone Number; (3) E-mail Address; (4) Web Site (http:// or www.).

The text includes information on organizations (their mission, activities, publications and director) and peace studies/conflict resolution programs (degree offered, courses, publications, director).

GENERAL AND UNITED STATES INTRODUCTION

by James Richard Bennett

Blessed are the peacemakers: for they shall be called the children of God. —Jesus

Those of us who love peace must learn to organize as effectively as those who love war.
—Martin Luther King, Jr.

To prevent war, to prevent the next crisis, we must begin right now. —Thich Nhat Hanh

Personal and Public Peacemaking

Meditative retreats (for example, the Vajrapani Institute, Wattle Hollow), activist organizations like WAND and Peace Action, and peace studies/conflict resolution programs at colleges share peaceful purposes. They hope to reconstitute the self and the structures of the world which inhibit our peaceful self-realization. Inseparable and collaborative, this personal and public nonviolent crusade to prevent the destruction of the future—from Anchorage, Vancouver, and Halifax, to Chiapas and Mexico City, and all over the world—inspires hope.

Nonviolence and the North American Peace Movement

In the word Satyagraha, the name Gandhi gave to a way of overcoming injustice, *satya* means the search for truth and *agraha* means persistence. Inseparable from Satyagraha is Ahimsa; that is, *a-himsa* (*hims:* desiring to kill): the effort to avoid killing until the desire to kill has been replaced by love for others and justice. Gandhi tried to teach people how to make Satyagraha/Ahimsa a way of life.

In *Love in Action*, Thich Nhat Hanh advocates an inclusive nonviolence. "We cannot be completely nonviolent," but we can pursue that goal. "If we divide reality into two camps—the violent and the non-

3

violent—and stand in one camp while attacking the other, the world will never have peace. We will always blame and condemn those we feel are responsible for wars and social injustice, without recognizing the degree of violence in ourselves."

Consequently, I have included some organizations not opposed to the use of military force for peaceful purposes, as, for example, supporters of armed U.N. peacekeeping forces such as the World Federalists. The guiding question for inclusion is Hanh's: Were the individuals, the organizations, the creators of the memorials seeking alternatives to violent force? The directory is not limited to pacifists.

Hope for Peace

As New Year's Day 2000 swept westward from time zone to time zone, city to city, the world rose in one voice of hope for the new century. The United Nations called the year 2000 the Year of Peace, and the ten years to follow, the Decade of Peace, and has issued a Manifesto for a Culture of Peace to define the goals of the envisioned future.

The "Statement on Violence" adopted by UNESCO at a meeting in Seville in 1986, despite its simplification of several problems, prepared for this hopefulness. The "Seville Statement" objects to the widespread assumption that organized violence is biologically determined, that humans are genetically programmed inevitably to do violence to each other by wars. Human biology, it argues, makes warfare possible, but not inevitable.

The twentieth century, only a moment in our species' evolution, deserves to be remembered for imagining peace as a global possibility. The League of Nations was an early, failed experiment. The United Nations is another attempt to actualize what we now imagine. The Universal Dec-

laration of Human Rights, for example, which argues for world amity based upon rights and laws, was promulgated only a half-century ago.

On December 10, 1948, the U.N. General Assembly ratified the UDHR, reaching back to preceding utopian declarations—the U.S. Declaration of Independence of 1776, the French Revolutionary Declaration of the Rights of Man and Citizen of 1789, the U.S. Constitution also of 1789, and its Bill of Rights. The U.N. Declaration's Preamble affirms "the inherent dignity ... and equal and inalienable rights of all members of the human family" to be "the foundation of freedom, justice, and peace in the world," and "should be protected by the rule of law."

The work ahead for the peace movement is to expand its numbers and effectively exert its political will based upon these principles, until believers in nonviolent peacemaking gain leadership in governments throughout the world, as in Denmark with Olaf Palme and Costa Rica with Oscar Arias, in order to *prevent* wars. As *Costs of Conflict* demonstrate, conflict prevention is cost-effective, by all economic, human, and environmental measures.

The good influence of the United Nations is inestimable. For example, the U.N. Year/Decade for a Culture of Peace and Nonviolence 2000/2010, endorsed by the Security Council in 1999, offers, in the words of Michael True, "an opportunity to revitalize the peace movement's language and program. It is a concrete effort to reclaim the dynamics of peace, after a century of world wars." The Culture of Peace movement urges "globalization from below," including education in nonviolence, grassroots democracy, citizen diplomacy, free media, more women in peacemaking, and sustainable development. Obviously, in this conception peace is no mere absence of war but a dynamic program for preventing wars and, when a war still occurs, healing its consequences.

Peace Memorials: From War to Peace

Many in the peace movement would make language—myth, symbolism, imagery—the cutting edge of resistance to violence. In order to gain access to the militarized majority, they would expand nonviolent image-making in all aspects of society, toward stopping the killing. For example, the propaganda of ethnic or national superiority—a major cause of wars—is a linguistic enterprise. That the celebration of war has militarized the language and landscape of many nations scarcely needs saying. Everywhere we encounter grassroots militarism reinforced by and reinforcing language/symbol control. For example, the millions dead in wars, potentially an obstacle to bellicose enthusiasms, have been patriotized—along with the nobility of arms and the dignity of dying for one's flag—by hundreds of solemnly grand and beautifully maintained cemeteries and monuments in the United States that cost with veterans during Fiscal Year 1999 over $42 billion. In contrast, the celebration of opponents of war and militarism is notably rare, one more factor in the grassroots militarism which dominates perception, thought, and speech.

Instead of a rhetoric of violence, the peace movement extends a rhetoric of mutual respect, cooperation, and learning. It has been a long time coming.

Human consciousness is moving from the traditional affirmations of patriotism to the bereavement for combatants killed, to sympathy for all civilians and soldiers as victims of wars, and finally, it is hoped, to admiration for resisters to war and to a genuine desire to abolish wars, following the Okinawan example with their Cornerstone

of Peace. Two responses to the patriotic memorializing of the nationalistic mass slaughter of World War I (and later wars) were possible. Antiwar writing and films emphasized the gruesome aspects of the war—such as the poems of Owen and Sassoon, the novel *All Quiet on the Western Front* by Remarque, the film *J'accuse*, and the similar play *Miracle at Verdun* by Chlumberg in which the dead soldiers rise up in protest. Also, in Berlin an antiwar museum appeared in 1924 to show the savagery of the war and its impact on the millions of victims, which the patriotic collections suppressed, but it was closed by the Nazis.

But another antiwar tradition exists in the United States and around the world—the representation of peace. The growing number of peace places—monuments, gardens, parks—counter the pervasive dominance of imagery and symbolism of chauvinism by the imagery and symbolism of nonviolence and negotiation.

Canada leads the way in peace places. For example, a project called "Peace Parks Across Canada," commemorating Canada's 125th anniversary as a nation, resulted in the dedication of a park to peace by some 400 cities and towns.

Herein are listed some 230 plaques, peace poles, monuments, sculptures, buildings, museums, pagodas, pavilions, plazas, gardens, and parks dedicated to alternatives to war violence (United States 178, Canada 44, Mexico 3), and over a dozen organizations devoted to building peace places, and these are only a fraction of the total, since unlisted are the thousands of peace poles, the over 150 nuclear weapons free zones, and the many private retreats.

Between the exaltation of warriors represented by the gigantic statues of generals and the celebration of peacemakers represented by parks and doves, lies the long transition from the victorious mode of commemoration—reflecting the heroic code of triumphing violently over enemies—

to the pacific mode. The shift from the war museum collections of artifacts of military victories, the larger-than-life monuments of generals, and the cemetery shrines to combatants, to the peace museums, parks, and poles for nonviolent peacemakers (and other indications, such as the Universal Declaration of Human Rights) reflects an evolution in moral consciousness so far scarcely recognized.

Much more, one is reminded of the beauty of nature and art and peacemakers, by bells, gardens, parks, groves, college campuses, homes and yards, sculptures, and murals. The large cooperative border parks and monuments deserve the world's emulation. The Prairie Peace Park (entry 582) offers two dozen significant displays indoors and outdoors for people of all ages, the achievement of one man. Salt Lake City, Utah (996), and Thunder Bay, Ontario (1318), have created similar international parks, each section of their parks representing a different nation. Lyndale Peace Park in Minneapolis (523) is a city pride. On Belle Isle, Detroit, the Peace Tower Carillon (498) rings out for peace; Chicago and New York City each have several memorials, as expected, but small towns have contributed remarkably. The central plaza of Salem, Oregon (848), is completely given over to peace—ceramic sculptures, international flags, a large mural. Newport, Kentucky's, World Peace Bell (355), the largest free-swinging bell in the world, rings for peace. The tiny town of Nederland, Colorado, has a peace park at each end of the town; one includes a peace pole, the other a sculpture. David Barr has linked Canada and the U.S. and Russia with his SunSweep and Arctic Arc sculptures.

Individual heroes have been widely recognized by sculptures, gardens, and parks: Peace Pilgrim, A. J. Muste, Sadako, Kroc, Gandhi, King, Pauling, Addams, Tolstoy, Samantha Smith, Gladdys Muir,

Jeannette Rankin, Elizabeth and John Baker, Emery Reves, Eleanor Roosevelt, Fannie Lou Hamer, William Penn, and many more in this directory. The Peace Abbey in Sherborn, Massachusetts (470), presents individual memorials to 60 men and women pacifists, surrounding a statue of Gandhi. The peace movement is trying to change our heroes, as Howard Zinn appealed, from "slaveholders, Indian-killers, and militarists" (Andrew Jackson, Theodore Roosevelt, Woodrow Wilson, John McCain) to peacemakers (Frederick Douglass, Mark Twain, Emma Goldman, Helen Keller, Philip Berrigan).

And nonviolent peacemaking has inspired some of North America's most original architecture: the World Peace Pavilion (1271) in Dartmouth, Nova Scotia, the Elizabeth Baker Peace Chapel, designed by Maya Lin, in Pennsylvania (869), and the Holocaust Museum in Houston (967).

Peace Organizations: A Power Yet to Be Realized

In *Avoiding Politics*, Nina Eliasoph documents the ways the U.S. public avoids civic engagement and the ways political apathy is produced. But the North American peace movement reveals another side of the public: organizing for peace. This directory lists some 1,200 peace organizations (academic programs and nonacademic groups, and museums). For Massachusetts alone, I have listed 55 nonacademic organizations, 24 peace studies/conflict resolution programs at colleges and universities, and 3 memorials (which do not include the many peace poles, sister cities, and nuclear free zones in that state).

Peace and Conflict Resolution Studies in Academia

A distinction should be made between "peace" and "conflict resolution" studies. Peace Studies was the original common designator in the 1970s and 1980s, usually referring to liberal arts courses on war and peace—the causes, consequences, and remedies of war. The first Peace Studies undergraduate courses in the U.S. began at Manchester College, Indiana, in 1948.

Gradually, emphasis shifted to the management of anger, violence, and disputes between individuals, groups, and nations. The more recent conflict resolution/management programs require fewer liberal arts and more practical courses. The Indiana Conflict Resolution Institute at Indiana University, Bloomington, for example, concentrates on understanding and solving conflicts. The Center for Peace and Conflict Studies at Wayne State University, originally the Center for Teaching about War and Peace, today emphasizes the management of conflicts as background needed for graduate work or employment in government and business (resolution, etc.) and a MS and Certificate in Conflict Management for professionals.

In Canada apparently practice leans toward conflict studies. Ontario has a Centre for Peace Studies and a Dispute Resolution program. Nova Scotia has a Peace and Conflict Studies program. But in Alberta, British Columbia, and Manitoba, apparently, only conflict resolution/management programs exist.

A further distinction must be made between peace education and peace/conflict resolution studies. Peace education programs—pedagogy and teacher training for schools and nonformal education—are located in schools of education. At present, only two education colleges provide programs for training future teachers: at Columbia University Teachers College and the College of Education, University of Cincinnati. The importance of peace education cannot be exaggerated, for if teachers lack education in peace, the next generation will repeat the same war patterns of the past.

Peace studies/conflict resolution programs, the usual labels for academic programs, have grown rapidly in number during the past few years, as made emphatically clear by the Year 2000 Edition of *COPRED'S Global Directory of Peace Studies and Conflict Resolution Programs*, which lists 381 colleges and universities with programs, an increase of almost 100 since the 1995-96 edition.

Nonacademic Organizations, National and International

UNITED NATIONS

On June 26, 1945, 51 war-weary nations created the United Nations, founded on the defense-only principle, and full of hope for world peace. But soon those hopes faded as the Cold War polarized the world and the U.N. became hostage to the veto power of Security Council members. Without a way of maintaining or imposing peace, the world witnessed 149 wars and the deaths of 123 million people by wars, the majority of them noncombatants, between the end of World War II and 1992. By 1992, over 18 million people were still refugees. The U.N. never was allowed to function for peace as it had been envisioned. During its first 45 years, there were only 18 U.N. peacekeeping missions. Despite underfunding and superpower unilateralism, however, U.N. achievements in humanitarian and direct relief roles are remarkable during this period. As a result,

North American public approval of the U.N. is strong.

But the U.N. should be more democratic, should receive a much larger and more certain financial base, and should have its own rapid deployment force, especially composed of civilian nation-building personnel. The world, if it is to become a community, needs a United Nations that is the first rather than the last resort in the quest for peace.

NATIONAL ORGANIZATIONS WITH CHAPTERS

Several peace organizations, such as Sister Cities International and Nuclear Free Zones, have extensive affiliation.

Sister Cities International, with headquarters in Washington, D.C., links communities from the U.S. with communities worldwide. Begun after President Dwight D. Eisenhower proposed a people-to-people program in 1956, SCI became an independent organization in 1967, and by 1998 it represented 1,200 U.S. cities, counties, and states and their 2,100 partners in 125 countries. Statistics for each state may be found in SCI's annual *Sister Cities International Directory.*

No central nuclear free zones (NFZ) organization exists at present, but the idea lives through the efforts of individual citizens in towns and cities throughout North America. From 1980 to 1991, 180 U.S. communities passed such a resolution in an effort to stop the proliferation of nuclear power and weapons. By 1995 more than 17 million U.S. citizens lived in NF zones along with 4,000 communities worldwide. Abolition 2000 provides a model NFZ resolution for colleges (*www.napf.org*).

Other nationwide peace initiatives, each coordinating a network of offices or chapters, include Peace Action, WAND, Pax Christi, Society of Friends, War Re-

sisters League, United Nations Association, the Catholic Worker, Fellowship of Reconciliation, the World Federalist Association, and Holocaust organizations.

The North American peace movement has always benefited from the moral bedrock provided by the pacifist churches and secular groups. If the ground of morality is the refusal to kill, to resolutely affirm life, then these churches' radical ethic is the peace movement's foundation: Quakers, Mennonites, Church of Brethren, Bahá'í, Buddhists, Doukhobors, Bruderhof, and conscientious objectors (not all of whom belong to a church).

The Quakers/Society of Friends have an extensive enterprise, especially in the United States. With headquarters in Philadelphia, regional branches throughout the U.S., a legislative office in Washington, D.C. (FCNL), several colleges and private schools, and several magazines (*Friends, Peacework*) and newsletters, the Quakers project a powerful voice against wars and militarism and for peace and justice.

The Mennonites have structured themselves similarly, with a central committee, regional offices, and colleges. The Bahá'ís are growing, especially in Canada, where they emphasize the creation of gardens and parks. The Doukhobors are very small in number, but their courageous history of nonviolence (like that of the Quakers and Mennonites) and their connection with Tolstoy give them a moral authority beyond their numbers. Since China's conquest of Tibet, many Buddhists have immigrated to the U.S., where they have constructed retreats, study centers, and pagodas.

Although the Roman Catholic Church, with its "just war" doctrine, is not pacifist, many of its adherents define a "just war" so strictly that often they seem indistinguishable from Quakers. Certainly this is true of members of Dorothy Day's Catholic Workers, and the Catholic peace organization, Pax Christi, opposes wars and violence. From the U.S. bishops' criticism of the Vietnam War to the leadership of Father Bourgeois against the School of Americas, the Catholics must be acknowledged as among the strongest forces for nonviolence in North America.

All of the mainstream Protestant churches have a peace and justice office—the Baptist Peace Fellowship, the Episcopal Peace Fellowship, and so on.

A nonsectarian religious organization is Fellowship of Reconciliation. Fellowship of Reconciliation (over 50 entries), a branch of International Fellowship of Reconciliation, has some 60 chapters and publishes a notable magazine, *Fellowship*.

National secular organizations include many large, active groups. The War Resisters League, with its broken rifle logo, its magazine *The Nonviolent Activist*, its many chapters, and its frequent public demonstrations, is the only national secular pacifist organization in the U.S. Peace Action, evolved from the old SANE/Freeze group, has chapters around the U.S. (e.g., the Peace House in Oklahoma City) and can generate an insistent voice locally, regionally, and nationally. The venerable Women's International League for Peace and Freedom, founded by Jane Addams, continues to persevere for peace. Another women's group, WAND, Women's Action for New Directions, founded by Helen Caldicott, and its chapters and active on-line newsletter, also help achieve both the short-run political actions and the long-run education to transform warrior into nonviolent values. Montessori schools generally follow the teachings for peace by their founder, Maria Montessori. Amnesty International, with its numerous members, Physicians for Social Responsibility, Veterans for Peace—large and small, the quality of life in North America and national foreign policies are conditioned by the energetic educational and activist programs of its national peacemaking groups.

Numerous other organizations have no chapters, no national network, but wield important influence nationally and even internationally.

Many organizations, both for profit and nonprofit, exist to assist schools in decreasing violence. Several magazines and journals invigorate critique and action—including the *Nuclear Resister, Peace Review, The Bulletin of the Atomic Scientists, PeaceZine,* and hundreds of local newsletters (see Index). Publishing companies for peace offer fresh ideas for thought and action—including *New Society, The Plough, Wellington,* and *Pittenbruach*. And film, video, and radio advance the cause of peace: including Ground Zero Minnesota, the Center for War, Peace, and the News Media, Enviro Video, Radio Free Maine, and the Video Project.

Single organizations which exert a wide impact include: Grandmothers for Peace International, Nuclear Age Peace Foundation, the Carter Center, Martin Luther King, Jr., Center, SOA Watch, Jonah House, Pastors for Peace, Voices in the Wilderness, the Union of Concerned Scientists, the Peace Abbey, and the Ground Zero nuclear protesters in Washington state. Foundations exist too, among which are the Muste Institute, Einstein Institute, Oak Street, and Earth Action. And there is the United States Institute for Peace (USIP), the U.S.-funded research and consultative center.

LOCAL ORGANIZATIONS

Perhaps the most important energy of the peace movement derives from the numerous nonacademic, nonchapter, local, ad hoc groups—some forty in California alone, such as the Chico Peace and Justice Center, Tri-Valley Cares, and the San Jose Peace Center. All over the U.S., local or area citizens have joined together to protest killing and oppression and to affirm life and love: the Pikes Peak Justice and Peace Commission, Colorado Springs; North Dakota Peace Coalition; the Peace Museum, Chicago; Swords into Plowshares Peace Center, Detroit; Rhode Island Mobilization for Peace and Justice. Many of these groups, as in North Dakota, reach out to other area local groups to form coalitions for coordinating effective action—another example is the Colorado Coalition for the Prevention of Nuclear War, Denver.

In Canada similarly, unique, local groups exist. In British Columbia there is the Committee for a Nuclear Free Nanoose, another coalition, End the Arms Race, Public Education for Peace Society, Society Promoting Environmental Conservation, Victoria Anti-War Coalition, and Victoria Peace Centre.

ENVIRONMENTAL ORGANIZATIONS

Included in this work is the environmental movement because sustainability is essential to a peaceful world. New mythologies are needed to supersede those of expansion through growth and development and wars. The peace movement is providing the new ways of seeing. Daniel Quinn in *Ishmael* points to indigenous peoples whose beliefs allowed them to last for thousands of years. One publisher alone, New Society of Gabriola Island, B.C., offers dozens of books which corroborate Quinn's fiction.

The war on animals is at last being acknowledged, and the old antivivisection protest has broadened into a general ethical condemnation of cruelty and genocide. Such books as Sue Coe's *Dead Meat* tackle the barbarity of slaughterhouses. A significant development is the confrontation of Christian views, as in *Good News for Animals*. "Thou shalt not kill" has assumed a tremendously intensified relevance in the context of genocidal speciesism.

The energy of the Peace Movement goes far beyond the organizations listed in this directory. Long as this directory is, there was not space, for example, for most of the nuclear free zones, sister cities, death penalty chapters, private retreats, and conflict mediation centers. The Movement is immense and vibrant.

There can be no better conclusion than the speech given by Oscar Arias at Nazareth College commencement, May 9, 1999. Entitled "Living the Way of Peace," Arias reminded his audience of the achievements during this century—the general increase of life expectancy, the decline of infant mortality in many countries, the ending of colonialism, the development of the United Nations, Panama's decision to emulate Costa Rica by abolishing its national army. But he also appealed to U.S. and world leaders to end the "vicious cycle of poverty and militarism" by everywhere supporting peaceful service. He urged those leaders, and the students, parents, and teachers in his audience, to wage peace instead of war, for human, not national, security.

CANADIAN INTRODUCTION

by John MacLeod

Why not try peace for awhile? If we find war is better, it will not be difficult to fight again... —Abdu'l-Baha

In the middle of a meeting in Québec City in December 1998, a colleague reached across the table and handed me a photocopy of a letter. It was addressed to the mayor of the suburban city of Beauport and was a request for information concerning the city's peace park. In several succinct lines the author presented a project similar to one on which I had been reflecting for years: "I am writing a book about memorials to nonviolent peacemaking in Canada and the United States, and I understand that Beauport has a peace park or garden. Will you please send me a description of it ... and photo?"

It was a Dr. Dick Bennett of the University of Arkansas who had written that letter and, I surmised, hundreds of others like it. I wrote to him in the days that followed and he quickly responded noting that he had found about 100 memorials/ museums/centers in North America so far. The scope of his project was destined to

expand considerably. While I tracked down details for some of the Canadian entries, Dick Bennett continued to gather scores of others from Canada and Mexico and hundreds from the United States. This is the work of a man driven by a profound sense of justice and the vision of peace.

While my particular interest has been the design of places dedicated to peace, collaboration on this directory has allowed me to grasp the significant breadth and depth of the community of peace organizations in Canada. I would like to amplify here several points already made in Dr. Bennett's general introduction and add a personal perspective.

Whatever our culture, creed, or homeland, world peace begins within each one of us with the affirmation that it is possible. Nobody expends her or his energy or resources without this vision/commitment, and nothing durable is accomplished without it.

The rich documentation of this directory and Dick Bennett's comprehensive introduction beg a question. Is the rise of the movement towards peace simply the reflection of a profound social reaction to and of general fatigue at the cost of war and violence? In the cyclical nature of movements, are these efforts towards peace doomed to being surpassed by more pressing, more engaging preoccupations in the years and decades to come? Or is something very significant happening, a social reconfiguration, a new perspective of human relationships and of all other life on the planet? What is the true significance of this preoccupation with peace?

We might ask why the concern for peace has become so widespread, growing in intensity with the advancement of the twentieth century and reaching an unprecedented level at its end. Might we be witnessing something largely unexplored and generally unanticipated, a phenomenon so dramatic that the words to describe it may sound simplistic but nonetheless engaging? Might we be living through a turning point in history, the maturing of our collective scientific and spiritual capacities, our nascent assuming of collective responsibility for each other's welfare and the well-being of the planet? Might this be the beginning of the stage of collective planetary endeavors upon which global efforts to find peace suggest we have embarked: humanity's coming of age?

In fact, might we find ourselves wondering if peace is not only possible, but if it is not, in fact, the natural next stage in the collective evolution of humanity? Like the inevitable development of an individual human being from infancy through childhood and adolescence to maturity, or of an oak tree from acorn to sapling to young tree to shade-providing biomass producing its own plentiful fruit, might humanity as an organic whole be moving toward a mature era of reconciliation and peace?

For many, perhaps most, this is not obvious. But it merits our deep reflection and perhaps challenges our notions of very slow evolutionary change. The analogy of the broad river quietly pursuing the same course for centuries comes to mind. In what is but a moment of historical time, in the reconfiguration brought on by heavy rainfall or unusually rapid snowmelt, the river leaps its banks, floods, then receding, seeks a new path. Scientific and spiritual discovery is also often like this: long periods of searching through routine experiments or experience till a spark lights up and new links are made between what has been known and new knowledge, opening new paths for human possibilities. Perhaps what we are learning about ourselves and communication, culture and human rights has the power to assist us in profoundly transforming our world, for perhaps we are entering an era where the human family will consciously decide for itself the course its collective evolution will take.

The twentieth century has undeniably witnessed the most generalized and devastating violence and wars ever. However, parallel to this destruction and sometimes in reaction to it, humanity's response has also been unprecedented. The creation of world-embracing bodies, particularly the League of Nations and the United Nations, has no historical antecedent, and the Universal Declaration of Human Rights, no global parallel. The U.N.'s gradual ability to influence world events and processes has marked the century. This fact alone provides a measure of hope for peace unknown to any other era of human history. There are many others: the nonviolent collapse of totalitarian regimes under their own weight, the dismantling of apartheid, the ongoing if tenuous quest for lasting peace in the Middle East, the beginning of the process of dismantling nuclear arsenals and the abolition of the armies of several sovereign nations. With the continuing advances in communications and the increasing recognition of the importance of the rule of law in international affairs, might something very important be happening?

Even before the twentieth century began, Canada had marked more than eight decades of uninterrupted peace with its neighbor, the United States of America. This continuing legacy of peaceful cooperation would be a major achievement of these two nations through the end of the millennium. It has inspired the individuals that have created a vast body of art, music, literature and places dedicated to the vision of world peace, and the organizations that nurture it.

In the years following World War I, the governments of the United States and Canada responded to the requests of private groups and service clubs and fostered the development of a host of places along the international boundary to commemorate the then-century-old peace between these two nations. First was the Peace Arch (1921) straddling the border with one of its supports in British Columbia and the other in Washington state. It was followed by the Peace Bridge (1927) across the Niagara River between Ontario and New York state, Waterton Lakes–Glacier International Peace Park (1932) uniting the two national parks situated in Alberta and Montana, and the International Peace Garden (also 1932) between Manitoba and North Dakota. Since then, and particularly in the final decades of the century, this model has inspired the creation of scores of transborder parks and nature preserves throughout the world.

Canada has been particularly fertile ground for the expression of the vision of peace. Through the dedication and persistence of individuals touched by this vision, numerous places and organizations continue to promote their legacy. A few of these memorable personalities are recalled: John George "Kootenai" Brown, pioneer ranger (warden) of Waterton Lakes National Park who promoted the idea of international collaboration between his park and Glacier National Park in Montana, which eventually led to the creation of the International Peace Park; Dr. Henry Moore of Islington, Ontario, whose suggestion led to the establishment of the International Peace Garden; Roy and Priscilla Cadwell, founders of the Lester B. Pearson Peace Park (1967) in Tweed, Ontario; Lou D'Amore of the International Institute for Peace Through Tourism, whose Peace Parks Across Canada project led to the dedication of parks in some 400 places in 1992, and Julia Morton-Marr, whose International School Peace Gardens have carried on that process.

Also noted are the continuing efforts of such organizations as Amnesty International, Servas, Mundialized Cities, Peace Research Institute (Dundas), CUSO, Friends of the Earth, the U.N. Association, World Federalists, Voice of Women for Peace, Canadian Coalition for Nuclear Responsibility, whose names constitute the foundation of the peace movement in Canada. Rights and Freedoms, the new name of the International Centre for Human Rights and Democratic Development established by Parliament in 1988, continues to offer counsel primarily to developing countries that are establishing the bases upon which human rights and democratic government can flourish. Faith communities including Bahá'ís, Doukhobors, Mennonites, Quakers and many others have contributed to elevating the consciousness of Canadians with regard to the efforts required and the benefits to be reaped from the cultivation of peace.

In the latter decades of the century, there has been a resurgence in dedicating places for peace in Canada and elsewhere, many inspired by the International Year of Peace in 1986. With the end of the Cold War and major changes taking place in society, renewed hope for peace has increasingly found expression through the medium of landscape. However, in contrast to the earlier international parks and gardens which were distant from population concentrations, this new wave is focused on highly visible, accessible sites in the heart of urban centers. In general, creating these places has involved the collaboration of many community groups and civil authorities. The results are very diverse expressions of place, layering local conditions and concerns with universal values. By 1995, most of Canada's major cities—Halifax/Dartmouth, Montréal, Ottawa (both the Peacekeeping Monument and Melvin Charney's Human Rights Tribute), Toronto, Winnipeg, Vancouver—and hundreds of smaller centers had created public squares, parks or gardens dedicated to the cause of peace.

But when the design process ends and the people associated with the initial creative endeavor are no longer involved, the peace place is "passed on" to its visitors and users who often have not been "initiated" into the meaning of the place. Their "reading" is conditioned simply by what the place evokes in them and the experience it offers. If the message is obscure or inaccessible, if the experience of the place lacks richness, or more importantly, if its location or design precludes it from becoming a part of a community's everyday life or its special occasions, it will lose the place the community had initially afforded it. This is unfortunately the lot of many of the places dedicated to peace in Canada in the last wave prior to the end of the millennium.

The successful places, such as the Peace Garden in Nathan Phillips Square in front of the Toronto City Hall, work well because they are situated where the public will use them in the normal course of their daily and special activities. One can imagine that over and above the message of peace and the symbolism which many visitors wouldn't be able to "read," the designers' intention was to create a peaceful place in the heart of the city, a place that would welcome individual visitors to stop and eat their lunch as well as the crowds participating in special events. The designers chose to nurture the culture of peace and the attitudes which encourage it as well as evoking collective memory and collective vision through the design of the garden.

The U.N.'s Manifesto 2000 for the Year of the Culture of Peace and Non-Violence challenges us: it's what we do, and how we do it that count. Designers are now called upon to take to a new level the creation of places for peace: to express the universal, remaining faithful to what characterizes the local, to layer carefully our aspirations on the places the past has created. In fact, whether or not peace is expressed directly in the project's name is not important. The places for peace of the new millennium will be created through processes that are inclusive and open, that reflect the people and the place, and that are by their nature and location integral parts of community life. In this way, housing complexes, recreation areas, city centers, traffic and service corridors of all kinds, as well as, of course, sculptures and monuments, parks and gardens, can take their place in any city's places for peace.

Having entered the twentieth century a fledgling nation, a broad band of lightly populated provinces newly strung together by a national railroad and lacking a strong sense of identity, Canada is embarking on the twenty-first as a mature participant in the global family of nations, deeply conscious of its community of individuals, groups and organizations dedicated to advancing the cause of universal peace not only in our country, but in the whole world. As in the past, one of the critical, determining factors in the process will be the role that youth choose to play. Through education for world citizenship, volunteer service projects in Canada and abroad, through its opening up to the world and peace-inspired values and attitudes, this generation of young citizens holds the future of the new world into which we are quickly moving.

Despite the dark clouds of injustice and intolerance that continue to lurk on the world's horizon, the forces of peace have made huge advances in the last century. Where such forces could be masked in other eras, the light now shines clearly enough for all who wish to, to see. World peace is emerging not as an option, but as the only way for humanity to progress: as one family in one world. For all the advances it has witnessed, for all the darkness from which humanity is struggling to emerge, for its place in history as the time when, in the face of its potential total destruction, humanity began to organize itself as one people living in one homeland, might the last century not be perceived as a century of light?

These fruitless strifes, these ruinous wars shall pass away, and the "Most Great Peace" will come.—Baha'u'llah

The
Directory

United States of America

According to the World Peace Prayer Society, as of October 29, 1998, the United States had 5869 Peace Poles.

—— *Alabama (AL)* ——

12 Sister Cities. / 22 Peace Poles.

See Davis, *Weary Feet, Rested Souls*, 20–132, for more Civil Rights Movement organizations and memorials.

BIRMINGHAM, AL

1. *Birmingham Civil Rights Institute* (1992) (org, mus, mem).

   520 16th St. North, Birmingham 35203; (205) 328-9696; *bcri.info@bcri.bham.al.us; http://bcri.bham.al.us*

   An exhibit on the second floor traces the history of African-American life and the struggle for civil and human rights. Its programs and services encourage research, provide information, and promote discussion: the Archives Dept. gathers documents for research; the Oral History Project documents Birmingham's role in the civil rights movement; the Education Dept. produces programs for the schools and public; also there are changing exhibits. The bars of King's cell from the City Jail and other significant artifacts are housed here. And out front a bronze statue of the Rev. Fred Shuttlesworth looks out over the Park. The Institute is part of a $15 million renovation encompassing Kelly Ingram Park and the Sixteenth Street Baptist Church. Dr. Lawrence Pijeaux, Jr., Exec. Dir.

2. *Civil Rights District* (1992) (mem).

   Between 15th and 19th Streets south of I-59 and I-20 (9th Ave.), Birmingham.

   This six-block tribute to the struggle for human rights includes the Birmingham Civil Rights Institute, Kelly Ingram Park (a focal point of resistance to Jim Crow), and the Sixteenth Street Baptist Church (site of the infamous bombing that killed four little girls). Kelly Ingram Park contains sculptures which depict attacks on demonstrators, children jailed for participating in the protests, and a tribute to the clergy's contributions to the movement (6th Ave. N. at 16th St.).

3. *Mary's House Catholic Worker* (1993) (org).

   2107 Ave. G, Birmingham 35218; (205) 780-2020.

   "We believe that it is each of our personal responsibility, right now, to build God's reign by caring for each person as we would care for Christ." Annual Hiroshima vigil, vigils and prayers for victims of other U.S. bombings, travel to Iraq with medicines, advocacy of nonviolence and disarmament. Newsletter: *Magnificat*. Contact Jim and Shelley Douglass.

HUNTSVILLE, AL

4. *International Association of Educators for World Peace* (1969) (org).

   PO Box 3282, Mastin Lake Station, Huntsville 35810-0282; (256) 634-5501;

*mercieca@hiway.net; www.earthportals.
com/Portal_Messenger/mercieca.html*

Promotes international understanding and peace through education, protecting the environment, and safeguarding human rights, through annual world congresses, workshops, conferences, and publications, with special advocacy of the U.N. Universal Declaration of Human Rights. Pubs: *UN News* monthly; *Peace Progress* (annual); *Peace Education* (annual); newsletter six times a year; newsletters in various countries. Also, books pub. by members; e.g., *Peace and Spirituality of the Third Millennium*, and many articles. Dr. Charles Mercieca, Pres.

LOWNDESBORO, AL

5. *Viola Liuzzo Marker* (1995) (mem).

Six-foot stone marker in Lowndes County, Highway 80, between mile

Viola Liuzzo Marker located near Birmingham, Alabama. Photograph courtesy of Peggy Collins, Alabama Bureau of Tourism & Travel.

markers 113 and 114, near Lowndesboro, about 20 miles west of Montgomery.

Inscribed: "In memory of our sister Viola Liuzzo, who gave her life in the struggle for the right to vote. March 25, 1965." The memorial marks the spot where Ms. Liuzzo, a Unitarian Universalist and housewife who had come from the North to defend racial equality nonviolently and was shuttling marchers back and forth, was murdered by Ku Klux Klansmen.

Stanton, Mary. *From Selma to Sorrow: The Life and Death of Viola Liuzzo.* Athens, GA: U of Georgia P, 1998.

MOBILE, AL

6. **Society Mobile-La Habana, Inc.* (1993) (org).

2507 Myrtle St., Mobile 36607; or PO Box 13220, Mobile 36663; (334) 675-5990, ext. 2312; *schaefer@zebra.net*

Created to "strengthen the cultural, educational, and political ties between the two cities." A member of (and helped create) the U.S.-Cuba Sister Cities Assoc. Robert Schaefer, Pres.

Mobile was the site of the U.S.-Cuba Sister Cities Association Conference in October 1999.

MONTGOMERY, AL

7. *Civil Rights Memorial Monument* (1993) (mem)

404 Washington Ave. in front of the Southern Poverty Law Center, overlooking downtown Montgomery.

Water cascades over a black granite table with the names of 40 civil rights martyrs radiating out like the hands of a clock that chronicles the bloody 1950s and '60s. On a facing wall are inscribed King's words: "...until justice rolls down like waters and righteousness like a mighty stream." Designed by Maya Lin, also the designer of the Vietnam War Memorial in D.C. Nearby are the Dexter Avenue King Memorial Baptist Church, where Martin Luther King, Jr., led the boycott of segregated public transportation, and the Greyhound Bus Station, where Freedom Riders were beaten.

"The Civil Rights Memorial: A Decade of Remembrance, 1989-1999." *SPLC Report* (Dec. 1999) Supplement.

Civil Rights Memorial Monument by Maya Lin. Photograph courtesy of Southern Poverty Law Center, Montgomery, Alabama.

8. *Dexter Avenue King Memorial Baptist Church* (1877) (org, mem).

On Dexter Ave. a block from the Capitol, Montgomery. Selma and the Edmund Pettus Bridge are 40 miles to the west, Tuskegee 30 miles to the east.

A small red-brick building. Martin Luther King, Jr., was its new pastor in 1955 when Rosa Parks was arrested for refusing to give her seat on a city bus to a white man. King was tapped to lead the boycott of the public transportation system; out of the yearlong boycott came the nonviolent civil rights movement and its leader. King preached his last sermon here, "The Meaning of Hope," on December 10, 1967, four months before his assassination. Dexter was renamed in his honor in 1978 and today is the only Civil Rights Movement church to be designated a National Historic Landmark.

9. **Southern Poverty Law Center* (1971) (org).

400 Washington Ave., Montgomery 36104 (on a hill overlooking downtown); (334) 264-0286; *www.splcenter.org*

Opposes discrimination, intolerance, and violence; dedicated to securing civil rights. The Center's legal team successfully sued to integrate the Alabama state police, and through litigation bankrupted several white supremacy groups. Its Klanwatch monitors organized racist activity across the nation, and its Militia Task Force keeps track of the activities of more than 400 unauthorized militia units; these activities are reported in the Center's *Intelligence Report.* The Center's Teaching Tolerance project, which is designed to counter hateful racist propaganda, has distributed over $4 million in free videos, books, and training materials to schools; for example, its *Teaching Tolerance* magazine is distributed free of charge twice a year to 400,000 educators. Another pub. is its quarterly newspaper, *SPLC Report.* Co-founded by Morris Dees and Joe Levin.

PERRY COUNTY, AL

10. *Jimmie Lee Jackson Gravesite and Highway 14* (1965) (mem).

Heard Cemetery, off Highway 14, Perry County.

Jackson was one of the several people murdered during the nonviolent protests of 1965. An annual service and pilgrimage is held here each February. This section of Highway 14, renamed the Martin Luther King Memorial Parkway, is possibly the longest road in the nation named for King.

SELMA, AL

11. *Brown Chapel AME Church* (1867) (mem, mus).

410 Martin Luther King St., Selma 36701.

The starting point for most of the civil rights marches in Selma and the site for numerous mass meetings. A plaque for the four people killed during 1965 in connection to the voting rights march from Selma to Montgomery (James Reeb, Jimmie Lee Jackson, Jonathan Daniels, and Viola Liuzzo) hangs to the left of the apse. The church is listed on the National Register of Historic Places. The adjoining parsonage, which served as a hospital during Bloody Sunday, is now an exhibition space for civil rights. A *bust of King* stands outside.

12. *Martin Luther King, Jr., Street* (1976) (mem).

Along the street ten mounted placards of text and photographs depict the most important events leading up to the march to Montgomery (containing some whitewashing of the repressive behavior of the white power structure).

13. *National Voting Rights Museum and Institute* (1992) (org).

Adjacent to the Edmund Pettus Bridge, 1012 Water Ave., PO Box 1366, Selma 36702.

Houses a collection of messages from Bloody Sunday, 1965, marchers, whose footprints are cast in plaster, and photos of the marchers; a small chapel; and other artifacts; and coordinates the annual commemorative Bloody Sunday bridge crossing. A marker about Bloody Sunday stands on the Selma side of the bridge.

Howlett, Duncan. *No Greater Love.* Boston: Skinner House, 1993. (Biography of Reeb.)

—— *Alaska (AK)* ——

19 Sister Cities. / 36 Peace Poles.

Alaska has many Sister Cities Partnerships: Anchorage (6), Fairbanks (3), Fairbanks North Star Borough (1), Girdwood (1), Homer (2), Juneau (4), Kenai (1), Ketchikan (2), Kotzebue (1), Nome (1), North Pole (1), Palmer (1), Petersburg (1), Savoonga (1), Seward (1), Sitka (1), Unalaska (1), Wasilla (1), Wrangell (1). Alaska also has three Sister State/Territory Relations.

ANCHORAGE, AK

14. *Peace Poles* (mem).

Thanks to the Girl Scouts, Anchorage has seven Peace Poles: located at Russian Jack Springs Park, Girl Scouts Susitna Council Office, Saturday Market, Old Federal Building, Anchorage Museum of History and Art, Bean's Café, and Midtown Park.

15. *Sister Cities* (org).

Anchorage has a Sister Cities Commission and six Sister Cities: Chitose, Japan (1969); Tromso, Norway (1969); Whitby, Eng. (1978); Darwin, Aus. (1982); Inchon, Korea (1986); Magadan, Russia (1991). Contact Peter Ginder (*pglaw@alaska.net*). Linda "Jay" Jackson, Alaska State Coordinator.

WALES, AK

16. *Arctic Arc* (1988) (mem)

"Arctic Arc," the conception of the sculptor David Barr, is composed of two sculptures, one in Wales (the U.S. community closest to the Russian border) and the other at Naukan, Chukotskiy Peninsula, Russia (1991). The sculpture in Wales has two elements: one suggests an incomplete bridge and a hand extended in friendship, created by Barr. In flight over the bridge and in front of the upraised hand is a dove, the work of Eskimo artist, Joe Senungetuk, born in Wales. The sculpture at Naukan, also by Barr, suggests an Eskimo sled. "The sculptures express the desire of individuals to promote international understanding with a

Arctic Arc in Wales, Alaska.

Arctic Arc in Naukan, Russian Far East.

concept that involves global citizenry," and a "faith in humanity and a faith that when we are united by the arts, the world community is most living, most sane, and most human." Barr also designed the multiple sculpture, "SunSweep," along the Canadian-U.S. border.

— *Arizona (AZ)* —

20 Sister Cities. / 93 Peace Poles.

PHOENIX, AZ

17. **André House of Arizona* (1984) (org).

PO Box 2014, Phoenix 85001; 213 11th Ave., Phoenix (soup kitchen/clothing bank), 1002 W. Polk St. (guest home); (602) 255-0580 or 252-9023.

This "community of hospitality" blends "the traditions of the Catholic Worker and the Congregation of Holy Cross" to "serve the poor and homeless" and strive for peace and understanding. Third Friday discussions pertain to peace and social justice; protests against capital punishment. *The Open Door* pub. three times/year. Rev. Brent Kruger, C.S.C., Director.

PRESCOTT, AZ

18. **Integrative Studies Program* (1997) (col).

Prescott College, 220 Grove Ave., Prescott 86301; (520) 778-2250 or 778-2090; *rdpadmissions@prescott.edu;* *www.prescott.edu/rdp/rdp_is.html#peace*

The ISP offers peace studies and conflict resolution as one of the program's graduation areas, including courses on the historical roots of war and on approaches to resolving conflicts on all levels of society. Contact Paul Smith, Assoc. Dean.

TEMPE, AZ

19. **Arizona Institute for Peace Education and Research* (1988) (org).

325 E. Broadway, Tempe 85282; (480) 967-3880; oracle@goodnet.com

Established by the World Family Trust, a partnership of Phoenix-area peace advocates who purchased the present property and the property adjacent at 329 E. Broadway for an expanded program of networking. Seeks "to take effective action on behalf of peace, social justice, and a sustainable environment." Hosts a film/discussion series on current issues (economic justice, nuclear weapons in space, etc.); a forum series with speakers from the U.N., World Federalists, American Indian Movement, etc.; a nonviolence program; a Latin American Committee; and other programs. Its Advocacy Committee promotes actions. And it has a library of printed and video materials. Pub. a newsletter; the Spring 2000 number includes articles on the People's Campaign for Nonviolence, Phoenix Hazardous Waste Facility, the School of the Americas, and Worker Rights, and it has a Directory of Supporting Organizations and a Calendar of Events. Contact Sherry Bohlen.

20. *Coalition for Justice and Peace* (1976) (col)

2354 E. Pebble Beach Dr., Tempe 85282-6035; (602) 831-7381; *rogeri49@aol.com*

Meets weekly for lunch with a speaker at Arizona State U. Founded by Roger Axford.

21. *School of Justice Studies* (1972) (col).

College of Public Programs, Arizona State Univ., Tempe 85287; (480) 965-7020; *david.goldberg@asu.edu*; *www.asu.edu/copp/justice/undgra1.htm*

Undergraduate BS focuses on both theories and the law of justice, as well as social and economic justice, crime, violence, and related subjects. Affil. with American University's Justice Semester Program in Washington, DC; internships available. David Goldberg, Dir. MS and Ph.D. in Justice Studies offered for professionals and scholars. Nancy Winn, Graduate Advisor.

TOPOCK, AZ

22. *Alliance of Atomic Veterans (IAAV)* (1984) (org).

Box 32, Topock 86436; (520) 768-6623; *aav1@ctaz.com*

Membership of international victims of nuclear weapons testing and war veterans who were exposed to fallout. Dedicated to ending all nuclear weapons testing and to curbing nuclear weapons proliferation. Anthony Guarisco, Dir.

TUCSON, AZ

23. *Heartsprings, Inc.* (1991) (porg).

PO Box 12158, Tucson 85732; (800) 368-9356; (520) 322-9977; *mik@heartsprings.org*

Creator of the "PeaceBuilders Violence Prevention Program"(1993). The goal of this company is to help schools become peaceful learning places. Of the 84 programs evaluated by the Substance Abuse and Mental Health Services Administration, PeaceBuilders was one of the ten to receive an "A" rating. Michael Krupnick, President.

Warren, Jenifer. "Salinas Schools Teach Their City the Path of Peace." *Los Angeles Times* (Dec. 5, 1998) A18.

24. *The Nuclear Resister* (1980) (org).

P.O. Box 43383, Tucson 85733; tel: (520) 323-8697; *nukeresister@igc.org*

Supports active nonviolent resistance to nuclear weapons and other expressions of violence by supporting men and women who spend time in jails and prisons for their acts of conscience (the Gods of Metal Plowshares, the School of the Americas, disarming Britain's Trident fleet, etc.). Pub.: *The Nuclear Resister*, newspaper format full of articles about resisters and the peace movement in general. Founded and directed by Felice and Jack Cohen-Joppa.

25. *Tucson Peace Center* (1983) (org).

POB 42843, Tucson 85733; (520) 795-8291; *lstage@pobox.com*

A networking organization for local groups involved in peace, justice, and environmental activities. The Center holds the annual Peace Fair every February in Reid Park, a day-long festival of music and booths representing up to 40 local peace and justice organizations, and it publishes the *Peace Calendar*, a monthly listing of local peace, justice, and environmental meetings and events. Lisa Stage, Dir.

—— *Arkansas (AR)* ——

7 Sister Cities. / 26 Peace Poles.

EUREKA SPRINGS, AR

26. *Center on War & the Child* (1987) (org).

P.O. Box 487, 36 Benton St., Eureka Springs 72632; (501) 253-8900.

Focuses on the militarization of children and children as victims in civil and international conflict; challenges the glorification of war and violence; studies the effects of war on children. Publishes the *War Child Monitor* newsletter and other writings. Latest project: "Kids Without Violence Program" to expose and oppose the socialization of children to violence. Founder and Exec. Dir.: Richard Parker.

FAYETTEVILLE, AR

27. **Fulbright Institute of International Relations* (1982) (col).

722 W. Maple, Fayetteville 72701; (501) 575-2006; *jpurvis@comp.uark.edu*

A center for research of foreign policy and international affairs within the J. William Fulbright College of Arts and Sciences of the University of Arkansas, where Senator Fulbright's papers reside. "The Institute is dedicated to the proposition that knowledge promotes tolerance and understanding among peoples." Sponsors Visiting Fellows, College Faculty Research Fellows, an annual symposium, the Fulbright School of Public Affairs (a summer program for high school gifted and talented students), and other activities. Hoyt Purvis, Dir. (1982-2000); Todd Shields, Dir.

28. *J. William Fulbright Peace Fountain and Statue* (1998) (mem, col).

At the center of the campus of the University of Arkansas, Fayetteville, just west of Old Main.

Honors the life of the former president of the University and U.S. Senator, for his initiation of the International Exchange Program of students, teachers, and researchers, often called the "Fulbright Program," and for his opposition to the Vietnam War and militarism in the United States and around the world, while Chairman of the Senate Committee on Foreign Relations during the 1960s and 70s. Fulbright wrote several books analyzing U.S. foreign and military polices, including *The Pentagon Propaganda Machine,* and *Arrogance of Power.* The memorial, costing almost $900,000, is composed in two parts: a fountain of cascading water below a brass sculpture representing a jet of water rising 41 feet, and a life-size statue of Fulbright. The fountain/sculpture was designed by Fay Jones

and Maurice Jennings, architects. Gretta Bader created the statue.

29. **Peace Links Papers* (1988) (lib).

University of Arkansas Libraries.

Peace Links, a movement of women committed to preventing nuclear war, founded by Betty Bumpers, wife of Arkansas' Senator Dale Bumpers, donated its 1977-1989 records to the University's Special Collections.

30. *Peace Pole and Garden* (1999) (mem).

Unitarian Universalist Fellowship, 901 W. Cleveland St., Fayetteville 72701; (501) 521-8839; *uufellow@comp.uark.edu*

The Pole is surrounded by flagstone patio and flower garden built by Fellowship members. The dedication ceremony was organized by the minister, Rev. Rhett Baird, with readings by members and poetry by Miller Williams.

J. William Fulbright Peace Fountain is on the campus of the University of Arkansas in Fayetteville.

Peace Rock sculpture by Hank Kaminsky.

31. *Peace Rock* (1998) (mem).

2582 Jimmie, Fayetteville 72703.

Sculpture by Hank Kaminsky with the names of 30 male and female peacemakers inscribed on its sides, in the yard of Dick Bennett. Photo, explanation, and description of the "Rock" available.

32. **PeaceWriting* (1998) (org).

2582 Jimmie, Fayetteville 72703;
jbennet@uark.edu

Awards for unpublished manuscripts about the causes, consequences, and solutions to violence and war, the ideas and practices of nonviolent peacemaking, and the lives of nonviolent peace activists.

33. **Sister City* (1996) (org).

Santiago de Los Caballeros, Dominican Republic. College student exchange.

FOX, AR

34. *Peace Pole* (1988) (mem)

Meadowcreek, PO Box 100, 1 Meadowcreek Lane, Fox 72051.

Meadowcreek is an educational center dedicated to a "sustainable future."

HOT SPRINGS, AR

35. **Sister City* (1997) (org).

Hanamaki, Japan. High School student exchange.

JONESBORO, AR

36. *Peace Pole* (1995) (mem).

Children's House Montessori School,
300 E. Nettleton Ave., Jonesboro

Located on the lawn of the property, used for outside kindergarten graduations and annual spring flower plantings. When the Pole was erected, the children buried a time capsule with their pictures and statements of their personal peace goal. The school employs the book *Our Peaceful Classroom*, based upon Maria Montessori's philosophy of mutual respect, acceptance, trust, and freedom.

LITTLE ROCK, AR

37. **Arkansas Coalition to Abolish the Death Penalty* (1985) (org).

904 W. 2nd St., Suite One, Little Rock 72201; (501) 374-2660; *arkclu@igc.org*

Affil. with the National Coalition to Abolish the Death Penalty (*www.nacadp.org*). ACADP has an educational program, an annual meeting/dinner, a library of books and films. Between 1990 and 1999, 21 persons were executed in Arkansas; forty-five people were on death row in June 1999. David Rickard, Chairperson.

38. **Central High Museum* (1997) (mus).

2125 W. 14th St., Little Rock 72202;
(501) 374-1957; *chmuseum@swbell.net;*
home.swbell.net/chmuseum/

Commemorates the closing and reopening of Little Rock's Central High School in 1957, testifying to the city's commitment to eliminating separate systems of education for blacks and whites. The Museum occupies a former Mobil service station, restored to its 1957 appearance, across from Central. The present exhibition is entitled: *"All the World Is Watching Us": Little Rock and the 1957 Crisis*, which is divided into six sections tracing Arkansas racial history up to

Central High School Visitors Center and Museum, Little Rock, Arkansas. Photograph courtesy of Central High Museum.

the present and the state's determination to end discrimination. Pub. a brochure. The "Little Rock Nine" received the Congressional Gold Medal in 1999 for their bravery as teen-agers.

39. *Women's Action for New Directions (WAND), Little Rock Chapter* (1980) (org).

2510 Hidden Valley Drive, Little Rock 72212; *jgordon@igc.apc.org*

Originally Women's Action for Nuclear Disarmament founded by Dr. Helen Caldicott. Seeks to empower women to act politically, to reduce militarism and violence, and to redirect military resources toward human and environmental needs. Contact: Jean Gordon. National office Arlington, MA; national field office: Decatur, GA.

40. *Women's Project* (1981) (org).

2224 Main St., Little Rock 72206; (501) 372-5113; *wproject@aol.com*.

Mainly strives to eliminate sexism and racism, which involves community education and assistance to women to end violence against women. Lending library; annual retreat; conferences; Women's Coffeehouse monthly. Monthly newsletter/calendar; *Transformation*, a quarterly journal. Judy Matsuoka, Exec. Dir.

PARTHENON, AR

41. *River Spirit* (1997) (porg and mem).

HCR 72, Box 85, Parthenon 72666; (870) 446-5642.

A retreat in mountainous Newton County creating an environment conducive to inner peace and dedicated to honoring diversity of race, religious preference, and lifestyle, and to living more gently and peacefully with the natural world. Has a *Peace Pole*.

Arkansas Democrat Gazette (November 6, 1998) cover of the NW Arkansas Weekend section.

WINSLOW, AR

42. *Wattle Hollow Retreat Center* (1989) (org).

Contact Joy Fox, 344 Combs. Ave., Fayetteville 72701; (501) 521-7148; *joyfoxwath@aol.com;* *www.WattleHollow.com*

Under construction from 1980, WH opened as a healing retreat. It offers a naturally beautiful environment, where people can reach inward towards a compassionate understanding for the creation of a saner, happier world. It has a meditation hall, a dozen outdoor meditation places, several cabins, and a dormitory. Joy Fox, founder and director.

— *California (CA)* —

219 Sister Cities. / 675 Peace Poles.

BEN LOMOND, CA

43. *The Video Project: Media for a Safe & Sustainable World* (1983) (org).

200 Estates Drive, Ben Lomond 95005; (800) 4-planet; (831) 336-0160; *videoproject@videoproject.org;* *www.videoproject.org/*

TVP offers a wide range of films on war, peace, the environment, and related subjects. In their early 2000 catalog, TVP quotes the 1992 declaration from over 1700 national academy scientists world wide sent out by the Union of Concerned Scientists, "World Scientists' Warning to Humanity," regarding the serious risk to human society and the plant and animal worlds caused by current economic and industrial practices. In response, TVP offers videos on war and peace, the atmosphere, water resources, soil, forests, species, population, human rights, women's rights, Vietnam War, nuclear threats, radiation, land mines, renewable energy, development and the environment, children, education, nature, and related topics.

BERKELEY, CA

44. *Buddhist Peace Fellowship* (1978) (org).

PO Box 4650, Berkeley 94704; (510) 525-8596.

Advances Buddhist practice as a way of peace and protection of all beings, and to raise peace, environmental, feminist, and social justice concerns among U.S. Buddhists. Initiates letter-writing campaigns in support of human rights around the world, supports refugees, sponsors retreats and conferences. Pub. quarterly magazine *Turning Wheel* and book of essays on socially engaged Buddhism, *The Path of Compassion.*

Chappell, David, ed. *Buddhist Peacework: Creating Cultures of Peace.* Boston Research Center, 1999.

45. *Butterfly Gardeners Association* (1993) (org).

1563 Solano Ave. #477, Berkeley 94707; (510) 528-7730; *bflyspirit@aol.com*

With the butterfly as their symbol for the evolution of the planet, world peace, sustainability, and the New Millennium, BGA promotes environmental education, wildlife gardening and conservation, nonviolence, and peace and environmental community organizing. Alan Moore, Dir.

46. *California Peace Action* (1990) (org).

2800 Adeline St., Berkeley 94703; (510) 849-2272; *capazaction@igc.apc.org;* *www.capa.org*

A branch of Peace Action (formerly SANE/Freeze), California Peace Action is "the largest grassroots peace organization in the state." It works especially "to end the production of nuclear weapons, reduce excessive military spending, and stop arms sales" by educating congresspeople and providing congressional voting report cards, but it also responds to global violence and militarism, as in protests against the sanctions and bombings in Iraq and Yugoslavia. Has "Canvass" branches in Santa Cruz, Los Angeles, and San Francisco. In July 1999 pub. a full-page ad in the *New York Times* exposing the military-industrial-congressional complex. Pub. "Report Cards" on the voting records of and military corporate contributions to congresspeople; and many informative pamphlets and posters. Pub. *The Catalyst* newsletter, which in its Spring 1999 number included articles on the Abolition 2000 Campaign, on its media campaign against military spending, arms spending, bombing Yugoslavia, Iraq sanctions, child soldiers, and two pages of "Action Alert." Peter Ferenbach, Exec. Dir.

47. *Center for Ethics and Social Policy* (1974) (col).

Graduate Theological Union, 2400 Ridge Rd., Berkeley 94709; (510) 649-2560; *cesp@gtu.edu; www.gtu.edu/centers/cesp/cesp.html*

Focusing on economic injustices, the Center works especially with labor unions, women's organizations, religious groups, and similar groups. Pub. *Ethics and Policy* newsletter. Robert Bellah, Faculty Rep.

48. *The Earth Proclamation* (1999) (org).

1563 Solano Ave., #477, Berkeley 94707; (510) 528-7730; *bflyspirit@aol.com; www.enter.net/~lemitchell/ proclamation.html*

Individuals and groups are invited to endorse this vision of a world transformed for peace. Contact Alan Moore. See also entry 45.

49. *Human Rights Center* (1994) (col).

Institute of International Studies, Univ. of California, Berkeley 94720; (510) 642-0965; *stover@globetrotter.berkeley.edu; http:// globetrotter.berkeley.edu/humanrights*

Research on human rights, rules of war, and humanitarian law. Summer fellowships available. Eric Stover, Dir.

50. *METTA* (see Tomales, CA).

2401 LeConte, Berkeley 94709; (510) 540-6689; *mnagler@igc.org*

Michael Nagler, Dir. See also entry 166.

51. *Peace and Conflict Studies Program (PACS)* (1983) (col).

International Studies, Univ. of California, Berkeley 94720; (510) 642-4466; *iastp@uclink.berkeley.edu; www.ias.berkeley.edu/iastp.pac.htm*

Offers an interdisciplinary BA through core courses, survey courses, an area of concentration, and a social diversity course. Students are encouraged to design their programs, and the Peace Studies Student Organization plays an active role. Michael Nagler, Chair.

52. *World Wall for Peace* (1989) (mem).

World Wall for Peace, 1427 Milvia St., Berkeley 94709; (510) 527-2356; *clightfoot@aol.com; www.wwfp.org*

Carolyna Marks, Founder and Pres., has developed walls around the world, composed of original tiles that express each artist's vision of peace. A central symbol is the Medicine Wheel of Love encircling the Earth, with connecting sections in different countries and cultures around the world. Her book about the Walls is entitled *Creativity in the Lions Den: Releasing Our Children from Violence*. (See: Oakland, CA.) (The Peace Wall concept is spreading. Clara Halter, painter, has built a wall for peace at the foot of the Eiffel Tower. It is made of glass and wood with the word Peace written in 32 languages and Braille. It also offers a variation on the Temple Wall of Jerusalem: people can come and slide a peace message in the wall.)

World Wall for Peace in Berkeley, California. Photograph courtesy of Carolyna Marks.

World Wall for Peace, founded in Berkeley, California. Photograph courtesy of Carolyna Marks.

53. **World Without War Council* (1958) (org).

1730 Martin Luther King Jr. Way, Berkeley 94563; (510) 845-1992; *www.wwwc.org/wwwc/wwwchome.html*

Seeks to make the U.S. a leader "toward a world that resolves mass political conflict without war." WWWC began with Acts for Peace under Robert Pickus, then was named Turn Toward Peace in 1961. During the Vietnam War the org. split into two, with WWWC turning its attention to the nonviolent resolution of political conflict. Today it works in conjunction with the James Madison Foundation of Washington, DC, for the Common Good/Immigrants and Citizenship project; and other projects.

BOULDER CREEK, CA

54. **Vajrapani Institute* (1975) (org).

PO Box I, Boulder Creek 95006; (831) 338-6654.

A Tibetan Buddhist teaching center and retreat in the Santa Cruz mountains. Has a 15-foot stupa.

CHICO, CA

55. **Chico Peace and Justice Center* (1960, inc. 1983) (org).

526 Broadway, Chico 95928, downtown Chico; (530) 893-9078; *peacefirst@aol.com; www.becnet.org/ChicoPeace*

Originated by women and Quakers who protested the planned Nike missile base in early 1960s. Weekly street peace vigil, monthly vigil for Abolition 2000, weekly radio program, annual Hiroshima-Nagasaki Remembrance; direct actions (Livermore, etc.). Pub. *Peaceful Action* monthly; the July-Aug. 1999 issue includes articles on Yugoslavia, Hiroshima, the June March on the Pentagon, the Commission of Inquiry hearing for an International War Crimes Tribunal initiated by Ramsey Clark, interview of Noam Chomsky. John Martin, Dir.

56. **Conflict Resolution Program* (col).

College of Behavioral and Social Sciences, California State Univ., Chico 95929; (530) 898-5986; *sosc@csuchico.edu; www.csuchico.edu/catalog.sosc/min_cr.html*

Offers an undergraduate minor in conflict management, especially the techniques of negotiation, accompanied by related electives. Contact Mark Morlock. The Political Science Dept. offers courses and internships in alternative dispute resolution. Robert Ross, Dept. Chair (530-898-5960; *rross@exchange.csuchico.edu; www.csuchico.edu/pols*).

DAVIS, CA

57. **Conflict Management and Resolution* (col).

PO Box 409, D-Q University, Davis 95616; (530) 758-0470, x1032; *www.dcn.davis.ca.us/go/dquaaa/cd.html*

This private two-year tribal college, in partnership with Indian Dispute Resolution Services, offers for improving personal communication and collaboration. The CM&R Certificate requires 13 units of courses. ("D" stands for the Great Peacemaker of the Iroquois Confederacy; "Q" represents Quetzalcoatl, Aztec prophet.)

58. *War-Peace Studies* (1990) (col).

International Relations Program,
Univ. of California, Davis 95616;
(530) 752-3063; *eogoldman@ucdavis.edu;*
www.registrar.ucdavis.edu/ucdwebcatalog/
webcatcrs/gc_warpeace.htm

Offers an interdisciplinary minor of 20 hours in War-Peace Studies organized around the concepts of causes, prevention, and resolution of wars. The university also has a 48-hour major in International Relations with a Peace and Security track that deals with alliances, diplomacy, etc. Emily Goldman, Dir.

ELK GROVE, CA

59. *Grandmothers for Peace International* (1982) (org).

9444 Medstead Way, Elk Grove 95758;
(916) 684-8744; *wiednerb@aol.com;*
www.GrandmothersForPeace.org

Began as a sustained protest against nuclear weapons at Mather Air Force Base and continues as a nuclear protest group (plutonium on the Cassini space probe in 1997, etc.), but has expanded to include diverse international conflicts and to presenting annual awards to students entering college who have committed themselves to promoting peace and justice (the Dorothy Vandercook Memorial Peace Scholarships). Included in *Ms. Magazine*'s report "Women Activists on Preventing War and Making Peace" (Aug./Sept. 1999) Founder/Director: Barbara Wiedner.

ENCINITAS, CA

60. *Project on Youth and Non-Military Opportunities (YANO)* (1984) (org).

PO Box 230157,
Encinitas 92023;
(760) 753-7518 or
(619) 283-3401;
projyano@aol.com

Offers youths in San Diego County a contrasting view on military enlistment, informs them about non-military alternatives for skills training and college financial aid, and promotes careers in peacemaking and social change. Many pubs., request resource list. Rick Jahnkow, Prog. Coord. (See: War Resisters League).

FRESNO, CA

61. *Center for Peacemaking and Conflict Studies* (1990) (col).

Fresno Pacific University,
1717 S. Chestnut Ave., Fresno 93702;
(559) 455-5840; *dreimer@fresno.edu;*
www.fresno.edu/dept/pacs

A minor program (1980s) designed for people preparing to work with people—church ministries, counseling, education, social work, etc.; also a graduate program (mid-1990s). Pubs. include: Roxanne and Ron Claassen, *Making Things Right: 32 Activities Teach Conflict Resolution & Mediation Skills* (1996) and Duane Ruth-Heffelbower, *Conflict & Peacemaking Across Cultures: Training for Trainers* (1999). Dalton Reimer, Co-Dir.

62. *Fresno Center for Nonviolence* (1992) (org).

985 N. Van Ness, Suite 11, Fresno 93728;
(559) 237-3223 (559-23PEACE);
fcnv2@juno.com

Fresno Center for Nonviolence located in Fresno, California.

Fosters the desire for peace, justice, equity, non-injury, inclusiveness, and simplicity in individuals, neighborhoods, and regions. Supports all groups and activities whose aims and methods are compatible with nonviolent peacemaking. Organizes forums, workshops, films, demonstrations, Hiroshima Day, and other activities, in coalition with many organizations. A branch of the Fellowship of Reconciliation. Richard Stone, Prog. Dir., Arthur Siegel, Pres.

63. *Martin Luther King, Jr., Bust* (1988) (mem).

Fresno, in front of the courthouse.

The Fresno branch of the WILPF celebrates King's birthday there each year.

64. **Peace and Conflict Studies Program* (1986) (org).

School of Social Sciences, Fresno State University, Fresno 93740-0091; (559) 278-2013; *bobfi@csufresno.edu; isabel_kaprielian@csufresno.edu*

A 21-unit minor degree to prepare students for leadership in conflict management, and special 12-unit Certificate in Peacebuilding and Mediation; courses on Peace and Conflict, Peacebuilding, Mediation, and Internship. Robert Fischer and Isabel Kaprielian, Co-Coordinators. Sudarshan Kapoor, former Dir. (*skapoor@zimmer.csufresno.edu*)

65. *Peace Garden* (1990) (mem).

On the campus of Fresno State University, adjacent to the Madden Library, north.

Statue of César Chávez located in Peace Garden on campus at Fresno State University. Photograph courtesy Sheri Osborn.

The garden, the idea of Sudarshan Kapoor, coordinator of the *Peace and Conflict Studies Program*, was dedicated with the installation of a large *bust of Gandhi*, created by the artist James Zerl Smith. (See MA and NYC). In 1996, a 9½-foot bronze *statue of César Chávez*, also an advocate of nonviolence, was added; the artist: Paul Suarez. A 6-foot *statue of Martin Luther King, Jr.*, by the artist Richard Blake, was erected in the fall of 1998. (See Tennessee.) The statues are surrounded by a variety of trees and shrubs (birch, crape myrtle, gingko, purple leaf plum, Canary Island pine, etc.).

66. **St. Benedict Catholic Worker* (1997) (org).

4022 Cheryl Ave., Fresno 93705-2201; (559) 229-6410; *bryanapper@juno.com*

Statue of Gandhi located in Peace Garden on the Fresno State University campus. Photograph courtesy Sheri Osborn.

A prisoner and homeless mission. Peace activities: vigils and other work against death penalty, support for Plowshares Movement, member of Vision of Micah Affinity Group (Oakland, CA), demonstrations against militarism. Pub. *Ora et Labora* newsletter (Dec. 1999 issue includes articles on the School of the Americas and "Ban the Bomb II"). Bryan and Liza Apper, Coordinators.

GARBERVILLE, CA

67. *Veterans Vietnam Restoration Project* (1988) (org).

PO Box 369, Garberville 95542; *vvrp@vvrp.org; www.vvrp.org*

Provides humanitarian assistance to Vietnam, the first U.S. NGO to be issued a license by the U.S. for construction in Vietnam. Its fourteenth team traveled in 1999. Film: *Hoa Binh: A Video Documentary*, traces the work of Team VIII. Founded by Fredy Champagne.

HEMET, CA

68. *Friends of Peace Pilgrim* (1982) (org). (recently moved to Somerset, CA)

7350 Dorado Canyon Rd., Somerset 95684; (530) 620-0333; *peacepilgrim@znet.com; www.peacepilgrim.com*

The woman now known as Peace Pilgrim (1908–1981) walked the world to teach love and inner peace. Her writings include: "Steps Toward Inner Peace," "Peace Pilgrim Book," and "Peace Pilgrim Offerings." Also: *Peace Pilgrim, Her Life and Work in Her Own Words*; newsletter: *Friends of Peace Pilgrim*. Several videos available, including *The Spirit of Peace* (71 min.); new video being prepared (contact *peacepilgrim@wakan.com*). Founders of *Friends*: Ann and John Rush. The Rushes display 10 translations of *Peace Pilgrim* and 25 translations of "Steps Toward Inner Peace."

IRVINE, CA

69. *Global Peace and Conflict* (1983) (col).

Univ. of California, Irvine 92697; (949) 824-1227; *pgarb@uci.edu; www.hypatia.ss.uci.edu/gpacs*

An undergraduate interdisciplinary minor dealing with international violence, the threat of

Peace Pilgrim. Photograph courtesy Friends of Peace Pilgrim.

global war, methods of cooperation, and related subjects, composed of core courses, a senior seminar, and upper division electives. Paula Garb, Assoc. Dir.

LAGUNA BEACH, CA

70. *Soulforce, Inc.* (1998) (porg).

PO Box 4467, Laguna Beach 92652; (949) 455-0999; *mel@soulforce.org; www.soulforce.org; www.melwhite.org*

"To create an interfaith, ecumenical network committed to applying the principles of nonviolence as taught by Gandhi and King to the liberation of sexual minorities."

LA HONDA, CA

71. *Peacemaker Community* (1996) (org).

Box 313, La Honda 94020-0313; (650) 747-0284; *marcury@tuna.net; www.PeacemakerCommunity.org*

Worldwide people practicing a vision of peace through study, spiritual practice, and social action.

Members subscribe to the Four Commitments agreed upon by representatives of 200 religions at the World Parliament of Religions held in Chicago in 1993: to a culture of nonviolence and reverence for life; to a culture of solidarity and a just economic order; to a culture of tolerance and a life based on truthfulness, and to a culture of equal rights and partnership between men and women. Since 1996 it has supported the Auschwitz-Birkenau Bearing Witness Retreat, hosted by the Zen Peacemaker Order. Co-founders: Sandra Jishu Holmes (1941–1998) and Bernie Glassman. Exec. Dir.: Grover Gauntt. See: Hudson River Peacemaker Center.

LA JOLLA *see* SAN DIEGO

LARKSPUR, CA

72. **Pathways to Peace* (1962) (org).

PO Box 1057, Larkspur 94977;
(415) 461-0500 (near San Francisco)

An international peacebuilding, educational, and consulting organization, Pathways' mission includes the expansion of the comprehension and expression of peacebuilding at all levels, the strengthening of existing organizations and programs, and support of the United Nations. Has initiated many projects, including the collaborative "Inquiry into Peacebuilding for the 21st Century." PTP also coordinates the "We the People" Initiative for the U.N., working to involve children in achieving peace in the 21st Century. This program includes the International Day of Peace/Hear the Children Day. Catherine Stone, Chief Administrative Officer.

LA VERNE, CA

73. **Peace Studies Program* (1996) (col).

1950 3rd St., University of La Verne,
La Verne 91750; (909) 593-3511, x4320;
*robertsd@ulv.edu; www.ulv.edu/acdem/
dept/inter/intp.html#psm*

The undergraduate, interdisciplinary minor teaches about the relationships between human and natural environments for mutual welfare and security, and requires 24 semester hours in core courses, colloquia, and related courses. Debbie Roberts, Coord.

LIVERMORE, CA

74. *Peace Monument* (1984) (mem).

On the grounds outside the Civic Center branch of the Livermore Library.

Two pieces of intertwining circles of teak wood, inspired by Leon Smith, a fatally ill Livermore Lab employee who badgered the city into installing it. The sculpture is approx. 18 feet high, sturdy enough for children to play on. The sculptor, Don Homan, also a Lab employee, believed it looks like Livermore would look from a space craft. TVC has gathered around it for various vigils and demonstrations.

Valley Times (July 5, 1984).

75. **Tri-Valley CAREs* (1983) (org).

2582 Old First St., Livermore 94550;
(925) 443-7148; *marylia@earthlink.net;
www.igc.org/tvc*

Located in the town which has one of the two major U.S. nuclear weapons design facilities, the Lawrence Livermore National Laboratory, this "Communities Against a Radioactive Environment" group protests plutonium dangers in Livermore (high levels in city parks) and throughout the world. The group's achievements include forcing the shutdown of a radioactive and toxic waste incinerator at the Lab and exposure of U.S. treaty violations. Member of the Alliance for Nuclear Accountability in the U.S. since 1989 and a co-founding member of the international Abolition 2000 network for the elimination of nuclear weapons. Marylia Kelley, Exec. Dir.

LONG BEACH, CA

76. **Long Beach Peace Network* (1999) (org).

PMB 471, 203 Argonne Ave., Suite B,
Long Beach 90803; (562) 438-6505 or
804-5564; *eruyle@csulb.edu*

Works to raise awareness and commitment at every level from individuals and homes to world affairs. Demonstrated at the Seal Beach Nuclear Weapons Station in August 1999 in memory of the atomic bombing of Hiroshima and Nagasaki; in October leafleted Madeleine Albright's appearance; and other activities planned. Gene Ruyle, organizer.

77. *Peace Pole* (1995) (mem).

California State University, Long Beach, next to the Multicultural Center.

Paid for by Globe, an environmental group on campus. Idea of Bob Rodgers.

Peace Pole located at California State University, Long Beach, California. Photograph courtesy of Susan Rice.

78. *Peace Studies Certificate Program* (1991) (col).

California State University, Long Beach, 1250 Bellflower Boulevard, Long Beach 90840-0902; *srice@csulb.edu*

A Program designed to enable students to define peace, discover the processes that create peace among peoples on this planet, learn about past and present conflicts that inhibit the achievement of peace, and promote peace by developing their thinking and communication skills to use in conflict situations. "Students will be empowered to believe that they can make a difference and will be encouraged in their activism." Susan Rice, Dept. of Social Work, and Ben Wisner, International Studies Program, Co-directors.

79. *Peter Carr Peace Center* (1981) (col).

c/o Eugene Ruyle, Dept. of Anthropology, California State University, Long Beach 90840; (562) 985-5364; *eruyle@csulb.edu; www.csulb.edu/~eruyle/pcpchome.html*

PCPC was founded in memory of Peter Carr—poet, artist, peace activist, and a founder of the Alliance for Survival. Its mission statement is Carr's 1977 work, "In the Summer We Went to the Mountains," in which he writes: "I keep telling [the managers] to quit messing with the stream beds and the sycamore flats and the redwoods up the coast. I keep telling everyone down here that we have to stop those nuclear businessmen and their helpers." The Center helped establish the Peace Studies Program at CSULB, and participates in demonstrations, sponsors lectures and forums, and other actions. Pub. occasional newsletter, the *Peter Carr Peace Center News*. Eugene Ruyle, organizer.

LOS ANGELES, CA

80. *Friendship Bell* (1976) (mem).

On the Upper Reservation of the old Fort MacArthur overlooking Point Fermin at the Port of Los Angeles near the San Pedro neighborhood of Los Angeles.

A bicentennial gift from South Korea, the Bell weighs seventeen tons and is twelve feet high, said to be the largest bell ever cast in Asia. Thirty workers came from Korea for the installation. (See KY.)

81. *Japanese American National Museum* (1985) (org).

In the Little Tokyo district of Los Angeles.

Originally a small former Buddhist temple, a $22 million pavilion named "Common Ground: The Heart of Community" was added in 1999 to house the collection of WWII Japanese-American internment in concentration camps around the nation. Gyo Obata, architect.

82. *National Committee Against Repressive Legislation* (1960) (org).

1313 W. 8th St., Suite 313, Los Angeles 90017; (213) 484-6661.

Originally the National Committee to Abolish HUAC. Frank Wilkinson, Exec. Dir. Emeritus; Kit Gage, Washington Rep.

83. **Pax Christi Southern California* (1970) (org).

St. Camillius Pastoral Center, 1911 Zonal Ave., Los Angeles 90033; (323) 223-9047; *cponnet.stcamillus@usa.net; www.circlesofhope.org*

Coordinating center for chapters in East L.A., San Pedro, Claremont, and Santa Monica. Among other activities: monthly liturgy peace and justice mass, weekly street demonstrations on current issues, especially nuclear, Las Vegas test site protests, Interfaith Campaign for Nuclear Free World. Fr. Chris Ponnet, Co-Coordinator.

84. **Peace and Conflict Studies Program* (1987) (col).

School of International Relations, Univ. of Southern California, Los Angeles 90089; *emgross@usc.edu; www.usc.edu/dept/admissions/undergrad/ minors3.html#PeaceandConflictStudies*

This minor degree program of 16 hours includes core courses, electives, and internship. The goal is to widen understanding of self and world in regard to violence and its alternatives. Contact JoAnn Baldwin (213-740-8630; jbaldwin@usc.edu).

85. **Peace Studies* (col).

College of Liberal Arts, Loyola Marymount University, Los Angeles 90045; (310) 338-2716; *dchristo@lmumail.lmu.edu; www.lmu.edu*

A minor and special programs promote student involvement in problems of war, violence, ethnic conflicts, and in values of nonviolence and toleration. Daniel Smith-Christopher, Dir.

86. *Peaceable Kingdom (Proposed).*

Los Angeles area.

Memorial to the Animal Rights Movement and the dream of a cruelty-free world, a joint project of The Peace Abbey (see MA) and Farm Sanctuary (see NY State). The memorial will include animal statues and bronze plaques with compassionate statements by great historical figures, such as Da Vinci, Tolstoy, Schweitzer, Gandhi, and Peace Pilgrim. Designed by Lado Goudjabidze.

87. **Simon Wiesenthal Center and Museum of Tolerance* (1977) (mus, org).

9786 West Pico Blvd., Los Angeles, 90035; (310) 553-8403; *www.wiesenthal.com.*

Not only dedicated to education about anti-Semitism and the Holocaust, the Center and Museum also expose the subjects of racism, prejudice, and discrimination in general. The Center is a human rights organization, with offices in several countries around the world. The Museum contains the Tolerancenter that focuses on intolerance in the U.S., a Holocaust display (letters of Anne Frank, artifacts from Auschwitz, artwork from Theresienstadt, etc.), a Multimedia Learning Center for research into the Holocaust (*www.motlc.wiesenthal.com*), an Exhibition Gallery with changing exhibitions, an auditorium for lectures, concerts, and films, a gift shop, and a cafeteria. The Museum has been the site for the International Human Rights Watch Film Festival and other film festivals. Pub. a brochure.

MILL VALLEY, CA

88. **The Light Party* (1999) (org).

20 Sunnyside Ave., Suite A-156, Mill Valley 94941; (415) 381-4061; *www.LightParty.com; www.GlobalPeaceFoundation.org*

A "holistic, synergistic 7-point program" for "health, peace, and freedom": demilitarization and abolition of nuclear weapons, establishment of global peace center at Alcatraz, sustainable global economy, a new TV network for health and peace, etc. Da Vid, M.D., founder.

MONTEREY, CA

89. **Center for Nonproliferation Studies, Monterey Institute for International Studies* (1989) (org).

425 Van Buren St., Monterey 93940; (831) 647-4154; *cns@miis.edu;bmonning@ miis.edu; asands@miis.edu; http:// cns.miis.edu/cns/projects/ionp/swords.htm*

The "world's largest non-governmental organization devoted to combating the spread of weapons of mass destruction," with over 50 specialists and five research programs. Trains graduate students. Publishes on-line databases and *The Nonproliferation Review*. Founded by William Potter; Am Sands, Dep. Dir.

90. *Monterey WILPF* (1964) (org).

POB 1851 Monterey 93942-1851; (408) 373-33475; *jvan@mbay.net*; *www.mabay.net/~jvan/wilpf*

Chapter of the Women's International League for Peace and Freedom, founded by Jane Addams. Lectures, workshops, protests. Diane Sammet, Chairperson; contact Joyce Vandevere.

MOUNTAIN VIEW, CA

91. *Center for Economic Conversion* (1975) (org).

222 View St., Mountain View 94041; (650) 968-8798; *cec@igc.org*; *www.conversion.org/about2.html*

Originally called the Mid-Peninsula Conversion Project, founded as a project of the Friends Service Committee, CEC became independent in 1978. Its mission is "to help build an economy that meets social needs and works in harmony with the environment." During the Cold War, CEC emphasized the transfer of military resources to civilian endeavors; today it concentrates on sustainable economic development, military conversion into revitalized local and regional economies, turning closed military base sites into eco-industrial parks. Joan Holtzman, Exec. Dir.

NEVADA CITY, CA

92. *T. D. Hopkins Peace Camp Fund* (1998) (org).

12959 Woolman Lane, Nevada City 95959; (530) 274-1862.

This small mini-grant fund in memory of Thomas David Hopkins supports Children's Peace Camp projects, a project of the Northern California Association for the Education of Young Children. The Peace Camps seek "to provide an alternative day camp experience which fosters an understanding of peace, justice, and environmental awareness."

T. D. Hopkins Peace Camp located at Nevada City, California. Photograph courtesy Susan Hopkins.

OAKLAND, CA

93. *Central Committee for Conscientious Objectors* (1968) (org).

630 20th St. #302, Oakland 94612; *info@objector.org; www.objector.org*

Promotes individual and collective resistance to war and preparations for war. Includes Military Out of Our Schools program to counter military recruiters in schools, focusing on youth in communities of color and the working class. Contact Alex Doty. (East Coast office in Philadelphia.)

94. *Community Peacemakers* (1996) (org).

2908 Madeline St., Suite 100, Oakland 94602-3337; (510) 530-1319; *compeace@concentric.net*; *www.compeace.org/sys-tmpl*

Co-partners with Bay Area educational and spiritual centers and social groups in search of a nonviolent, equal, and just society. Variety of programs: Peace Ambassadors Network, Brother Peacemaker, Bay Area Peace Power Alert, monthly Internet Express, etc. Don Marx, Exec. Dir.

95. *Food First* (1975) (org).

Institute for Food & Development Policy, 398-60th St., Oakland 94618; (510) 654-4400; *www.foodfirst.org*

Exposes the root causes of hunger in a world of plenty and defends the right to be free from hunger that claims some 40,000 children in the world every day. Pub. books about hunger to awaken and move people to take effective action against the concentrated economic and political power that creates hunger. Some of FF's books: *America Needs Human Rights*, *The Paradox of Plenty*, *Dark Victory: The United States and Global Poverty*, *Basta! Land and the Zapatista Rebellion in Chiapas*. Founded by Frances Moore Lappé and Joseph Collins. See also Hunger.

96. *Institute in Cultural and Creation Spirituality* (col).

Holy Names College, 3500 Mountain Blvd., Oakland 94619; (510) 436-1317; *garner@admin.hnc.edu*; *www.hnc.edu/gradcs.html*

Offers both a MA and a Certificate on the spiritual dimensions of peace and creativity. Contact Cathryn Farrell.

97. *Peace Brigades International/USA* (1983) (org). (recently moved to Washington, D.C.)

428 8th St. SE, Washington, D.C. 20003; *pbiusa@igc.apc.org*; *www.igc.org/pbi* See: Toronto, Canada.

PBI sends unarmed peace teams, "protective accompaniment," into areas of violent conflict or repression, at the request of local individuals or organizations under threat. Winner of several peace prizes. First team in Guatemala (1983–1999), followed by El Salvador (1987–1992) and Sri Lanka (1989–1998), North America (1992, Native Americans), Colombia (1994–), and now in Mexico. The teams also make reports on human rights and give training in nonviolence (Haiti Project). Pub. *Unarmed Bodyguards* and *PBI/USA Report* quarterly newsletter. Articles in the Fall 1999 *Report* include reports on Colombia and East Timor; the Winter 1999 issue has the same and articles on, "Diplomatic Relations,"

"Training Future Peacemakers," and "The Balkan Peace Team in Kosovo/a." Videos: *Unarmed Commitment*, *In the Company of Fear* (Columbia). Pete Stanga, Dir.

98. *World Wall for Peace, Oakland* (1988–) (mem).

Oakland is "a city with more peace walls than any other city in the world," says their founder, Carolyna Marks. (See: Berkeley, CA.) According to her brochure, there are a total of 9,000 Peace Tiles in Oakland, created mainly by Oakland residents. Chabot Elementary School, 6686 Chabot Road: 644 tiles (1989). Merritt College, 1200 Campus Drive, 1000 tiles located in the cafeteria. Fruitvale BART Peace Wall, East Oakland: 3500 tiles, painted by 3,000 youth and 600 adults (1994). Fruitvale Elementary School, 3200 Boston Ave.: 2000 tiles (1999). Jack London Square, 98 Broadway, composed of five Peace Walls with 3000 tiles: U.N. Peace Wall (1996); Peacemaking Power of Non-Violence Peace Wall (1997); Community Peace (done by five artists from northern Finland) (1998); Our Work Place a Peace Place (1999); and Our Families and Friends a Reservoir of Peace (1999). Around the world, there are 33 Walls in 6 U.S. states and internationally in three other nations. Marks conceives of these walls as part of one World Wall for Peace, and she believes that this and all creativity releases us from violence.

ORANGE, CA

99. *Peace Studies* (col).

Dept. of Peace Studies, Chapman University, Orange 92866; *will@chapman.edu*; *www.chapman.edu/wilkinson/socsci/peace_studies*

Offers both a BA (1989) and minor (1981) in peace studies, requiring core courses and encouraging an area specialization. The program has an endowed chair, a Peace Lecture series, a Peace Club, and an internship. Donald Will, Chair.

ORINDA, CA

100. *Conflict Resolution* (1993) (col).

Graduate School of Professional Psychology, John F. Kennedy University, Orinda

94563; (925) 258-7263; *mapsych@jfku.edu; www.jfku.edu/psych/index.html*

MA programs in counseling and organization psychology include specializations in conflict resolution, and a certificate program is also available.

PALM BEACH, CA

101. **Pax Christi Palm Beach Area* (1986) (org).

4855A Equestrian Road, Boynton Beach 33436-4310; (561) 731-4605; *dorney@juno.com*

Activities include School of Americas Watch lobbying and vigils, death penalty abolition letter writing and information, ending Iraq sanctions march, petitions. Contact Maureen Dorney.

PALM DESERT, CA

102. **Unitarian Universalist Peace Fellowship* (1941) (org).

48365 Prairie Dr., Palm Desert 92260; *dendawnh@worldnet.att.net*

A clearinghouse on conscientious objection for UUs and other issues. In 1999 working with other organizations on demonstrations in Washington, DC, during the summer of 2000 in support of the Decade for a Culture of Nonviolence for the Children of the World, approved by unanimous vote of the U.N. General Assembly. Presents an annual Adin Ballou Peace Award (in 1999 to Rev. Daniel Berrigan), named after the 19th-century Universalist and founder of the utopian Hopedale community in Massachusetts. Affil. with Fellowship of Reconciliation, and participated in the Fellowship of Reconciliation initiated "People's Campaign for Nonviolence" July 1–August 9, 2000, in Washington, DC. Pub. *UNIPAX* newsletter (print and e-mail). Rev. Dennis Davidson, Pres.

PALO ALTO, CA

103. **Computer Professionals for Social Responsibility* (1981) (org).

PO Box 717, Palo Alto 94302; *cpsr@cpsr.org; www.cpsr.org/home.html*

Works to educate computer professionals, policymakers, and the public about the relationship of computers and nuclear weapons and related issues. Pub. *CPSR Newsletter* quarterly. Annual conference.

104. **Peninsula Peace and Justice Center* (1965) (org).

In historic Westminster House, 457 Kingsley Ave., Palo Alto 94301; (650) 326-8837; hotline: (650) 321-4464; *paul@peacecenter.com; ppjc@peacecenter.com; www.peacecenter.com*

Committed to: changing U.S. foreign and domestic policies to meet human needs and rights; a demilitarized society and economy; end to all forms of discrimination; building coalitions; empowering citizens through information. Demonstrations, petition campaigns, vigils, meeting with elected officials; a speakers bureau; resources center. Pub. *PeaceWORKS* semi-monthly newsletter. Recent actions: demonstrations against the bombings of Yugoslavia and a concert and rally to raise money for both Kosovar and Serbian victims of the bombings. Paul George, Dir.

Workman, Bill. "Palo Alto Man Has Arresting Record on Peace Work." *San Francisco Chronicle* (June 10, 1999) A19.

PASADENA, CA

105. **American Friends Service Committee (AFSC), Pacific Southwest Region* (1942) (org).

980 N. Fair Oaks Ave., Pasadena 91103-3097; (626) 791-1978; *Lbrusseau@afsc.org; www.afsc.org/psro/pasa2.htm*

A Quaker organization of people of various faiths committed to peace, social justice, and humanitarian service. Local offices in Tucson, AZ, Honolulu, HI, Espanola, NM, and San Diego, CA. (National office: Philadelphia, *www.afsc.org*).

PETALUMA, CA

106. **Petaluma Progressives* (1995) (org).

PO Box 445, Petaluma 94953; (707) 763-8134; *shermuse@sonic.net*

Monthly meetings at Copperfield's Books,

140 Kentucky St. Peace, justice, and economic actions; for example, spring of 1999 weekly vigils against the bombings of Iraq and Yugoslavia. Monthly video series. Coord.: Chuck Sher.

PORT HUENEME, CA

107. *The Atomic Mirror* (1994) (org).

PO Box 220, Port Hueneme 93044; (805) 985-5073; *pmeidell@igc.org*; *bruyne@antenna.nl*; *www.antenna.nl/nukeatlas*

Founded in Malibu, Atomic Mirror is an umbrella for independent projects aiming for a world free from nuclear pollution. Provides an *Internet Atlas* for information pertaining to world-wide military and commercial nuclear facilities, and to facilitate exchange of research on environmental protection and nuclear disarmament. AM is part of Abolition 2000. Pamela Meidell and Suzanne Bruijne, Directors.

REDWOOD CITY, CA

108. *Catholic Worker House* (1976) (org).

545 Cassia St., PO Box 513, Redwood City 94064; (650) 366-4415.

A home for troubled teens but also vigils, leaflets, and talks for peace. Newsletter eight times a year. Larry Purcell, Coordinator.

RIVERSIDE, CA

109. *Conflict Management and Mediation Training* (col).

University Extension Center, Univ. of California, Riverside 92521; (909) 787-4111 x1616; *law@ucx.ucr.edu*; *www.unex.ucr.edu/law/mediation.html*

A Certificate in Conflict Management provides the basics of negotiation through core courses and electives, intended for counselors, attorneys, law enforcement officers, and related people. Elaine Rosen, Dir.

110. *Conflict Resolution for Educational Environments Certificate* (1995) (col).

University Extension Center, Univ. of California, Riverside 92521; (909) 787-4361, x1660; *moreinfo@unx.ucr.edu*; *www.unex.ucr.edu/certificates/conflict-resolution.html*

Designed for school administrators, teachers, and all personnel in the schools, to increase their skills in conflict and violence prevention, intervention, and resolution. Dr. Margi Wild, Dir.

111. *Frank A. Miller Testimonial Peace Tower* (1925) (mem).

On top of Mount Rubidoux near Riverside.

Built in appreciation of Frank Augustus Miller's lifetime dedication to his community and world peace. The tower bears the names and coats of arms of all nations at that time. Carved on the keystone are the words: "World Peace" and on a bronze tablet a portrait of Miller and the inscription" "Peace and Justice for All Men—1925." The architect was Arthur Benton.

SACRAMENTO, CA

112. *California Center for Public Dispute Resolution* (1992) (org).

1303 J St., Suite 250, Sacramento 94814; *sherryse@saclink.csus.edu*; *www.csus.edu/ccpdr/*

CCPDR offers services to regional, state, and local groups seeking assistance in solving conflicts, through mediation, consensus building, etc. Internships available. Susan Sherry, Exec. Dir.

113. *Center for African Peace and Conflict Resolution* (1996) (col).

California State University, School of Health and Human Services, 6000 J St., Sacramento 95819-6085; (916) 278-6282; *uwazieee@csus.edu*

"Providing conflict resolution, conciliation, and peace-building services and research for African (Diaspora) groups, governments, organizations, and families." Annual summer institute on Conflict Resolution; workshop on court mediation in West Africa; etc. Pub.: newsletter. Ernest Uwazie, Dir.

114. **Peace and Conflict Resolution Program* (1970) (col).

California State University, Sacramento 95819; (916) 278-6202; *dormanw@csus.edu;* *www.csus.edu/catalog/cat98/C8.htm*

This minor degree of 21 units prepares students for peaceful citizenship and for advanced studies in the peace professions. (The program arose in response to the invasion of Cambodia in 1970.) William Dorman, Coord.

115. **Sacramento-Yolo Peace Action* (1982) (org).

909 12th St., #118, Sacramento 95814; (916) 448-7157; *pasacramento@igc.org.*

Established as the Sacramento Nuclear Weapons Freeze, in 1987 became branch of SANE/ Freeze, then in 1993 a branch of Peace Action. Monthly discussions, quarterly member meetings, public programs, demonstrations, protests, lobbying. Pub.: monthly newsletter. Mario Galvan, Pres., and contact Winnie Detwiler.

SAN DIEGO, CA

116. **Committee Opposed to Militarism and the Draft (COMD)* (1979) (org).

PO Box 15195, San Diego 92175; (760) 753-7518, (619) 265-1369; *comdsd@aol.com; ProjYANO@aol.com*

San Diego's oldest active peace organization, COMD is "an anti-draft organization which also challenges the military institution, its effect on society, its budget, its role abroad and at home, and the racism, sexism, and homophobia that are inherent in the armed forces and Selective Service System." It co-founded Project YANO; promotes the AFSC report *Trading Books for Soldiers: The True Cost of JROTC*; supports the Peace on Earth Carolers; etc. Pub. bimonthly newsletter, *Draft Notices*; its 15th Anniversary Issue (July-Aug. 1994) includes articles on the history of COMD, JROTC, family life of military personnel; and other pieces; its Sept.-Oct. 1999 issue has articles on the draft, Yugoslavia and Kosovo, military recruiting, U.S. culture of violence, JROTC, women in the military, child soldiers. Contact Rick Jahnkow.

117. **Institute on Global Conflict and Cooperation* (1983) (col).

Univ. of California—San Diego, 9500 Gilman Drive, La Jolla 92093; (858) 534-3352; *pcowhey@ucsd.edu;* *www-igcc.ucsd.edu*

A research center in support of instructional programs in peace and security studies throughout the Univ. of California system. Also hosts conferences and pub. a newsletter. Peter Cowhey, Dir.

118. **International Security and Conflict Resolution Program (ISCOR)* (1995) (col).

Dept. of Political Science, San Diego State Univ., San Diego 92182; (619) 594-2778; *djohns@mail.sdsu.edu;* *www.sdsu.edu/academicprog/iscor.html*

This interdisciplinary program drawn from three colleges examines global systems and security and leads to a BA degree in liberal arts. The Institute for International Security and Conflict Resolution (IISCOR) (1989) pub. annually the *Institute for International Security and Conflict Resolution Newsletter*. David Johns, Coord.

119. **Kroc Institute for Peace and Justice* (1999) (col).

University of San Diego, 5998 Alcalá Park, San Diego 92100-2492; (619) 260-2358; *daker@acusd.edu; www.acusd.edu/peace*

The 90,000 square foot Institute will stand on the west point of the campus looking out to San Diego, Mission Bay, and the Pacific Ocean, amid courtyards, gardens, and reflection pools.

"To foster harmony, safety, and hope in a context of mutual respect and fairness in international, national, and local communities" is the purpose of the Kroc Institute, a place where "scholars, students, activists, and leaders can study, reflect, engage in dialogue, and work to promote peace and justice in the world." Both undergraduate and graduate programs are planned. Philanthropist Joan B. Kroc donated $25 million to the University for the Institute building and programs. Ground breaking October 6, 1999, open in 2001. Contact Dee Aker, Planning Coordinator.

Kroc Institute for Peace and Justice, University of San Diego, California. Courtesy of University of San Diego.

120. **Peace Resource Center of San Diego* (1980) (org).

PO Box 15307, San Diego 92175; (619) 265-0780; *prcsandiego@igc.org*; *www.activistsandiego.org*

A clearinghouse of over 40 member organizations devoted to peace and social justice education and activities in San Diego County. PRC is guided by the principles of nonviolence, tolerance, compassion, and respect for diversity. Current emphases: Central Clearinghouse, with books, videos, news; Children Nonviolence Project; Peace Writing Contest for High School Students; disarmament; military toxics; counter-recruitment. Pubs.: *Peace Center News* and *Peace Calendar* bi-monthly. Carol Jahnkow, Exec. Dir.

121. **San Diego F.O.R.* (1983) (org).

Box 1, Bonita 91908; (619) 479-4125.

Branch of the Fellowship of Reconciliation. Steve and Molly Gassaway.

SAN FRANCISCO, CA

122. **American Friends Service Committee (AFSC), Pacific Mountain Regional Office* (1942) (org).

65 Ninth St., San Francisco 94103; (415) 565-0201; *www.afsc.org/afscpmhp.htm*

A Quaker organization striving for peace and social justice, headquartered in Philadelphia. Pacific Mountain satellite offices in Oakland, Stockton, Visalia, and Davis.

123. **Association of World Citizens* (1975) (org).

55 New Montgomery St., Suite 224, San Francisco 94105; (415) 541-9610; *info@worldcitizens.org*; *www.worldcitizens.org*

The mission of AWC is to build the global village. The first priority for this task is to end the nationalistic war system, which killed 100 million people during this century, including 23 million in the past 45 years, most of whom were civilians. The way to this peaceful future is through world law, a democratic United Nations, a Peoples Assembly representing Non-Government Organizations (NGOs), an end to the arms trade, limitations on standing armies, elimination of nuclear, biological, chemical, and other weapons of mass destruction. Current projects: Peoples' Assembly in the U.N., World Citizenship Day, World Citizens Award, World Citizen Centers, World Citizen Assemblies. Doug Mattern, Pres.

124. *Center for Justice and Accountability* (1998) (org).

588 Sutter St., No. 433, San Francisco 94102; (415) 544-0444.

Established to close off the U.S. to torturers and other violators of human rights by helping torture victims sue perpetrators residing in the U.S. The Alien Torts Act of 1789, the first Congress, allows foreigners to sue if they are victims of crimes committed "in violation of the law of nations," reaffirmed in 1992 by the Torture Victim Protection Act, allowing U.S. citizens to file suit. By October 1998 approximately 35 suits had been filed and almost all have won, though few have collected the money (including a victory of $2 billion awarded to 10,000 victims of Philippine's dictator, Ferdinand Marcos). Founded by Gerald Gray.

125. *Committee for Nuclear Responsibility* (1971) (org).

PO Box 421993, San Francisco 94142; (415) 776-8299; *www.ratical.com/radiation/CNR/*

Dedicated to alerting people of the consequences from radiation pollution. Publications include *Preventing Breast Cancer*. Founded and directed by John W. Gofman.

126. *Committee of Atomic Bomb Survivors in the U.S.* (1971) (org).

1759 Sutter St., San Francisco 94115; (562) 698-0855.

After failing to gain medical assistance from the U.S. government or the State of California, the group focuses on helping the survivors. Membership made up of survivors. Mitsuo Tomozawa, President. See entry 132.

127. *Community and Global Studies* (1996) (col).

777 Valencia St., New College of California: World College Institute, San Francisco 94110; *jgarfield@ncgate.newcollege.edu; www.newcollege.edu/humanities/com_glob.htm*

This undergraduate BA program studies global economy, world cultures, and social movements. Fieldwork and internships emphasized. Jon Garfield, Coord.

128. *Earthjustice Legal Defense Fund* (1970) (org).

180 Montgomery St., Suite 1400, San Francisco 94104-4209; (415) 627-6700; *www.earthjustice.org*

The "law firm for the environment," active in creating and enforcing environmental laws in court. Vawter "Buck" Parker, Pres.

129. *Episcopal Peace Fellowship of San Francisco* (1983) (org).

Community of St. Francis, 3743 César Chávez St., San Francisco 94110; (415) 824-0288; *csf@sfo.com*

Occasional meetings. Sr. Pamela Clare, CSF, Convenor.

130. *Family Violence Prevention Fund* (1980) (org).

383 Rhode Island St., Suite 304, San Francisco 94103-5133; (415) 252-8900; *fund@fvpf.org; www.fvpf.org/*

Advocates domestic violence prevention, education, and public policy reform. One of its programs is the National Workplace Resource Center on Domestic Violence, which brings employers and unions together to inform employees and union members about domestic violence. This initiative sponsors the annual Work to End Domestic Violence Day, October 1. The Fund was founded by Esta Soler.

131. *Food Not Bombs* (1987) (org).

PO Box 40485, San Francisco 94140; (415) 675-9928; *sffnb@iww.org; www.foodnotbombs.org*

Challenges the system of militarism and inequality that creates violence and poverty "in the process of generating profit and privilege," and distributes free vegetarian food at open community meals in public places.

Crass, Chris. "FNB: Cooking for Peace and Social Change." *Peacework* (June 1999) 19-20.

Ziman, Jenna, and Hugh Mejia. "Food Not Bombs—Part of the International Struggle for Economic Human Rights." *Peacework* (June 1999) 17-18.

132. *Friends of Hibakusha* (1981) (org).

1832 Buchanan St., Ste. 206, San Francisco 94115; (415) 567-7599.

Supports survivors of WWII atomic bombings of Hiroshima and Nagasaki in U.S., informs public of effects of nuclear war, encourages research into radiation exposure, supports the Committee of Atomic Bomb Survivors. Pub. *The Paper Crane* quarterly.

133. **Global Peace, Human Rights Justice Studies* (1989) (col).

Dept. of Philosophy, San Francisco State Univ., San Francisco 94132; (415) 338-1598; *aanton@sfsu.edu; www.sfsu.edu/~bulletin/current/programs/global.htm*

This undergraduate minor degree program concentrates on the causes of violence, wars, and related topics, and on prevention and solutions to conflicts, especially international law of human rights. Anatole Anton, Co-Director.

134. **Health Science and Human Survival* (1986) (org).

Dept. of Anthropology, History, and Social Medicine, Univ. of California, San Francisco 94143; *ckiefer@itsa.ucsf.edu; www.ucsf.edu/global*

Deals with the links among health, international politics, poverty, human rights, violence, and similar subjects, especially in regard to the developing world. Chris Kiefer, Dir.

135. **Institute for Global Communications* (1987) (org).

Presidio Building #1012, First Floor, Torney Ave., PO Box 29904, San Francisco 94129-0904; (415) 561-6100; *support5@igc.apc.org; www.igc.apc.org*

Provides PeaceNet and EcoNet, a worldwide computer network connecting progressive activists in over 100 countries. Helped create the Association of Progressive Communications for low-cost computer networks in non-industrialized countries, as well as Alternex (Brazil), Nicarao (Nicaragua), and GlasNet (USSR) nonprofit computer networks. Now developing computer networks in other countries, to empower local, indigenous organizations. IGC Division of the Tides Foundation. Marci Lockwood, Dir. Charlie Rosenberg, Technical Support.

136. **Martin de Porres House of Hospitality* (1971) (org).

225 Potrero Ave., San Francisco 94103; (415) 552-0240

A house of the Catholic Worker Movement, Martin's is a free restaurant, on the principle that food is a right and feeding the hungry a matter of justice. Members have protested the Gulf War and the Nevada Test Site, and some have been arrested. Two members performed music and led liturgy at the test site for Millennium 2000 with the Nevada Desert Experience. They have marched and vigiled against the bombings of Yugoslavia and the bombings and sanctions against Iraq, and vigiled at the Pentagon and San Quentin at executions, and at other locations. Quarterly newsletter, *Martin de Porres House of Hospitality*. Barbara Collier, Director.

137. **Montessori Institute* (1972) (org).

678 Portola Drive, San Francisco, 94127; (415) 731-8188; *pax102@aol.com; www.3000.com/montessori_sf*

Publishes "Peace 101, Implementing the Vision" by Ursula Thrush that promotes Nobel Peace Prize Nominee Dr. Maria Montessori's belief that "establishing peace is the work of education" by combining academic skills that lead to intellectual understanding with the hands-on practice of peace-making skills.

138. **Pax Christi Bay Area* (1991) (org).

1086 Guerrero St., San Francisco 94110; (415) 285-2281; *twebb@woodsidepriory.com*

Pax Christi represents the growth of a nonviolent stance in the Roman Catholic church in the last half of the 20th century. Tom Webb, Regional Rep.

139. **Peace and Justice Studies Program* (1990) (org).

2130 Fulton St., University of San Francisco, San Francisco 94117-1080; (415) 422-6981; *zunes@usfca.edu*

An undergraduate interdisciplinary program. Courses include: Nonviolence in Theory and Practice, Global Conflict Resolution, Politics of War & Peace. Stephen Zunes, Dept. of Politics, Coordinator.

140. **Peace Review* (1989) (jour).

Politics Department, U. of San Francisco, 2130 Fulton St., San Francisco 94117; *watkinsr@usfca.edu*

A quarterly, transnational, multidisciplinary journal publishing essays in peace studies, broadly defined. Topics include war, violence, human rights, political economy, and related issues.

141. *Peaceworkers* (1978) (org).

721 Shrader St., San Francisco 94117; (415) 751-0302; *peaceworkers@igc.org*; *www.peaceworkers.org*

Promotes acceptance of nonviolent methods of peacemaking by individuals and by world bodies, including the United Nations. Arranges for individuals and teams to be on call for service in conflict areas, cooperates with likeminded organizations, like Peace Brigades, U.N. Volunteers, and Fellowship of Reconciliation. Working for the establishment of an international nonviolent Peace Force. Assisting nonviolent peace groups in Mexico. David Hartsough, Exec. Dir.

142. *Ploughshares Fund* (1981) (org).

Fort Mason Center, Bldg. B, Suite 330, San Francisco 94123; (415) 775-2244; *ploughshares@igc.org*; *www.ploughshares.org/about.html*

Founded to provide financial support to the best ideas and practices working to eliminate the threat of nuclear war. Now the Fund additionally strives to prevent nuclear and conventional weapons proliferation and regional conflicts. PF has made over 1,400 grants totaling more than $18,000,000 since its inception. Founded by Sally Lilienthal. Naila Bolus, Exec. Dir.

143. *Rainforest Action Network* (1985) (org).

221 Pine St., Suite 500, San Francisco, 94104; (415) 398-4404.

Works to protect tropical rainforests and the human rights of those living in and around those forests.

144. *Saybrook Graduate School and Research Center* (1971) (org).

450 Pacific, 3rd Fl, San Francisco 94133-4640; (415) 433-9200; *saybrook@saybrook.edu; www.saybrook.edu*

Saybrook "was founded on the view that human consciousness...is a work in progress for which we are each responsible." Offers a Concentration in "Peace, Conflict Resolution, and Community Development," in which students can learn "to be activist/scholars, to link theory to practice, and to contribute to a body of knowledge which can directly lead to a process of social change based on humanistic values and democratic processes." Gerald Bush, Pres.

145. *Sierra Club* (1892) (org).

85 Second St., 2nd Fl., San Francisco 94105-3441; *information@sierraclub.org*; *www.sierraclub.org*

Large membership org. (over half a million with more than 65 Chapters and 400 local groups) dedicated to a sustainable environment, especially the protection and preservation of wild lands in the U.S. Pubs.: books, calendars, *Sierra Magazine*. Founded by John Muir. SC and Amnesty International joined forces in 1999 to protect environmental journalists, and issued their first joint report: *Environmentalists Under Attack*.

146. *United Religions Initiative* (1996) (org).

PO Box 29242, San Francisco 94129-0242; (415) 561-2300; *office@united-religions.org*; *www.united-religions.org*

Its goal is to create the United Religions in June 2000—"a permanent public forum where people of many faiths gather in mutual respect to pursue justice, healing, and peace, with reverence for all life." Many projects are already under way. Pub. *United Religions Initiative*. Founder: Rt. Rev. William Swing, Bishop of the Episcopal Diocese of California.

SAN JOSE, CA

147. *San Jose Peace Center* (1957) (org).

The "Collins House," 48 S. 7th St., San Jose 95112, downtown between San Fernando and Santa Clara Streets; (408)297-2299; *sjpc@sjpeace.org*; *www.SJpeace.org/SJPC*

Begun by citizens concerned about the growth of nuclear arsenals and atmospheric testing. In the late 1960s SJPC spearheaded local efforts to end the war in Vietnam. Today the Center deals with nuclear disarmament, war, human rights, racial and social justice, environment, and other

San Jose Peace Center, downtown San Jose. Photograph courtesy San Jose Peace Center.

issues, to promote nonviolence. The Center offers meeting space, a library of books, audio, and video, resource files, a gift/book shop, a high school peace essay contest, and a monthly newsletter. The Center also supports such groups as the California Coalition for Alternatives to the Death Penalty, the Conflict Resolution Program, Women's International League for Peace and Freedom, Food Not Bombs, Abolition 2000, Peace for Cuba, the San Jose Peace Chorale, and others. The home of the Peace Center, the "Collins House," is owned by the Collins Foundation, named in honor of Evelyn and Rev. George Collins, tireless peace and justice advocates. The front of the building has a peace banner in the window, a peace dove flag flies outside, and two Peace Posts stand in the front yard.

SAN PEDRO, CA

148. *Children for Iraq* (1998) (org).

PO Box 1141, San Pedro 90733-1141;

iraqikids@aol.com; *http://members.aol.com/hamzaha/iraqichildren*

Campaign to send one million postcards to the President of the U.S. The AFSC has a 12-min. film about the campaign: *One Million Postcards*, dir. by Joan Mandell Kouthar and Marwa Al-Rawi.

Arnove, Anthony, ed. *Iraq Under Siege*. Cambridge, MA: South End, 2000.

149. *San Pedro Catholic Worker* (1993) (org).

1149 Crestwood St., San Pedro 90732; (310) 831-3480; *spcw@juno.com*

Weekly vigils at LOGICON military contractor. Pub. quarterly *In the Breaking of the Bread*; the Autumn 1999 issue featured Peter Maurin and the Catholic Worker Movement. Helen and Curt Grove, Coordinators.

SAN RAFAEL, CA

150. *Rotary Peace Cities* (1996) (org).

PO Box 6632, San Rafael 94903; *jreiss11@hotmail.com*; *www.peacecities.org*

Local Rotary Clubs have initiated peace cities in Parksville, Canada, and in Honolulu, East Los Angeles, Port Washington, and Milledgeville/Baldwin Country, GA, USA. Local Rotary Clubs are urged to become a Peace City and to purchase a Plaque, a bronze Dove Peace Symbol, and a Charter. Jeffrey Reiss, Coord.

SANTA BARBARA, CA

151. *Abolition 2000* (1995) (org).

Nuclear Age Peace Foundation, 1187 Coast Village road, PMB 121, Suite 1, Santa Barbara 93108; (805) 965-3443; *a2000@silcom.com*; *www.wagingpeace.org/abolition2000*

A global network working for a treaty to eliminate nuclear weapons. In 1995 activists from around the world drafted a statement calling for a treaty, by the conclusion of the year 2000, requiring the phased elimination of all nuclear weapons. This movement became known as "Abolition 2000." The Abolition 2000 statement has been endorsed by more than 1,400 citizen groups in 89 countries. Carah Ong, Coordinator. See entry 153.

152. **Global Peace and Security Program*
(1982) (col).

Univ. of California, Santa Barbara 93106;
juergens@alishaw.ucsb.edu;
www.gps.ucsb.edu

Interdisciplinary courses on global war and
peace provide a minor degree or certificate. Required: six upper division courses, monthly colloquia, research essay. Pub. include two books of
essays edited by Wolfram Hanreider: *Global
Peace and Security: Trends and Challenges* and
Technology, Strategy, and Arms Control. Mark
Juergensmeyer, Chair.

153. **Nuclear Age Peace Foundation*
(1982) (org).

PMB 121, 1187 Coast Village Rd.,
Suite 1, Santa Barbara 93108-2794;
(805) 965-3443; *wagingpeace@napf.org;*
www.wagingpeace.org

Activities: lecture series, peace retreat, Artists
for Peace!, Sadako Peace Day, Peace Heroes,
Peace Curriculum, Nuclear Age History. Awards:
Distinguished Peace Leadership Award (1983,
Dalai Lama, Tutu, Cousteau, Sagan, Turner,
Caldicott, et al); Peace Essay Contest for high
school students worldwide; scholarships; Peace
Poetry Prizes. Helped create the Abolition 2000
Global Network and the International Crimi-
nal Court; founding member of the Interna-
tional Network of Engineers and Scientists for
Global Responsibility (INES). Pubs: *Waging
Peace Worldwide* journal; Waging Peace Series
(booklets, e.g.: General George Lee Butler, *End-
ing the Nuclear Madness,* 1999); *Waging Peace;
The Sunflower* electronic newsletter on nuclear
weapons abolition and other peace issues. David
Krieger, Pres.

154. *Sadako Peace Garden* (August 6,
1995) (mem).

La Casa de Maria, 800 El Bosque Road,
Santa Barbara 93108.

Dedicated to Sadako Sasaki, the young sur-
vivor of Hiroshima who died of leukemia at age
12 after folding 646 paper cranes to achieve her
wish for health and world peace. A project of the
Nuclear Age Peace Foundation (1187 Coast Village Rd., Suite 123, 93108-2794) and La Casa
de Maria, the Garden was designed by Isabelle
Greene and Irma Cavat.

**Sadako Peace Garden, Santa Barbara, Califor-
nia. Photograph courtesy Nuclear Age Peace
Foundation.**

Santa Cruz, CA

155. *Collateral Damage: A Reality of War*
(August 6, 1995) (mem).

Downtown Santa Cruz near the town
clock.

Sculpture depicting a man, woman, and child
in a final embrace during wartime in memoriam
to all civilians who have died in all wars. "Collateral damage" is the military's public relations
doublespeak for civilian casualties of war. Between the end of World War II and 1995, 85
million civilians had been killed in wars throughout the world (U.N. statistic). Created by the
artist E. A. Chase. The project includes a meditative area with benches and landscaping. An
inspiring video about the community project is
available: Friends of Collateral Damage, 515
Broadway, Santa Cruz 95060; (408) 423-1626.
The Santa Cruz Resource Center for Nonviolence and the Santa Cruz Veterans of Foreign
Wars, Bill Motto Post #5888, were especially

Collateral Damage sculpture by E. A. Chase, Santa Cruz, California. Photograph by Ella Seneres.

instrumental in making the placing of the sculpture possible.

156. *Program in Alternative Dispute Resolution* (1994) (col).

UCSC Extension, Univ. of California, Santa Cruz 95064; (831) 384-4900; *gluce@cats.ucsc.edu; extension.edu/ knowledge_is_timeless/legal/index.html; www.ucsc.edu*

Offers a Certificate through U. of California Extension based upon five courses and a skills unit, for ADR professionals, teachers, counselors, attorneys, and related professionals. Contact Gordon Luce.

157. *Resource Center for Nonviolence* (1976) (org).

515 Broadway, Santa Cruz 95060; (408) 423-1626; *rcnv@cruzio.com; www.rcnv.org*

Education in nonviolence as a force for personal and social change: study groups, workshops, camps, direct action training for demonstrations, conscientious objection and draft counseling, films. A program of the Eschaton Foundation. Special projects: Latin American Nonviolence Support Program, Racial and Economic Justice Program. Pub. *Resource Center for Nonviolence—Center Update,* semiannual. Provides also the Roy C. Kepler Library on Nonviolence and Social Change, books and handcrafts for sale at their New Society Bookstore, and the Santa Cruz Hostel. Occasional notable "residents" stay at the center for varying periods of time: Daniel Berrigan, Wally and Juanita Nelson, Danilo Dolci, Gary Zimmerman, and others.

158. *Servicio Internacional Para La Paz/International Service for Peace (SIPAZ)* (1994) (org).

Box 2415, Santa Cruz 95063; (408) 425-1257; *sipaz@igc.org*

Coalition of organizations world-wide in support of human rights in Mexico.

159. *Women's International League for Peace and Freedom, Santa Cruz County Branch* (1961) *(WILPF)* (1915) (org).

PO Box 61, Santa Cruz 95063; (408) 429-8221, 459-8078; *www.wilpf.got.net*

Engages in diverse peace actions. Pub. the newsletter *Undaunted Dove.* Coord.: Marjorie Boehm.

SANTA ROSA, CA

160. *Sonoma County Center for Peace and Justice* (1986) (org).

540 Pacific Ave., Santa Rosa 95404; (707) 575-8902; *peacentr@sonic.net; www.sonic.net/~peacentr*

Vigils against bombings of Iraq and Yugoslavia, weekly programs or discussion groups, maintains a video, audio, and print library. Assoc. with the Fellowship of Reconciliation. Also the meeting place for other organizations: Veterans for Peace, Taxes for Peace. Pub. the *Sonoma County Peace Press.* The June/July issue had three articles on Yugoslavia, and notes on nonviolence, the School of Americas, Peace Rose, East Timor, Iraqi sanctions, the Los Alamos National Lab, arms trafficking, and other topics. Suzanne Regalado, Dir.

SOMERSET, CA *see* HEMET, CA

SONOMA COUNTY, CA

161. *Peace Circle Developing Peace Site* (1988) (mem).

In Ragle Park, Sonoma County, halfway between Ft. Ross and Sonoma Mission, just west of Sebastopol.

Originally a circle 100 feet in diameter with a Chestnut tree at the center, the circle became an evolving work of art (see *Finite and Infinite Games* by James Carse) and now encloses an Olive tree planted by veterans, a Peace Rose planted by Jewish and Palestinian people, a rock garden to honor a man who worked for peace in Northern Ireland, and a birch tree in honor of a Ukrainian Sister City. Initiated by Arthur Lisch.

STANFORD, CA

162. *Stanford Center on Conflict and Negotiation* (mid-1980s) (col).

Stanford University, Stanford 94305; (650) 723-2574; *byron.bland@leland.stanford.edu; www.stanford.edu/group/sccn/*

Interdisciplinary research and seminars develop theory regarding barriers to prevention and resolution of conflicts, and regarding solutions to the barriers, in the conflicts between individuals, groups, corporations, nations, and others. Annual award for the best paper on conflict resolution by a Stanford student. Pubs.: see *www.stanford.edu/group/sccn/general/wps.html*, and *Barriers to Conflict Resolution* by Arrow, et al. Byron Bland, Assoc. Dir.

STOCKTON, CA

163. *Peace and Justice Network of San Joaquin County* (1984) (org).

PO Box 4123, Stockton 95204; (209) 467-4455; *morearty@sonnet.com*

Impelled by a vision of a world of equality, adequate and fairly shared food, nonviolent resolution of conflicts, and a nurtured environment. Organizes Earth Day, Peaceful Holiday Gift Fair, Thinking Globally Conference, PeaceWords Peace Essay Contest. Pub., media: *Connections* (1986) monthly newsletter, 8000 circ., Bruce Giudici, editor (*bgiudici@caltel.com, www.sonnet.com/usr/pjc*). "Talking It Through" (1991), a weekly one-hour TV show on public access cable, John Morearty, Producer (209-464-3326). Eric Parfrey, Chair (209-462-4808; *eric@baseline-env.com*).

TECOPA, CA

164. *Healing Global Wounds* (1991) (org).

PO Box 420, Tecopa 92389; (760) 852-4175; *hgw@scruznet.com; heal@kay-net.com; www.shundahai.org/hgw*

Organizes spring and fall demonstrations at the Nevada Nuclear Test Site. May 7–10, 1999, about 700 people met for the 7th annual Spring Gathering, demanding an end to all nuclear weapons development programs and the radioactive poisoning of Mother Earth, and a halt to the dumping of nuclear waste on native sacred lands, especially honoring mothers' contributions to the environmental and native sovereignty movements. 198 people entered the site. Fall Gathering Oct. 8–11, 1999: daily Sunrise Ceremony to remember the theft of NTS land from the Western Shoshone in 1948; workshops on Yucca Mt. Waste Repository and alternatives; Indigenous Peoples' Day; etc. Coordinator: Jennifer Viereck.

TOMALES, CA

165. *Blue Mountain Center of Meditation* (1961) (org).

PO Box 256, Tomales 94971; *info@nilgiri.org; www.nilgiri.org*

Offers instruction in meditation and allied living skills, following the Eight-Point Program developed by Sri Eknath Easwaran, founder (1911-1999). Sponsors retreats all year long. Pub. *Blue Mountain: A Journal for Spiritual Living*, quarterly.

166. **METTA: Center for Nonviolence Education* (1981) (org).

PO Box 183, Tomales 94971; office in Berkeley; *mnagler@igc.org; www.fhb.org/Gardenia*).

METTA (a Buddhist term for nonviolence) promotes nonviolence through education, emphasizing the value of spiritual disciplines to the practice of nonviolence. Michael Nagler, Dir.

VALYERMO, CA

167. **High Desert Catholic Worker* (1998) (org).

PO Box 62, Valyermo 93563-0062; (661) 944-2655; *www.awadagin.com/cw/index.html* or *www.catholicworker*

One of twelve sister houses of the Los Angeles Catholic Worker, HDCW, in the wilderness near St. Andrew's Benedictine Monastery, is dedicated to integrating CW love in action with Benedictine work contemplation. It serves local detention facilities, laborers, and the poor. Peace and justice: anti-death penalty campaign, for closing the School of the Americas and the Nevada Nuclear Test Site. Pubs.: *Locusts and Wild Honey* newsletter; *Finding My Way: A Journey Along the Rim of the Catholic Worker Movement* by Toni Flynn. Contact Toni Flynn.

VISTA, CA

168. **Unitarian Universalists Against the Death Penalty* (1996) (org).

1600 Buena Vista Dr., Vista 92083; *jrabenold@aol.com; www.richmonduu.org/uuadp*

An independent affiliate of UUA that works to implement the mandate of UUA resolutions to abolish capital punishment. Pub. quarterly newsletter *Witness for Life*. Jean Rabenold, Founder and Pres.

WALNUT CREEK, CA

169. **Mount Diablo Peace Center* (1969) (org).

55 Eckley Lane, Walnut Creek 94596 (next to Shell Ridge Open Space); (925) 933-7850; *www.wenet.net/~mdpc/*

MDPC "strives to end violence by nurturing peace on all levels, between nations, communities, individuals, and within ourselves." Provides a monthly newsletter, public education programs, and a weekly television program, and protests militarism and nuclear weapons through non-violent demonstrations and by contacting government officials.

—— *Colorado (CO)* ——

26 Sister Cities. / 156 Peace Poles.

AURORA, CO

170. **Mediation Program* (1998) (col).

Community College of Aurora, 16000 East CentreTech Parkway, Aurora 80011; (303) 360-4700; *sharon.halford@cca.cccoes.edu; www.cca.cccoes.edu/aca/_academic.html*

A Certificate includes basic theory and skills courses, an emphasis in one of four areas (Business, Community, Criminal Justice, or Domestic Relations), and an internship. Contact Sharon Halford.

BOULDER, CO

171. **Center for the Study and Prevention of Violence* (1992) (col).

Institute of Behavioral Science, Campus Box 439, Univ. of Colorado, Boulder 80309-0442; (303) 492-1032; *cspv@colorado.edu; www.colorado.edu/cspv*

An interdisciplinary research foundation developing educational programs with technical assistance and databases. The Information House, the nucleus of the Center, maintains four primary databases. Pub. quarterly *Program Evaluation Newsletter*, books, and pamphlets; for example: *What Works in Reducing Adolescent Violence* and *Drugs, Alcohol, and Adolescent Violence* Delbert Elliott, Dir.

172. *Conflict Research Consortium* (1988) (col).

Campus Box 327, Univ. of Colorado, Boulder 80309; (303) 492-1635; *burgess@colorado.edu; www.colorado.edu/conflict*

Unites researchers, educators, and practitioners for theory-building, testing, and applying conflict management techniques particularly to long-term and intractable conflicts. CRC has published over 200 working papers, listed on web site, and 2 books: Burgess and Burgess, *Encyclopedia of Conflict Resolution* and Wehr, Burgess and Burgess, *Justice Without Violence*. Guy and Heidi Burgess, Dirs.

173. *Peace and Conflict Studies* (1968) (col).

Campus Box 471, Univ. of Colorado, Boulder 80309; (303) 492-2623; *paul.wehr@colorado.edu; www.csf.colorado.edu/orgs/pacs*

To acquire this undergraduate Certificate, students must complete 24 hours, consisting of core courses, a Senior Seminar, and related courses. They can also participate in the International and National Voluntary Service Training program. Paul Wehr, Acting Co-Dir.

174. *Rocky Mountain Peace and Justice Center* (1983) (org).

1520 Euclid Ave., Boulder 80302; (303) 444-6981.

Dedicated to research, education, and action in nonviolence as a way of life and as a means for personal and social change: nuclear disarmament, peacekeeping, conflict resolution, advocacy in the struggle against injustices. Activities include: Disarmament Action/Rocky Flats Group, Nonviolence Education Collective, Prisoner Rights Project, International Collective, Environmental Activist Resource, Food Coop. Pub. include a monthly newsletter and *Citizen's Guide to Rocky Flats, Colorado's Nuclear Bomb Factory*.

Colorado Springs, CO

175. *Citizens for Peace in Space* (1987) (org).

PO Box 915, Colorado Springs 80901; (719) 389-0644; *bsulzman@juno.com*

Originally STARS (Committee to Stop the Arms Race in Space, 1983), CPS opposes the U.S. military takeover of space and NASA's plans to use plutonium on deep space probes. Activities: Education of local and national leaders through theater, bannering, newsletters, artwork, letters; political networking with the Florida Coalition for Peace and Justice, the Denver AFSC, and groups abroad—the Global Network Against Weapons and Nuclear Power in Space—that also oppose U.S. world domination through space/spying facilities; and direct action against facilities (two members sentenced to prison for long terms). Contact Donna Johnson or Bill Sulzman. See entry 216.

176. *Life Foundation School of Therapeutics USA* (1989) (org).

5004 Sunsuite Trail South, Colorado Springs 80917; (719) 574-5452 or 597-7929.

Has sponsored peace-related seminars in several cities, especially self-help techniques for reducing stress. Established its center in Colorado Springs in 1998. Sponsored the installation of a *Peace Pole* at the Horticulture Arts Society Demonstration Garden in Monument Valley Park in downtown Colorado Springs. A Vigil was held in conjunction with the unveiling of the Pole. International headquarters in Bangor, North Wales. Contact Ned Hartfiel and Jeanne Katz.

177. *Pikes Peak Justice and Peace Commission* (1978) (org).

The old Firehouse on St. Francis Hospital grounds, E. Pikes Peak and Institute, Colorado Springs 80903; (719) 632-6189.

A Christian group committed to reverence for all creation, nonviolence, solidarity with the poor and oppressed, opposition to systemic injustice, and the transforming qualities of relationship, reconciliation, and community. Sponsors The Rose and Thorn Program of workshops in the study and practice of nonviolent preparedness in crisis situations; Dir.: Esther Kisamore. Pub. monthly *Active for Justice* newspaper: the May number suggested ways of stopping the bombing in Yugoslavia; the June/July number stresses active resistance especially by noncooperation and civil disobedience; the August no. includes articles on patriotism, Hiroshima and Iraq/Kosovo, Chiapas, School of Americas, militarism in schools. In 1999 Dorothy Schlaeger, osf, became new Director, following Jennifer Finn.

178. *Studies in Nonviolence* (1988) (col).

Dept. of Geology, Colorado College, Colorado Springs 80903; (719) 389-6516; *jnoblett@coloradocollege.edu*; *www.ColoradoCollege.edu/ThematicMinors/ ThematicConcentration/non-violence*

Undergraduate minor covers war and peace, interactions among people, and relations between humans and the natural world. Contact Jeffrey Noblett.

178a. *War and Peace in the Nuclear Age* (1985?) (col).

Dept. of History, Colorado College, Colorado Springs 80903; (719) 389-6523; *bhochman@coloradocollege.edu*; *www.coloradocollege.edu/thematicminors/ thematicconcentration/warandpeace*

Undergraduate minor dealing with nuclear weapons in context of science, ethical theory, and history. Contact William Hochman.

DENVER, CO

179. *American Friends Service Committee (AFSC),* Colorado Office (1955) (org).

901 14th Ave., Suite 7, Denver 80204; (303) 623-3464; *www.afsc.org/colorado.htm*

Concentrates on economic justice, human rights, and disarmament. Program examples in 1999: Colorado Campaign for Middle East Peace monthly meeting; Coloradans against NATO Aggression weekly vigils against the bombings; prayer service against Iraq economic sanctions; opposition to space warfare; Nuclear Abolition 2000; First Strike Theatre; peace education. Pub. *Footsteps* newsletter.

180. *Catholic Worker House* (1978) (org).

2420 Welton St., Denver 80205; (303) 296-6390; *denvercw@juno.com*

Serves the homeless, protests U.S. actions in Cuba, Iraq, Yugoslavia, and other actions for peace.

181. *Colorado Coalition for the Prevention of Nuclear War* (1984) (org).

1738 Wynkoop St., Suite 1, Denver 80202; (303) 388-4954.

The Coalition seeks to bring people together to find alternatives to nuclear weapons and militarism and to promote disarmament. It offers speakers and workshops, participates in campaigns—e.g., for a Comprehensive Test Ban Treaty—, vigils, rallies. It provides a monthly calendar of peace and justice events in the Denver area and fact sheets for political action. Member organizations: AFSC, Citizens for Peace in Space, Colorado Council of Churches, Denver Presbytery, First Universalist Church, Iliff School of Theology, New Jewish Agenda, Physicians for Social Responsibility, Pikes Peak Justice & Peace Commission, Rocky Mountain Peace & Justice Center, The Conflict Center, United Church of Christ, United Methodist Church, United Nations Assoc., WILPF, and WFA. Tom Rauch, Pres.

182. *Colorado Council of Churches: World Peace & Global Affairs Commission* (1984) (org).

1234 Bannock St., Denver 80204-3631; (303) 825-4910; *council@diac.com*

An ecumenical body of representatives from member denominations and other religious bodies to "witness the gospel of peace and justice by offering an alternative vision of the things which make for Shalom in a warring world, and by working for the realization of that vision. Further, the Commission seeks to address the spiral of violence as evidenced by a growing militarism and an increasing oppression and economic exploitation of the peoples of the world." It carries these goals through reflection, prayer, dialogue, education, and public witness. For example, members of the Commission traveled to Chiapas, Mexico to gather facts and support the oppressed. Rev. Bob Hunter, Chair.

183. *Conflict Resolution MA Degree* (1988) (col).

Graduate School of International Studies, Univ. of Denver, Denver 80208; (303) 871-2418; *kfeste@du.edu*; *www.du.edu/con-res*

Students apply alternative theories and case lessons to individual, national, and cultural conflicts. The 70 quarter credits program includes core, related area, and practical techniques courses, a methodology course, a thesis, and an internship. See web site for publications. Karen Feste, Director.

184. **Denver Presbytery: Social Justice and Shalom Peacemaking Committee* (1931) (org).

1710 S. Grant, Denver 80210; (303) 777-2453.

Contact: Rev. John Piper.

185. **Justice and Peace Studies* (1990) (org).

Iliff School of Theology, 2201 S. University Blvd., Denver 80210; (303) 765-3191, (303) 777-0164; *gvaleta@iliff.edu; www.iliff.edu*

"The Justice and Peace Studies concentration educates students in the analysis of social justice issues within an international order which has now been irrevocably shaken. Building upon strong spiritual foundations, the program stands as Iliff's commitment to education that responds to the challenges of race and racism, class and economic exploitation, sexism, and militarism." Degrees: M.A. in Conflict Resolution; Masters of Specialized Ministry (M.A.S.M.) Justice and Peace Studies Concentration; M. Div. with Peace Studies Concentration. Pub.: *Justice and Peace Newsletter.* Affil.: United Methodist Church. Rev. Gail Erisman Valeta, Contact.

186. **National Coalition Against Domestic Violence* (1978) (org).

PO Box 18749, Denver 80218-0749; (303) 839-1852; *www.webmerchants.com/ncadv*

Grassroots org. working to end violence in the lives of women and children. Provides a national network for state coalitions and local programs serving battered women and their children; sponsors a national conference every two years; is developing a national registry of women killed as a result of domestic violence; publishes a poster annually in October, Domestic Violence Awareness Month, listing the names of victims the previous year. Also has a Washington, DC, office. Rita Smith, Exec. Dir.

187. **Physicians for Social Responsibility, Colorado Chapter* (1984) (org).

1738 Wynkoop, Denver 80202; (303) 298-8001; *pascote@earthlink.net*

Dedicated to nuclear disarmament, preserving a sustainable environment, and violence prevention. Also known as the *Colorado Coalition Against Gun Violence.* Exec. Dir.: Ted Pascoe.

188. **World Federalist Denver Chapter* (1947) (org).

2180 S. University Ave., Denver 80210; (303) 744-2278.

WF brings speakers, pub. newsletter, sends postcards for actions and events, in support of stronger United Nations and international law. Supports WF's Partners for Global Change, dedicated to dialogue, law, the United Nations. Several members attended the Hague Appeal for Peace in May 1999. Stan Lefkowitz, Pres.; Judy Snyder, Treas. (101 Jersey St., 80220). WF (1947) national office in D.C.

FORT COLLINS, CO

189. **Center for Justice, Peace, and Environment (CJPE)* (1998) (org).

604 Sycamore, Fort Collins 80521; P.O. Box 400, 80522; (970) 221-0240; *centerjpe@aol.com.*

Serves to achieve progressive, nonviolent social change in Larimer County and the world; dedicated to political and economic democracy to achieve peace and justice for the environment and all creatures. Contact: John Kefalas.

LAKEWOOD, CO

190. **World Constitution and Parliament Association, Inc. (WCPA)* (1958) (org).

1480 Hoyt St., Suite 31, Lakewood 80215; (303) 233-3548 or 526-0463.

Because armed national sovereignty has killed millions of people and also in other ways has produced international anarchy in this century, an elected world parliament is needed to implement peaceful solutions to the world problems. Pubs.: "Why the U.N. Must Be Replaced," "A Constitution for the Federation of Earth," and other documents.

NEDERLAND, CO

191. *Mountain Forum for Peace* (1985) (org).

PO Box 1233, Nederland 80466.

Programs in 1998-9 included Nuclear Abolition 2000, Death Penalty, School of Americas, political refugees; activities included Kosovo vigil and refugee relief, Liz Caile essay contest on peace and environment, funds for books on peace theme to public schools, annual Mothers' Day vigil for peace, maintained two peace gardens, annual picnic. Julie Harris, Chairperson; Phillys Wright, Vice-chair.

192. *Nederland Peace Garden #1* (1989) (mem., garden).

The Garden by the pedestrian bridge across from the Visitors' Center contains a blue spruce in memory of Liz Caile, a local writer on peace and environmental subjects. The garden also displays a *Peace Pole* (1991) with its message, "May Peace Prevail on Earth" in four languages, made by woodcarver Scott Harrison, in memory of Stanley Wright.

193. *Peace Garden #2 and Sculpture* (1990) (mem., garden).

The second Peace Garden is located on Colorado State Highway 119 just inside Nederland town limits. It is home to a life-sized bronze sculpture depicting a Native American girl presenting a feather, symbolic of peace, to a pioneer child, entitled "Simple Gift." The sculpture was created by Nederland artist David Current.

Top: Nederland Peace Garden 1 with Peace Pole. *Bottom:* Nederland Peace Garden 2 with sculpture, "Simple Gift." Both photographs courtesy Phillys Wright.

PUEBLO, CO

194. *Mahatma Gandhi Center for Peace and Nonviolence* (1998) (org).

PO Box 11336, Pueblo 81001; (719) 561-0728, 564-7176; *roldandr@aol.com*

Seeks to become "a well-spring of those ideas that bring about a respect for all humans so that:

dialogue replaces violence, understanding replaces hatred, and compassion replaces condemnation." The Center initiates peace and nonviolence projects in the schools and community and works with state, national, and international peace objectives. For example, the Center sponsors a peace writing competition for students in Pueblo County, brought Arun and Sunanda to speak, and Mary Ann Roldan, Coordinator of the Center, has prepared a K-12 resource unit on peace and nonviolence

194a. *Peace Pole* (1997) (mem).

Mineral Palace Park, Pueblo.

"May Peace Be in Our Homes and Communities" and "May Peace Prevail on Earth." (Some citizens were constructing a Peace Place for children at the foot of Goat Hill. Contact Frank Arteaga, 719-560-7931.)

— *Connecticut (CT)* —

3 Sister Cities. / 84 Peace Poles.

COLUMBIA, CT

195. *Horace Porter School Peace Pole* (1998) (mem).

Next to the flagpole in front of the school, Columbia.

Displays the message "May Peace Prevail on Earth" in seven languages.

FAIRFIELD, CT

196. **Peace and Justice Studies* (1986) (col).

Politics Dept., Fairfield Univ., Fairfield 06430; (203) 254-4000, x2862; *kjcassidy@fair1.fairfield.edu; www.fairfield.edu/academic/artsci/majors/ faith/ugfphome.htm*

This minor degree of 15 credits reflects Jesuit commitment to the establishment of a just social order. Kevin Cassidy, Dir.

HARTFORD, CT

197. **St. Martin De Porres Catholic Worker Community* (1993) (org).

26 Clark St., Hartford 06120; (860) 724-7066; *cdoucot@erols.com*

A lay community of Catholics living in the north end of Hartford, "working and praying for an end to violence and poverty." Regular vigils to end war against Iraq; monthly vigil at Senator Joseph Lieberman's office; opposed war in Yugoslavia; civil disobedience at Electric Boat Co.; members have participated in Plowshares and peacemaking trips to Bosnia, Chiapas, the Test Site in Nevada, and Iraq. Pub. the *Hartford Catholic Worker* six times a year.

NEW HAVEN, CT

198. **City of New Haven Peace Commission* (1989) (org).

20 Mumford Rd., New Haven 06515; (203) 387-0370; *amistad@ct1.nai.net.*

Supports education for peace and non-violence, conflict resolution, gun control, peaceful domestic policies, reduced military budget, United Nations, and all activities within the City that augment a peaceful community. Alfred Marder, Chairman.

199. **Greater New Haven Peace Council* (1977) (org).

PO Box 3105, Westville Station, New Haven 06515; (203) 387-0370; *amistad@ct1.nai.net*

Deals with issues of disarmament; international solidarity; racism and national liberation; interrelations of domestic and foreign policies and peace. Alfred Marder, Pres.

200. Deleted.

201. **New Haven/Leon, Nicaragua Sister City Project* (1984) (org).

608 Whitney Ave., New Haven 06511; (203) 562-1607; *newhavenleon@igc.apc.org; www.igc.org/newhavenleon*

Promotes sustainable development and cultural exchange. Ongoing projects include: building construction, bicycle distribution, economic development, education and teacher training, art projects, mental health, diverse agricultural projects, and delegations. Tina Fiasconaro, Prog. Dir.

202. **Peace and Justice Studies* (col).

Philosophy/Religious Studies Dept., Albertus Magnus College, New Haven 06511; (203) 773-8554; *icecof@hotmail.com; www.albertus.edu/cc_plan.htm*

A minor undergraduate degree composed of five courses and one practicum. Jeremiah Coffey, Dir.

203. **Peace Messenger Cities, International Association of* (1987) (org).

20 Mumford Rd., New Haven 06515;

Now 78 cities strong throughout the world, PMC organizes peace gardens, exchanges, Peace Days, U.N. Days, workshops. The purpose is to encourage local authorities to strive for world peace. Contact Alfred Marder (*amistad@mail1. nai.net*).

204. **U.S. Peace Council* (1977) (org).

20 Mumford Rd., New Haven 06515; (203) 387-0370; *amistad@ct1.nai.net*

Member of the World Peace Council. Works on disarmament, racism and national liberation, international solidarity, military budget and domestic peace issues.

NORWICH, CT

205. **War Resisters League/New England* (1985) (org).

PO Box 1093, Norwich 06360; (860) 889-5337; *wrlne9@idt.net*

As a regional office of WRL, WRL/NE extends WRL programs, including Day Without the Pentagon and YouthPeace. Also nonviolence training, nonviolent campaign building, and feminism. Joanne Sheehan and Rick Gaumer, Staff.

RIDGEFIELD, CT

206. **Veterans for Peace, Western Connecticut Chapter #18* (1986?) (org).

289 Old Stagecoach Rd., Ridgefield 06877; (203) 438-2529.

Various actions (SOA), and award-winning weekly hour cable access TV program, "Earth Matters," dealing with peace, justice, and environment, going on some 15 years. Walter Hrozenchick, Pres.

STORRS, CT

207. *Peace Studies (1986) (col).

Philosophy Dept., University of Connecticut, Storrs 06269; *luyster@uconnvm.uconn.edu; www.ia.uconn.edu/pstx2.html*

Teaches creative solutions to war and violence through an individualized major degree that includes courses such as Global Militarism and Human Survival and Violence: Sources and Alternatives. Robert Luyster, Dir.

WEST HARTFORD, CT

208. **Peace and Justice* (1984) (col).

Religious Studies Dept., Saint Joseph College, West Hartford 06117; (860) 232-4571, x5299; *jthompson@sjc.edu; www.sjc.edu/?homepage*

An 18 credit minor composed of required (Christian Peacemaking and Christianity and Social Justice) and related courses and an internship. Contact J. Milburn Thompson.

— *Delaware (DE)* —

4 Sister Cities. / 3 Peace Poles.

FREDERICA, DE

209. **Kent County Peace Fellowship* (mid-'70s) (org).

3052 Andrews Lake Road, Frederica 19946-1940; (302) 335-4330; *erpjohn@aol.com*

A group seeking to enlarge nonviolence through local conflict resolution programs, community forums of peace education, arms control, and other avenues. Monthly meetings. Affil. with Pacem in Terris in Wilmington. Contact Ruth Johnson.

WILMINGTON, DE

210. **Delaware Pacem in Terris* (1967) (org).

1304 N. Rodney St., Wilmington 19806-4227; (302) 656-2721; *pinterris@aol.com*

The "oldest and largest grassroots organization on the Delmarva Peninsula" working to "educate the public about global peace and justice issues": ending the Vietnam War, stopping the nuclear arms race, improving US/USSR relations, altering U.S. policies in Central America, opposing the death penalty, providing conflict resolution training for elementary school children, and many other issues. Current major projects: reconciling Northern Irish Catholic and Protestant youth, and nuclear disarmament, racial justice, peaceable classrooms, opposing death penalty, film series, Resource Center. The Ulster Project, founded in 1976 by Charles and Josephine Robinson, brings Catholic and Protestant teenagers to Wilmington every year and sends an equal number of U.S. teens to N. Ireland. Pub. *Delmarva Peacework* newsletter with circulation of over 1500. The Sept.-Oct. 1999 number of *DM* included articles on SOA, Kosovo, conflict resolution in schools, Jubilee 2000, CTBT, capital punishment. Sally Milbury-Steen, Exec. Dir.

—— *Florida (FL)* ——

62 Sister Cities. / 274 Peace Poles.

BRADENTON, FL

211. *Peace Pole* (1998) (mem).

At Bashaw Elementary School, Bradenton.

Eight hundred students dedicated the Pole, paid for by student donations, in a ceremony which included sending the wish "May Peace Prevail" to countries around the world.

CORAL GABLES, FL

212. **Rights International, The Center for International Human Rights Law* (1994) (org).

600 Biltmore Way, No. 1117, Coral Gables 33134; (305) 446-7334; *ricenter@igc.org; www.rightsinternational.org*

"Fights for those rights recognized by the Universal Declaration of Human Rights and other international human rights treaties." Provides legal assistance to victims of human rights violations before international tribunals and trains lawyers and law students in international human rights and humanitarian law through the Frank C. Newman Internship Program, Cooperating Attorneys program, and Law School Consortium Program. Pub.: *International Human Rights Law & Practice: Cases, Treaties, and Materials* (1999); *Rights International Companion Series on Constitutional Law, Property Law, and Criminal Law & Procedure* (1999). President: Francisco Martin.

DAYTONA BEACH, FL

213. *Howard Thurman House* (1990) (mem).

614 Whitehall St., Daytona Beach; *www.cr.nps.gov/nr/travel/civilrights/f2.htm*

Thurman's *Jesus and the Disinherited*, which laid much of the philosophical foundation for a nonviolent civil rights movement, was often read by Martin Luther King, Jr.

FORT LAUDERDALE, FL

214. **Dispute Resolution and Peacemaking* (1992-2000) (col).

School of Social and Systemic Studies, Nova Southeastern Univ., Fort Lauderdale 33314; (954) 262-3000; *cr@nova.edu; www.nova.edu/ssss/dr*

Offers graduate Certificate (24 credits), MS (45 credits), and Ph.D. (82 credits) degrees both by residence and on-line. (MS and Graduate Certificate, 1992; Ph.D. 1994; Online Ph.D. 1999; Online MS and Graduate Certificate 2000). Online Newsletter *Center-Pointe* (*www.nova. edu/ssss/center-pointe*). Sean Byrne, Dir. (*sjbyrne@ nova.edu; sjbyrne@nsu.acast.nova.edu*). Hong-gang Yang, Dean.

GAINESVILLE, FL

215. **Florida Coalition for Peace and Justice* (1983) (org).

PO Box 90035, Gainesville 32607; (352) 468-3295; *fcpj@juno.com; earthweaver@juno.com*

Clearinghouse for peace, justice, church, environmental, and campus groups, with statewide meetings. Pub. *Just Peace* quarterly newspaper distributed statewide. Carol Mosley (Gainesville), State Coord.

216. *Global Network Against Weapons and Nuclear Power in Space* (1992) (org).

PO Box 90083, Gainesville 32607; (352) 337-9274; *globenet@afn.org; www.globenet.free-online.co.uk/*

Brings together activists who oppose the extension of war, greed, exploitation, and environmental contamination into space, and especially the nuclearization and weaponization of space. Space militarization took a leap in the year 2000 Pentagon budget with funding hikes in many programs, including the Space-Based Infrared Satellite; Milstar Satellite; Space-Based Laser Project; National Missile Defense Program; and the Navy Theater Missile Defense Project. An example of GN's activities is the 1997-99 Cancel Cassini Campaign, to stop the use of 72.3 pounds of plutonium to fuel a satellite. GN has 81 affiliates around the world (see website). Promotes the film *Nukes in Space II*, which reveals U.S. plans for military space domination, and the book *The Wrong Stuff*, by Karl Grossman, which documents the NASA, DoE, and Pentagon roles in militarizing space. Pub. a newsletter. Membership meetings are held in the U.S. and abroad. Contact Bruce Gagnon.

JUPITER, FL

217. *Pax Christi Florida* (1984) (org).

6062 Robinson St., Jupiter 33458; (561) 575-1795; *cricchio@juno.com*

"We witness to and imitate the example of the nonviolence of Jesus" through 8 local groups around the state. Pub. *Peacemaker* newsletter three times a year. Sandra Baran, Regional Rep. Founded by John and Patricia Frank.

LAKE WALES, FL

218. *Bok Tower Gardens* (1922) (mem).

1151 Tower Blvd., Lake Wales 33853, near U.S. Highway 27 three miles north of Lake Wales.

Among the many philanthropies established by Edward William Bok is the Bok Tower Gardens, a 157-acre "sanctuary for humans and birds," a retreat for strolling and listening to the carillon music from the 57 bronze bells in the tower ranging from 17 pounds to 12 tons. In 1923 he created the American Peace Award, a one-time award providing $100,000 for the best practicable plan by which the United States might cooperate with other nations to achieve and preserve the peace of the world (it was won by Dr. Charles H. Levermore of the New York Peace Society).

LAKE WORTH, FL

219. *Lake Worth F.O.R.* (1998) (org).

915 N. Lakeside Dr., NE, Lake Worth 33460-2709; (561) 588-2909.

Branch of the Fellowship of Reconciliation. Focuses on countering racism and building bridges by celebrating Martin Luther King's birthday, expanding their Sister Cities program, and establishing discussion groups in precincts. Contact Susan Glaser.

MIAMI, FL

220. *Center for Justice and Peace* (col).

Institute for Pastoral Ministries, St. Thomas Univ., Miami 33054; (305) 628-6717; *rrufo@stu.edu; www.stu.edu/relph/IPM/peace%20and%20 justice.htm*

Disseminates Catholic social justice teachings and confronts racism and violence through workshops and lectures at St. Thomas and in the parishes of South Florida. The Institute has a quarterly newsletter in which the Center has a column. Ray Rufo, Coord.

221. *Justice & Peace Studies* (col). Email

Institute for Pastoral Ministries, St. Thomas Univ., Miami 33054; *crose@stu.edu; www.stu.edu/relph/IPM/ institute_for_oastirak_ministrie.htm*

Offers both BA and MA degrees in pastoral ministries specializing in justice and peace, and both require a practicum involved in the local community or beyond and through workshops conducted by the University's Center for Justice and Peace. Mercedes Iannone, Dir.

MIAMI SHORES, FL

222. **Peace Studies* (1984) (col).

School of Arts and Sciences, Barry University, Miami Shores 33161; (305) 899-3472; *jmendez@mail.barry.edu; www.barry.edu/vpaa-intrdisc*

Undergraduate minor degree based on Catholic principles requiring 21 credits. Jesus Mendez, Chair.

PALM BEACH, FL

223. **Pax Christi Palm Beach* (1983) (org).

4855 A Equestrian Rd., Apt. 438A, Boynton Beach 33436; (561) 731-4605; *dorney@juno.com*

Concerned especially for the School of the Americas, capital punishment, Iraq sanctions, and militarism. Maureen Dorney, Coord.

224. **Pax Christi USA* (org).

442 33rd St., West Palm Beach 33407; (561) 842-7701; *paxwpb@gate.net*

National Section of the International Catholic Peace Movement (see Erie, PA). Phyllis Jepson, Local/Regional Coord. Eileen Egan, co-founder of PCUSA, author of *Peace Be With You: Justified Warfare or the Way of Nonviolence* (Orbis, 1999).

ST. AUGUSTINE, FL

225. *Lincolnville Historic District* (mem).

Bounded by DeSoto Place and Cedar, Riberia, Cerro, and Washington Streets; *www.cr.nps.gov/ nr/travel/civilrights/fl.htm*

Lincolnville, the major black residential subdivision in St. Augustine (one of the most segregated cities of the South), was a center of civil rights protests during the 1960s.

ST. PETERSBURG, FL

226. **Florida Holocaust Museum* (1998) (mus).

55 5th St. South, in downtown St. Petersburg 33701; (727) 820-0100; *dmtindell@flholocaustmuseum.org; www.flholocaustmuseum.org*

Opened in 1992 as the Tampa Bay Holocaust Memorial Museum. The fourth largest of about 100 Holocaust museums and resource centers in the U.S. (27,000 square feet), the FHM is dedicated to advancing public awareness, education, and understanding of the Holocaust. It offers study guides, teacher training, seminars, and workshops for all levels of students. Its first floor contains the permanent exhibit divided into 12 areas, from pre-war life to the birth of Israel, an auditorium, a Meditation Court, Memorial Chapel, a Store for the sale of books, posters, and other items. The second floor is for special exhibitions. In 2000 the Museum presented the exhibit "Anne Frank: A History for Today," following up "Anne Frank in the World: 1929-1945." The exhibits were created by the Anne Frank Center USA in NYC. And the third floor is the Education Center, with a large auditorium, a Learning Center with two classrooms,

Florida Holocaust Museum located in St. Petersburg, Florida. Photograph courtesy Diane Tindell.

the Murray Tolerance Center with computer facilities, and the Library and Resource Center. The Museum was designed by Nick Benjacob, architect, and L. David Von Thaden, interior design. Stephen Goldman, Dir.

227. *International Relations and Global Affairs* (1995) (col).

Eckerd College, St. Petersburg 33711; (727) 864-8994; *felicewf@eckerd.edu; www.eckerd.edu/academics/bes/irga/*

Courses offered on international law, political economy, and related areas. No specific peace program. Contact William Felice.

TALLAHASSEE, FL

228. *Wellington Press* (1982) (org).

PO Box 13939, Tallahassee 32317-3939; (877) 390-4425; *www.peacegames.com.*

Publishes books and games on peacemaking, conflict management, and mediation; for example, books: *From Conflict to Consensus: Reasoning Skills for Handling Conflict, How to Work for Peace*; games: Balkans Conflicts, Middle East Peace, Teenage Conflicts. David and Judy Felder, publishers.

TEQUESTA, FL

229. *Citizens United for Alternatives to the Death Penalty (CUADP)* (1997) (org).

PMB 297, 177 U.S. Highway #1, Tequesta 33469; (800) 973-6548; *cuadp@cuadp.org; www.cuadp.org*

Works to end the death penalty in the U.S. through public education and grassroots activism. Abraham Bonowitz, Dir.

—— *Georgia (GA)* ——

25 Sister Cities. / 64 Peace Poles.

See Davis, *Weary Feet, Rested Souls*, 138–190, for more Civil Rights Movement organizations and memorials.

ALBANY, GA

230. *Albany Civil Rights Movement Museum* (1998) (mus).

In Mount Zion Baptist Church, 324 Whitney Ave., Albany 31707; (912) 432-1698; *www.cr.nps.gov/nr/travel/civilrights/g3.htm*

Mount Zion was a center of the nonviolent Albany Movement. It is now a civil rights museum and features the work of SNCC photographer Danny Lyon.

231. *Albany Movement Monument* (1992) (mem).

West Highland and Jackson Streets, Albany, between the former black business district and the graveyard on Jackson St.

Four black granite slabs with historical chronologies and quotations surround a fountain. The names of local Movement activists are etched in white stones around a brick periphery.

232. *Albany State College* (org).

504 College Drive, Albany 31701.

A center of Movement protest.

233. *King Family Plot* (mem).

Oakview Cemetery, 200 Cotton Ave., Albany 31701.

No relation to the Atlanta Kings, the Albany Kings also made great contributions and sacrifices for the Movement (see Davis, *Weary Feet*, 176–78). C. B. King and his father are buried in the family plot; Slater King is buried at Roselawn Cemetery.

ATLANTA, GA

234. *American Friends Service Committee (AFSC), Southeast Region* (1980) (org).

92 Piedmont Ave., NE, Atlanta 30303; (404) 586-0460; *afscser@afsc.org*

Relocated from Highpoint, NC in 1980. Programs include: Central America Political Asylum Project (South Miami, FL, afsccapap@ msn.com), Middle East Peace Education

Program (Atlanta, ilisec@aol.com), Southern Africa Peace Education Program (Atlanta, kderuga@aol.com), Orita Youth Program (Winston-Salem, NC, annglennon@aol.com). National Office in Philadelphia (afscinfo@afsc.org).

235. *Atlanta Fellowship of Reconciliation* (1991) (org).

678 Park Dr. NE, Atlanta 30306; (404) 892-7353; *lbaxter@emory.edu*

This branch of the Fellowship of Reconciliation offers nonviolence, conflict resolution, and peace education in the schools and community. Contact Lili Baxter.

236. *Atlanta University Center* (org).

A cluster of institutions in Atlanta that have shared ideas and resources since their founding: Morehouse (men), Spelman (women), and Morris Brown colleges, Clark College and Atlanta University (now Clark Atlanta University), and the Interdenominational Theological Center. Martin Luther King, Jr., his father, and his grandfather attended Morehouse (830 Westview Drive SW). Students began protests against Jim Crow laws in 1960, and King joined them in a march to downtown in October of that year, which resulted in his first night in jail. A statue of King with his right arm extended stands in front of the Martin Luther King, Jr., International Chapel on Westview Drive across from the Spelman College parking lot.

237. *Auburn Avenue Historic Site and Preservation District* (1980) (mus).

Between Courtland and Randolph streets, Atlanta. From I-75/I-85, exit at Freedom Parkway/Carter Center; turn right at the first stoplight onto Boulevard; follow signs. From I20, take I-75-/I-85 north and proceed as above.

Designed to preserve the remnants of King's childhood and youth. The National Parks Service Visitor Center (450 Auburn, NE, 30312-1515; 404-331-5190; www.nps.gov/malu) contains an exhibition of King and the Movement.

238. *The Carter Presidential Center* (1982) (org).

One Copenhill, 453 Freedom Parkway, Atlanta 30307. Located in a wooded, 35-acre park 5 minutes from downtown Atlanta (go east on North Avenue for approximately 1.5 miles to Freedom Parkway, turn right on Freedom parkway and follow signs).

The Center is dedicated to creating a world where everyone has the opportunity to live in peace. It strives to relieve suffering in the U.S. and around the world by focusing on the causes and consequences of war, hunger, disease, poverty, tyranny, and human rights abuses. Nearby are the Jimmy Carter Library and Museum.

239. *Ebenezer Baptist Church* (1980, built 1914-22) (mus).

407-13 Auburn Ave. downtown Atlanta.

Beginning in 1931 this church was pastored by King's father, Martin Luther King, Sr. Martin, Jr., preached his first sermon here at age 17 and joined his father as co-pastor from 1960 to 1968. Here King, Jr. became the first president of the Southern Christian Leadership Conference (SCLC); here in April 1968 his body lay in state following his assassination, and here his mother was murdered by an assassin in 1974. On March 7, 1999, the Ebenezer congregation turned over the site to the National Park Service and moved across the street.

240. *Freedom Quilt Mural* (1988) (mem).

92 Piedmont Ave., NE, Atlanta 30303.

On one outside wall of the American Friends Service Building, Atlanta. Artist: David Fichter.

Depicts 16 men and women committed to the nonviolent struggle for peace and justice: Mubarak Awad, Nelson Mandela, Oscar Romero, et al.

241. *Martin Luther King, Jr., Birth Home* (1980) (mus).

501 Auburn Ave., Atlanta.

Part of the historic district of "Sweet Auburn" Avenue now maintained by the National Park Service.

242. *Martin Luther King, Jr., Center for Nonviolent Social Change* (1968) (org).

449 Auburn Ave., NE, Atlanta 30312-1590; (404) 526-8900; *mlkctr@aol.com; www.thekingcenter.com*

Houses the King Library and Archives and the King Papers Project; conducts the Commu-

Freedom Quilt Mural by David Fichter, Atlanta, Georgia. Courtesy AFSC Atlanta office.

nity Empowerment Initiative and workshops on nonviolence education and training. The Center plans to install state-of-the-art technologies to teach people better about Dr. King. The Center is located in the Martin Luther King, Jr. national historical district (his birth home and Ebenezer Baptist Church, where he, his father, and grandfather preached) and is the permanent site for Dr. King's tomb. Formerly headed by King's widow, Coretta Scott King, it is now run by their son, Dexter King.

243. *Southern Christian Leadership Conference* (1957) (org).

334 Auburn Ave., Atlanta.

Martin Luther King, Jr., headed this nonviolent civil rights organization from its beginning in 1957 until his death in 1968. The SCLC promoted voter registration, massive demonstrations, the March on Washington in 1963, and the Poor People's Campaign of 1968, mainly focusing on cities. Following King, Rev. Ralph Abernathy became its head. Now it is run by Rev. Joseph Lowery. There is also now the SCLC Women (1979, 328 Auburn Ave.), founded by Lowery's wife, Evelyn.

244. *Violence Studies Program* (1997) (col).

Dept. of Sociology, Emory Univ., Atlanta 30322; (404) 727-7502; *bagnew@emory.edu*; *www.emory.edu/COLLEGE/VS/index.htm*

Undergraduate minor involves numerous faculty and departments to focus on the causes,

effects, representations, and prevention of violence. Has an annual newsletter on website. Robert Agnew, Dir.

245. *West Hunter Street Baptist Church* (org).

1040 Ralph David Abernathy Boulevard SW, Atlanta.

Long pastored by Rev. Ralph Abernathy, King's most trusted friend in the Nonviolent Movement. Abernathy is entombed in Lincoln Cemetery on Simpson Road in west Atlanta. West Hunter was one of several churches in west Atlanta that advanced the Movement for black civil rights.

COLUMBUS, GA

246. *SOA Watch* (1990) (org).

PO Box 3330, Columbus 31903.

The ongoing protest of the School of Americas at Fort Benning begun by Father Roy Bourgeois.

Hodge, James, and Linda Cooper. "Priest Testifies to School of Americas Ties to Pinochet." *National Catholic Reporter* (January 15, 1999) 11.

Streb, Richard. "A Statement of My Experiences in Latin America." *www.flash.net/~aonstad/streb.htm*

See School of Americas Watch homepage.

DECATUR, GA

247. *Women's Action for New Directions (WAND)* (1996) (org).

139 Candler Oaks Lane, Decatur 30030; (404) 370-0448; *membership@wand.org*; *www.wand.org*

WAND National Field Office. Mission: "to empower women to act politically to reduce militarism and violence, and redirect military resources toward human and environmental needs." Director: Bobbie Wrenn Banks. The National Office is in Arlington, MA; *info@ wand.org*

GAINESVILLE, GA

248. *Conflict Resolution and Legal Studies* (1998) (col).

Humanities Dept., Brenau Univ., Gainesville 30501; *kfrank@lib.brenau.edu; www.brenau.edu/humanities/frank/ default.htm*

Undergraduate major offers courses in resolving conflicts through law, and requires an internship. Kenneth Frank, Dir.

KENNESAW, GA

249. *Alternative Dispute Resolution* (1998) (col).

Dept. of Political Science and International Affairs, Kennesaw State Univ., Kennesaw 30144; (770) 423-6299; *kohlsson@ksumail.kennesaw.edu; www.kennesaw.edu/pols.adr/index.htm*

Offers a Certificate requiring 25 quarter hours of courses. At present implementing an MS in Conflict Management. Karen Ohlsson, Admin. Coord.

MABLETON, GA

250. *Atlanta WAND* (1984) (org).

6126 Driftwood Trail, Mableton 30126; (770) 745-0465; *mkmclendon@msn.com*

Chapter of Women's Action for New Directions. Contact Marci McClendon.

SAVANNAH, GA

251. *First African Baptist Church* (1773, 1859).

23 Montgomery St., Franklin Square, Savannah.

The oldest autonomous black church in North America and a center for nonviolent rights activities from the 1940s to the present (see Davis 184-5).

—— *Hawaii (HI)* ——

5 Sister Cities. / 13 Peace Poles.

HONOLULU, HI

252. *Center for Alternative Dispute Resolution* (1985) (org).

The Judiciary, State of Hawaii, 417 S. King St., Rm. 207, Ali'iolani Hale, Honolulu 96813; (808) 539-4ADR; *www.state.hi.us/jud.*

Most of the cases affect the agencies of state and local government: public disputes, complex litigation, policy "roundtables." Hawaii Chapter of the Society of Professionals in Dispute Resolution Council (SPIDR).

253. *Liberty Bell of Aloha* (1985) (mem).

Civic Center Grounds, City Hall, 530 S. King St., Honolulu 96813.

Remembers the 5th World Peace Youth Cultural Festival, the 100th Anniversary of Japanese Immigration to Hawaii, and the United Nations International Youth Year, "that there be no more Pearl Harbor, no more Hiroshima, and no more war."

254. *Matsunaga Institute for Peace* (1986) (col).

University of Hawaii, 2424 Maile Way, Porteus 717, Honolulu 96822; (808) 956-7427; *uhip@hawaii.edu; www.hawaii.edu/uhip/*

The Program on Conflict Resolution seeks to advance theory and practice by producing a book of case studies, a colloquium series, summer research grants to graduate students and faculty, and creating an interdisciplinary graduate Certificate in Dispute Resolution and specialization within the MA in Political Science. Also, MIP sponsors a Resource Center for research; the International Center for Democracy to foster democratic values and practices around the globe; the nonviolence Program for research on the cause of violence and conditions for nonviolence; and an undergraduate program in Peace and Conflict Education. Other activities: Invites distinguished peacemakers to visit: Jose Ramos-Horta, Nobel Peace Prize winner, Jamyang Sakya, Buddhist teacher, Mubarak Awad of Nonviolence International, and other speakers; helped Hokulani Elementary School begin a peace-centered school and to create a peace garden. Pubs.: guest edited issues of *Social Alternatives*, *Peace Review*, and *Pacifica Review*; several monographs (www2.soc.hawaii.edu/peace). Offers three peace awards: to promote peacemaking among students, to recognize peace projects at community colleges, and to fund a graduate student during his/her writing of a peace or conflict resolution dissertation. Ralph Summy, Former Dir. Brien Hattett, Acting Dir.

255. *Rhoda Miller Peace Memorial* (1997) (mem).

Located between the Social Sciences building, Hawaii Hall, and the new Student Center, University of Hawaii, Honolulu.

Consists of three wide v-shaped concrete forms surrounded by palm trees, a quiet place to sit, meditate, and talk. Miller was associate director of the Matsunaga Institute for Peace from 1989–1993, authored *Institutionalizing Peace* (1994) on the history of the United States Institute for Peace, and dedicated her life to peacemaking.

255a. *Toda Institute* (1996) (org).

1600 Kapiolani Blvd., Suite 1111, Honolulu 96814; (808) 955-8231; *toda@toda.org*

Founded by Daisaku Ikeda, president of Soka Gakkai International, to honor Josei Toda, second president of Soka Gakkai. Toda staunchly opposed militarism and nuclear weapons. The Institute works for "global citizenship." Majid Tehranian, Dir. (Headquarters in Tokyo).

——— *Idaho (ID)* ———

10 Sister Cities. / 19 Peace Poles.

BOISE, ID

256. * *Idaho Human Rights Education Center* (under construction: year 2002 est. completion).

Boise Greenbelt next to the Public Library and the Log Cabin Literary Center,

801 Capitol Blvd., Boise 83702; (208) 345-0304; *lesbock@idaho-humanrights.org*

Features of the *Human Rights Memorial and Education Park* will include: 175 foot Human Rights Wall made of granite slabs etched with human rights quotations and stories from human rights heroes, past and present. In the highest granite slab, a small "attic" window will frame a life size bronze sculpture of Anne Frank. Children's Attic Plaza area with quotes, visuals, and activities. Granite writing table and bronze replica of Anne's famous diary. The Center was already in 1999 an active educational organization with programs for the schools in support of human dignity and diversity. Les Bock, Exec. Dir. (See New York City, Florida, and other places for Anne Frank memorials).

COTTONWOOD, ID

257. **Benedictines for Peace* (1980) (org).

HC 3 Box 121, Cottonwood 83522-9408; (208) 962-3224.

"BFP gives a common voice to a vision of peace as we confront the violence of our day with the love of Christ." Begun in 1980 in response to the threat of nuclear war, BFP was "revitalized in 1995" to witness against the multifarious violence in the world through prayer, services, petitions, special projects like the celebration of the 50th Anniversary of the U.N. Declaration of Human Rights. Thirty-three Benedictine communities, monasteries, oblates, and individual monastics compose the BFP network. Pub.: newsletter. Sr. Carol Ann Wassmuth, OSB, Correspondent.

MOSCOW, ID

258. *Borah Foundation International Peace Grove* (1993) (mem).

University of Idaho, Moscow 83844-3229; *www.martin.uidaho.edu*

The Foundation has planted one tree for the past 7 years in a permanent Peace Grove on the grounds of the University of Idaho Arboretum, representative of the theme of each year's program; for example, in relation to the Borah Symposium on China, a species native to China was planted, accompanied with a brass plaque. Richard Naskali, Dir of the Arboretum.

259. **Borah Outlawry of War Foundation* (1929) (col).

Martin Institute (see next entry).

Named for the former U.S. Senator from Idaho, William Edgar Borah, the Foundation shares the mission of the Martin Institute by continuing the work of Senator Borah to remove the causes of war and to understand the conditions necessary for world peace. The Foundation sponsors speakers and programs, and it purchases books about peace and conflict for the Univ. of Idaho Library.

260. **Martin Institute for Peace Studies and Conflict Resolution* (1979) (col).

University of Idaho, Moscow 83844-3229; (208) 885-6527; *martin@uidaho.edu; www.martin.uidaho.edu*

Founded to advance research and teaching into the causes especially of global and regional conflict and to provide conflict resolution services. Offers an inter-disciplinary undergraduate major in International Studies, and training institutes and workshops in dispute solving. Pub. newsletter, *Martin Institute News*, twice a year; the *Martin Journal of Peace Research* (theoretical, historical, and empirical research relating to peace and war in the international system); the Martin Monograph Series and three electronic journals. Editor of journal and monograph series: Jack Vincent, Political Science. Richard Slaughter, Dir. (*richards@uidaho.edu*).

—— *Illinois (IL)* ——

48 Sister Cities. / 89 Peace Poles.

CARBONDALE, IL

261. **Peace Coalition of Southern Illinois/ Fellowship of Reconciliation* (1983) (org).

1702 Taylor Dr., Carbondale 62901-2115; (618) 549-7193; *mparker@srellim.org*

Affil. with FOR in 1992. Pub. *SI Peace Coalition Newsletter* monthly. Monthly meetings, annual Tax Day Action April 15, annual July 4th Picnic, Annual Hiroshima Day, forums, films, phone tree. Contact Margie Parker.

CHAMPAIGN, IL

262. **International Coalition Against Violent Entertainment* (1980) (org).

PO Box 2157, Champaign 61825; (310) 278-5433.

Disseminates information on violence in the media and other areas of entertainment—TV, sports, music video, cartoons, war toys, etc. Pub. bi-monthly press release. Carole Luberman, Chm.

263. **Program in Arms Control, Disarmament, and International Security (ACDIS)* (1978) (col).

University of Illinois at Urbana-Champaign, 359 Armory building, 505 E. Armory Ave., Champaign 61820; (217) 333-7086; *acdis@uiuc.edu; http://acdisweb.acdis.uiuc.edu*

Devoted "to advancing and disseminating knowledge about the problems of war and peace in our time, including weapons of mass destruction, ethnic conflict, genocide, and strategies for conflict resolution and peace-making." Maintains a research library, organizes seminars, workshops, conferences, and produces publications of faculty and student research. Pub. an annual bulletin *Swords and Ploughshares* and *Occasional Papers*. Not a degree program. Prof. Clifford Singer, Director; Merrily Shaw, Asst. Dir.

CHICAGO, IL

264. **American Friends Service Committee (AFSC), Great Lakes Region* (1950) (org).

59 E. Van Buren St., Suite 1400, Chicago 60605; (312) 427-2533; *afscchi@igc.org* (National office: Philadelphia).

Represents the Quakers in Illinois, Indiana, Kentucky, Ohio, Michigan, and Wisconsin, working for peace and social and economic justice in programs that include Middle East peace, prisoner advocacy, and anti-racism. Michael McConnell, Dir.

265. *The Angel of Peace* (1999) (mem).

St. James Cathedral, Chicago Episcopal Diocese and Plaza, 65 East Huron, Chicago.

A nine-foot bronze Angel in honor of the 60th anniversary of the founding of the Episcopal Peace Fellowship (Armistice Day 1939) and of Bishop Persell, member of EPF and long-time supporter of peace and justice. A gift from Episcopal Peace Fellowship members and sculpted by EPF member and New Hampshire artist William H. Kieffer. The text which inspired the sculptor is from Psalm 46, verse 10: "It is God who makes war to cease in all the world; who breaks the bow, and shatters the spear, and burns the shields with fire."

Skidmore, David, and Meigan Thiel, "Angel Inspires Witness for Peace." *Anglican Advance* (Dec. 1999) 15–16.

The Angel of Peace sculpture by William Kieffer, Chicago, Illinois. Photograph courtesy Sunny Lopez.

266. *The Bulletin of the Atomic Scientists* (1945) (org, mag).

6042 S. Kimbark Ave., Chicago 60637; *jmike@interaccess.com;* *www.bullatomsci.org/nuclear/Bulletin.html*

The *Bulletin* came out of the "Manhattan Project," the WWII program that developed the atom bomb. Some of the participating scientists opposed dropping the atom bomb on a civilian city and urged the government to push for international control of nuclear energy after the war. The journal was created to advance international cooperation in relations among nations and especially for atomic weapons. "The goal of the *Bulletin* is to render obsolete the statement by Einstein, one of the *Bulletin's* godfathers: "The unleashed power of the atom has changed everything save our modes of thinking, and thus we drift toward unparalleled catastrophe." Today the journal is committed to evaluating wide-ranging war-and-peace issues related to nuclearism—U.N. peacekeeping, international sanctions, military spending, worldwide arms trade, militarism, secrecy. Its famous Doomsday Clock dramatizes the nuclear peril. Monthly pub.

266a. *Certificate in Conflict Resolution* (1998) (col).

Department of Sociology, Anthropology and Criminal Justice, St. Xavier Univ., Chicago 60655; (773) 298-3000, x3281; *ade@sxu.edu;* *www.sxu.edu/academ/artsci/ criminal_justice*

Courses and off-campus internships. Christopher Cooper, Dir.

267. *Christian Peacemakers Teams* (1993) (org).

PO Box 6508, Chicago 60680-6508; (312) 455-1199; *cpt@igc.org*

The idea of a Christian nonviolent peacekeeping force to intervene in unjust situations and violent conflicts was inspired by a speech by Ron Sider in 1984, "God's People Reconciling." From 1993 to 1997 CPT had a violence reduction team in Haiti and briefly in other countries. CPT now has year-round violence reduction projects in Hebron, West Bank, Richmond, Va., and most recently in Chiapas, Mexico. CPT also sends delegations abroad and to Canada and the U.S. to witness oppression and assist the teams. Pub. *Signs of the Times* quarterly newsletter. CPT received the 1998 "Award for Social Courage" for its work in Hebron from COPRED. CPT has also produced a resource packet called "Sing Out Against Violent Toys: How to Organize a Public Witness at Your Local Toy Store." Gene Stoltzfus, Director. Participating denominations: Church of the Brethren, Friends United Meeting, General Conference Mennonite Church, Mennonite Church.

268. *Episcopal Peace Fellowship of Northern Illinois* (1960s) (org).

3115 W. Jerome Ave., Chicago 60645; (773) 989-1349 or 262-0606; *frasudoda@juno.com*

Monthly meetings at Bethany Homes (773-989-1349) for prayer and advancing peace and justice ministries. Currently focusing on the death penalty and gun control. Rev. Sunny Lopez, Convenor.

269. *The Fountain of Time* (1922) (mem).

Stands at the west end of the Midway Plaisance at Cottage Grove Avenue in Washington Park.

The statue, recently restored, commemorates

a century of peace between England and the United States that began with an 1814 treaty settling all border disputes with Canada. Not actually a fountain, but rather a relief behind a pool. "The 'lone sentinel,' Time, stands across a pool of water from an enormous 110-foot-long wave of humanity peopled with 100 figures (composed from over 4,500 pieces) including a central soldier on horseback surrounded by soldiers with banners, by refugees, camp-followers, lovers, youths, the aged, and even the sculptor and his assistants." The sculptor, Lorado Taft (1860–1936) worked 14 years to complete what was said at the time to be the "largest single group of statuary in existence." "The material is steel-reinforced, hollow-cast concrete. More than 4,500 pieces comprised the finished mold, reportedly the largest plaster piece-mold ever made."

270. *Illinois Peace Action* (1982)

202 S. State St., #1500, Chicago 60604; (312) 939-3316; *ilpeace@igc.org; www.webcom.com/ipa*

A branch of Peace Action. Focuses on abolishing nuclear weapons, ending sanctions on people of Iraq, stopping weapons sales to human rights abusers, and cutting the military budget. Pub. a newsletter twice a year; the summer 1999 issue included articles on Kosovo and a report

The Fountain of Time sculpture by Lorado Taft, Chicago, Illinois. Photograph courtesy Michael Lash, Director of Public Art, City of Chicago.

from the Hague Appeal. Kevin Martin, former Dir. Roger Romanelli, Exec. Dir. Carrie Benzschawel, Prog. Asst.

271. *International Physicians for the Prevention of Nuclear War/Physicians for Social Responsibility* (org).

59 E. Van Buren St., Chicago 60605; (312) 663-1777.

272. *Jane Addams Memorial Park* (1996) (mem).

600 N. Lake Shore Drive, bordered by Navy Pier, Lake Shore Drive, Grand Avenue, and the Ohio Street beach, Chicago.

The 5-acre park honors the first U.S. woman to win a Nobel Prize, the Nobel Peace Prize in 1931. The focal point of the park is a sculpture in black granite by Louis Bourgeois of a series of outstretched hands symbolizing people, old and young, whom Addams helped in her Hull House.

O'Brien, Dennis. "City Memorializes Own Jane Addams." *Chicago Tribune* (August 27, 1996) 3.

"Park District Honored for Addams." *North Loop News* (July 24, 1997).

Jane Addams Memorial Park and Sculpture by Louis Bourgeois, Chicago, Illinois.

273. *Mexico Solidarity Network* (1998) (org).

4834 N. Springfield, Chicago 60625; (773) 583-7728; 1247 E St., SE,

DC 20003; (202) 544-9355; *www.mexicosolidarity.org*

Dedicated to finding alternatives to capital-centered globalization as applied to Mexico, especially in Chiapas, through fact-finding delegations to Mexico, speaking tours in the U.S. by Mexicans, educating people about legislations in Congress, and other activities. Tom Hansen, National Coordinator. Sr. Pat Krommer staffs the DC office. Supporting organizations: Global Exchange, Alliance for Global Justice, Maryknoll Office for Global Concerns, NACLA, Episcopal Peace Fellowship, SOA Watch.

274. *Pastors for Peace* (1996) (org).

Interreligious Foundation for Community Organizing (IFCO). PO Box 408130, Chicago 60640-8130; (773) 272-4817 or 271-5269; *p4p@igc.apc.org*

Sends caravans with supplies to Central America and the Caribbean. National office in NYC. Rev. Lucius Walker, Jr., Exec. Dir.

275. *Pax Christi Illinois* (1979) (org).

Sacred Heart Monastery, 1910 Maple Ave., Lisle 60532; (630) 969-7040; *knykiel@aol.com*

Pub. newsletter three times a year. Sr. Karen Nykiel, OSB, is the contact person.

276. *The Peace Museum* (1981) (mus, org).

314 W. Institute Place, Chicago, IL, 60610-3043, one-half block north of Chicago Avenue between Franklin and Orleans Streets; (312) 440-1860; *virginiaa@peacemuseum. org; www.peacemuseum. org*

The Museum is an art and history museum dedicated to peace. Founded by Marjorie Craig Benton and Mark Rogovin, it is the first museum of its kind in the United States. Its programming includes on-site and traveling exhibitions, regular public programs, a permanent collection, an archive and library of peace books, audio, and visual tapes. More than 10,000 individual artworks, artifacts, and historical items are accessible to the public. Among its 16 traveling exhibits are "Martin Luther King, Jr., Peacemaker" and "Via Crusis de Solentiname." "The Peace Museum is actively committed to exploring creative non-violent solutions to social issues, through education, community involvement, and exhibitions chronicling local, national, and international efforts to attain peace." Pub. *The Peace Release.* Virginia Albaneso, Exec. Dir.

United Nations Publications on Peace. *Peace Museums Worldwide.* Geneva: United Nations Library, 1998. P. 70.

277. *Peace License Plate* (1995) (org).

State of Illinois, *www.ivpa.org*

Illinois sponsors a Prevent Violence license plate, part of the proceeds going to the Illinois Violence Prevention Authority.

278. *The Peace School* (1972) (org).

3121 N. Lincoln Ave., Chicago 60657; (773) 248-7959; *www.peaceschool.org.*

The School strives to bring peace into the lives of people by improving their physical and mental capabilities and helping them become part of the peace-making process in society. Conducts classes in World Peace Breathing, World Peace Exercise, massage, and other activities. Initiated Peace Day in Chicago, an idea which has expanded to Peace Month in Chicago and elsewhere. Named a U.N. Peace Messenger org. in 1987. Charles Hwi-Chul Kim, Dir.

279. *Peace Studies* (1994) (col).

Peace Studies Office, Loyola University Chicago, Lake Shore Campus, Center for Interdisciplinary Programs, Damen 110, 6525 N. Sheridan Road, Chicago 60626; (773) 508-3377 or 508-8995;

An undergraduate minor degree on violence and peacemaking in political and environmental spheres. Encourages internships, field studies, and international exchanges. Pub. intercampus newsletter, "Peace Studies News and Notes" quarterly. Hannah Rockwell, Dir.

280. *Transform Society Mural* (1994) (mem).

In the Delcia Torres Conference Room of the Chicago Center of the American Friends Service Committee, 59 E. Van Buren St.; (312) 427-2533.

Reflects the history of AFSC's work for peace and justice in Chicago and abroad, and its view of a society transformed by courage and vision. (See Pennsylvania: Quakers).

281. *The Triumphs of Peace Endure—The Triumphs of War Perish* (1926) (mem).

Elks National Memorial (Benevolent and Protective Order of Elks, BPOE), 2750 N. Lakeview Ave. at Diversey, Chicago 60614-1889; (773) 755-4700; *mikek@elks.org*; *www.elks.org*

Transform Society Mural located in Chicago. Photograph courtesy AFSC Chicago Center.

The Triumphs of Peace Endure—The Triumphs of War Perish sculpture by Adolph Weinman, Chicago. Photograph courtesy Mike Kelly, BPOE Hq, Chicago.

This motif is incorporated in all the murals and artwork throughout the building, but especially in the frieze above the entranceway. Adolph Weinman's 5 foot high and 168 foot long relief, composed of more than seventy figures in the style of classical Greek sculpture, encircles the building. To the left (south) "a procession of joyful humanity in peace versus to the right (north) a mournful and agonized collection of victims and combatants in brutal confrontations." Contact Mike Kelly.

Riedy, James. *Chicago Sculpture*. Urbana: U of Illinois P, 1981. Pp. 169–171.

282. *Voices in the Wilderness* (1996) (org).

1460 W. Carmen Ave., Chicago 60640; (773) 784-8065; *kkelly@igc.apc.org*; *www.nonviolence.org/vitw*

A campaign to end the economic sanctions and bombings against the people of Iraq, which in 1999 were in their ninth year, and which violate international laws prohibiting crimes against humanity. The war against Iraq in 1991 destroyed 85% of the country's infrastructure; the sanctions have prevented reconstruction of water and sewage facilities and other essential services. Voices had sent some 25 delegations to Iraq by the year 2000 to document the deaths of over two million people by malnutrition, dehydration, and preventable disease, with 4,500 Iraqi children dying each month for lack of food, clean water, and medicine, according to UNICEF estimates. And thousands of civilians have been killed by the continual bombings since 1991. Contact: Kathy Kelly or Rick McDowell, (978) 544-9021 (*rjpmcd@aol.com*). Kelly was nominated for the Nobel Peace Prize May 1, 2000 (along with Denis Halliday, former U.N. Humanitarian Coordinator in Iraq).

Pilger, John. "Collateral Damage: Ten Years of Sanctions in Iraq." *In These Times* (May 15, 2000) 14–17.

Talvi, Silja J.A. "Voice in the Wilderness." *In These Times* (March 6, 2000) 10.

283. *War and Peace Studies* (1988) (col).

Depaul University, Fullerton near Halstead, Chicago 60604; (312) 362-7460; *rrotenbe@wppost.depaul.edu*; *http://condor.depaul.edu/~rrotenbe/warpeac.html*

Undergraduate students develop their own 5-course concentration in consultation with an advisor. Contact Robert Rotenberg.

EDWARDSVILLE, IL

284. *Peace and International Studies Program* (1974) (col).

Southern Illinois University, Edwardsville 62026 (618) 650-2250; *tpaxson@siue.edu; www.siue.edu*

A 21-credit minor with a concentration in one of four areas: world peace, western European, Latin America, and African. Contact Tom Paxson.

EVANSTON, IL

285. **Ethics Center* (col).

Garrett-Evangelical Theological Seminary, Evanston 60201; (847) 866-3887; *ken.vaux@nwu.edu; www.garrett.nwu.edu*

Affil. with United Methodists. Offers an MA in Ethics and Society and Christian Education. Courses on ethics of peace. Contact Ken Vaux.

286. **Rotary International* (1905) (org).

1560 Sherman Ave., Evanston 60201; *www.rotary.org*

Rotary Clubs have a long history of encouraging amity among nations. They have built plaques along the U.S.-Canadian border, for example, celebrating the enduring peace between the two countries. Beginning in the fall of 2002, the Rotary Foundation will fund seventy scholars at seven international studies centers for learning diplomacy and skills to resolve conflict and promote international understanding. Rotary hopes the scholars will become leaders in preventing and resolving conflicts. The institutions chosen for the two-year graduate programs are: Duke U/U of North Carolina-Chapel Hill (joint hosts), U of California-Berkeley, and universities in France, England, Australia, Japan, and Argentina. Applications available in the fall of 2000. The Rotary Foundation operates the largest privately funded scholarship program in the world—1,300 students yearly studying worldwide. The chairman of the Foundation, Robert Barth, declared: "Wars in the Balkans, Sierra Leone, Angola, and other regions underscore the urgent need for conflict resolution skills in the world's leaders and diplomats."

LOMBARD, IL

287. **West Suburban F.O.R.* (1940) (org).

1 S. 171 Pine Ln., Lombard 60148; (630) 342-2762.

Branch of the Fellowship of Reconciliation. Special attention to Latin America. Contact Betty Clegg.

NORMAL, IL

288. *Peace and Conflict Resolution* (1987) (col).

Illinois State University, Normal 61790; (309) 438-7935; *dgentry@ilstu.edu; www.cast.ilstu.edu/fcs/faculty/dgentry.htm*

Offers a minor degree drawn from five colleges in the University, with courses from world conflicts to nonviolent ethics. Contact Deborah Gentry.

OAK BROOK, IL

289. **Lions Club International, Peace Poster Contest* (1988) (org).

300 22nd St., Oak Brook 60523-8842; (630) 571-5466, ext. 358 or 372; *pr@lionsclubs.org; jmcmahan@ lionsclubs.org; www.lionsclubs.org*

This annual contest aims to give young people (ages 11–13) the opportunity to think about world peace and express what it means to them in an original artwork. Submissions must be sponsored by a local Lions club.

QUINCY, IL

290. *Peacemaking* (1999) (col).

College of Arts and Sciences, Quincy University, Quincy 62301; (217) 228-5573; *chasemi@quincy.edu;*

*www.quincy.edu/
academics/programs.
html?courses=
PMKandkey=32*

Offers a minor, a certificate, and a BA. The BA includes a seminar, 43-hours of general education, and 5–7 courses closely related to peacemaking. Contact Michael Chase.

ROCKFORD, IL

291. *Peace and Conflict Studies Program* (col).

Rockford College, Rockford 61108; (815) 226-4077; *ptobias@rockford.edu; www.rockford.edu/ academic/catalog/peace/ peace.htm*

Bahá'í House of Worship located in Wilmette. Photograph courtesy L. Caswell Ellis, BHW.

A minor degree of courses mainly in the social sciences with focus on causes of conflict and violence and their management. Off-campus learning and study abroad are available. Peter Tobias, Chair.

WILMETTE, IL

292. **Bahá'í House of Worship* (1921, 1931).

Wilmette 60091.

Construction began in March, 1921; superstructure was finished in 1931. The cost was over $1,300,000 up to January 1, 1947, with total cost estimated as $2,000,000. The height of the Temple from the foundation floor is 192 feet; its diameter is 204 feet at the foundation floor. The auditorium will seat approximately 1200 people. The dome's outside diameter is 90 feet; its outside height is 45 feet. The radiant white of the Temple's exterior derives from a combination of crystalline and white opaque quartz and white Portland cement. The Temple's nine sides and nine doors symbolize Bahá'í belief in the unity of all religions and of all mankind and their welcome to all people, regardless of race, nationality, or creed, to worship the One God. Archi-

tect: Louis J. Bourgeois. The special designation of the Temple for Bahá'ís is "Dawning-Point of the Remembrance of God." The Temple resides on 6.97 acres surrounded by trees, shrubs, and flowers, the gardens designed by Hilbert Dahl.

—— *Indiana (IN)* ——

33 Sister Cities. / 85 Peace Poles.

ANDERSON, IN

293. **Church of God Peace Fellowship* (1966, going back to the 1930s) (org).

1826 St. James Place, Anderson 46012.

"An international community of Christ's followers, peacemakers, compelled by the Biblical vision of shalom, peace with justice, for all of God's creation; committed to the clear New Testament peace witness of our pioneers; commissioned by Christ to eliminate violence, racism, oppression, and militarism, and to be

His agents of reconciliation." Recently raised $100,000 endowment for a course at Anderson University. Affiliate of the Fellowship of Reconciliation. Sponsors an annual conference and the newsletter *Peace Fellowship*.

BLOOMINGTON, IN

294. *Indiana Conflict Resolution Institute (ICRI)* (1997) (col).

School of Public and Environmental Affairs, Indiana University, Bloomington 47405; (812) 855-1618; *lbingham@indiana.edu; www.spea.indiana.edu/icri*

A teaching, research, and service institution for understanding and solving conflicts. Lisa Bingham, Dir.

295. **Tibetan Cultural Center (Tibet Society)* (1967) (org).

3655 S. Snoddy Rd., Bloomington 47401; (812) 334-7046.

Includes stupa, library, visitors' center, gardens, and assembly hall.

COLUMBUS, IN

296. **Columbus Peace Fellowship* (1967) (org).

11820 W. Youth Camp Rd., Columbus 47201; (812) 342-3443.

Affil. with the Fellowship of Reconciliation in 1996. Focuses on death penalty, international solidarity, racial and economic justice through speakers at regular meetings. Contact Sarah Kramer.

ELKHART, IN

297. *Peace Studies (MAPS)* (1975) (col).

Associated Mennonite Biblical Seminary, Elkhart 46517; (219) 295-3726; *tkoontz@ambs.edu; www.ambs.edu*

Offers an MA and M.Div. peace major based

upon the historical peacemaking of Mennonites, with a strong biblical and theological emphasis. One course in Ministry is required for the 60-hour MA; the full M. Div. requires 90 hours. Contact Ted Koontz.

FORT WAYNE, IN

298. *Peace and Conflict Studies* (1989) (col).

Indiana University-Purdue University, Fort Wayne, Fort Wayne 46805; (219) 481-6638; *johnsonr@ipfw.edu; www.ipfw.edu*

Began offering an undergraduate Certificate in 1993, with courses including Dr. King and the Civil Rights Movement and The Vietnam War. Richard Johnson, Dir.

299. *Peace Pole* (mem).

In the sanctuary of the Unitarian-Universalist Church, 5510 Old Mill Road, Fort Wayne 46805.

300. **Fort Wayne F.O.R.* (1999) (org).

2505 Florida Dr., Forth Wayne 46805; (219) 484-4741(h) or 422-5561 x2285(w); *kilgore@indtech.edu*

Activities: disarmament, Chiapas, annual Hiroshima Day, annual Fall Retreat. Branch of the Fellowship of Reconciliation. Contact Bill Kilgore.

GOSHEN, IN

301. **Fourth Freedom Forum, Project Abolition* (1999) (org).

803 N. Main St., Goshen 46528; (800) 233-6786, x21 or (219) 534-3402; *kmartin@fourthfreedom.org*

FFF initiated Project Abolition to increase public awareness of nuclear danger and build grassroots support in the U.S. for the reduction and elimination of nuclear weapons, in collaboration with the Disarmament Clearinghouse and other organizations. Kevin Martin, Director.

302. *Peace, Justice and Conflict Studies* (1973) (col).

Goshen College, Goshen 46526; (219) 535-7466; *ruthek@goshen.edu; www.goshen.edu/peace*

Peace education in the Anabaptist-Mennonite tradition offers a major and a minor. The major has two areas of concentration: conflict management and peace and justice. The minor can be combined with any major. Study abroad and scholarships available. Ruth Krall, Dir.

GREENCASTLE, IN

303. *Conflict Studies* (col).

Sociology and Anthropology Department, Depauw University, Greencastle 46135; (765) 658-4519; *gkuecker@depauw.edu; www.depauw.edu/acad/conflict/confmajor.htm*

The major and minor have core courses, a Senior Seminar, and workshops. Assoc. with the United Methodist Church. Glen Kuecker, Coord.

HUNTINGTON, IN

304. **Huntington F.O.R.* (1991) (org).

3596 W. 544 N, Huntington 46750; (219) 356-4444; *dbeery@netusa1.net*

Started in 1988 as "People for Peace and Justice," then became a branch of the Fellowship of Reconciliation. Promotes nonviolence and reconciliation in individuals and society, peace and justice through love and faith. Monthly meetings, community meetings, sponsored a peace pole, letter writing campaigns, annual picnic, community prayer services, etc. A *Peace Pole* (1995) with the words "Let Peace Prevail on Earth" in eight languages is located in a rose garden in Memorial Park in Huntington, about 100 yards from a tank and a jet plane. Dean and Susan Beery and Sr. Joan Arnold, Co-chairs.

INDIANAPOLIS, IN

305. **Disciples Peace Fellowship* (1935) (org).

Disciples Center, PO Box 1986,

Indianapolis 46206; (317) 635-3113; *ccosby@dhm.disciples.org*

"Its original covenant includes working to abolish war and to create the conditions of peace and justice among all people and nations." It has supported conscientious objectors, Pastors for Peace in Cuba, nuclear disarmament, conflict resolution education, and other causes. "Present foci includes working to abolish the death penalty, education about the maquiladoras, and corporate responsibility in investments." Summer peace internships. A quarterly newsletter. Carol Cosby, staff.

306. **Indianapolis Peace & Justice Center* (1982) (org).

3808 N. Meridian St., Indianapolis 46208; (317) 955-8121.

A coordinating and communications network for area nonviolent groups committed to ending all forms of social oppression. Sponsors a conflict resolution service known as Reaching Common Ground (317-955-8369). Provides a speakers bureau. Maintains a library of books, pamphlets, and videos. Holds seminars, workshops, and coffee houses. Pub. a monthly newspaper and a monthly community calendar of events. Kenni Washington, Pres.; Leah Di-Maria, Office Coordinator.

307. **Organization Development Institute* (1986) (org).

425 Univ. blvd., POLS, Indianapolis 46202; (317) 924-5965; *ssachs@iupui.edu*

Seeks to help network the peace community. Pub. newsletter *Nonviolent Change.* Stephen Sachs, Co-Chair, Co-Editor.

MUNCIE, IN

308. **Studies and Conflict Resolution* (1989) (col).

Department of History, Ball State University, Muncie 47306; (765)-285-8739; *oopazimmerma@bsuve.bsu.edu; www.bsu.edu/csh/history/program/id1.htm*

A minor introduces students to the main issues of war and violence and the creation of peace both personally and in the world. Phyllis Zimmerman, Dir.

NEWBURGH, IN

309. *Conflict Management* (col).

Trinity College and Seminary,
Newburgh 47629; (812) 853-0611;
75413.22@compuserve.com;
www.trinitysem.edu/tccm.html

Offers a Certificate, MA, Dr. Ministry, and
Ph.D. in a Christian context. Terry Wise, Dir.

310. **Trinity Center for Conflict
Management* (col).

See preceding entry.

Training in biblical methods of conflict management especially in the church through seminars and workshops. Pub. the quarterly *The Consultant.*

NORTH MANCHESTER, IN

311. *Gladdys Muir Peace Garden* (2000)
(mem).

Northwest corner of College Ave. and
Wayne St., across from Helman Hall,
Manchester College, North Manchester.

The garden honors the founder of the first
Peace Studies program in the U.S. (1948) at
Manchester College. Adjacent to the "Meeting
House" for conflict resolution. "If God's peaceful city should ever come on earth, Gladdys
Muir has provided brick and mortar, and laid
well a small part of its foundation."

312. *Martin Luther King, Jr., Plaque and
Photo* (1997) (mem).

Manchester College.

Noting his speech there shortly before his
death in 1968.

313. **North Manchester F.O.R.* (1979)
(org).

Box 25, N. Manchester 46962;
(219) 982-1605; *ecri@ctlnet.com*

Branch of the Fellowship of Reconciliation.
Activities include: monthly meeting, annual Fall
Retreat, Tax Day protests, Annual Hiroshima-
Nagasaki commemoration. Pub. monthly newsletter, *The Climate Changer.* Contact Paul Pierce.

314. **Peace Poles.*

Manchester College displays several Peace
Poles (at the entrance to the president's residence, in front of the library). In addition Peace
Poles can be found in the Manchester City
Park, at a retirement home, and at several residences.

315. **Peace Studies* (1948)
(col).

Manchester College, Box 27,
N. Manchester 46962;
(219) 982-5343;
klbrown@manchester.edu;
www.manchester.edu

The Peace Studies Institute
and Program for Conflict Resolution, which explore nonviolent alternatives to conflict and
injustice, "pioneered as the first
undergraduate peace studies
program in the United States."
The College offers both a major
and minor in peace studies,
which extends beyond the classroom through internships with
peace organizations and the
January interim courses. The
Institute sponsors conferences
and programs for college and
community, and its *Bulletin of*

"If God's peaceful city should ever come
on earth, Gladdys Muir has provided brick
and mortar, and laid well a small part of its
foundation."
                        — Allen Deeter '53

Gladdys Muir Peace Garden, North Manchester, Indiana. Photograph courtesy Manchester College Peace Studies Program.

the Peace Studies Institute and Program in Conflict Resolution publishes academic papers and news of the program. It is also the principal sponsor of the Graduation Pledge Alliance, which invites students to pledge: "I _____ pledge to take into account the social and environmental consequences of any job I consider or any organization for which I work." Ken Brown, Director.

Notre Dame, IN

316. **Joan B. Kroc Institute for International Peace Studies* (1986) (col).

Hesburgh Center for International Studies, U of Notre Dame, PO Box 639, Notre Dame 46556-0639; (219) 631-6970; *www.nd.edu/~krocinst*

Seeks "to understand the causes of violence and the conditions for peace and to contribute to just and demilitarized international relations." The Institute is housed on the University of Notre Dame campus, along with the Helen Kellogg Institute for International Studies, in the Hesburgh Center, which includes also an auditorium, conference rooms, a restaurant, and an apartment residence for visiting faculty. The graduate program provides two full-scholarship paths leading to the M.A. degree in peace studies: the Kroc Scholars Program for young students living together in International Peace House and the Hesburgh Scholars without residential requirement. The undergraduate Concentration in Peace Studies is a 15-hour multidisciplinary program. The Institute also sponsors research projects whose results are reported in scholarly books and articles (19 books 1997-98), and conferences; for example, "The Sacred, the Sword, and Global Society: Religious Dimensions of Violence, Peace, and Security" (1998). Pubs.: semi-annual newsletter *Report*, about the Institute's programs and activities. Hal Culbertson, Asst. to the Dir.; Carolyn Nordstrom (219-631-8819; *nordstrom.1@nd.edu*), Dir. Of Graduate Studies; George Lopez, Dr. of Undergraduate Studies.

Richmond, IN

317. **Peace and Global Studies* (1972) (col).

Earlham College, Richmond 47374-4095; (765) 983-1200;

dortham@earlham.edu; (Richmond is 70 miles east of Indianapolis).

Earlham's commitment to peace education derives from its Quaker roots. PAGS seeks to make the world more respectful of the dignity of human life and to increase nonviolent means in resolving conflicts. Majors are required to take courses in Women's Studies and African American Studies, and a course in Twentieth Century conflicts, among others, and an off-campus internship for applying methods of peacemaking. Peace studies infuse the entire curriculum of Earlham through the general education requirements and numerous alternative courses that help students understand the structures of society as part of a global system of war and injustice. Anthony Bing, Director.

318. *Peace and Justice Studies* (1963, 1980, 1992) (col).

Earlham School of Religion, Richmond 47674; (765) 983-1353; *valenlo@earlham.edu;* *www.earlham.edu/~esr*

The Earlham School of Religion was founded in 1963 as the graduate program of Earlham College. This Quaker and Ecumenical affil. school started a MA in Religion and a MA of Ministry/Divinity with a peace and justice emphasis in 1980 and 1992 respectively. Both require courses in Christian foundations, peace and justice and thesis, and the M.Div. adds an internship. Pub. "ESR Reports" regularly. Contact Lonnie Valentine.

319. **Peace Studies Association* (1987) (col).

Earlham College, Drawer 105, Richmond 47374-4095; (765) 983-1386; Fax: (765) 983-1229; *psa@earlham.edu;*

A consortium of individuals and programs from over 200 institutions in North America, Latin America, and Europe where Peace Studies is offered. PSA serves to assist academic programs through workshops and seminars, an annual conference, and collaboration among programs. Tony Bing, Earlham, Exec. Dir., Dortha Meredith, Earlham, Exec. Secretary. (At the CO-PRED/PSA Conference, April 2000 in Austin, TX, the two organizations voted to merge.)

320. **Peace Studies Program* (1980) (col).

Bethany Theological Seminary, Richmond 47374; (765) 983-1800;

bachje@earlham.edu;
www.brethren.org/bethany/peace.htm

A Church of the Brethren institution. Since 1971 the Seminary had given an M.A. degree in theology with a peace studies emphasis. In 1980 John and Elizabeth Baker funded an expanded program (Baker Peace Fund). Today Bethany offers also a Master of Arts in Theology, a Master of Divinity, and a Doctor of Ministry all in peace studies, one of the few graduate-level programs in peace studies in the U.S. The Fund also enables the Seminary to bring Brethren faculty and pastors to campus for seminars, to send students to peace meetings, and to bring lecturers to campus, and it supports a weekly Peace Studies Seminar. Contact Jeff Bach.

321. *Richmond F.O.R.* (1991) (org).

Peace and Global Studies Program, Earlham College, Richmond 47374; (317) 983-1305 (w), 962-1741 (h); *tonyb@earlham.edu*

Branch of the Fellowship of Reconciliation. Focuses on the Conflict Resolution Center in Richmond. Also active on specific issues, e.g. Iraq. Contact Anthony Bing.

SOUTH BEND, IN

322. *Michiana War Resisters League* (1994) (org).

1036 N. Niles Ave., South Bend 46617; (219) 289-2126; *psmith@saintmarys.edu*

Leafletting every Tues. at Federal Building, and other work.

TERRE HAUTE, IN

323. *Conflict Resolution Program* (1994) (col).

Department of Sociology, Indiana State University, Terre Haute 47809; (812) 237-3446; *soschel@scifac.indstate.edu;* *http://spot.indstate.edu/crp*

A MS degree in conflict resolution for professionals provides mediation training; or a Certificate for those who do not want the full master's program. An interdisciplinary undergraduate course, Social Conflict and Conflict Resolution, is available in the general education program. Brief newsletter twice a year, "Conflict Resolution Notes." James Schellenberg, Coord.

WEST LAFAYETTE, IN

324. *IR/Peace and Conflict Resolution/IR Peace Studies* (col).

Department of Political Science, Purdue University, West Lafayette 47907; (765) 494-8762; *carroll@polsci.purdue.edu;* *www.purdue.edu*

The BA degree draws upon diverse departments and sponsors internships and field studies. A scholarship for a peace related research project is available. The MA and Ph.D. in peace studies are also available. Contact Berenice Carroll (a founder of COPRED).

——— *Iowa (IA)* ———

16 Sister Cities. / 22 Peace Poles.

CEDAR RAPIDS, IA

325. *Clare House* (1996) (org).

514 McKinley St. SE, PO Box 1183, Cedar Rapids 52403; (319) 364-4101.

A Catholic Worker residence for persons with HIV/AIDS that also addresses peace and justice issues. Contact Jim Foxwell.

326. *Conflict Resolution* (1992) (col).

Department of Sociology, Anthropology and Criminology, University of Northern Iowa, Cedar Falls 50614; (319) 273-6217; *ronald.roberts@uni.edu;* *http://csbsnt.csbs.uni.edu/dept/sac/*

The Certificate consists of a core course and four electives. Ronald Roberts, Coord.

DAVENPORT

327. *Peace and Justice Program* (1978) (col).

Theology Department, Saint Ambrose University, Davenport 52803;

(319) 333-6442; *edunn@saunix.sau.edu; www.sau.edu/academic/theology/mpj.html*

Offers an 18-hour minor in peace and justice in the tradition of St. Ambrose and Catholic social teaching. Contact Ed Dunn. (The university also has another peace organization, called PAX (1995), Bud Grant, Dir.).

DECORAH, IA

328. *Luther College Global Concerns* (1971) (col).

Decorah 52101.

Offers diverse courses oriented around peace-making. Contact Michael Blair, Campus Pastor, Center for Faith and Life (319) 387-1040, *blairmic@luther.edu*; or Kent Simmonds, *simmonke@martin.luther.edu*

DES MOINES, IA

329. *American Friends Service Committee (AFSC), North Central Region* (1948) (org).

4211 Grand Ave., Des Moines 50312; (515) 274-4851; *afscdesm@afsc.org*; *www.afsc.org/afscnchp.htm*
National office: Philadelphia

This Quaker regional office for peace and justice covers eleven midwestern states from Texas and Arkansas to North Dakota and Minnesota, with satellite offices in St. Louis, Kansas City, Colorado, Tucson, Oglala, SD, and a sub-regional office for Texas/Arkansas/Oklahoma (TAO) in Austin. Some of their programs are: immigrant/refugee assistance, education in peace and nonviolence (conflict resolution training in schools, economic conversion of military/nuclear industries, Comprehensive Nuclear Test Ban Treaty, opposition to Junior ROTC in public schools, countering violence in the media, education about peace and justice problems in countries abroad, civil and human rights advocacy (death penalty, etc.). Pub. *AFSC Now: Central Regional News & Views*. Eloise Cranke, Regional Dir. National office in Philadelphia (*afscinfo@afsc.org*).

330. *Des Moines Catholic Worker* (1976) (org).

PO Box 4551, Des Moines 50306; (515) 243-0765.

Serves the poor and needy at Dingman House and engages in social justice actions. Msgr. Ligutti House contains the Peace & Justice Library, 1301 8th St., Des Moines 50314; (515) 246-9887. Pub. *Via Pacis* quarterly newsletter; Resistance notes in each issue: regular Ploughshares Update, information for example about *The Nuclear Resister*, Voices in the Wilderness, protest at Strategic Air Command Headquarters, Hiroshima-Nagasaki remembrance. Contact Fr. Frank Cordaro.

331. *Iowa Peace Network* (1979) (org).

4211 Grand Ave., Des Moines 50312-2496; (515) 255-7114; *ipnet@earthlink.net*

Five denominations support the Network: The Church of the Brethren, the Iowa-Nebraska Mennonite Conference, the Iowa Yearly Meeting of Friends (Quakers) (Conservative and United), and the United Methodist Church. IPN's mission includes educating members about peace initiatives on the local, national, and international level, and educating the community about alternatives to violence. IPN has a "Peace Resource Center" available to the community—books, films, t-shirts, bumper stickers, curricula, visual arts; offers a speaker's bureau; sponsor's an annual "Tax Day Bake Sale" to inform the public about military expenditures; conducts a "Muslim and Christian Dialogue" every two weeks; and has workshops on nonviolence. Pub. *Dovetail* quarterly (16 pp.). 1200 members, full-time coordinator. Susan Myers, Coordinator.

DUBUQUE, IA

332. *Father Ray Herman Peace and Justice Center* (1982) (col).

Loras College, Dept. of Campus Ministry, Alumni Campus Center, 1450 Alta Vista, PO Box 178, Dubuque 52004-0178; (319) 588-7572; *jgoodman@loras.edu*; *www.loras.edu* under "Campus Ministry."

Named after Fr. Ray Herman, a missionary of the Archdiocese of Dubuque, who was murdered in Bolivia in 1975 after 13 years of serving the needs of that country's poor, the Center is not only an information clearinghouse (courses of study, a resource library) but is also a place for service by Loras students to the greater community. Students take annual trips to Appalachia and Washington, DC, among other actions. Scholarships allow junior students to spend their summers in social service around the country. The major activity each year is Peace with Justice Week, which includes a guest lecturer to speak on nonviolence, peace making, and community change (Colman McCarthy, Rev. John Dear, SJ) and a Peace Pole ceremony. The *Peace Pole* is located in front of Christ the King Chapel at Loras (1996). James M. Goodman, Dir. of Campus Ministry.

333. *Hope House Catholic Worker* (1996) (org).

1592 Locust St., Dubuque 52001; (319) 582-9079.

HH participants live in pursuit of peace and justice through the Catholic Worker philosophy of personalism. Monthly sessions for thought, public witnessing during national military operations, simple living, hospitality to the homeless. Contact Mary Moody.

334. *Justice and Peace Studies* (1988) (col).

Dubuque 52001; (319) 588-6543; nfreund@keller.clarke.edu; www.clarke.edu/academics/departments/ justice&peacestudies/index.htm

A minor degree from a Christian perspective. Affil. with the Iowa Peace Institute. Norman Freund, Chair.

GRINNELL, IA

335. *Iowa Peace Institute* (1986) (org).

917 Tenth Ave., PO Box 480, Grinnell, 50112; (515) 236-4880.

Promotes alternatives to violence through conflict management, global education, international development, and world trade. Encourages global education and conflict resolution curricula in public schools, peace studies programs in institutions of high learning, community dispute resolution centers in Iowa, inclusion of environmental issues, etc. $1 million endowment.

IOWA CITY, IA

336. *Center for Human Rights* (col).

Univ. of Iowa, Iowa City 52242; (319) 335-3900; uichr@iowa.edu

Research and education for human rights in Iowa and globally. Burns Weston, Dir. (burns-weston@iowa.edu); Rex Honey, Assoc. Dir.

336a. *Global Studies Program* (1972) (col).

Geography Dept., University of Iowa, Iowa City 52242; (319) 335-0154; rex-honey@uiowa.edu; www.uiowa.edu/~gsp/index.html

Began as World Order Studies. Provides a Certificate and a Major in War, Peace, and Security, or Human Rights and Social Justice. Rex Honey, Dir.

KIRKWOOD, IA

337. *Peace Pole* (1998) (mem).

Kirkwood Community College, Kirkwood.

Dedicated during Kirkwood's "Beauty of Diversity Days." Students and staff recited "May Peace Prevail on Earth" in some 60 languages.

LAMONI, IA

338. *Peace Studies* (1992) (col).

Division of Social Studies, Graceland University 50140; (515) 784-5185; juhnke@graceland.edu; www2.graceland.edu

The minor consists of core courses on the principles and practices of peace. Affil. with Reorganized Latter Day Saints. William Juhnke, Chairperson.

MALOY, IA

339. *Strangers & Guests Catholic Worker* (1986) (org).

108 Hillcrest Dr., Maloy 50836; (515) 785-2321.

Emphasizes serving the poor through manual arts and crafts and growing their own food. Peace activities: demonstrations at S.A.C./STRATcom in Omaha, missile silos, and E.L.F. in Wisconsin and D.C.; support at Plowshares trials. One member participated in the Walk for a Peaceful Future in the Middle East Voices in the Wilderness trip to Iraq. Contact Betsy Keenan.

MUSCATINE, IA

340. *Stanley Foundation* (1956) (org).

209 Iowa Ave., Muscatine 52761; (319) 264-1500; *info@stanleyfdn.org*; *www.stanleyfdn.org*

Sponsors diverse programs intended to provoke thought and encourage dialog on international relations and world affairs, especially international policy conferences and the publication of the conference reports. Also organizes global education programs for youth. Current topics: the U.N., countries in or emerging from conflict with the U.S., human rights, sustainable development, and global education. Publishes *World Press Review*, a monthly magazine (pub. in New York), and the *Courier*, a newsletter. Also sponsors a weekly radio program on world affairs, *Common Ground*. Founded by C. Maxwell and Elizabeth Stanley to further the effective management of global problems. President: Richard H. Stanley.

SIOUX CITY, IA

341. *Alternatives for Simple Living* (1973) (org).

5312 Morningside Ave., PO Box 2857, Sioux City 51106; (800) 821-6153; (712) 174-8875; *Alternatives@SimpleLiving.org*; *www.SimpleLiving.org*

ASL started as a protest against the commercialization of Christmas. Sells books mainly and some videos for children and adults on making peace, preserving the environment, and reducing consuming. Some titles: *How to Teach Peace to Children, 1000 Paper Cranes: The Story of Sadako & Children's Peace Statue, Circles of Hope, Circles of Peace, Hands Around the World, Play Lightly on the Earth*. Catalog of 46pp. Gerald Iversen, Nat. Coord.

342. *Peace Studies* (col).

Sociology Department, Briar Cliff College, Sioux City 5114; (712) 279-5488; *fields@briar-cliff.edu*; *www.briar-cliff.edu/majors/sociology.htm#PeaceStudies*

An interdepartmental minor, internships encouraged. Sample courses: War, Peace, and the Human Condition, Theology of Peace. Contact Grace Ann Witte.

—— Kansas (KS) ——

16 Sister Cities. / 22 Peace Poles.

MEDICINE LODGE, KS

343. *Peace Treaty Pageant* (1927) (org).

Located in *Memorial Peace Park* in a natural amphitheater where the Medicine River and Elm Creek flow together. PO Box 128, Medicine Lodge 67104, 72 miles southwest of Wichita at the intersection of highways 160 and 281; *ptreaty@cyberlodg.com*; *www.idir.net/~ourtown/*

The Pageant compresses 300 years of history into two hours and particularly commemorates

Medicine Lodge Peace Treaty Pageant, Medicine Lodge. Photograph courtesy Peace Treaty Association.

the great peace council of 1867 between the Peace Commission of the U.S. government and the five tribes of the Plains Indians: the Kiowa, the Comanche, the Kiowa-Apache, the Arapahoe, and the Cheyenne. A monument of a U.S. soldier and an Indian facing each other, the Indian holding a peace pipe, also commemorates the Treaty.

Jones, Doug. *The Treaty of Medicine Lodge.* Norman, OK: U of Oklahoma P, 1966.

NEWTON, KS

344. *Newton Area Peace Center* (1983) (org).

116 West 6th St., PO Box 185, Newton 67114; (316) 284-2828; *peace@southwind.net*

An ecumenical, Christian church-based organization promoting peace through social justice. Assists local peacemaking efforts, provides peace education resources, disseminates alternative news, a voice for peace. Annual actions: commemorates Hiroshima/Nagasaki bombings, peace toys Fair, summer Peace Camps. Pub. monthly newsletter. Palwasha Kakar, Interim Dir.

NORTH NEWTON, KS

345. *Conflict Management Certification Program* (1998) (col).

Bethel College, 300 E 27th St., North Newton 67117; (316) 284-5217; *gflory@bethelks.edu*

Consists of 12 credit hours of courses from the Social Sciences, Business, and Social Work departments and an internship. Offered through the Kansas Institute for Peace and Conflict Resolution. Gary Flory, Director.

346. *Global Peace and Justice Studies* (1973) (col).

Bethel College, North Newton 67117; *jhart@bethelks.edu;* *www.bethelks.edu/academics/globaljustice*

Undergraduate major and minor especially to prepare for international development. Internships required and study abroad encouraged. Contact Julie Hart.

347. *Kansas Institute for Peace and Conflict Resolution* (1985) (col).

Bethel College, North Newton 67117; (316) 284-5217; *gflory@bethelks.edu*

Bethel represents an Anabaptist/Christian perspective of "reconciliation, service, appreciation of diversity, personal transformation and integrity, and nonviolence and peacebuilding within the context of social justice." Offers an undergraduate Conflict Management Certificate (1998), a Community Mediation Center (1999), a Summer Mediation Training Institute (1999), a Peace Lecture Series. The original Bethel College Peace Lecture Series (1972) and KIPCOR merged in 1992. The Institute endeavors to strengthen conflict resolution and peacebuilding in communities; encourages research and education to prepare students and groups to be peacemakers. Gary Flory, Dir.

348. *Mennonite Central Committee/ Central States* (1944) (org).

121 East 30th St., Box 235, North Newton 67117; (316) 283-2720; *centralstates@mcc.org*

Their Peace and Justice Education section (1999) is engaged in education, advocacy, and organizing for peace. Contact Rachel Stutzman (*rachel_e_stutzman@mail.mcc.org*).

SALINA, KS

349. *The Land Institute* (1976) (org).

2440 E. Water Well Rd., Salina 67401; (785) 823-5376; *www.LandInstitute.org*

The Institute seeks to relate people, land, and community and to develop an agriculture that will save soil from being lost or poisoned while promoting a community life both prosperous and enduring. Its Prairie Festival 2000 was held on May 26–28.

TOPEKA, KS

350. *Topeka Center for Peace and Justice* (1986) (org).

1248 SW Buchanan St., Topeka 66604-1263; (785) 232-4388; *topekacpj@aol.com*

Promotes justice and peace through education and action for social change in the greater Topeka community. Racial dialogue programs, victim-offender mediation, annual summer Peace Camp, annual Tax Day education. Pub. *Cooperation Times*. Contact Bill Beachy, Exec. Dir., or Wendy Perlman.

WICHITA, KS

351. *Churches United for Peacemaking* (1981) (org).

1407 N. Topeka, Wichita 67214; (316) 263-5886; *hplenert@southwind.net*

Promotes peace among churches and Christians. Annual conference. Harold Plenert, Coord.

352. *Peace and Social Justice Center of South Central Kansas* (1992) (org).

1407 North Topeka, Wichita 67214; (316) 263-5886; *peacecenter@igc.org*; *www.ewichita.com/peacecenter*

Seeks to establish justice and peace for all people and to care for the earth, by educating, networking and community-building, and organizing for action. Year 2000 emphases: peace and justice for children and families, Food and Forum monthly program, Iraq, peace education, livable wage campaign, school violence, militarism, and related issues. Pub. *Peace & Social Justice Center of South Central Kansas Newsletter*, e-mail Action Alerts, Member Updates. Patrick Cameron, Dir.

353. *Peace Pole* (1998) (mem).

Students from the Pioneers for Peace and Justice club at West High School planted the first peace pole at a public school in Wichita.

—— *Kentucky (KY)* ——

19 Sister Cities. / 39 Peace Poles.

LOUISVILLE, KY

354. *Louisville F.O.R.* (1975) (org).

242 Clover Lane, Louisville 40207; (502) 899-5989.

Branch of the Fellowship of Reconciliation.

Monthly meetings, committees on demilitarization, economic justice, and editorial. Newsletter *FORsooth* ten times a year. Activities include a Bosnian Student Project, protesting JROTC, annual Tax Day actions, annual Hiroshima/Nagasaki commemoration, public meetings, rallies. Contact Erik Reinhart-Vidal.

NEWPORT, KY

355. *World Peace Bell* (1999) (mem).

Next to the Millennium Monument Tower, Fifth and York streets, Newport, across the Ohio River from Cincinnati; *www.milleniummonument.com*

An inscription engraved on the bell's side reads: "The World Peace Bell is a symbol of freedom and peace honoring our past, celebrating our present, and inspiring our future." The "largest free-swinging bell in the world" (33 tons/66,000 pounds, swinging from a yoke of 13 tons) was rung for the first time in the United States on New Year's Eve, 1999, every hour on the hour for all 24 time zones in the world, broadcast world wide. It rang again as the "Prelude" to the "International Day of Peace" in September, 2000, as part of the "Bells Ringing for Peace" project of *Symposium 2000*, to celebrate the year 2000 as the International Year for a Culture of Peace. Designed and cast in Nantes, France, in 1998, rung first in March, and then shipped across the Atlantic to New Orleans and up the Mississippi River to Newport. The bell hangs permanently in a glass-and-steel pavilion. The bell was the idea of Wayne Carlisle and David Hosea. Contact Cindy Goodman (606-655-9500).

Flynn, Terry. "Bell's Journey Is Over." *Cincinnati Enquirer* (Aug. 2, 1999)

Lord, Ellen. "Peace Bell Touches Hearts." *Cincinnati Post* (Aug. 2, 1999).

—— *Louisiana (LA)* ——

15 Sister Cities. / 34 Peace Poles.

BATON ROUGE, LA

356. *Baton Rouge Catholic Worker* (1993) (org).

1275 Laurel St., Baton Rouge 70802;

(225) 389-9572 or 343-3045;
timvining@mindspring.com

A gospel-based multiracial and ecumenical community offering hospitality and resistance to economic and racial injustice. Peace activities include: vigils against NATO bombing, opposition to militarism, resistance to Iraq sanctions, and anti-death penalty education. Pub.: bimonthly newsletter, *Baton Rouge Catholic Worker.* Contact Tim Vining.

357. *Louisiana Coalition to Abolish the Death Penalty* (1984) (org).

PO Box 64635, Baton Rouge 70896;
(225) 344-5483;
timvining@mindspring.com

Committed to abolishing state sanctioned executions and to informing the public about death penalty facts and issues, through forums, speakers, and materials. Contact Tim Vining.

LCADP chapters also in Monroe (POB 762, 71210; 318-325-1253; Dot Brown) and Shreveport (939 Jordan St.; 318-221-5296).

358. *Martin Luther King, Jr., Memorial* (1997) (mem).

Between the Government Building and the Theater for Performing Arts, St. Louis St., Baton Rouge.

An abstract sculpture composed of a central blue form with a human shape and cross in red-orange on each side. Inscribed on plaque at the base of the monument are King's words: "We must learn to live as brothers or we will perish as fools." The sculpture as a whole is described as symbolic of King's famous line, "Free at last." Sculptor: Arthur Silverman.

BROUSSARD, LA

359. *Montessori Children's House* (1996) (org).

Broussard 70518; (337) 837-1841.

Their Peace Pole is located in an herb garden within the children's playground. The school holds a combined celebration of Peace Day and Children's Day each year on October 24 around their Peace Pole, when each child (ages 3 to 5) brings some symbol or costume of a country. Mary Leblanc, Dir.; Ann Langston, Teacher.

MONROE, LA

360. *Northminster Peace & Justice Group* (2000) (org).

1991 Winnsboro Rd., Monroe 71202;
(318) 398-9817; *tamaram@bayou.com*

Arose out of discussions generated by the

Martin Luther King, Jr., Memorial sculpture by Arthur Silverman, East Baton Rouge Parish. Photograph by Hugh Shankle, courtesy Dennis McCain.

Pursuing Justice Series of the Alliance of Baptists. Began new group with racism discussion, moving toward war/peace issues with viewing and discussion of CBS video *Fail Safe*. Contact Tammy Powell.

NEW ORLEANS, LA

361. **Pax Christi New Orleans* (1983) (org).

PO Box 50304, New Orleans 70150; (504) 522-3751 or 944-6069; *yanktonjan@aol.com*

Diverse nonviolent advocacy: death penalty vigils, Iraq sanctions, globalization/economic justice, Jubilee 2000, etc. Judy and Pete Yuslum, Regional Representatives.

362. **Twomey Center for Peace Through Justice* (1991) (org).

Loyola University, 502 Pine St., New Orleans 70118; mailing: 7214 St. Charles Ave., Campus Box 907, 70118; (504) 861-5830; *quant@loyno.edu; www.loyno.edu/twomey/*

Credo: "...to create a Society in which the dignity of the human person, in whomsoever found, shall be acknowledged, respected, and protected." Father Louis J. Twomey S.J. (1906–1969). Father Twomey's work for economic justice, workers' rights, human rights, educational opportunities, and toleration led to the Human Relations Institute, which became the Twomey Center. Coord.: Ted Quant.

SHREVEPORT, LA

363. **Pax Christi Shreveport* (1984) (org).

Katherine Credeur, 824 Elmwood, Shreveport 71106; (318) 221-5296; *mhicks@shreve.net; http://207.78.168.4;* or Catholic Center, 2500 Line Ave., Shreveport 71104; (318) 222-2006.

Among other activities: Annual Vow of Nonviolence to the people of Shreveport; Way of the Cross/Way of Justice, on Good Fridays. Katherine Credeur, Dir.; or contact Mark Hicks. Also: Fr. Murray Clayton (at Sacred Heart, 318-635-2121) or Fr. Mark Watson (at Catholic Center).

—— *Maine (ME)* ——

9 Sister Cities. / 22 Peace Poles.

AUGUSTA, ME

364. **Radio Free Maine* (1988) (org).

PO Box 2705, Augusta 04338; (207) 622-6629; *www.radiofreemaine.com*

Offers recordings by Brian Willson, Howard Zinn, Noam Chomsky, Jonathan Schell, Staughton Lynd, among a host of other advocates of peace and justice. Roger Leisner, Dir.

365. *Samantha Reed Smith Statue* (1986) (mem).

In front of the Maine Cultural Building and next to the State Museum and Library in Augusta.

The statue, entitled "Maine's Young Ambassador of Goodwill," sculpted by Glen Hines, commemorates the life of the Maine girl (1972–1985) who sought to foster better relations between the Soviet Union and the United States in the 1980s. A dove symbol of peace is poised in her hand, ready to fly, and a bear cub sits at her feet (representing the state of Maine and the Soviet Union). (See Nebraska).
Smith, Samantha, and Arthur Smith. *Samantha Smith: A Journey to the Soviet Union.*

BANGOR, ME

366. **Peace and Justice Center of Eastern Maine* (1989) (org).

170 Park St., Bangor 04401; (207) 942-9343; *peacectr@mint.net; www.bairnet.org/organizations/peacectr/*

Peace, justice, and environmental network center for 5 counties in eastern Maine. Sponsors educational programs, films, resource library, training workshops, annual HOPE Festival, and works in coalition with other peace groups. Monthly newsletter/calendar, *Peace and Justice News and Views*. Stephen Souci, Office Manager; Ilze Petersons, Prog. Coord.

Samantha Reed Smith Statue by Glen Hines, Augusta. Photograph courtesy Earle Shettleworth, Jr., Maine Historic Preservation Commission.

BRUNSWICK, ME

367. *Women's International League for Peace and Freedom (WILPF)* (1991) (org).

43 Willow Grove, Brunswick 04011; (207) 729-0023; PO Box 81, Ogunquit 03907; (207) 646-5772.

Since 1915, WILPF has worked for nonviolent resolution of conflicts. Recent activities here have centered on peoples of this hemisphere, including building a Sister City in Cuba. Contact Christine De Troy, founder. A Southern Maine group meets in York (contact Betty Williams, PO Box 81, Ogunquit 03907; 207-646-5772)

for education and action about gun control, violence against women, and the environment.

FARMINGTON, ME

368. *Peacemakers* (1997) (org).

72 Perham St., Farmington 04938; (207) 778-6609.

Affil. with the Fellowship of Reconciliation. Activities during the past few years include candlelight vigils for nonviolence and workshop on nonviolence. Contact Joel Hayden.
Thistle, Scott. "Vigils to Focus on Ending Hate." *Lewiston Sun-Journal* (Sept. 30, 1999) B1.

MONROE, ME

369. *INVERT: Institute for Nonviolence Education, Research, and Training* (1977) (org).

PO Box 776, Monroe 04951; (207) 525-7776; *invert@acadia.net*

Promotes nonviolent social change through education and statewide and regional organizing and coalition-building. Programs in 1999: Alternatives to Violence projects (workshops at prisons), Maine Draft and Military Counselors (for high school youth), Grass-Roots Organizers' Workshop (GROW), Nonviolence Training, Changing Maine (day-long gatherings of organizers), and more. Pub. quarterly report and a directory of nonprofits and social change groups, *The Maine Alternative Yellow and Green Pages* (1200 orgs. in Maine). Larry Dansinger, Coord.

370. *Maine Draft and Military Counselors* (1985) (org).

PO Box 776, Monroe 04951; (207) 525-7776.

Provides information about alternatives to military service and draft registration especially to high school age youth. Contact Larry Dansinger (Monroe), Norm Meldrum (Wilton).

371. *Maine War Tax Resistance Resource Center* (1982) (org).

PO Box 776, Monroe 04951; (207) 525-7776.

Counsels and supports individuals concerned about government spending on the military and war/war preparations and who are opposed to their own income and telephone taxes going for those purposes. Information packet available. Contact Larry Dansinger.

ORONO, ME

372. *Maine Peace Action Committee* (1974) (org).

Philosophy Dept., The Maples, Univ. of Maine, Orono 04469; (207) 581-3860; *dallen@maine.edu*

A student/faculty/community organization, anti-militarist, anti-imperialist, pro-environment, peace and justice, anti-nuclear Abolition 2000, WTO issues, Central America, CIA recruiting, etc. Public education through weekly lecture series, films, and a newsletter, *Maine Peace Action Committee Newsletter*, twice a year. Contact Doug Allen.

373. *Orono Peace Group* (1990?) (org).

64 Gardner Rd., Orono 04473; (207) 866-4785(h) or 581-2315(w); *shirley_davis@umit.maine.edu*

Promotes peace education in the Orono-Bangor area. Affil. with the Campaign for Global Change and World Federalist Association. Contact Shirley ("Lee") Davis.

374. *Peace Studies Program* (1988) (col).

University of Maine, 5725 East Annex, Orono 04469; (207) 581-2609.

Focuses on the roots of violence and conflict through its academic concentration, lending library, lectures, and conferences to increase peace and nonviolent conflict resolution on campus and in the community. Also offers an annual summer institute on "Teaching Conflict Resolution K-8," conflict resolution training and consultation, an annual Peace Week in October, an annual Spring Lecture Series. Pub.: newsletter *Changing Ways/Building Skills*, twice a year. Phyllis Brazee, Dir.

PORTLAND, ME

375. *Maine Veterans for Peace* (1985) (org).

One Pleasant St., Portland 04101; (207) 772-0680.

Advocates ratification of the Comprehensive Test Ban and Landmines Treaties, abolition of nuclear weapons, reduction of U.S. arms sales abroad, normalization of U.S.-Cuba relations, closing the School of Americas, nonviolent resolution of conflicts, and oppose secret wars, black budgets, and covert operations. Chapter 001 of Veterans for Peace (Washington, D.C.). Tom Sturtevant, Pres.

376. *Pax Christi Maine* (1981) (org).

242 Ludlow St., Portland 04102-1808; (207) 773-6562 or 767-4193.

Opposes violence on all levels of society and seeks a just world order by sponsoring speakers, sending representatives to Central America, and assisting hunger projects. Offers a Romero Award; coordinates Quest for Peace collections. Pub. a newsletter. Bill Slavick, Coordinator and Regional Rep., or Denise Ewell.

377. *Peace Action Maine* (1982) (org).

PO Box 3842, 1 Pleasant St., 4th fl, Portland 04104; (207) 772-0680; *peaceactionme@ctel.net; www.peaceactionme.org*

A branch of Peace Action, PAM concentrates on disarmament (abolition of nuclear weapons, end to international arms trade, substantial reduction in military spending, economic conversion from military to civilian production) and conflict resolution (education for creative ways of responding to conflict without violence). Quarterly newsletter *Peace Talk*: June 1999 articles include rebuilding the Balkans, arms race, U.S. supported massacres in Chiapas, campaign to abolish nuclear weapons, companies which profit from the air strikes on Iraq, book reviews, and a list of new or rejoined members by towns. Contact Wells Staley-Mays.

378. *Peace and Justice Center of Southern Maine* (1996) (org).

1 Pleasant St., 4th Fl, Portland 04101; (207) 772-0680 or 774-6936.

The Center supports peace and justice groups and promotes networking by providing a library and equipment for several organizations, including Veterans for Peace and Peace Action Maine.

379. *Physicians for Social Responsibility—Maine Chapter* (1980) (org).

PO Box 1771, Portland 04104; (207) 772-0680; *psr_maine@yahoo.com*

Committed to eliminating weapons of mass destruction, preserving a sustainable environment, and reducing violence and its causes. Programs include: Campaign to Protect Sane Gun Laws, providing health professionals with training in violence awareness, the nuclear disarmament campaign: Abolition 2000, and climate change. Co-chairs: Peter Wilk (207-787-2158) and Dan Oppenheim.

RANGELY, ME

380. *TRANET* (1976) (org).

PO Box 567, Rangely 04970; (202) 864-2252); *tranet@igc.apc.org*; *www.nonviolence.org/tranet/*

Helps concerned global citizens exchange ideas and techniques which empower individuals and communities to make the transition from the homocentric Industrial Culture based on self-interest, survival of the fittest, and materialism to an ecocentric Gaiain Culture based on belonging, community, and mutual respect. Pub. bi-monthly newsletter.

WATERVILLE, ME

381. *Oak Institute for the Study of Human Rights* (1997) (org).

Colby College, Waterville 04901; (207) 872-3270; *oakhr@colby.edu*; *www.colby.edu/oak*

A grant from the Oak Institute enabled the Institute to provide Fellowships for respite to front line human rights workers, and to sponsor lectures and events centered around the Fellow's work. The first Fellow was a Pakistani journalist who was arrested for exposing child bonded labor; the second was a Congolese monitor of abuses by the security and militias. Offers the Oak Human Rights Fellow, a one semester appointment for human rights professionals as a scholar-in-residence. Ken Rodman, Dir.

WAYNE, ME

382. *Winthrop Area People for Peace* (1982) (org).

RR 1 Box 423, Wayne 04284; (207) 685-9604; *tkerchner@iname.com*

Educational activities about war, peace, and the environment. Annual Peace Recognition Award to a group committed to reducing violence in society. Monthly meetings. Contact Theresa Kerchner or Tom and Mary Sturtevant (207-377-2370).

WILTON, ME

383. *Maine Draft and Military Counselors.*

PO Box 106, Wilton 04294; (207) 645-2162. See Monroe.

— *Maryland (MD)* —

14 Sister Cities. / 46 Peace Poles.

ANNAPOLIS, MD

384. *Anne Arundel Peace Action* (1982) (org).

310 Riverview Ave., Annapolis 21403; (410) 263-7409; *mkeller@mhec.state.md.us*; *www2.ari.net/leeirwin/peaceannapolis*

This Chapter of Peace Action works for alternatives to war through the U.N. and other international organizations, community peacemaking, peace studies in educational curriculum, handgun control, overcoming racism and other bigotries, reduction in military spending, conversion to a peace economy, and abolition of nuclear weapons beginning with a cessation of nuclear bomb testing. Sponsors educational programs, including a half-hour cable TV show; gives an annual Martin Luther King Peacemaker

Award to a person who follows the ideals of Dr. King; lobbies public officials; actively campaigns for pro-peace political candidates; and other activities. Quarterly newsletter, *Strength Through Peace*. Mike Keller, Coordinator.

BALTIMORE, MD

385. *American Friends Service Committee (AFSC), Middle Atlantic Region* (1968) (org).

4806 York Road, Baltimore, 21212; (410) 323-7200; *mar@afsc.org*; *ggillespie@afsc.org; www.afsc.org*

Focuses on peace building, demilitarization, social and economic justice, and youth, in local programs in Baltimore, Washington, DC, Syracuse, NY, Lancaster, PA, and West Virginia. Pub. *MARSTAR Newsletter* online. Sandy Rappeport, Regional Dir. (National office: Philadelphia, *afscinfo@afsc.org*).

386. *Baltimore Emergency Response Network (BERN)* (1985) (org).

311 E. 25th St., Baltimore 21218; (410) 243-7695 or 323-7200 or 377-7987; *mobuszewski@afsc.org*

This group is resolved "to live nonviolently, to promote justice through direct action and to continue to speak out against the ills of the National Security Agency and all government institutions bent on world domination." Begun as part of the national Pledge of Resistance against aid to the Contras, BERN now acts on many issues—anti-war, CIA, nuclear weapons, torture, refugees, and more. For four consecutive years members protested the National Security Agency at Fort Meade on site.

387. *Center for Negotiations and Conflict Management* (1977) (col).

Yale Gordon College of Liberal Arts, University of Baltimore, 1420 North Charles St., Baltimore 21201; (410) 837-5320; *dmulcahey@ubmail.ubalt.edu; www.ubalt.edu/cncm/*

Offers mediation training, provides mediators, assesses conflict management systems. Developed the MS curriculum in Negotiations and Conflict Management. Pub. a newsletter, *Resolutions*. Donald Mulcahey, Dir.

388. *Help Increase the Peace Network (HIP)* (1991) (org).

4806 York Road, Baltimore 21212; (410) 323-7200; *lchico@mail.afsc.org*

A project of the AFSC Regional Office, HIP covers 19 states, working to reduce violence and intolerance in schools and communities, through workshops and follow-up. Laura Chico, Coord.

389. *Jonah House* (1973) (org).

1301 Moreland Ave., Baltimore 21216; *disarmnow@erols.com*

Home of Plowshares activists. For example, on December 19, 1999, they "converted" the A-10 Warthog attack plane, which fired depleted uranium in the Gulf War. JH advocates abolition of nuclear weapons and war, and seeks peace via community-making and education in nonviolence. Contact Philip Berrigan, Stephen Kelly, SJ, Elizabeth Walz, Susan Crane

390. *Peace Studies* (1990) (col).

Goucher College, 1021 Dulaney Valley Rd., Baltimore 21204; (410) 337-6278; *jmorton@goucher.edu; www.goucher.edu/academics/academics_index.html*

A 21-credit minor can be combined with any major in the college. The International Studies major can combine a peace studies concentration. Internships encouraged. Courses include: Building a Just and Peaceful World, Human Rights. Contact Joe Morton.

391. *Shriver Peaceworker Program* (1994) (org).

Shriver Center, 1000 Hilltop Circle, Baltimore 21250; (410) 455-2493; *www.umbc.edu/shriver*

Founded by the Shriver Center "to honor Sargent Shriver's leadership in developing pathbreaking initiatives for promoting peace and social justice." The Program enables returned Peace Corps volunteers to adapt their experiences abroad to the challenges of urban USA through a graduate degree combined with community service and ethical reflection. Dr. James Price, III, Dir.; Dr. Peter Antoci, Assoc. Dir.

392. *Viva House* (1968) (org).

26 S. Mount St., Baltimore 21223; (410) 233-0488.

The Baltimore Catholic Worker House, dedicated to living "in accordance with the justice and charity of Jesus." Site of the Festival of Hope, March 19, 2000 in support of Philip Berrigan, Susan Crane, Rev. Steve Kell S.J., and Elizabeth Walz, who went on trial the next day for protesting the weapons at Maryland Warfield Air National Guard Base in December of 1999. The July 1999 issue of its quarterly newsletter, *Enthusiasm*, includes articles on poverty, "cleansing" in Baltimore (woven with bombings of Yugoslavia), and nonviolent alternatives to the bombings.

BETHESDA, MD

393. **Lion & Lamb Project* (1995) (org).

4300 Montgomery Ave., Suite 104, Bethesda 20814; (301) 654-3091; *lionlamb@lionlamb.org; www.lionlamb.org*

Provides information to parents, teachers, day care providers, and others about the effects of violent entertainment, toys, games, and domestic conflicts on children's behavior, seeking to teach nonviolent values to children. Provides Parent Action Kits, workshops, and violent toy trade-ins. Daphne White, Exec. Dir.

BOWIE, MD

394. **Center for Alternative Dispute Resolution (CADR)* (1986) (col).

Dept. of Business, Public Administration, and Economics, Bowie State University, Bowie 20715; (301) 464-3000; *center_for_adr@bowiestate.edu; www.bowiestate.edu/academics/profess/adr.htm*

Offers a Certificate for eight courses in managing conflicts in the workplace, community, schools, family, and beyond. Marvin Johns, Dir.

COLLEGE PARK, MD

395. **Center for International Development and Conflict Management* (1983) (col).

Dept. of History, Univ. of Maryland, College Park 20742; (301) 314-7703; *cidcm@cidcm.umd.edu; www.bsos.umd.edu/cidcm*

Supports scholarly research on war, conflict, development, and ethics. For example, one focus is upon "state failure," a range of extreme political conflicts and regime crises: revolutionary wars, ethnic wars, disruptive regime transitions, genocides, and politicides (*www.bsos.umd.edu/cidcm/stfail*).

Also, CIDCM offers an evening and weekend program of conflict transformation and peacebuilding in ethnic, nationalist, or religious conflicts, as well as conflicts over borders, water, or other resources, using the techniques of "second track" or citizen diplomacy (*edanzer@cidcm.umd.edu*). CIDCM enjoys two distinguished chairs. The Anwar Sadat Chair for Population, Development, and Peace (1997) works to further peace especially in the Middle East. The Bahá'í Chair for World Peace develops alternatives to violent conflict and shares Bahá'í world views and community; in 1999 it coordinated The First International Conference on Kahlil Gibran. Ernest J. Wilson, III, Director.

395a. **International and Inter-Ethnic Conflict* (col).

Dept. of Government and Politics, Univ. of Maryland, College Park 20742; (301) 405-4161; *jwilkenf@bss2.umd.edu; www.bsos.umd.edu/gvpt*

Ph.D. in political science includes a specialized field of international and inter-ethnic conflict. Jonathan Wilkenfeld, Chair.

396. **March for Peaceful Energy* (1998) (org).

UMCP Student Union Box 73, College Park 20740; (301) 345-3454; *plantseedk@aol.com; www.peacefulenergy.org*

Tries to turn the world away from nuclear and fossil fuels and toward clean alternative sources of energy by marching in Washington, DC, to promote the Citizens Peaceful Energy Plan, to avoid wars over oil supplies, to implement the "Million Solar Rooftops Initiative," to ban new nuclear power plants, and other aims. Richard Lasken, Dir.

GERMANTOWN, MD

397. *World Peacemakers* (1978) (org).

11427 Scottsbury Terrace, Germantown 20876-6010; (301) 916-0442; *worldpeacemakers@compuserve.com*; *www.nonviolence.org/worldpeacemakers/*

"Founded in the Church of the Saviour." Beginning with the aim to understand how to attain real security without nuclear weapons, WP joined with Fellowship of Reconciliation, New Call to Peacemakers, Pax Christi-USA, and Sojourners to abolish nuclear weapons. Today it continues its nonviolent struggle against the Pax Americana, among other ways by distributing its Handbooks for World Peacemakers Groups and quarterly newsletter and by its Global Demilitarization Campaign "to disable all nuclear weapons in the world." Pub.: *World Peacemakers* quarterly; the "Trinity Season" issue paid much attention to Jonathan Schell's *The Gift of Time*, printed a talk by Richard Barnet, reviewed two books by Walter Wink, and more. Bill Price, Coordinator.

HYATTSVILLE, MD

398. *Moratorium Now!* (1997) (org).

C/o Quixote Center, PO Box 5206, Hyattsville 20782; (301) 699-0042; *ejusa@quixote.org; www.quixote.org*

Originated by Equal Justice USA. Seeks "to foment a grassroots dialogue on how unjustly the U.S. death penalty is applied and to organize grassroots pressure to stop executions." Pubs.: *Equal Justice Under Law? How Racism Riddles the U.S. Death Penalty* (1998), *A Saga of Shame* (1999), newsletter *Moratorium News*.

399. *Quest for Peace* (1984) (org).

C/o Quixote Center, PO Box 5206, Hyattsville, 20782; (301) 699-0042; *quixote@igc.apc.org; www.igc.apc.org/quixote.*

Project of the Quixote Center. Organizes aid to the people of Nicaragua and Haiti.

400. *Quixote Center* (1975) (org).

PO Box 5206, Hyattsville 20782; (301) 699-0042; *quixote@quixote.org; www.quixote.org*

A "community of collaborators who dream and plan practical ways to bring justice and peace to our world." Catholic affiliation. Raises funds for Moratorium Now!, Quest for Peace, Nicaraguan Cultural Alliance, Prison Radio Project, and other activities. Pub.: newsletter *Rocinante*. Coord.: Dolores Pomerleau, William Callahan.

POOLESVILLE, MD

401. *Kunzang Odsal Palyul Changchub Choeling Stupa and Peace Park* (1982) (org, mem).

18400 River Road, Poolesville 20837; (301) 428-8116.

The 35-foot stupa is surrounded by a 65-acre park containing meditation gardens, walking paths, and additional stupas.

SALISBURY, MD

402. *Center for Conflict Resolution, Inc.* (1991) (col).

See next entry.

Teaches mediation skills to judges, lawyers, government officials, teachers, and others. Contact Brian Polkinghorn.

403. *Conflict Analysis and Dispute Resolution* (1991) (col).

Sociology Department, Salisbury University, 1101 Camden Avenue, Salisbury 21801; (410) 219-2873; *bdpolkinghorn@ssu.edu; www.conflict-resolution.org*

Offers both a minor and a major (with 2000-01 academic year), focusing on the history and analysis of conflict and peacemaking techniques. Sponsors internships, workshops, and exchange programs with the Univ. for Peace in Costa Rica and Hiroshima Jogakuin Univ. in Japan. Contact Brian Polkinghorn.

SANDY SPRING, MD

404. *Friends Peace Teams Project* (1993) (org).

c/o BYM, 17000 Quaker Lane,

Sandy Spring 20860; (301) 774-6855;
fptp@igc.apc.org;
www.quaker.org/fptp/start.html

"Assists individual Quakers, Friends Churches, Yearly and Monthly Meetings in developing and/or supporting peace team projects." "As Friends, we believe that faithfulness to the injunction to love our neighbor, including our enemy, and to do good for those who may hate us, requires more than statements abhorring war and violence: we must actively search for alternatives that will enable all to learn to peacefully and creatively resolve conflict and overcome differences." Also supports volunteers to Christian Peacemaker Teams and Peace Brigades International.

TAKOMA PARK, MD

405. **Creative Response to Conflict, Capital Area Branch* (1973) (porg).

7710 Carroll Ave., Takoma Park 20912; (301) 270-1005; *ccrcca@juno.com*

Seeks to increase the number of people skilled in conflict resolution—children, youth, and adults. Training sessions include affirmation, cooperation, communication, problem-solving, bias awareness, and mediation.

– *Massachusetts (MA)* –

36 Sister Cities. / 15 Peace Poles.

AMHERST, MA

406. **Amherst Pax Christi* (1991) (org).

Rolling Green Dr., Amherst 02174; (413) 253-7710.

Monthly meetings, sponsors lectures, weekly leafletting on nuclear and other current issues. Marion Frazier, Founder and Dir.

407. **Earth Action* (1992) (org).

30 Cottage St., Amherst 01002; (413) 549-8118; *amherst@earthaction.org; www.earthaction.org.*

A global network of over 1,500 organizations and community groups dedicated to educating citizens and influential people—especially political leaders and journalists—about peace and the environment and to mobilizing them to take action. Several times a year EA distributes an "Information-Action Kit" focused on a critical environment, development, peace, or social justice issue. In the summer of 1999, among other issues, EA campaigned for strict limitations on the arms trade and for nuclear disarmament. Lois Barber, International Coordinator.

408. *Peace and World Security Studies (PAWSS)* (1983) (col).

c/o Hampshire College, Box SS Five College Consortium, Suite D, Prescott Center, Amherst 01002; (413) 559-5367; *pawss@hampshire.edu; www.pawss.hampshire.edu*

Engaged in developing new courses, sponsoring public lectures and symposia, publishing resource materials, and supporting student internships. The PAWSS Summer Faculty Institute on World Security Affairs and the Winter Workshop draw faculty from all across the U.S., and its January Term and Spring-break activities enable students to gain knowledge through travel. Pubs.: *Guide to Careers, Internships, and Graduate Education in Peace Studies, Peace and World Security Studies: A Curriculum Guide,* annual journal *Peace and World Security Report,* undergraduate text *World Security: Challenges for a New Century,* and *College Peace Studies,* a guide to undergraduate programs. Michael Klare, Dir. The five colleges are: Amherst, Hampshire, Mount Holyoke, Smith, and the U of Mass.

409. **WAND of Western Massachusetts* (1998) (org).

252 West St. #15, Amherst 01002; (413) 584-9556; *laura@natprior.org; wand_wmass@hotmail.com*

Branch of Women's Action for New Directions. Contact Laura Beavers.

ARLINGTON, MA

410. **WAND: Women's Action for New Directions* (1982) (org).

691 Massachusetts Ave., Arlington 02476; (781) 643-6740; *info@wand.org; wand@world.std.com; www.wand.org;*

Washington Office: 110 Maryland Ave. NE, Ste. 205, 20002; (202)-543-8505; *wandwill@wand.org*

Mission: "to empower women to act politically to reduce violence and militarism and redirect military resources toward human and environmental needs." Founded as Women's Action for Nuclear Disarmament by Dr. Helen Caldicott, WAND continues the struggle to abolish nuclear weapons, to handle nuclear waste responsibly, to reduce militarism and violence, to redirect military resources toward human and environmental needs, and to empower women politically. Projects: Women Legislators' Lobby (WiLL), connects with women state legislators; Women Take Action! (WTA), focuses on shifting federal budget priorities away from Pentagon excesses; WAND PAC, support for WAND and WiLL members running for Congress. Pub. *WAND Bulletin* quarterly, Nancy Cole, Ed. Susan Shaer, Exec. Dir.; Rep. Kathryn Bowers (TN), Pres.

411. *WiLL: Women Legislators Lobby* (1990) (org).

(same address as WAND). Also Washington, DC office: (202) 543-8505; *will@wand.org*

The only national network of women state legislators seeking to redirect excessive military spending towards domestic needs and to curb the proliferation of weapons. Rep. Nan Grogan Orrock, Pres.

BOSTON, MA

412. *Boston Fellowship of Reconciliation* (1999) (org).

183 Central St., Somerville 02145; (617) 776-9452; *vickyi@earthlink.net*

Priorities: nonviolent communication, peace curriculum in high school. Contact Vicky I.

413. *Boston Pax Christi* (1995) (org).

Paulist Center, 5 Park St., Boston 02108; (617) 742-4460; *fiveparkst@aol.com; www.paulist.org/Boston*

Vigils against death penalty and SOA. Correspondence with death row inmate. Contact Cornelia Sullivan, Michael Burke.
E. Cerino (617-246-2627), Kate Prendergast (617-859-1872).

414. *The Brudnick Center on Violence and Conflict* (1998) (col).

Department of Sociology and Anthropology, Northeastern University, 360 Huntington Avenue, Boston 02115; (617) 373-4983; *jlevin1049@aol.com; www.violence.neu.edu/*

Initiates research and educational endeavors. An undergraduate minor in Conflict and Violence Studies is new (2000), and graduate students can select the Sociology of Conflict and Violence as an area of specialization. Jack Levin, Dir.

414a. *Campus Green Vote* (1999) (org).

19 Cortes St., #5, Boston 02116; (617) 290-8927; *rani@envirocitizen;org; www.envirocitizen.org*

An activity of the Center for Environmental Citizenship in DC to stimulate student political activism for the environment. Rani Corey, Dir.

415. *Center for Campus Organizing* (1995) (org).

165 Friend St., #1, Boston 02114-2025; (617) 725-2886; *cco@igc.org; www.cco.org*

"Dedicated to building progressive activism on college campuses." Pub. *Infusion: The National Magazine for Progressive Campus Activists.*

416. *Citizens for Participation in Political Action (CPPAX)* (1962) (org).

25 West St., Boston 02111; (617) 426-3040; *cppax@cppax.org; www.cppax.org*

Massachusetts citizens working for peace, democracy, and economic justice. From opposition to the Vietnam War (CPPAX organized the Vietnam Moratorium in 1968) to resisting the deportation of Salvadorian refugees, cutting the military budget, and other activities. Pub. a newsletter, voting records, lobbying alerts, and more.

417. *Grassroots International* (1983) (org).

179 Boylston St., 4th fl., Boston 02130; (617) 524-1400; *grassroots@igc.apc.org*

Seeks to strengthen grassroots movements for social change in Brazil, Eritrea, Haiti, and other countries. Pub. quarterly newsletter, *Insights.* Tim Wise, Dir.

418. *Infact* (1977) (org).

46 Plympton St., Boston, 02118;
(617) 695-2525; *infact@igc.org;*
www.infact.org

Works to stop life-threatening activities of transnational corporations, including the production and promotion of nuclear weapons (General Electric campaign 1986-1993). Pub.: *Infact Update* newsletter.

419. *Institute for the Study of Conflict, Ideology and Policy* (1988) (col).

Boston University, 121 Bay State Road, Boston 02215; (617) 353-5815;
mlanskoy@bu.edu;
www.bu.edu/iscip/index.html

Not primarily engaged in conflict resolution but in the study of the contemporary transformation of post-Soviet states. Pub. *Perspective* bimonthly during academic year, and the biweekly *NIS Observed: An Analytical Review.* Miriam Lanskoy, Prog. Manager.

420. *National Foundation to Improve Television* (1969) (org).

50 Congress St., Suite 925, Boston 02109; (617) 523-5520; *wabbott1@aol.com*

Formulates strategies and implements programs to reduce the amount of television violence during hours when children are significantly watching. William Abbott, Pres.

421. *Oxfam* (1975) (org).

26 West St., Boston 02111;
www.oxfamamerica.org

Supports grassroots self-development by grants and technical assistance to landless peasants, indigenous people, women, refugees, and survivors of war and natural disasters. Raymond Offenheiser, Pres.

422. *Physicians for Human Rights* (1986) (org).

100 Boylston St., Suite 702, Boston 02116; (617) 695-0041; *phrusa@phrusa.org;*
www.phrusa.org/

Works to prevent violations of international law and human rights, to stop torture, disappearances, and political killings by governments and factions, to improve health and sanitary conditions in prisons and detention centers, and other activities. Shared the *1997 Nobel Peace Prize* for its work on the steering committee of the International Campaign to Ban Landmines. Leonard S. Rubenstein, J.D., Exec. Dir.; Robert Lawrence, M.D., Pres. See entry 436.

423. *Program in Dispute Resolution* (1985, 1995) (col).

University of Massachusetts, Boston, 100 Morrissey Boulevard, Boston 02125; (617) 287-7421; *disres@umbsky.cc.umb.edu;*
www.umb.edu/academic_programs/
Graduate_Programs/Dispute_Resolution/
dispute_resolution_home.html

A MA (1995) requires 36-credits, and two graduate Certificate options (1985) assist professionals to upgrade their training. One Certificate is for K-12 educators. David Matz, Dir.

424. *Program on Negotiation (PON)* (col).

Simmons College, 300 The Fenway, Boston 02115-5898; (617) 521-2000 or (800) 345-8468; *www.simmons.edu*

See Harvard Univ.

CAMBRIDGE, MA

Has several *Peace Poles*: One at the Episcopal Divinity School near Harvard Sq., one at the Fitzgerald School with a garden area surrounding it, and others.

425. *Albert Einstein Institution* (1983) (org).

50 Church St., Cambridge, Massachusetts 02138; (617) 876-0311.

Offers grants in support of conferences and studies of past and present nonviolent struggles, for projections of the future usefulness of nonviolent techniques and for more effective means of communicating existing knowledge more widely. The long-range goal of the Einstein Institution is to develop nonviolent sanctions and expand their capacity as effective alternatives to violence. Programs: Fellows Program (books and dissertations), Program on Nonviolent Sanctions at Harvard University, South Africa Program, Civilian-Based Defense Policy Studies, Publications Program (quarterly newsletter, *Nonviolent Sanctions*, monograph series, and *An*

Encyclopedia of Nonviolent Action), and Educational Outreach and Consulting Program. Bruce Jenkins, Exec. Dir.

426. *American Friends Service Committee (AFSC), New England Regional Office* (1923, 1949) (org).

2161 Mass. Ave., Cambridge, 02140; (617) 661-6130; *afscnero@igc.apc.org; www.afsc.org/nero/nepq.htm*

The AFSC works to relieve the suffering of war and poverty, to foster peace and reconciliation, and to promote social justice. Several projects on peacebuilding. Provides a large video and film library. Publishes *Peacework* (1972) eleven times a year to serve the movements for nonviolent social change by covering social justice and peace issues (*pwork@igc.org; www.afsc. org/peacewrk.htm*). The Sept. 1999 issue includes articles on prisons, the Middle East, the toxic aftermath of NATO bombings, walks of protest and affirmation, a culture of peace. Patricia Watson, Ed.

427. *Boston Research Center for the 21st Century* (1993) (org).

396 Harvard St., Cambridge 02138-3924; *center@brc21.org; www.brc21.org*

Promotes dialog among scholars and activists for the prevention of violent confrontation through enhanced mutual understanding, life-affirming values, and the appreciation of differences. In 1999 organized three conferences on Cultures of Peace to prepare for the year 2000, the United Nations International Year for the Culture of Peace. Pubs.: *Abolishing War*, dialog between Elise Boulding and Randall Forsberg; *Earth Charter Studies Kit* (three books); and *Subverting Hatred*; newsletter (brc21c@aol.com). Founded by Soka Gakkai International President Daisaku Ikeda; Virginia Straus, Exec. Dir.

428. *Cambridge Peace Commission* (1982) (org).

51 Inman St., Cambridge 02139; (617) 349-4694; *choffman@ci.cambridge.ma.us*

Formerly: *Cambridge Commission on Nuclear Disarmament and Peace Education*. Promotes peace and challenges violence and its causes on all levels of Cambridge society. Creates programs to resolve conflicts and promote peace-making in the classroom; has an affirmative action diversity working group; creates anti-bias, anti-vio-

lence elementary education initiatives; supports a summer Youth Peace and Justice Institute; offers a Youth Peace and Justice Corps; gives annual Peace and Justice Awards Dinner and networking teas for activists; participates in the anti-violence Shoe Gun Project, the annual Holocaust remembrance, and the Cambridge/ El Salvador Sister City project; opposes the death penalty; and more. Cathy Hoffman, Exec. Dir.

429. *Cambridge/San Jose las Flores Sister Cities* (1987) (org).

c/o Cambridge Peace Commission; *jwallace@igc.org*

Part of U.S. El Salvador Sister Cities (in Kendall Park, NJ).

430. *Cambridge WAND* (1999) (org).

18 Maple Ave., Cambridge 02139; (617) 876-5485; *jrk1956@shore.net*

Informs people about the military budget, militarism, peace initiatives, nuclear disarmament, violence and women, and other issues. Co-chairs: Judy King and Suleigken Walker.

431. *Cambridge/Yerevan Sister City Project* (1986) (org).

PO Box 382591, Cambridge, MA 02238; *spearce@igc.org*

Contact Suzie Pearce for newsletter. Armand Andreassian, Acting Pres.

432. *Center for Peaceable Schools* (1991) (col).

Lesley College, 29 Everett Street, Cambridge 02139; (617) 349-8491; *peace@mail.lesley.edu; www.lesley.edu/peace.html*

Helps schools develop curricula and pedagogies. Sarah Grant, Prog. Coord.

433. *Concerned Educators Allied for a Safe Environment* (1979) (org).

17 Gerry St., Cambridge, 02138; (617) 864-0999.

Early childhood educators and parents concerned with the danger of nuclear war, nuclear arms production, and nuclear power. Seeks to inform the public on peaceful alternatives to nuclear arms.

434. *Conflict Resolution and Peaceable Schools* (1997) (col).

School of Education, Lesley College, Cambridge 02139; (617) 349-8393; *peace@mail.lesley.edu; www.lesley.edu/ academic_centers/peace/masters/faculty.html*

A MA and Certificate program to prepare teachers, administrators, and youth workers. A collaboration between Lesley and the Resolving Conflict Creatively Program, an initiative of Educators for Social Responsibility. Employs innovative residency design with Saturday meetings and internet. Sarah Grant, Prog. Coord.

435. **Global Action to Prevent War* (1998) (org).

IDDS, 675 Massachusetts Ave., Cambridge 02139; (617)354-4337; *globalaction@idds.org*

Works to build a war-prevention system and reduce military spending and militarism by strengthening the rule of law and international institutions for conflict resolution, peacekeeping, and peace enforcement, to replace national, unilateral interventions outside of national borders. Initiated by Dr. Randall Forsberg, Amb. (Ret.) Jonathan Dean, and Prof. Saul Mendlovitz.

436. **International Physicians for the Prevention of Nuclear War* (1980) (org).

727 Massachusetts Ave., Cambridge 02139; (617) 868-5050; *ippnwbos@ippnw.org; www.ippnw.org*

Dedicated to research, education, and advocacy relevant to the prevention of nuclear war, and thus seeks to prevent all wars, to promote nonviolent conflict resolution, and to minimize the effects of war on health, development, and the environment. Recipient of the 1985 Nobel Peace Prize. Publishes *Vital Signs* quarterly; included in its Aug. 1998 number articles on Abolition 2000, banning land mines, the nuclear energy/nuclear weapons complex, and South Asian nuclear security. Bernard Lown, MD, is founding co-president of IPPNW. See entry 422.

437. **Massachusetts Peace Action* (1986) (org).

11 Garden St., Cambridge 02138; (617) 354-2169; *masspa@gis.net; www.gis.net/~masspa*

Originally MA Freeze, now state office of Peace Action. Seeks nuclear abolition, a peacetime economy for civilian needs, exposure of U.S. unilateralism in foreign policy, and other objectives. Contact Shelagh Foreman. One affil. in MA: Watertown Citizens' for Environmental Safety.

438. **Middle Powers Initiative* (1998) (org).

727 Massachusetts Ave., Cambridge 02139; (617) 492-9189; *mpi@igc.org; mpi@ippnw.org; www.middlepowers.org*

The purpose of the MPI is to mobilize key "middle-power" states to press the nuclear weapons states to commit themselves to the elimination of their nuclear arsenals. Founded and chaired by Canadian Senator Douglas Roche, former Canadian Ambassador for Disarmament to the U.N. Pub.: *Fast Track to Zero Nuclear Weapons* by Robert Green. Suzanne Pearce, Coord.

439. *Negotiation and Conflict Resolution* (col).

Master of Management Program, Cambridge College, 1000 Massachusetts Avenue, Cambridge 02138; 800-877-4723, est. 163; *mbelden@idea.cambridge.edu; admit@idea.cambridge.edu; www.cambridge.edu/programs.html*

A Certificate program for adult learners. Contact Martha Belden.

440. **Program on International Conflict Analysis and Resolution (PICAR)* (1986, 1993) (col).

Weatherhead Center for International Affairs, Coolidge Hall, Harvard U, 1737 Cambridge St., Cambridge 02138; (617) 496-0680 or 496-7370; *picar@cfia.harvard.edu; leitzman@cfia.harvard.edu*

Scholar-practitioners work toward the resolution of international and intercommunal/ethnic conflicts through the interactive problem-solving method in the Middle East, Sri Lanka, Northern Ireland, Cyprus, urban U.S. Herbert Kelman, Director; Donna Hicks, Deputy Director.

441. *Program on Negotiation (PON)* (1983) (col).

Harvard Law School, Cambridge 02138; (617) 495-1684; *cobb@law.harvard.edu; www.pon.harvard.edu*

A consortium of Boston area schools, including MIT, Simmons, and Tufts, for research to improve theory and practice. Sponsors conferences and maintains a library of books and videos. Pub. *Negotiation Journal* (1985), J. William Breslin, Ed. Sara Cobb, Exec. Dir.

442. *Program on Nonviolent Sanctions and Cultural Survival* (1995) (col).

Weatherhead Center for International Affairs, Harvard University, Cambridge 02138; (617) 495-5580; *pns@cfia.harvard.edu; http://data.fas. harvard.edu/cfia/pnscs/index.htm*

Established from two existing organizations, the Program on Nonviolent Sanctions (1983) and the Cultural Survival Center (1972). Opportunities for pre- and post-doctoral visiting scholars to explore nonviolence theory and case studies. Pubs.: see web site. Contact Doug Bond.

443. **Union of Concerned Scientists* (1969) (org).

2 Brattle Square, Cambridge, 02238-9105; (617) 547-5552; *ucs@ucsusa.org; www.ucsusa.org.*

Arms control and the environment are among its many activities deriving from its concern about the impact of technology on society. Pubs. include *Nucleus*, a quarterly magazine, and *Cool Energy: The Renewable Solution to Global Warming.*

444. **World Peace Foundation* (1910) (org).

104 Mount Auburn St., Cambridge, 02138; (617) 491-5085.

Founded and funded by Edwin Ginn, the Foundation seeks to advance the cause of world peace through study, analysis, and action. Supported the League of Nations and the United Nations. At present focuses on large-scale human suffering engendered by ethnic, religious, and other conflicts. Has pub. books on world order, regional security, transnational relations, reducing arms proliferation, role of media for peace, role of NGOs in conflict prevention, and other

subjects. Also pub. the journal *International Organization.*

CENTERVILLE, MA

445. **Cape Cod Pax Christi* (1991) (org).

77 Old Post Road, Centerville 02632; (508) 771-6737.

Meets monthly. Edouard and Francoise Rocher, Co-leaders.

446. **Pax Christi Massachusetts* (1990) (org).

20 Tomahawk Dr., Centerville 02632; (508) 771-1106 or 775-6662; *jmlees@mediaone.net*

Assembly in spring and Retreat in fall; Board meets four times a year. Newsletter two times a year, ed. by John Stella (in Arlington) and Brian Keaney (Worcester). Mary Lees, Coordinator and Regional Rep.

CHESTNUT HILL, MA

447. **Faith, Peace and Justice Program* (1983, 1989) (col).

Boston College, Chestnut Hill 02467; (617) 552-3886; *mullanmd@bc.edu; www.bc.edu/bc_org/avp/enmgt/stserv/acd/ specprogs/fpj_study.html*

This concentration (1983) and minor program (1989) explore how the major faith traditions relate to the advancement or hindrance of peace and justice. Student retreats and annual trip to the Navajo Nation are special features. Jesuit affiliation. Matthew Mullane, Dir.

CONCORD, MA

448. **Zaltho Foundation* (1994) (org).

Box 312, 60 Thoreau St., Box 312, Concord 01742; (978) 369-6112; *anshin@sprynet.com; www.access.ch/spuren/claudethomas; www.peacemakercommunity.org/Zaltho*

"Committed to ending violence by encouraging and establishing socially engaged projects in schools, communities, organizations, and facilities, with an emphasis on the most important ingredient, the individual." Focuses: support to veterans and victims of war and violence; workshops and retreats teaching meditation; public talks on mindfulness, healing aggression, roots of war, etc. Founder: Claude Anshin Thomas, Zen Priest.

DEERFIELD, MA

449. *Traprock Peace Center* (1979) (org).

103A Keets Rd., Woolman Hill, Deerfield 01342 (1/2 mile south of Greenfield off Route 5 & 10); (413) 773-7427; *www.crocker.com/~traprock*

Explores nonviolence, fosters community, works to end war, promotes communication, and takes initiatives for peace, justice, and sustainable environment. Monthly meetings, several working groups; Peacemakers Exhibit, MLK, Jr., celebration, Earth Connection 2000, Young Peacemaker Awards, War Resisters Clinic, travel delegations (Iraq, Chiapas), prison visit, Nonviolence Film Festival, etc. Pub. *Traprock Peace Action Report* (Fall-Winter 1998 issue included articles on UDHR, death penalty, Plowshares actions, Chiapas, Tibet, and civilian-based defense). Sunny Miller, Dir.

EASTON, MA

450. *Religious Studies/Institute for Justice and Peace* (1976) (col).

Stonehill College, 320 Washington St., Easton 01257; (508) 565-1444.

The undergraduate Religious Studies offers a few courses in peace studies. Gregory Shaw, Chair (gshaw@stonehill.edu). The Institute is a resource center for the college and community, providing a large videotape library and internships. Contact Peter Beisheim (pbeisheim@stonehill.edu).

GARDNER, MA

451. *Gardner Fellowship F.O.R.* (1993) (org).

500 Colony Rd., Gardner 01440; (978) 632-2000.

The Gardner Branch of the Fellowship of Reconciliation is located in a prison. Contact Steve Hirons, Recreation Officer.

GRAFTON, MA

452. *Grafton Center for Inner Peace* (1990) (org).

13 Sartell Rd., Grafton 01519; *TashaHal@aol.com*; *http://members.aol.com/PeaceNow4U*

A meditation and healing center, with a unique "Spiral Garden." The garden is about 80 feet across, full of herbs, perennials, and shrubs that border the grassy path. Associated with the Peace branch of the Theosophical Order of Service, which has a Peace Garden division. Tasha and Stephen Halpert, Dir. (Tasha is author of *Heaven Is Now, a Guide to Living in the Kingdom of Heaven*).

GREAT BARRINGTON, MA

453. *Sheffield F.O.R.* (early 1980s) (org).

4 Manville St., Great Barrington 01230; (413) 528-4170.

Branch of the Fellowship of Reconciliation. Mary Carter.

HARWICH, MA

454. *Cape Cod F.O.R.* (1980) (org).

Box 595, Harwich 02645; (508) 945-9238; *ccforjuliet@earthlink.net*

Branch of the Fellowship of Reconciliation, which seeks to "replace violence, war, racism, and economic injustice with nonviolence, peace, and justice." The Cape Cod Chapter has monthly meetings, frequent speakers, sponsors the annual Clarence Althouse Peace Essay Competition for local high school students, created a traveling exhibition on land mines, opposes the death penalty and nuclear proliferation, participates in the annual Martin Luther King, Jr., memorial march, pub. a newsletter ten times a year, and other activities. Contact Juliet Bernstein.

Grafton Center for Inner Peace and Spiral Garden, Grafton. Photograph courtesy Tasha and Stephen Halpert, directors.

HAYDENVILLE, MA

455. **WAND of Western Massachusetts* (1998) (org).

PO box 324, Haydenville 01039; (413) 268-7628; *wand_wmass@hotmail.com*; *www.geocities.com/wand_wmass*

Provides educational forums with women at the five surrounding colleges, participates in local activities for WAND's goals, distributes WAND's alerts to local network. Laura Beavers, Dir. (*www.natprior.org*).

LAWRENCE, MA

456. **Greens/Green Party USA* (1991) (org).

PO Box 1134, Lawrence, MA 01842; (978) 682-4353; *gpusa@greens.org*; *www.greens.org/gpusa*; *www.greenparty.org/*

Inspired by the German Green Party, some U.S. activists formed the Green Committees of Correspondence, which evolved into Greens/ Green Party USA at its first Congress in 1991. Today Green locals are organized in 46 of 50 states, where they run candidates, rebuild inner cities, oppose nuclear waste dumps, challenge undemocratic governments, try to change polluting industries, support labor unions, educate communities about environmental and social justice, take nonviolent direct action for Green principles. GP uses electoral politics and direct action to bring about ecological wisdom, grassroots democracy, social justice, and peace/nonviolence. Pub. *Green Program: An Evolving Vision.* Tamara Trejo, Clearinghouse Coordinator.

LEVERETT, MA

457. **Karuna Center for Peacebuilding* (1992) (org).

49 Richardson Rd., Leverett 01054; (413) 367-9520; *karunapg@aol.com*

Founded on "the principles of nonviolence, loving-kindness, and the interdependence of all life,", the Center provides education and training to transform conflict through dialogue and reconciliation. Affil. with Buddhist Peace Fellowship. Karuna means "compassion." Paula Green, Dir. (member of faculty of the School for International Training).

458. *Peace Pagoda* (1985) (mem, org).

Nipponzan Myohoji, New England Sangha: Buddhist Religious Society, 100 Cave Hill road, Leverett 01054; (413) 367-2202; *www.peacepagoda.org* (linked to *www.interfaithpilgrimage.org*).

One of many domed structures—over seventy around the world by 1985—initiated by the Buddhist order, Nipponzan Myohoji, and built as shrines to Lord Buddha and his teachings of inner and world peace. The founder of the order, the Most Venerable Nichidatsu Fujii (1885–1985), taught the renunciation of violence and affirmation of compassion, gentleness, and simplicity. The Leverett Peace Pagoda (or Stupa) is approximately 160 feet in diameter with four niches around the outside each containing a statue of the Buddha representing historical moments in his life. It was built by volunteers from several nations who were united by their desire for world peace.

Carter, Clare. "To Embody Peace: The Building of Peace Pagodas Around the World." *Unwinding the Vietnam War*. Ed. Reese Williams. Seattle: Real Comet Press, 1987. Pp. 416–26.

Fujii, Nichidatsu. *Beating Celestial Drums*. Los Angeles: Nipponzan Myohoji/Peace Press, 1982.

____. *Buddhism for World Peace*. Miyazaki, Yumiko, tr. Tokyo: Japan Bharat Sarvodaya Mitra Sangha, 1980.

____. *My Non-violence*. Tokyo: Japan Buddha Sangha Press, 1975.

____. *The Time Has Come*. Tokyo: Bharat Sarvodaya Mitrata Sanga, 1982.

Montgomery, Daniel. *Fire in the Lotus*. London: Mandala, 1991.

LOWELL, MA

459. *Peace and Conflict Studies Institute (PACSI)* (1988, 1991) (col).

U Massachusetts, One University Ave., Lowell 01854; (978) 934-3903; *robert_gamache@uml.edu; John_MacDougall@uml.edu*

Buddhist Peace Pagoda located in Leverett, Massachusetts. Photograph courtesy Toby Keyes, lay devotee.

Promotes peace education in the University and the community. Offers a minor degree with special attention to the structural origins of violence and war. Organizes workshops on topics such as conflict resolution and economic conversion; participates in annual Days Without Violence honoring the death of Martin Luther King, Jr. Has a resource area in the Library. Co-Directors: Robert Gamache, John MacDougall, Imogene Stulken.

MARBLEHEAD, MA

460. *North Shore WAND* (1999) (org).

99 Front St., Marblehead 01945;
(781) 631-7998.

Branch of Women's Action for New Directions. Hiroshima-Nagasaki vigil, sponsors speakers. Contact Bonnie Howard, Lanie Pryor.

MEDFORD, MA

461. *Peace and Justice Studies* (1985) (col).

Tufts University, PJS/109 Eaton Hall, Medford 02155; (617) 627-2261; 627-2470; *debryan@tufts.edu; www.jumbohub.com/pjs*

PJS "provides an interdisciplinary structure for examining the obstacles, conditions, and paths to achieving a just global peace." Emphasizes four areas: 1) causes of war, techniques of war prevention, conditions of just peace; 2) origins, strategies, and visions of social movements seeking justice and ecological sustainability; theory and practice of conflict resolution; study of peace culture, particularly in education and literature. Offers both a Major (10 courses) and Certificate. Paul Joseph, Dir.; Dale Bryan, Assist. Dir

NATICK, MA

462. *Metro West Pax Christi* (1993) (org)

24 Grove St., Natick 01760; (508) 655-0268; fmadzar@wellesley.edu

An offshoot of the parish Peace & Justice Ministry. Monthly meetings. Sponsors annual retreat for all Pax Christi groups in the state. Strives to end sanctions against Iraq by vigils and educational meetings. Contact Faith Madzar.

NORTHAMPTON, MA

463. *Peace and World Security Studies (PAWSS)* (col).

Member, Five College Program in Peace and World Security Studies, Smith College, Northampton 01063; (413) 584-2700.

See Hampshire College, Amherst.

464. *Pittenbruach Press* (1986) (org).

15 Walnut St., PO Box 553, Northampton 01061-0553; (413) 584-8547; *tmilne@crocker.com; www.crocker.com/~tmilne*

Quaker publishing company: *Shambala Warriors: Nonviolent Fighters for Peace, Satyagraha: The Gandhian Approach to Nonviolent Social Change*, the *Peace Porridge* books, *Wars Must Cease*, etc. Teddy Milne, publisher and author.

PITTSFIELD, MA

465. *Global Issues Research Organization* (1979) (org).

Berkshire Community College, Pittsfield 01201.

The campus peace group has organized many conferences on such topics as "Alternatives to Violence" and "We the People" (about peace activists).

466. *Never Again Campaign* (1986) (org).

1350 West St., Pittsfield, 01201-5786; (413) 499-4660 ext. 351; *dlathrop@cc.berkshire.org*

A volunteer program of Berkshire Community College, one of the College's outreach programs, begun by Prof. Don and Marion Lathrop to spread the message of the Hiroshima and Nagasaki A-bomb survivors and promote international understanding through sharing Japanese culture. NAC volunteers live with hosts in one area of the U.S. or Canada for up to six months to speak to clubs, schools, etc. Donald and Marion Lathrop, Dir.

467. **Peace and World Order Studies* (1982) (col).

Berkshire Community College, Pittsfield 01201-5786; (413) 499-4660, ext. 351; *dlathrop@cc.berkshire.org; www.cc.berkshire.org*

The first peace and war course was taught in 1979, "the first peace studies course at a Community College in the United States." Now the program has four basic courses. A Peace Pole on campus in English, Russian, Spanish, and Japanese, was erected in honor of Dr. Lathrop's 35 years at the college. Donald Lathrop, Dir.

RUTLAND, MA

468. *Peace Pole* (1998) (mem).

Overlook Farm, Rutland.

Guests carried flags of 35 countries while repeating "May Peace Prevail in the World" in many languages.

SALEM, MA

469. *Peace Studies Minor* (1982) (col).

Peace Institute, Department of Philosophy, Salem State College, 352 Lafayette Street, Salem 01970; (978) 542-6298; *krishna.mallick@salem.mass.edu; www.salem.mass.edu/peaceinstitute/index.htm*

Eighteen hours of courses chosen by the student in consultation with an advisor and cooperation with the Peace Institute. Krishna Mallick, Dir.

SHERBORN, MA

470. *Memorial Stone to Unknown Civilians Killed in War* (1994) (mem).

Originally at The Peace Abbey, near The Pacifist Memorial.

A 1400 pound granite stone engraved with the words "Unknown Civilians Killed in War," the only memorial to civilian war dead in the U.S., was accompanied by an eternal flame, a smaller stone with a quotation from the poetry of Thich Nhat Hanh, and nearby a stone commemorating all Victims of Violence with words of St. Francis. "On average, 2,174 people die every day as a direct result of war. Nine out of ten of these are civilians. Half of these are children." In the summer of 1999 the Memorial Stone for Unknown Civilians Killed in War traveled through 81 cities and towns for 33 days from Massachusetts to Arlington National Cemetery, Washington, DC ("Stonewalk"). The journey of pulling the stone was intended to increase awareness of the full cost of wars, and to heighten our resolve as a nation to settle disputes peacefully. The police impounded the Stone on its arrival at Arlington, but the Landas hope Congress will give permission for its permanent placement there.

471. *The Pacifist Memorial* (October 2, 1994, the 125th birth anniversary of Mahatma Gandhi) (mem).

On the grounds of The Peace Abbey.

In the center of the Memorial stands a statue of Mahatma Gandhi, created by the sculptor Lado Goudjabidze. Radiating outward are six brick walls on which are recorded the names of and quotations from sixty peacemakers, thirty men and thirty women who contributed courageously to peace (other names are to be added). *Men:* Adin Ballou, Stephen Biko, Elihu Burritt, César Chávez, David Darst, Albert Einstein, Stephen Foster, George Fox, St. Francis of Assisi, Gandhi, Siddhartha Gautama (the Buddha), Paul Goodman, Michael Harrington,

Plaque quoting William Stafford on The Pacifist Memorial statue, Sherborn. Photograph courtesy Lewis and Meg Randa.

Herman Hesse, Franz Jagerstatter, Jesus of Nazareth, Toyohiko Kagawa, Krishnamurti, John Lennon, Martin Luther King, Jr., Thomas Merton, A. J. Muste, Vardhamana Nataputta, Scott and Helen Nearing, Oscar Romero, Jalai-din Rumi, Bertrand Russell, Albert Schweitzer, Chief Seattle, Mulford Sibley, Glenn Smiley, William Stafford, Leo Tolstoy, Lao Tzu. *Women*: Jane Addams, Susan Anthony, Hannah Arendt, Emily Balch, St. Catherine of Siena, Carrie Catt, St. Claire of Assisi, Maura Clarke, Dorothy Day, Jean Donovan, Ida Ford, Abigail Foster, Anne Frank, Frances Harper, Jessie Hughan, Mother Jones, Frances Kent (Sister Corita), Mother Ann Lee, Dorothy Kazel, Margaret Mead, Lucretia Mott, Peace Pilgrim, Rosika Schwimmer, Samantha Smith, Muriel Lester, Muriel Rukeyser, Baroness Bertha von Suttner, Sojourner Truth, Annabel Wolfson. (See the web site for more information about these peacemakers and the quotations.) At the heads of each wall are engraved one of the Peace Seeds, a condensed form of the Sacred Office of Peace. These prayers for peace from each of the world's major faith traditions were first prayed at a convocation of religious leaders at Assisi. Italy, in 1986. The Memorial was designed by Lewis Randa.

The Pacifist Memorial designed by Lewis Randa, Sherborn. Photograph courtesy Lewis and Meg Randa.

472. **The Peace Abbey* (1988) (org).

2 North Main St., Sherborn 01770; (508) 435-4077; *http://www.peaceabbey.org/pacmem.htm*

Founded by Lewis and Meg Randa for education, retreats, and conferences for peace. The Abbey also provides the Courage of Conscience Award, the Greater Boston Vegetarian Resource Library, the National Registry for Conscientious Objection, the Pacifist Living History Museum and Archives, and a farm for animals escaped from slaughterhouses. The Randas earlier, in 1971, had founded and still operate the Life Experience School for disabled and terminally-ill students, from which the Peace Abbey developed. With these students, the Randas are developing a Special Peace Corps.

SOMERVILLE, MA

473. **Peace Games* (1992) (org).

249 Elm St., Sommerville 02144; (617) 628-5555; *www.peacegames.org*.

Strives to create safe, peacemaking schools by mobilizing AmeriCorps members and college volunteers to collaborate with elementary schools in the Boston area. Eric Dawson, Exec. Dir.

474. **RESIST* (1967) (org).

259 Elm St., Suite 201, Somerville 02144; (617) 623-5110; *www.resistinc.org*

Gives grants to progressive organizations pursuing a more just society.

SOUTH HADLEY, MA

475. *Peace and World Security* (col).

Mount Holyoke College,
South Hadley 01075; (413) 538-2000;
www.mtholyoke.edu

Member, Five College Program in Peace and World Security Studies (PAWSS). See Hampshire College, Amherst.

VINEYARD HAVEN, MA

476. *Martha's Vineyard Peace Council* (1980?) (org).

PO Box 4069 Vineyard Haven 02568;
(508) 693-3930.

The Council seeks to disseminate ideas for peace, justice, and good will by writing and calling media and public officials. The members also demonstrate, vigil, and hold meetings with speakers such as J. K. Galbraith, Howard Zinn, and Noam Chomsky. Rev. Alden Besse, Chairman.

WALTHAM, MA

477. *International Center for Ethics, Justice, and Public Life* (1998) (col).

Brandeis University, MS 086
PO Box 9110, Ridgewood 20, Waltham
02454-9110; *ethics@brandeis.edu*;
www.brandeis.edu/ethics

The Center, established through a gift of $13 million to Brandeis by Abraham Feinberg, supports the work abroad of International Fellows, Student Fellows, seminars at Brandeis and abroad, and other peacemaking activities. Daniel Terris, Dir.

478. *International Nonviolent Initiatives* (1975) (org).

PO Box 515, Waltham, 02254;
(781) 891-0814.

Promotes nonviolent means to resolve disputes. Member of War Resisters International.

479. *Peace and Conflict Studies Program* (1984) (col).

Brandeis Univ., Waltham 01454-9110;
(781) 736-2642; *fellman@brandeis.edu*

This interdisciplinary program studies the causes of war and nonviolent resolution of conflicts. The program examines the meanings of "security," the nature of power, alternatives to violence, and the roads to disarmament and ending war. Core requirements: War and Possibilities of Peace, Internship in Peace and Conflict Studies, International Nonviolent initiatives, Introduction to inter-Communal Coexistence. Gordon Fellman, Chair (Sociology Dept., MS 071). (Fellman is the author of *Rambo and the Dalai Lama: The Compulsion to Win and Its Threat to Human Survival*, 1998; http://stanley.feldberg.brandeis.edu/~fellman).

WARE, MA

480. *Agape* (1982) (org).

2062 Greenwich Road, Ware 01082-9309; (413) 967-9369.

Simple living, educational ministry based on nonviolence, conducting retreats for inner city colleges, parishes, and youths. Pub. *Servant Song* bi-annually. Co-founded by Suzanne Shanley and Brayton Shanley.

WATERTOWN, MA

481. *School Mediation Associates* (1984) (porg).

134 W. Standish Rd., Watertown 02472;
(617) 926-5969; *sma@world.com*

SMA would "transform schools into safer, more caring, and more effective institutions" by teaching conflict resolution skills and processes in the curriculum and other ideas.

WELLESLEY, MA

482. *Peace and Justice Studies Program* (1984) (col).

Wellesley College, 106 Central Street,
Wellesley 02481; (781) 283-2685;
vkazanji@wellesley.edu;
www.wellesley.edu/rellife/peace/index.htm

Both a major and minor offered, of core courses, related electives, and practicum. Victor Kazanjian and Sally Merry, Co-Directors.

WOODVILLE, MA

483. *Metro West WAND* (1989) (org).

PO Box 214, Woodville 01784
(part of Hopkinton); (508) 435-5104;
louiseina@gateway.net;
onclearwater@aol.com

A chapter of Women's Action for New Directions, covering area west of Boston. Films, letters to Congresspeople, information tables at events, national lobby days. Meets at the Peace Abbey in Sherborn. Contact Louise Falkoff.

WORCESTER, MA

484. *Conflict Management* (1996) (col).

College of Professional and Continuing Education, Clark University, Worcester 01610; (508) 793-7217/7742;
ekyle@clarku.edu; www.copace.clarku.edu

A MS and Certificate for mid-level professionals in both theory and practice. Contact Elena Kyle.

485. *Holy Cross Pax Christi* (1986) (org, col).

College of the Holy Cross, 1 College St., Box 16A, Worcester 01610;
(508) 793-2448.

Weekly meetings for prayer and planning actions. Contact Kim McElaney.

486. *Peace and Conflict Studies* (1985) (col).

Center for Interdisciplinary and Special Studies, College of the Holy Cross, Worcester 01610; (508) 793-3485;
pcicovac@holycross.edu;
www.sterling.holycross.edu/departments/ciss/website/homepage/peace.html

Undergraduate concentration to complement the student's major field, consisting of a core course, electives, and a research project or internship. David O'Brien, Founder; Predrag Cicovacki, Dir., Philosophy Dept. (508-793-2467).

487. *Peace Studies* (1987) (col).

Department of Psychology, Clark University, 950 Main St., Worcester 01610; (508) 793-7663; *jderivera@clarku.edu; www2.clarku.edu/departments/peacestudies*

An undergraduate concentration of 24 semester hours focusing on alternative ways to promote peace and justice. Internships and study abroad encouraged. Joe de Rivera, Prog. Dir.

488. *Saints Francis and Therese Catholic Worker* (1986) (org).

52 Mason St., Worcester 01610;
(508) 753-3588 or 799-6228.

Shelters the homeless, operates a bakery, and promotes peace and justice. Pub. newspaper *The Catholic Radical* with the motto: "to foster a society based on creed instead of greed."

—— *Michigan (MI)* ——

58 Sister Cities. / 1112 Peace Poles.

489. Canceled.

ANN ARBOR, MI

490. *Birth of the Peace Corps* (mem).

Michigan Union, University of Michigan, 53 S. State St., Ann Arbor, MI.

A plaque marks the place where President John F. Kennedy first introduced the idea for the Peace Corps on October 14, 1960.

491. *Interfaith Council for Peace & Justice* (1965) (org).

730 Tappan, Ann Arbor 48104;
(734) 663-1870.

An educational and social action organization of people of various faiths committed to belief in the world as one family, love, future generations, wise stewardship of the environment, and promoting social, political and economic justice. Contact Tobi Hanna-Davies.

DELTON, MI

492. *Circle Pines Center* (1938) (org).

8650 Mullen Rd., Delton 40046 (between Kalamazoo and Grand Rapids);

(616) 623-9054; *circle@net-link.net;*
www.circlepinescenter.org

Summer camp for ages 8–17 and year-round retreat center teaching cooperative principles and values of peace, justice, and ecology. Has 40 buildings, including a Lodge, on 294 acres and 1/3 miles of lakefront. Pub. *Pine Needles* quarterly newsletter.

DETROIT, MI

493. **Center for Peace and Conflict Studies* (1965, 1987) (col).

2320 Faculty/Administration Bldng., Wayne State University, Detroit 48202; (313) 577-3453; *ab3440@wayne.edu; www.pcs.wayne.edu*

Originally the Center for Teaching about War and Peace. The present Center seeks to advance "the search for ways to understand and manage domestic and international conflict, diminish violence, and study the modalities of conflict resolution and management," by academic programs, conferences, research, workshops, and publications. The Peace and Conflict Studies curriculum offers an undergraduate co-major or minor, providing tools and background

needed for graduate work or positions in government or business related to conflict management, and thus prepares for the MA in dispute resolution. Sponsors several community programs, including Harmony III (racial conflict), Peaceful Schools, and the Multicultural Experience in Leadership Development (MELD). Frederic Pearson, Director.

494. *International Peace Monument* (1941) (mem).

Belle Isle Park in the Detroit River, Detroit.

This large granite bench celebrates the many years of amity between the U.S. and Canada. It is inscribed with these words: "With This Everlasting Witness We Keep Peace with Our Neighbors As They Have Kept Peace with Us Throughout the Years." Carved also on the back of the Bench is an eagle with 13 stars to the left for the U.S. and a crown and lion to the right for Canada.

495. **Mediating Theory and Democratic Systems Program* (1991) (col).

College of Urban, Labor, and Metropolitan Affairs, 3248 Faculty/Admin. Bldng., Wayne State Univ., Detroit 48202;

International Peace Monument (Bench), Belle Isle Park, Detroit. Photograph by Joe Crachiola, courtesy Jo Bristah.

(313) 993-7482; *www.mtds.wayne.edu/campus.htm*

Founded with assistance from William and Flora Hewlett Foundation. Pub. *Conflict Management in Higher Education Report.* Frederic Pearson, Dir.

496. **Metro Detroit WAND* (1986) (org).

PO Box 2577, Southfield 48037; (313) 545-1862; *arfwand@mich.com*

A branch of Women's Action for New Directions. Active with WiLL, Women Legislators Lobby, women state legislators concerned about national spending priorities, esp. military spending vs. human and environmental needs (Michigan's 3 Congressional women are members of WiLL). Annual Mothers' Peace Day Award Breakfast. Periodic newsletter, Claire Colman, ed. Contact Kim Bergier (*kimroman49@hotmail.com*), Claire Colman (*claire@oeonline.com*). National WAND: *www.wand.org*

497. **Michigan People of Faith Against the Death Penalty* (1999) (org).

c/o Groundwork for a Just World, 11224 Kercheval, Detroit 48214-3323; (313) 822-2055; *groundwork@aol.com; jbnels@gateway.net*

Brings together religious leaders to uphold the sacredness of life, to educate and advocate against capital punishment, and to work for worldwide abolition. Jeff Nelson, Dir.

498. *Peace Carillon* (1940) (mem).

Belle Isle, Detroit.

The Carillon resounds with the music from a 49-bell, four-octave electronic instrument. The 85-foot Tower contains messages affirming peace, including: "A just and lasting peace among ourselves and with all nations" (Lincoln) and "As on the sea of Galilee/The Christ is whispering, 'Peace'" (Whittier). The journalist Nancy Brown inspired readers to raise funds for the construction of the Peace Tower, which is near the International Peace Monument (Bench).

499. **Swords into Plowshares Peace Center* (1985) (org).

Central United Methodist Church, 33 East Adams, Detroit, 48226; (313) 963-7575 (w) or 393-1437 (h).

Contains a 5000-square-foot art gallery, gift

Swords into Ploughshares Peace Center, Detroit. Photograph courtesy Jo Bristah.

shop, children's corner, and reference library, all related to the theme of peace. Every two years the Center sponsors a juried art exhibit by Ontario and Michigan artists on the theme of transition from war to peace. Provides three to five exhibits a year: for example, "Hiroshima Panels," "Children of War," "U.S. Detention Camps of WWII," and several exhibits of children's art. Publishes *Harbinger* quarterly magazine on the Center's activities. Initiated by the Central United Methodist Church. Dir.: James and Jo Bristah.

United Nations Publications on Peace. *Peace Museums Worldwide.* Geneva: United Nations Library, 1998. P. 71.

EAST JORDAN, MI

500. **Little Traverse League for Peace and Freedom* (1980) (org).

1790 Sanderson Road, East Jordan, 49727; (616) 582-7592.

As branch 100 of Women's International League for Peace and Freedom (WILPF), LTLPF deals with national and international issues, disseminating information, mounting protests. Contact Bruce and Char Sanderson.

501. **Wagbo Peace Center* (1992) (org).

5745 North M-66, East Jordan 49727; (616) 536-0333; *wagbo@juno.com*

Founded when Martha Wagbo willed her family homestead to become a peace education center: "To model peaceable, sustainable living and to teach the related concepts of peace, nonviolence, sustainable agriculture, and environmental stewardship through experiential education programs, conferences, retreats, and community activities." "We know that the roots of international violence stem from the stealing of raw materials through the use of military force." They have interns, work with at-risk teens on the farm, and mount a full summer program. Pub.: *Centerpeace* newsletter. Steve Maniaci, Chair. Contact Tracy Meisterheim.

FERNDALE, MI

502. *Michigan Peace Action* (1993) (org).

195 W. Nine Mile Road, #208, Ferndale 48220; (248) 548-3920; *peaceactmich@earthlink.net*

Originally the Detroit area Freeze campaign, then Michigan SANE/Freeze (1987), and now Peace Action of Michigan with a broadened agenda: abolition of nuclear weapons, human rights, ending international arms trade, converting U.S. militarized economy to peaceful production, promoting nonviolent conflict resolution on all levels. Pub.: *Flash!* quarterly. Brad van Guilder, State Organizer (*pamiorganize@ earthlink.net*).

HOLLAND, MI

503. *Stop, Look, and Listen* (1991) (mem, col).

The Muste alcove of the Van Wylen Library, Hope College, Holland 49422-9000.

A memorial to the radical union organizer and pacifist Abraham Johannes Muste (1885–1967), sometimes called the father of the nonviolent movement for peace and justice in the United States. He actively opposed every U.S. war in this century, including the Cold War and "police actions," and he pioneered the application of Gandhian techniques of nonviolent resistance ranging from a major textile strike he helped organize in 1919 to opposition to nuclear weapons bases in the 1950s and 1960s. The

Stop, Look, and Listen Muste Memorial by John Saurer, Hope College, Holland, Michigan. Photograph courtesy Donald Cronkite.

sculpture at Hope College (Muste's alma mater) is composed of three objects finished in green chalk board with chalk and erasure provided for comment by any student, faculty member, or campus visitor, and was created by John Saurer.

Collum, Danny. "A. J. Muste: The Prophetic Pilgrim." *Sojourners* (December 1984) 12–14.

Robinson, Jo Ann. *Abraham Went Out: A Biography of A. J. Muste.* Philadelphia: Temple UP, 1982.

Also: A. J. Muste Memorial Institute, 339 Lafayette St., N.Y., N.Y. 10012.

HOUGHTON, MI

504. *Copper Country Peace Alliance* (1980) (org).

PO Box 767, Houghton 49931; (906) 487-2149.

The Alliance works for the nonviolent resolution of local and world conflicts and for the eventual end of war. It opposes the "alarming increase in world militarism and the increasing proliferation of nuclear arsenals," the "proposition that war is a just and legitimate means by which governments may achieve their will," the "increased reliance on technologies that pose dangers to human health and the environment," and the "increasing ability of large, impersonal and irresponsible multi-national corporations to dictate policies which serve primarily the interests of short-term profits for the few." Coord.: Dana Richter.

LANSING, MI

505. *Michigan Coalition Against the Death Penalty* (1979) (org).

300 N. Washington Square, #102, Lansing 48933; (517) 482-4161; *miccd@aol.com*

Organized by the Michigan Council on Crime & Delinquency. Pub. brochure and bulletins. Elizabeth Arnovits, Pres.

506. *Michigan Faith & Resistance Peace Team* (1993) (org).

1516 Jerome St., Lansing 48912-2220; (517) 484-3178;

michpeacteam@peacenet.org; *www.traverse.com/nonprof/peaceteam*

Offers nonviolence training for peace teams. In 1999 sent volunteers to Chiapas to provide protective accompaniment to rural residents of Tila municipality and other communities. Rev. C. Peter Dougherty, Coord. of training. (See: Peace Brigades).

507. *Pax Christi Michigan* (1970s) (org).

934 Cleo St., Lansing 48915; (517) 482-2558; *tirakpaxmi@aol.com*

Joan Tirak, Coordinator and Regional Rep.

ORCHARD LAKE, MI

508. *Peace & National Priorities Center of Oakland Co.* (1971) (org).

PO Box 240344, Orchard Lake 48324; (248) 683-3363.

Develops teaching materials, trains staffs in teaching non-violent conflict resolution in elementary schools. Maintains free film/video/audio library. Pub. a newsletter. Bill & Mary Carry, Coordinators.

PORT HURON, MI

509. *Children's Peace Committee of the International Institute/Museum of Arts & History* (1984) (org).

1115 Sixth St., Port Huron, 48060-5346; (810) 982-0891; *phmuseum@tir.com*

Involves young people in arts programs, U.N. events, and other peace projects, and creators of the Samantha-Katerina Children's Peace Garden in Port Huron.

510. *Samantha and Katerina Children's Peace Garden* (1985) (mem).

Pine Grove Peace Park, Port Huron, on the bank of the St. Clair River.

Named for Samantha Smith, the young girl from Maine who initiated a dialog with the Soviet Union and visited as their guest, and Katerina Lycheva, who brought greetings to the

Samantha and Katerina Children's Peace Garden, Pine Grove Peace Park, Port Huron, Michigan. Photograph courtesy Mary Davis, Port Huron Museum.

U.S. after Samantha was killed in a plane crash in 1985. The garden of 1140 sq. ft. is in two sections, one for Samantha, one for Katarina. In 1990 the garden became the official Children's Peace Garden of Michigan. A sign displays Einstein's statement on achieving peace through understanding, not force.

SAGINAW, MI

511. *Mustard Seed Catholic Worker* (1995) (org).

721 E. Holland Ave., Saginaw 48601-2619; (517) 755-4741 or 790-4380; *riegle@svsu.edu* and *LeonaSull@cs.com*

Activities include weekly vigil against the Iraqi blockade and other issues, yearly commemoration of Hiroshima and Nagasaki bombings, and sometimes participates in national demonstrations, as at the Nevada Test Site. Pub. *The Seed* newsletter. Contact Sr. Leona Sullivan, Rosalie Riegle.

——— *Minnesota* ———

32 Sister Cities. / 134 Peace Poles.

AMERICAN POINT ISLAND, MN

512. *SunSweep* (1985) (mem).

Located where the U.S. border stretches above the 49th parallel to enclose a few islands and a peninsula projecting into Lake-of-the-Woods at the most northern point in the contiguous United States.

A pair of wedge-shaped slabs of black granite with engraved hands surrounded by circles on the inside surfaces. One of three sculptures conceived and sculpted by David Barr along the U.S./Canadian Border, the other two at Point Roberts, Washington, and Campobello Island, New Brunswick. Barr's mother is Canadian, and he grew up in Detroit.

BEMIDJI, MN

513. **Peace and Justice Studies* (col).

School of Integrative Studies, Bemidji State Univ., Bemidji 56601; (218) 755-2829; *admissions@vax1.bemidji.msus.edu*; *www.bemidji.msus.edu/Catalog/ SemesterCatalo/PJST/index.html*

A minor program of four major components: economy, ecology, justice, and nonviolence. Dean Bowman, Acad. Dir.

COLLEGEVILLE, MN

514. **Peace Studies* (1988) (col).

St. John's Univ., Collegeville 56321; (320) 363-3047; *janderson@csbsju.edu*; *www.csbsju.edu/prospective /academics/ areasofstudy/majorsminors/peacestudies/ peace_studies.htm*

St. John's Univ. for men offers both major and minor degrees in Peace Studies in alliance with the College of St. Benedict for women. Examples of course offerings: Philosophies of Nonviolence/Violence, International Law and International Organization. Jeff Anderson, chair.

DULUTH, MN

515. **Center for the Study of Peace & Justice* (1987) (col).

College of Saint Scholastica, Duluth 55811; (218) 723-6442; *tmorgan@css.edu*; *www.css.edu*

Undergraduate minor following the Benedictine tradition of peace, service, and scholarship. The Center also encourages peace studies across the disciplines and sponsors workshops. Contact Thomas Morgan.

516. **Loaves and Fishes Community* (1989) (org).

1614 Jefferson St., Duluth 55812; (218) 728-0629 or 724-2054.

Follows the teachings of Jesus and the Catholic Worker tradition in serving the homeless and opposing the war on Iraq, the Navy's ELF Trident triggers, military recruiting in the schools, war toys. Contact: Joel Kilgore

MANKATO, MN

517. **Kessel Institute for the Study of Peace and Change (KISPC)* (1995) (col).

Minnesota State University-Mankato, Mankato 56002-8400; (507) 389-5315; *donald.strasser@mankato.msus.edu*; *www.mankato.msus.edu/depts/Kessel*

Named after Abbas Kessel, MSU Political Science professor and peace activist, the institute sponsors seminars, lectures, and cultural events and supports curriculum development and research. Contact Donald Strasser.

MARINE ON ST. CROIX, MN

518. **Growing Communities for Peace* (1982, 1993) (org).

16542 Orwell Rd., N, Marine on St. Croix 55047-9754; (612) 433-4303; *peace@peacemaker.org*; *www.peacemaker.org*

A division of Hudson Human Potential Institute (1982). "Dedicated to the process of empowering children and the adults who care for them, to develop skills to live and interact nonviolently and in harmony with the Earth, in order to create communities capable of peace." Some goals: increase abilities to employ nonviolent living skills and to interact compassionately; guide teachers in developing curricula for developing nonviolent living skills for students. Pubs.: quarterly *Peacemaker's News*. Books and other resources available for purchase. Rebecca Janke and Julie Peterson, Co-directors, who are available for workshops.

MINNEAPOLIS, MN

519. **Center for Global Education* (1982) (col).

Augsburg College, 2211 Riverside Ave., Minneapolis 55454; (612) 330-1159, (800) 299-8889; *globaled@augsburg.edu*; *www.augsburg.edu/global*

The Center provides "cross-cultural educational opportunities in order to foster critical analysis of local and global conditions…leading to a more just and sustainable world."

Through the support of the Lutheran Church, "the Center has coordinated programs in the Two-Thirds world for more than 6,500 students and adults." It "coordinates five undergraduate semester programs in Mexico, Central America, and Southern Africa," and "over 25 short-term educational programs each year for institutions, churches, community groups and other adults." Pubs.: quarterly newsletter: *Global News & Notes*; semi-annual newsletter *Global Connections* for alumni/ae of semester programs; on-line journal, "Peace Matters" (www.augsburg.edu/peace). The College is a Peace Site with a designating flag.

520. *Conflict and Change Center/
Conflict Management* Minor (1986)
(col).

Hubert H. Humphrey Institute of Public Affairs, University of Minnesota, Minneapolis 55455; (612) 625-3513; *tfiutak@hhh.umn.edu; www.hhh.umn.edu/centers/conflict-change*

The Center seeks innovative ways to resolve conflicts nonviolently. It helped create the graduate minor program in conflict management (1993). Tom Fiutak, Dir.

521. *Friends for a Non-Violent World*
(1981) (org).

Meridel Le Sueur Center for Peace & Justice, 1929 @. 5th St., Minneapolis 55454; (612) 321-9787; *FNVW@mm.com; www.mm.com/fnvw/*

Inaugurated "to build a world of Peace and Justice" through such programs as the Alternatives to Violence Project (AVP) in the community, schools, churches, and prisons; Customized Non-Violence Trainings; the People Camp, a week-long camp for experiences in cooperation, conflict resolution, consensus building, and non-violence theory and action; the Peace Breakfast, a monthly gathering; the Minnesota Military Tax Resistance Network for expressing conscientious objection to military spending; the Coalition to Demilitarize Our Schools to Resist J-ROTC; Summer Interns; the twice yearly Newsletter. Michael Bischoff, Dir.

522. *Ground Zero Minnesota* (1983)
(org).

PO Box 13127, Minneapolis, 55414. (651) 690-5357; web site: *www.gzmn.org*

Slogan: "Education for Informed Democracy and Human Survival." GZM emphasizes the connections between resource competition worldwide and violent conflicts. Organized some 150 programs at colleges, high schools, and churches, mainly on nuclear weapons issues. Created 48 videos on peace and justice topics: "War and Peace Around the World," "Military Budgets and the Arms Trade," "The War on 'Drugs,'" "The Causes of War," etc. Now focusing on nuclear weapons and the Comprehensive Test Ban Treaty. Michael Andregg, Director (author of "On the Causes of War").

523. *Lyndale Park Peace Garden* (1998)
(mem).

By Lake Harriet in Minneapolis.

The Garden is the recreation of the Lake Harriet Rock Garden (1985). It contains relic stones from both Hiroshima and Nagasaki, which are placed at either end of a foot bridge designed with two ninety-degree turns, which according to Japanese lore, protect pedestrians from evil spirits. Also has a *Peace Pole*. The only park in the U.S. with relics from both cities, it was developed by Marj Wunder and others in Minneapolis and Japan. The park has come to sym-

Lyndale Park Peace Garden and International Peace Site, Minneapolis. Photograph courtesy Marj Wunder, Minneapolis-Hiroshima Friendship Cities, Inc.

bolize not only peace, but the ability of ordinary people worlds apart to work together for peace. Dedicated as an International Peace Site in May, 1999. Contact Marj Wunder (4508 Arden Ave. So., Minneapolis 55424; 612-920-3439).

Griffin, Dave. "Building a Peace Park." *Minnesota Parent* (August 1998) 21–23.

Porter, Louis. "'Peace Stone' spans 2 Nations." *St. Paul Pioneer Press and Dispatch* (Aug. 6, 1985).

524. *Midwest Institute for Social Transformation (MIST)* (1991) (org).

2615 Park Ave., #404, Minneapolis 55407; (612) 874-7715

"Seeks to promote social change through programs and actions based on the principles of radical nonviolence and self-determination." Examples: Helped the Prairie Island Coalition Against Nuclear Storage/Mdewakanton Sioux stop the nuclear waste dump at Prairie Island; demonstrations against Alliant Tech Systems, Hopkins, MN (Alliant makes depleted uranium shells and rocket propulsion systems); conference on peace conversion; Committing to Peace conference on nonviolent dissent in the U.S., Oct. 1999. Pub.: *The Rising* newsletter. Marv Davidov, Dir.

525. *Minneapolis-Hiroshima Friendship Cities, Inc.* (1997) (org).

4508 Arden Ave. So., Minneapolis 55424 (612) 920-3439.

Sponsor of the Lyndale Park Peace Garden. Marj Wunder, Coord. (See: Sister Cities.)

526. *Minnesota Alliance of Peacemakers* (1995) (org).

511 Groveland at Lyndale, Minneapolis 55403; (612) 591-0388 or 374-3594; *natchison@igc.apc.org*.

A coalition of 26 Minnesota peace organizations, formed to enable them to pool resources and ideas for common goals set out in their extensive mission statement (primacy of justice

Lyndale Park Peace Garden and International Peace Site, Minneapolis. Photograph courtesy Marj Wunder, Minneapolis-Hiroshima Friendship Cities, Inc.

and law, disarmament, support of the U.N., healthy ecosystem, unity in diversity, human rights, education). Lyle Christianson, Pres.

527. *Minnesota Fellowship of Reconciliation* (1946) (org).

PO Box 14792, Minneapolis 55414-0792; (612) 458-7745; *dcady@piper.hamline.edu*

Local Fellowship of Reconciliation. Monthly exec. meeting, quarterly membership meeting, annual fall conference, landmines project, non-violence training for high school and college youth, Hiroshima-Nagasaki Day, FOR actions. Pub. *North Country Peace Builder* quarterly newsletter. Contact Michael Brown.

528. *Northern Sun Merchandizing* (porg).

2916 E. Lake St., Minneapolis 55406-2065; (612) 729-2001.

Shirts, posters, bumper stickers, etc.

529. *Women Against Military Madness* (1982) (org).

310 East 38th St., #225, Minneapolis; (612)827-5364; *wamm@mtn.org*

A nonviolent feminist organization that works in solidarity with others to create a system of social equality, self-determination, and justice through education and empowerment, and to oppose militarism, the degradation of Earth's environment, and the malevolence of the global economy. Publishes a newsletter *W.A.M.M.*, 8 pp. Founded by Mary Shepard, Polly Mann, and other women.

MOORHEAD, MN

530. *Dorothy Day House of Hospitality* (1983) (org).

714 8th St. S, Moorhead 56560; (218) 233-5763; *fmdd@juno.com*

Refuge for homeless men and "committed to nonviolence and its insistence on a personalist response to political problems....in solidarity with nonviolent movements for peace and social justice the world over."

PIPESTONE, MN

531. *Pipestone National Monument* (1937) (mus).

36 Reservation Ave., Pipestone 56164, on US 75, 23, 30, near north boundary of Pipestone; *pipe_superintendent@nps.gov; www.nps.gov/pipe/*

A quarry from which Indians obtained materials for making peace pipes used in ceremonies, where all who came there were able to quarry in peace. Offers a Cultural Center, Museum, self-guiding trail, demonstrations of Indian pipes being made. 283 acres in all.

SAGINAW, MN

532. *The Mustard Seed* (org).

721 East Holland, Saginaw 48601-2619; (517) 744-4741; *riegle@tardis.svsw.edu*

Holds a Picnic for Racial Unity in July and commemorates the victims of Hiroshima and Nagasaki in August with a public prayer service. A Catholic Worker House.

ST. JOSEPH, MN

533. *Peace Studies* (1988) (col).

College of Saint Benedict, Saint Joseph 56374; (320) 363-2770; *janderson@ csbsju.edu; www.csbsju.edu/peacestudies/*

This women's college, in collaboration with St. John's Univ. for men, offers an undergraduate major on the history of human conflict and its resolution through violent and nonviolent struggle, in a Judeo-Christian context. Jeff Anderson, Chair.

ST. PAUL, MN

534. *Community of Peace Academy* (1995) (org).

471 Magnolia Ave. E., St. Paul 55101-3849; (612) 776-5151.

A public charter school dedicated to racial and cultural diversity and a peaceful environment "in which each person is treated with unconditional positive regard" and encouraged to "practice a nonviolent lifestyle." Eritrian, Hmong, African American, Hispanic, and European children.

535. *Global Citizens Network* (1992) (org).

130 N. Howell St., St. Paul 55104; (651) 644-0960; (800) 644-9292; *gcn@mtn.org; www.globalcitizens.org*

Seeks to bring together people "committed to the shared values of peace, justice, tolerance, cross-cultural understanding and global cooperation" by sending teams to live and work with rural people in other countries for brief periods of time. Pub.: newsletter *Harambee* (Swahili word for "unite" or "work together"). Kim Regnier, Program Director.

536. *Hamline Students FOR Peace
(1978) (org).

Hamline U Mail #252, 1536 Hewitt Ave.,
St. Paul 55104; (651) 523-2316;
dcady@gw.hamline.edu

Affil. with Fellowship of Reconciliation (FOR).
Promotes discussion of peace and justice issues
(Iraq, Kosovo, landmines, School of the Amer-
icas, etc.); annually sponsors MLK memorial
lecture on nonviolence. Duane Cady, Faculty
Advisor.

537. *International Journal on World
Peace (1984) (jour).

2700 Univ. Ave. West, Suite 200,
St. Paul 55114; (651) 644-2809;
gordon@pwpa.org; www.pwpa.org/IJWP

Concerned with national interests, ethnic
rivalries, hunger, the environment, ideology,
human nature, economics, and all aspects of the
search for peace, this scholarly publication cuts
across all disciplines and cultures from around
the world in articles and reviews. Abstracted,
indexed, or made available on CD-ROM by
several agencies. Gordon Anderson, Editor.

538. *Justice and Peace Studies (Minor
1987, Major 1991) (col).

University of St. Thomas, #4137,
St. Paul 55105-1096; (651) 962-5325;
dwsmith@stthomas.edu; www.
stthomas.edu/www/juspce_http/justpeac.htm

JPS "teaches students how to criticize societies responsibly and how to act effectively for
the common good, both to relieve suffering and
to make positive changes in social structures."
Both major and minor degrees include "The-
ologies of Justice, Peace, Prosperity, and Security," "Active Nonviolence," "Justice and Peace
Methods and Resources." David Smith, Dir.

539. *Pax Christi Minnesota (1982)
(org).

1440 Randolph Ave., #213,
St. Paul 55105; (612) 696-1642;
steichen@tcfreenet.org

Consists of PC groups in the 6 dioceses of
MN. Annual State Assembly their chief activity; also responds to alerts by PC USA and co-
sponsors events with other groups. Sr. Florence
Steichen, CSJ, Coordinator and Regional Rep.

540. *Pax Christi Twin Cities Area
(1982) (org).

328 W. Kellogg Blvd., St. Paul 55102;
(651) 699-8565.

Annual retreat, prayer services to commemorate those who died for peace (Bishop Oscar
Romero and others), collaboration with other
groups, quarterly newsletter. Jennie Downey,
Marilyn Schmit, Co-chairs.

541. *Peace Site Project (1982) (org).

2145 Ford Pkwy., #300,
St. Paul 55116; (651) 695-2587;
www.bloomington.k12.mn.us/peacesite/index

The Peace Site Project facilitates the creation
of public and private places as peace sites. As of
May 2000, there were some 180 Peace Sites in
Minnesota—e.g. the Governor's mansion—and
over 700 worldwide. A marker is available for
indoors or out. (See below: World Citizen, Inc.).
Lynn Elling, Founder and Dir.

542. Vision of Peace (1936) (mem).

The Memorial concourse of the St. Paul
City Hall and Courthouse.

This huge statue carved of Mexican white
onyx represents a god of peace holding a sacred
pipe and extending a hand in a friendly gesture.
At its base are carved five Native American
figures sitting around a campfire with their sacred ceremonial pipes. It was named Vision of
Peace in 1994 at a special ceremony involving
three major Minnesota Native American tribes.
The design in plaster was by Carl Milles (1875–
1955), noted Swedish sculptor; Giovanni Garatti
and 19 craftsmen sculpted the marble. Weigh-
ing about 60 tons and standing some 36 feet
high, the statue is the largest carved onyx figure
in the world. It oscillates 66 degrees to the left
and 66 degrees to the right, each rotation requiring two and one-half hours. More than
100,000 persons view it each year. Although the
statue was dedicated to the war veterans of
Ramsey County, Milles, a pacifist, stipulated
that it should symbolize world peace. Memorial Hall, constructed entirely of blue Belgian
marble, provides an appropriate setting for the
impressive statue. The City has a brochure.

543. *World Citizen, Inc. (1982) (org).

2145 Ford Parkway, Suite 300, Saint Paul
55116; (651) 695-2587, 729-5133;
ellin017@marroon.tc.umn.edu;

Vision of Peace sculpture designed by Carl Milles, City Hall, St. Paul. Photograph courtesy Andrea Oelrich, District Court.

www.bloomington.k12.mn.us/peacesite/ peacesite.html

Mission: "To involve as many people as we can, starting with children, in activities that promote a Peaceful Healthy World." WC pursues this goal especially through the Peace Site Project, which was founded by Louis Kousin of New Jersey. A Peace Site is any place—school, church, business, park, home, etc.—that is committed to protecting the environment, promoting intercultural understanding, seeking peace within self and among others, and "working towards world law with justice through a strong, effective U.N." As of Feb. 1999 there were 714 Peace Sites worldwide. WC also sponsors a Peace Prize Festival, an annual afternoon-long celebration of Nobel Peace Prize Laureates. The 1999 Festival was held at Augsburg College, with representatives of the International Campaign to Ban Landmines, 1997 Nobel Peace Prize co-recipient, as guests of honor. Lynn Elling, Chair.

St. Peter, MN

544. **Peace Studies* (1970) (col).

Gustavus Adolphus College, 800 West College Ave., Saint Peter 56082; (507) 931-7398; *ghmason@gac.edu; www.gac.edu/oncampus/academics/ General_Catalog*

Major of 13 courses and minor of 6 complements the college's co-curricular peace education program, which works campus wide. Study or work abroad recommended; annual lectures in honor of Martin Luther King, Jr., and Raoul Wallenberg; three scholarships available; annual grant for a delegation of Model U.N. students. Gregory Mason, Dir.

Winona, MN

545. **Dorothy Day Library on the Web* (1998) (lib).

251 E. Wabasha St., Winona 55987; (507) 452-7224; *jallaire@rconnect.com; www.catholicworker.org/dorothyday*

An online archive of Day's writings from *The Catholic Worker* and elsewhere. Brouse summaries or do full text research. Also included is an interactive forum for discussing her work. Links are provided to other Catholic Worker communities, bibliographies, and archives. Jim Allaire, Compiler. See: Catholic Worker Roundtable on the Internet (*www.catholicworker.org/roundtable*).

— *Mississippi (MS)* —

7 Sister Cities. / 17 Peace Poles.

See Davis, *Weary Feet, Rested Souls*, 190–308, for more Civil Rights Movement organizations and memorials.

Belzoni, MS

546. *Swords into Plowshares* (1979) (mem).

Humphreys County Library, 105 S. Hayden, Belzoni, 39038.

Sculpture of wooden plow handles and welded iron plowshares approx. 39 by 27 by 22 inches on a stone base 19 by 16 by 82 in. Donated by the Belzoni Garden Club. Mildred Love Pepper, Sculptor.

HATTIESBURG, MS

547. **Mount Carmel Baptist Church* (1886) (mem, org).

641 Mobile St., Hattiesburg.

This sanctuary and headquarters for civil rights activists in the 1960s continues actively engaged in the struggle.

JACKSON, MS

548. **Tougaloo College* (1869) (org).

500 County Line Road, Jackson

Many faculty and students of this college risked their safety for the civil rights Movement. Backed by the United Church of Christ and with roots in the abolitionist American Missionary Association, the college provided a rare sanctuary in the state for rights protesters. (Davis 216–218). The College archives contain extensive materials on the Movement and on Medgar Evers' nonviolent philosophy.

549. *Benjamin Brown Park* (1995) (mem).

1400 John R. Lynch St., Jackson.

A long-time worker for civil rights in Jackson, Brown was killed by the police during a confrontation between them and students. (Davis 226).

550. *Evers-King Monument* (mem).

Intersection of Medgar Evers St. and Martin Luther King Blvd., Jackson.

Stone slab with pictures of Evers and King and inscriptions.

551. *Medgar Evers Statue* (1992) (mem).

4215 Medgar Evers Blvd., just north of the Medgar Evers Branch of the Jackson Public Library, Jackson.

A life-size, 500-pound, bronze statue of Evers, advocate of nonviolence, NAACP civil rights leader, assassinated on June 12, 1963, at age 37.

Inscribed on the base: "Dedicated to Everyone Who Believes in Peace, Love and Non-violence; Let's Keep the Torch Burning." The statue was created by Thomas Jay Warren.

Evers, Mrs. Medgar, with William Peters. *For Us, the Living*. Garden City, NY: Doubleday, 1967.

Gates, Jimmie. "McRae's Donation Gilds Drive for Evers' Memorial." *Clarion-Ledger* April 10, 1992) 1A.

McKenzie, Danny. "What Can Statue of Medgar Evers See from Vantage?" *Clarion-Ledger* (July 5, 1992) 18.

Morris, Willie. *The Ghosts of Medgar Evers: A Tale of Race, Murder, Mississippi, and Hollywood*. New York: Random House, 1998.

552. *Medgar Evers United States Post Office* (1994) (mem).

Downtown Jackson.

Mitchell, Jerry. "Naming Post office for Medgar Evers 'Fitting Tribute.'" *Clarion-Ledger* (Sept. 4, 1994) B1.

553. *Medgar Wiley Evers House Museum* (mem).

2332 Margaret Walker Alexander Drive (formerly Guynes St.), Jackson, not far from the Evers Branch Library.

Where the NAACP's first full-time field secretary in Mississippi lived and was murdered in

Evers-King Monument, Jackson. Photograph courtesy Mississippi Department of Archives and History.

1963. The house is now owned by Tougaloo College. Museum not yet dedicated, but tours available.

LONGDALE, MS

554. *Mount Zion Methodist Church Memorial* (1964) (mem).

County Line road, Neshoba County (Longdale), near Philadelphia.

This church was burned down in 1964 for supporting the civil rights Movement. Chaney, Goodman, and Schwerner had investigated the arson before they were killed. A *plaque* near the front door of the rebuilt church pays tribute to the slain three.

MERIDIAN, MS

555. *James Chaney Gravesite* (1964) (mem).

Okatibbee Cemetery, Fish Lodge road off Valley Road, Meridian.

Murdered at the age of twenty-one while carrying on his work for civil rights (along with Goodman and Schwerner).

PHILADELPHIA, MS

556. *Chaney, Goodman, and Schwerner Memorial* (1976) (mem).

Mount Nebo Missionary Baptist Church, 257 Carver Ave., Philadelphia.

A memorial to the three Movement workers slain in Longdale stands in front of the church, which was active in the struggle for civil rights. Lillie Jones headed the fund-raising for the memorial.

RULEVILLE, MS

557. *Fannie Lou Hamer House, Gravesite, and U.S. Post Office* (1994) (org).

721 Fannie Lou Hamer Drive (formerly James St.), Ruleville.

Mrs. Hamer was a leader of the nonviolent civil rights Movement in the 1960s: SNCC field secretary; speaking at the Democratic Convention in 1963 of her beating in jail; using her house as a Freedom Summer headquarters in 1964; founding a co-op Freedom Farm in 1969; etc. Mrs. Hamer was buried on land formerly held by the Freedom Farm, now the property of the city. The Ruleville Post Office was named for her in 1994.

Mills, Kay. *This Little Light of Mine: The Life of Fannie Lou Hamer.* New York: Dutton, 1993.

— *Missouri (MO)* —

19 Sister Cities. / 47 Peace Poles.

COLUMBIA, MO

558. **Columbia-Mid Missouri FOR* (1961) (org).

Box 268, Columbia 65203; (573) 449-4585; *jstack@mail.coin.missouri.edu*

Fellowship of Reconciliation local group, working on the death penalty, Iraqi sanctions, military in High Schools, weekly peace vigils, workshops on nonviolent action, and other issues. Gives attention to international problems, sponsoring 2 Bosnian students, programs on various countries, etc. Contact Jeff Stack.

559. **Mid-Missouri Peaceworks* (1982) (org).

804-C E. Broadway, Columbia 65201; (573) 875-0539; *peacewks@coin.org*; *http://peaceworks.missouri.org*

Holds "a vision of an ecologically sound, sustainable world and a violence-free community in which human equality and justice flourish." Sponsors classes, speakers, programs, and events for peace and justice. Operates a non-profit store called the Peace Nook. Pub. *Peaceworks Monitor* newsletter. Mark Haim, Director.

560. *Peace Park, Symbol, and Kent State Stone* (1960s and 70s) (mem).

Park and Peace Symbol are located at the southwest corner of 8th and Elm next to the Historic North Entrance to the University of Missouri Campus.

McAlester Park was nicknamed "Peace Park" by anti-war protesters in 1970. Near the Peace Symbol lies a stone with the words: "Peace will be the dawn of civilization," followed by a list of the students killed at Kent State, May 4, 1970.

"Antiwar Groups Urge Boycott of Classes." *The Maneater* (May 4, 1971).

Beahler, John. "Something's Happening Here." *Missouri Alumnus* (Summer 1990) 20–21.

"Moratorium Marchers Chant, 'Peace Now.'" *The Maneater* (May 7,1971), 1,4.

Peace Park, Symbol, and Kent State Stone, Columbia. Photograph courtesy David Snead and Carl Lingle, University of Missouri Archives, and Chris Cotton.

561. *Peace Studies* (1970) (col).

College of Arts and Sciences, University of Missouri-Columbia, Columbia 65211; (573) 882-6060; *socgall@showme.missouri.edu; www.missouri.edu/~peacewww*

A minor (15 credit hours) and a concentration (33 hours) (1978). John Galliher, Dir.

KANSAS CITY, MO

562. *American Friends Service Committee (AFSC), Kansas City Office* (1981) (org).

4405 Gillham Road, Kansas City 64110; (816) 931-5256; *afsckc@oz.SunFlower.org*

Provides conflict resolution workshops for public school students, builds community through listening projects and a Forum Theatre, counters military recruiting in public schools, exposes media violence, explores issues through newsletters, coffeehouse discussions, and special events. Ira Harritt, Program Coord.

563. *PeaceWorks Kansas City* (1982) (org).

4509 Walnut St., Kansas City 64111; (816) 561-1181 or 523-7666; *peaceworkskc@earthlink.net; http://home.earthlink.net/~peaceworkskc*

Chapter of Peace Action. Lobbying by phone and mail, multicultural reading program for 5th grade students in 10 schools, scholarships for two students each year enrolled in peace studies at Park College, and annual production of updated directory of about 100 area environmental and social justice groups. Lynn & Kris Cheatum, Co-chairs.

564. *People to People International* (1956) (org).

501 E. Armour Blvd., Kansas City 64109-2200; (816) 531-4701; *ptpi@ptpi.org; www.ptpi.org*

A "cultural and educational exchange organization dedicated to advancing international understanding and friendship through the exchange of ideas and experiences directly among peoples of different countries and cultures." At first government supported, in 1961 PTP switched to private sector. Programs: Youth: Collegiate and Professional Studies Program for college students, Student Ambassador Program for high school/middle school students, U.S. Heartland Communication and Culture Program for international students to practice the English language, Sports Division. Adults: International Exchange Programs. PTP's 14th Worldwide Conference was in Hong Kong in 2000. Pubs: *People* magazine; *Communiqué*, yearly magazine for Student Ambassadors and their parents; *Delegate*, newsletter for Citizen Ambassador Program. Dwight D. Eisenhower, Founder. Dr. Alan Warne, Chief Exec.

565. *Western Missouri Coalition to Abolish the Death Penalty* (1987) (org).

PO Box 45302, Kansas City 64171;
(816) 363-3968; *burnettc@umkc.edu*;
www.qni.com/~billw/death/wmcadp.html

Pen pal program with death row inmates; advocating changes in laws, especially regarding mentally retarded; pushing for a moratorium on capital sentences, following the decision of the Illinois governor. Cathy Burnett, Pres.; Ted Wilson, Sec't. (816-822-7455).

OAK RIDGE, MO

566. *Southeast Missouri F.O.R.* (1988) (org).

126 Hart Ave., Oak Ridge 63769;
(573) 266-3696; *stahl@showme.net*

Local Fellowship of Reconciliation. Annual Martin Luther King, Jr. Day, annual Central America Week, annual Hiroshima Day, annual Hunger Day, etc. Contact Janet Smith.

PARKVILLE, MO

567. *Peace Studies* (1990) (col).

Park University, 8700 River Park Drive, Parkville 64152; (816) 741-2000 ext 6352; *jglauner@mail.park.edu*; *www.park.edu/catalog/Coursesinstruction/Minors/peace_study.htm*

A minor gives an introduction to the causes and consequences of violence, values, and peacemaking. Contact Jeff Glauner.

ROLLA, MO

568. *Rolla Peace Issues Group* (1982) (org).

PO Box 2046, Rolla 65402;
(573) 368-5551; *tomsager@umr.edu*

Occasional programs. Contact Tom Sager.

RUTLEDGE, MO

569. *Fellowship for Intentional Community* (1948) (org).

Rt. 1, Box 155-B, Rutledge 63563-9720;
(660) 883-5545; *fic@ic.org*; *www.ic.org/*

FIC "fosters connections and cooperation among communitarians and their friends," including co-housing groups, ecovillages, community networks, and similar undertakings. Pub. *Communities Directory* (1996) and *Communities, Journal of Cooperative Living*.

ST. JOSEPH, MO

570. *Peace Pole* (1998) (mem).

Unity Church of Practical Christianity, 1202 Felix St., St. Joseph, 64501; (816) 279-4075; *unity@ccp.com*

The Pole in eight different languages was planted on the "World Day of Prayer" to celebrate Unity's dedication to peace.
"World Day of Prayer Celebrated." *Saint Joseph Telegraph* (Sept. 17, 1998) 7.

ST. LOUIS, MO

571. *American Friends Service Committee, St. Louis Office* (1968) (org).

438 N. Skinker, St. Louis 63130;
(314) 862-5773;
lreed@afsc.org; *www.afsc.org*

Three areas of work: Economic Justice (economic literacy, Jobs with Justice, police brutality), International Affairs (Iraq sanctions, Ogoni rights, opposing militarism), Ujima Development (leadership training for young African-Americans). *Step by Step* quarterly newsletter. Virginia Druhe, Coord. Lori Reed, Admin. Assoc.

572. *Center for the Study of the Holocaust, Genocide, and Human Rights* (1999) (col).

Department of Behavioral and Social Sciences, Webster University, St. Louis 63119; (314) 968-7062; *woolflm@webster.edu*; *www.webster.edu/~woolflm/cshghr.html*

Supports undergraduate and post-graduate education through a library of books and films, lectures, conferences, exhibits and other activities, on the St. Louis campus and at four campuses in Europe and in the community. Contact Linda Woolf.

573. **Institute for Peace and Justice* (1970) (org).

4144 Lindell Blvd., Suite 408, St. Louis 63108; (314) 533-4445; *ipj@ipj-ppj.org; www.ipj-ppj.org*

Wide range of peace and justice activities. In 1996 created the Family Pledge of Nonviolence, the School/Classroom Pledge, the Campus Pledge, and the Congregation/Parish Pledge, as part of the founding of the Families Against Violence Advocacy Network (FAVAN). Kathleen McGinnis, Dir.

574. **World Holiday for Peace, United Nations Day, October 24* (1971) (org).

PO Box 78189, St. Louis, 63178-8189.

A campaign by Dorothy Schneider to create a world holiday for peace. She initiated U.N. General Assembly Resolution 2782 (Dec. 6, 1971), declaring October 24 United Nations Day an international holiday, and she has spent the rest of her life persuading governments to make the occasion official.

— *Montana (MT)* —

4 Sister Cities. / 26 Peace Poles.

HELENA, MT

575. **Helena Service for Peace and Justice (SERPAJ)/FOR* (1990) (org).

PO Box 11, Helena 59624; (406) 443-5671 or 433-0843; *serpaj@aol.com; fkromkowsk@aol.com; elliep@hotmail.com*

Affil. with Fellowship of Reconciliation in 1995. Offers nonviolence training, regular educational programs on nuclear weapons, etc., and a resource library. Has *Sister City*: Riveas, Nicaragua (since 1988). Pub. *Helena SERPAJ News.* Contact Frank Kromkowski or Ellie Parker.

576. *Jeannette Rankin Statue* (1980) (mem).

A larger-than-life statue of Rankin, created by the artist Terry Mimnaugh, stands in the Montana State Capitol, Helena, and in Statuary Hall, U.S. Capitol (1985).

Jeannette Rankin Statue by Terry Mimnaugh, Helena. Photograph courtesy the sculptor.

MISSOULA, MT

577. **Jeannette Rankin Peace Resource Center (JRPRC)* (1987) (org).

519 S. Higgins, Missoula, Montana, 59801; (406) 543-3955; *peace@jrpc.org; www.jrpc.org*

Jeannette Rankin (1880–1973), born in Missoula, was the first woman elected to the U.S. House of Representatives and the only member of Congress to oppose the entry of the United States into both world wars. Her leadership in the suffrage and other women's movements was always combined with the quest for peace. She campaigned against U.S. involvement in all wars. According to Joan Hoff-Wilson: "Her life epitomizes the experience of a western woman among a generation of female pacifists who, like Jane Addams, believed in a global society of peace—one they conceived of in terms of 'community and world housekeeping.' There has probably never been such an influential generation of pacifists and Jeannette Rankin remains one of its most memorable representatives." The JRPRC works for "community peace and social justice through action and education projects that promote tolerance and an understanding of diversity." Some activities: monthly book discussion group, discussions with young people about violence, sustainable living workshops, compassion activities, "World Passport Program": children learning about other cultures, "SISS Program": visits with international students and scholars. Sally Thompson, Exec. Dir.

Bayly, Ronn, Nancy Landgren, Susan Regele. "The Woman Who Voted No" (video). Univ. of Montana Materials Service.

Giles, Kevin. *Flight of the Dove: The Story of Jeannette Rankin.* Beaverton, OR: Touchstone Press, 1980.

Hoff-Wilson, Joan. "Peace Is a Woman's Job." *Montana: The Magazine of Western History* 30.1&2 (Jan. and April 1980).

McCarthy, Colman. *All of One Peace.* New Brunswick, NJ: Rutgers UP, 1994.

State of Montana. *Acceptance and Dedication of the Statue of Jeannette Rankin. Proceedings in the Rotunda, United States Capitol, Wednesday, May 1, 1985.* Washington, D.C.: United States Government Printing Office, 1987.

White, Florence. *First Woman in Congress: Jeannette Rankin.* New York: Messner, 1980. For young readers.

578. *World War I Opposition Painting* (1936).

This painting by Karl Yens (reported by Baber, location undetermined) is a tribute to the legislators who refused to vote for World War I. The inscription reads: "To the Memory of those Heroic Men, Senators and Representatives, who, having ignominy heaped upon them by a frenzied people, victims of mendacious propaganda, dared stand forth on those fateful days of April, 1917, to cast their votes against the resolution driving us into an iniquitous foreign war." Rankin's name is displayed prominently.

—— *Nebraska (NE)* ——

6 Sister Cities. / 16 Peace Poles.

LINCOLN, NE

579. *Nebraskans for Peace* (1969) (org).
941 'O' St., Suite 1026, Lincoln, 68508; (402) 475-4620; *nfpstate@aol.com*

NFP describes itself as the oldest statewide peace and justice organization in the nation. NFP goals are anti-war, non-violence, equality, anti-nuclear, and economic justice. Their motto: "there is no Peace without Justice." One of NFP's projects is their annual *Cat Lovers Against the Bomb* wall calendar fund-raiser (*catcal@aol.com; http://expage.com/page/CLAB*). (Three people and four cats came up with the idea in 1982, and the first calendar appeared in 1984). The Year 2000 calendar is dedicated to the Nobel Peace Prize laureates/United Nations "Decade for a Culture of Peace and Nonviolence." (Send your cat photos for calendar 2002). NFP also has a tax-deductible foundation, Nebraska Peace Foundation.

580. *Peace Memorial* (1995) (mem).
Antelope Park near 23rd & N St., Lincoln.

Dedicated to Albert and Idella Campbell Schrekinger by their families. The Schrekingers were devoted peaceworkers. Al was the Nebraska Assoc. of Social Workers representative on the Nebraskans for Peace Board for many years.

581. *Peacemaking Workshop* (1981) (org).
First United Methodist Church, 50th and St. Paul Ave., Lincoln.

An annual event that brings people together to seek ways to make peace a way of life. *Community Peacemakers*, an organization focusing on peace and justice, is an outgrowth of the Peacemaking Workshop and meets monthly at New United Methodist Church.

Peace Memorial, Lincoln. Photograph courtesy Jerry Shorney, Parks Operations, and Ben Knauss, Nebraskans for Peace.

582. *Prairie Peace Park* (1994) (mem & org).

Seven miles west of Lincoln on I-80, north side of highway off exit 388; office: 129 N. 10th St., #423. P.O. Box 95062. Lincoln, 68509; (402) 466-6622; *peace.lnk@ispi.net; www.igc.apc.org/PeacePark*

Open May 15–Sept. 15. Designed for both children and adults, the Park offers about forty indoor and outdoor interactive peace displays on its 27 acres to encourage visitors to create new ways to overcome violence, resolve conflicts, and heal the planet. "This Park offers visitors a vantage point to gain perspective to see that war, violence, and exploitation are not permanent, that we can develop a peaceful world, and how this is possible as we unite our minds together." Founded and directed by Don Tilley. Some features are:

Artistic replicas of 30,000 *Nuclear Weapons* covering 10,000 sq. ft.

200 feet long *World Population Exhibit.*

Seven Imperatives for the Creation of a Peaceful World.

The Samantha Smith Show: slides based on the story of a 10-year-old girl from Maine who helped inspire peace between the U.S. and the Soviet Union (see Maine).

Sadako Sculpture Display: 16 sculptures designed by children throughout the world inspired by the story of a Japanese girl's desire to live after the atomic bomb fell on Hiroshima (see New Mexico, Utah).

80 × 10 feet ceramic *World Peace Mural* created in Flagstaff, AZ, by over 40 international artists.

Children's Maze with over 50 large paintings from children from around the world.

Prairie Peace Park, west of Lincoln, Nebraska. Photograph courtesy Don Tilley, Director.

Human Body as Model for World Cooperation Exhibit.

Path of Hope: 13 violent practices the world has overcome.

War-Peace Path with 40 signs of destructive consequences of war, and suggested solutions.

Esperanto Exhibit: learn about Dr. Zamenhof, founder of this international language.

New exhibits in 1998 include *Eleanor Roosevelt* and *Peace Pilgrim*. And many more exhibits. The Park also sponsors a children's "Peace Camp" and has a traveling educational display for peace programs in schools in the mid–West. The Park's web page (over 100 pages) includes an International Forum with current issues discussed from a futuristic perspective: *http://www.igc.apc.org. PeacePark* Many publications available, including "Pursuit of Peace Path," "Thirteen Violent Practices We Have Overcome," "Visions: Artwork from the Prairie Peace Park" (accompanied by quotations by great peacemakers), "Interpretive Manual" (commentary on the "Visions" book by Don Tilley).

OMAHA, NE

583. *Justice and Peace Studies Program* (1993) (col).

Creighton University, Administration 425A, 2500 California Plaza, Omaha 68178; *rbjps@creighton.edu; http://puffin. creighton.edu/ccas/centers/jps.htm*

As a Catholic, Jesuit University, Creighton "is committed to 'the promotion of justice.'" JPS offers a co-major degree program and a Certificate program, and JPS courses are required for the Major in Sociology and Anthropology and the Major in Ministry. The Program also sponsors the annual Social Justice Lecture and other programs and speakers. Roger Bergman, Dir.

—— *Nevada (NV)* ——

4 Sister Cities. / 27 Peace Poles.

CACTUS SPRINGS, NV

584. *Madre del Mundo* (mem).
Located in The Temple of Goddess Spirituality, highway 95 south, Cactus Springs; PO Box 946, Indian Springs 89081; (702) 879-3263; *goddess@anv.net; www.sekhmettemple.com*
Mother and Child sculpted by Marsha Gomez.

LAS VEGAS, NV

585. *Nevada Desert Experience (NDE)* (1982) (org).
PO Box 46645, Las Vegas, 89114-6645; (702) 646-4814 or 631-5538; *nde@igc.org; www.shundahai.org/nde*

Nevada Desert Experience. Photograph courtesy Marc Page, Cindy Pile.

Same people who performed the Lenten Desert Experiences prior to naming themselves the NDE. Opposes the production and testing of nuclear and other weapons of mass destruction through a campaign of prayer, dialogue, and nonviolent direct action. Organizes two yearly gatherings at the Nevada Nuclear Test Site: the Lenten Desert Experience during the Christian season of Lent, and the August Desert Witness during the anniversary of the bombing of Hiroshima and Nagasaki, August 6 and 9. Dec. 29, 1999-Jan. 2, 2000, "Millennium 2000: Walking the Ways of Peace," candlelit procession at midnight Dec. 31. NDE is endorsed by many faith and peace organizations. Pub. *Desert Voices* newsletter and "Notes on Faith and Strategy: The Nevada Desert Experience Campaign to End Nuclear Testing" (23 pp.). Cindy Pile, Dir. (Oakland); Marc Page, Las Vegas Manager for NDE.

586. *Pace e Bene Franciscan Nonviolence Center* (1989) (org).

1420 W. Bartlett Ave., Las Vegas 89106; (702) 648-2281; *paceebene@compuserve.com*

Founded "to address the escalating plague of violence in our society through a deepening understanding and incarnating of the spirituality and practice of active nonviolence." The program, called "From Violence to Wholeness," includes workshops, retreats, and various resource materials. Pubs.: quarterly newsletter, *The Wolf*; book: *Roots of Violence in the US Culture: A Diagnosis Towards Healing.*

RENO, NV

587. *Center for Holocaust, Genocide, and Peace Studies* (1994) (col).

University of Nevada/402, Reno 89557; (775) 784-6767; *center@scs.unr.edu*; *www.unr.edu/chgps/blank.htm*

The Univ. of Nevada responded to the genocidal attacks and global escalation of intolerance and violence in the early 1990s by creating this Center, which offers public programming, research, publications, conferences, and interdisciplinary courses of study. A 19-credit minor program is designed to cover many disciplines and to challenge students to think critically about prejudice, hatred, dehumanization, geno-

cides, ways to resolve conflict, and nurturing peaceful social and political relationships. Pub. *Center News* (1995). Viktoria Hertling, Dir.

588. *Sierra Interfaith Action for Peace* (1988?) (org).

c/o Barbara Scott, MPH, RD, Dept. of Pediatrics, U of Nevada School of Medicine, 411 West 2nd St., Reno 89503; (775) 784-1945; *scottbj@scs.unr.edu*

Affil. with Fellowship of Reconciliation in 1998. Special concerns include nuclear testing, nuclear waste transport and storage, Jubilee 2000. Contact Barbara Scott.

— *New Hampshire* — *(NH)*

6 Sister Cities. / 59 Peace Poles.

CONCORD, NH

589. *Certificate in Conflict Resolution and Mediation* (1996) (col).

New Hampshire Technical Institute, Concord 03301; (603) 271-6951; *epedersen@tec.nh.us*; *www.conc.tec.nh.us/cert_crm.htm*

Supports career and community improvement in mediation. Courses include: Mediation with Youth and Families in School Systems. Contact Elizabeth Pedersen.

DURHAM, NH

590. *War and Peace Studies* (1992) (col).

English Dept., University of New Hampshire, Durham 03824; (603) 862-3973; *mferber@cisunix.unh.edu*; *www.unh.edu/undergrad-catalog/webspecial.html#*

A minor offers core and elective courses, internships, speaker's bureau, and events. Contact Michael Ferber.

HANOVER, NH

591. *War/Peace Program* (1984, 1986) (col).

Dartmouth College, Hanover.

Elise Boulding and Peter Bien had founded a "War/Peace Course" by 1984. In 1986 John and Elizabeth Baker endowed two new academic offerings: an interdisciplinary "Introduction to War/Peace Studies" and a War/Peace Seminar for the instructors. Later developed a course on International Conflict Negotiation and the Dartmouth Community Mediation Center. By 1988 the Baker endowment had grown to over $340,000, and John Baker's last gift of $50,000 in 1998 was the occasion for renaming the Endowment to the Jean Monnet Endowment for War/Peace Studies (Monnet was a hero to Baker). The Program now has an undergraduate minor, a monthly public speaker series, and student War and Peace Studies Fellows.

592. *World Federalist Association, NH and VT Chapter* (1992) (org).

80 Lyme Rd., Apt. 368, Hanover 03755; (603) 643-1787.

Recently campaigned successfully to persuade three towns to approve Abolition 2000, a resolution on eliminating all nuclear weapons, through the Town Meeting approach. Contact Anne Orton.

NASHUA, NH

593. *Center for Peace & Social Justice* (1997) (col).

Rivier College, 420 Main St., Nashua 03060; (603) 897-8481; *jannis@rivier.edu;akubick@rivier.edu*

Endeavors to put Catholic Social Teaching into practice, through teaching, scholarship, service, and outreach. Guest lectures (e.g., Nobel Peace Laureate Robert Muller, Congressman John Lewis) and workshops (e.g., with Colman McCarthy in Oct. 1999). Dr. Arthur Kubick, Dir.

PLYMOUTH, NH

594. *Peace and Justice Studies* (1999) (col).

Plymouth State College, Plymouth 03264; (603) 535-2287;

lsandy@mail.plymouth.edu; oz.plymouth.edu/~lsandy/home.html

The minor includes core and elective courses and an independent study. Leo Sandy, Coord.

—— *New Jersey* ——

21 Sister Cities. / 101 Peace Poles.

CAMDEN, NJ

595. *Leavenhouse* (1981) (org).

644 State St., Camden 08102; (609) 966-4596.

A Catholic Worker House for the poor, and supports Abolition 2000 and the South Jersey Campaign for Peace and Justice, while opposing the embargo and war against Iraq and the embargo against Cuba. Pub. annual newsletter *Leavenhouse*; the July 1999 number includes articles on the Pastors for Peace Cuba Caravan and the School of Americas; several articles in Spanish.

596. *National Stop the Violence Alliance* (1991) (org).

PO Box 1293, Camden, 08105-0339.

Promotes the end of violence in the U.S., through increased self-esteem, enhanced economic and educational opportunities, and community services.

COLTS NECK, NJ

597. *Dorothy Day Statue* (1996) (mem).

St. Mary Roman Catholic Church, Hwy. 34 and Phalanx Rd., Box H, Colts Neck, 07722.

Statue of Day seated on bench outside the church and dressed in a poor housedress and sweater and holding a book, indicating her many writings about the poor. The sculpture was executed by Brian Hanlon. The donor of the statue intended it to gaze at parishioners as they left the church. Day founded the Catholic Worker Movement. (Her papers are in the Marquette University Archives, Milwaukee, WI.). See PA.

JERSEY CITY, NJ

598. *Dorothy Day House* (1982) (mem).

35 Glenwood Ave., St. Peter's College, Jersey City, NJ 07306-5997.

Day founded the Catholic Worker Movement, dedicated to service to the poor and to world peace. A plaque inside the building has a photograph of Day on one side, and a written tribute to her on the other. The building houses several academic departments.

KENDALL PARK, NJ

599. **U.S./El Salvador Sister Cities* (1985) (org).

11 Cambridge Rd., Kendall Park 08824; (732) 398-9600; *usessc@igc.org; www.us-elsalvador-sisters.org*

A network of 24 U.S. groups in partnership with rural communities in El Salvador to further social justice, democracy, peace, and dignity there. Contact Michael Ring.

KEYPORT, NJ

600. **St. Joseph's Haiti Parish Twinning Program* (1994) (org).

St. Joseph's Church, 376 Maple Place, Keyport 07735; (732) 264-0322; *toniepax@aol.com*

Through the Parish Twinning Program of the Americas, St. Joseph's is coupled with the Catholic parish of Pignon in Haiti, to provide microcredit loans, money for teachers' salaries, the salary of an agronomist/veterinarian, and other projects. Antonia Malone, Coord.; Rev. Ronald Cioffi, Pastor. See: Sister Cities.

LINWOOD, NJ

601. **Coalition for Peace & Justice* (1981) (org).

321 Barr Ave., Linwood 08221; (609) 601-8537 or 601-8583; *norco@bellatlantic.net; http://members.bellatlantic.net/~norco*

A Chapter of Peace Action and affil. with Coalition for Peace Action. Covers the greater Atlantic City area (the southern coastal counties, 2nd Congressional District). Congressional lobbying, teachers convention booth, UN Week, Tax Day, Hiroshima Day. Norm Cohen, Exec. Dir.

MAPLEWOOD, NJ

602. **South Mountain Peace Action* (1957) (org).

101 Plymouth Ave., Maplewood 07040.

Originally SANE and then SANE/Freeze, now a chapter of Peace Action. Public meetings (e.g., a lecture by a visitor to Iraq), fund raisers, annual picnic. Contact Paul Surovell. Also: Betty Duffey (973) 763-6970.

MIDDLETOWN, NJ

603. *St. Francis of Assisi Statue* (1991) (mem).

St. Leo's The Great Church, Lincroft section of Middletown.

St. Francis (1181?–1226) founded the Franciscan order of the Roman Catholic Church, devoted to a life of poverty, service to the poor, and celebration of all life, the animals his "brothers and sisters."

MONTCLAIR, NJ

604. **New Jersey Peace Action* (1957) (org).

89 Walnut St., Montclair 07042; (973) 744-3263; *njsane@igc.apc.org; www.njpeaceaction.org*

Goals: abolish nuclear war, promote peaceful economy, end weapons trafficking, encourage non-military solutions to international conflicts, promote conflict resolution at all levels. NJPA lobbies for policy changes from UN and Congress to local towns, pub. a hotline on federal legislation and an annual voting record for every member of Congress on peace and justice issues, distributes fact sheets, holds public meetings on important issues, and works through the press.

Pub. *The New Jersey Peacemaker*, quarterly. Virginia Ahern, Dir.

NEW BRUNSWICK, NJ

605. *Center for Negotiation and Conflict Resolution (CNCR)* (1987) (col).

Bloustein School of Planning and Public Policy, Rutgers, The State University of New Jersey; New Brunswick 08901; (732) 932-2487; *cncr@rc.rutgers.edu*; *lstamato@rci.rutgers.edu*; *http://policy. rutgers.edu/CNCR/*

Provides education, research, service, and training in all aspects of mediation, through lectures, seminars, conferences, working groups, and assistance to state governments and courts, and to organizations abroad. Pub. a working papers series and a newsletter, *CNCR News*. Linda Stamato, Dep. Dir.

POMONA, NJ

606. **Conflict Resolution* (1981) (col).

Richard Stockton State College of New Jersey; Pomona 08240; (609) 652-4872; *Robert.Helsabeck@stockton.edu; www2. stockton.edu/academics/undergraduate/ social_and_behavioral/socy.html*

Undergraduate minor offered by the Sociology and Criminal Justice departments, five courses and a practicum. Undergraduate minor in Conflict and Peace Studies started in 1993. Contact Robert Helsabeck.

PRINCETON, NJ

607. **Coalition for Peace Action* (1980) (org).

40 Witherspoon St., Princeton 08542-3208; (609) 924-5022; *cfpa@eticomm.net*; *www.eticomm.net/~cfpa*

Began as the Coalition for Nuclear Disarmament, now a Peace Action Chapter (1988) serving central and south Jersey. CFPA lobbies elected representatives and organizes demonstrations, vigils, briefings, and similar activities. Has standing with the UN as a NGO. It sponsors a Youth for Peace program, the annual Interfaith Service and Conference, the Peaceful Toys Fair, and other educational events—speakers, fact sheets, videos. Its Concert Committee organizes occasional concerts for peace and funds. It presents inter-racial workshops on violence, RAVE (Real Alternatives to Violence for Everyone). To commemorate Hiroshima and Nagasaki 1999, CPA organized an evening of paper crane folding, music, dance performance, speakers, and candle floating on the pond. In Nov. 1999 CPA sponsored "The Challenge of Peace in the 21st Century" conference and interfaith service. Rev. Bob Moore, Exec. Dir.; L.L. Morgan-DuBreuil, Assoc. Dir.

608. **World Citizen Diplomats* (1991) (org).

PO Box 1484, Princeton 08541; (732) 556-9562; *loispeace@aol.com*; *www.worldpeace2000.com/wcd*

Organizes Peace Caravans to promote greater understanding among people worldwide through citizen to citizen engagement, staying in homes of local families. In 1998, WCD conducted its third Peace Caravan through 19 cities in 9 countries in Europe. Chapters in 9 countries throughout the world. Lois Nicolai, founder and director.

RIDGEWOOD, NJ

609. **Root and Branch Collective* (1991) (org).

10 East Ridgewood Ave. #19, Ridgewood 07450; (201) 251-9591; *bweiss@carroll.com*; *www.nonviolence.org/~nvweb/rbc*

Affil. with Fellowship of Reconciliation, promoting nonviolence in diverse ways—demonstrations, monthly coffeehouse meetings, tax resistance, street theater, etc. Contact Melissa Jameson

RUTHERFORD, NJ

610. **Pax Christi New Jersey* (1986) (org).

20B Hastings Ave., Rutherford 07070-1810; *cfay@worldnet.att.net*; *bgd@inpro.net*

Combines 15 local chapters, three of which are on college campuses and two in high schools.

Has an annual assembly in the Spring and annual retreat in the Fall. Offers a video lending library and pub. a newsletter twice a year. Carol Fay and Geri Braden-Whartenby, Coordinators.

SOUTH ORANGE, NJ

611. *School of Diplomacy and International Relations* (1997) (col).

Seton Hall University, 400 S. Orange Ave., South Orange 07079; (973) 275-2425; *diplomat@shu.edu;* *www.shu.edu/diplomacy*

Offers global studies and international management training for a Bachelor of Science and a Master of Arts in Diplomacy and International Relations for careers in global leadership. Internships with international organizations, diplomatic missions, governmental agencies, non-governmental organizations, and international businesses available. Clay Constantinou, Dean.

UPPER MONTCLAIR, NJ

612. *Dispute Resolution* (1995) (col).

Department of Legal Studies, Montclair State University; Upper Montclair 07043; (973) 655-7292; *nagleb@mail.montclair.edu;* *www.chss.montclair.edu/leclair/LS/dr.html*

A MA concentration of 8 courses consisting of core courses, a seminar in legal studies, and electives. Barbara Nagle, Coord.

VINCENTOWN, NJ

613. *South Jersey Campaign for Peace and Justice* (1982) (org).

PO Box 2366, Vincentown 08088; (609) 859-2785; *smilingjc@aol.com*

Began as the South Jersey Campaign for a Nuclear Weapons Freeze, affiliated with New Jersey SANE/FREEZE. Now affil. of New Jersey Peace Action. Serves the greater Camden area (Burlington & Camden Counties). Works to reduce military aggression and spending and to increase health care, education, housing, and other human needs through education and political action—demonstrations, rallies, lobbying Congresspeople. SJCPJ mounted weekly protests in front of Rep. Andrew's office against US/NATO bombing of Yugoslavia; commemorated the bombing of Hiroshima and Nagasaki, August 6, 1999; etc. Pub. a newsletter. Rick Walnut, Dir.

WAYNE, NJ

614. *Peace Pole* (1998) (mem).

At the Rainbow Montessori School in Wayne.

The school dedicated their Pole with a Parade of Nations, international foods, and a medley of peace songs.

— *New Mexico (NM)* —

7 Sister Cities. / 43 Peace Poles.

Many *Buddhist centers:* Racicot, Anna, "Stupas Along the Rio Grande," *Tricycle: The Buddhist Review* (Summer 1997) 59–63; "Buddhist Stupas Grace the Landscape," *New Mexico Magazine* (December 1998) 34–39.

ALBUQUERQUE, NM

615. *Dispute Resolution* (1997) (col).

School of Public Administration, University of New Mexico, Albuquerque 87131; (505) 277-3312; *tzane@unm.edu; spagrad@unm.edu;* *www.unm.edu/~spagrad/5AREAS1.htm*

Offers a concentration with MPA of 15 units and internship/practicum. Students in other graduate programs can take the certificate program. T. Zane Reeves, Dir.

ANTHONY, NM

616. *Peace Pole* (1998) (mem).

At the Casa de Ninos Montessori School in La Union, RR1, Box 537, Anthony, 88021; (505) 589-3756.

Peace Pole, Montessori School, La Union/Anthony. Photograph courtesy Mercedes Thrush.

An original Pole with the message "May Peace Prevail on Earth" in four languages (English, Spanish, Italian, Hindi). The messages are constructed of ceramic tiles carved and stained by the children. The tiles are attached to a wooden post topped by a dove and set in the middle of a Peace Garden, where the children plant flowers and plants from all over the world. The school celebrates three peace parades a year: United Nations Day, Martin Luther King's Day, and on March 31st, the conclusion of the peace curriculum. The projects were under the general direction of Mercedes and Ed Thrush.

ESPANOLA, NM

617. **International Peace Prayer Day* (1999) (porg).

Rt. 2, Box 132-D, Espanola 87532; (505) 753-4454, ext. 251; *www.peacecereal.com*

June 17, 2000, Jemez Mountains above Española, the 15th annual event, from sunrise (Aztec prayer) to sunset festival: broadcast on the Internet via Yahoo; music by Seal and Boukman Eksperyans; Kundalini Yoga; conflict resolution workshops; The World Peace Prayer Ceremony with flags of every nation; Breathwalk; creating the Peace Prayer Day Millennium sculpture; afternoon and evening concerts; dances; Woman of Peace Award and Man of Peace Award; the Sacred Healing Circle at sunset. Sponsored by Sikh Dharma of the Western hemisphere and Golden Temple Natural Foods. Siri Ram Kaur Khalsa, Exec. Dir.

SANTA FE, NM

618. *Children's Peace Statue, "A Peace Garden"* (1995) (mem).

Plaza Resolana, 401 Old Taos Hwy, Santa Fe 87501-1203; (505) 982-8539; 1-800-821-5145; *macnewmex@aol.com* or *kmj@aol.com; www.newmexico.com/ resolana*

The first U.S. peace statue initiated, designed, and paid for by children and teens. It began with a group of elementary school students in Albuquerque inspired by Sadako Sasaki. More than 50,000 names of young people who participated from 63 countries were read at the dedication. The statue, designed by Noe Martinez of Dallas,

Left: Children's Peace Statue, Santa Fe. Photograph courtesy Annabelle Patton. *Right:* Kagyu Shenpen Kunchab Buddhist Center Stupa, Santa Fe. Photograph courtesy Christina Stephenson.

Texas, was selected from among hundreds of drawings submitted (the sixteen final models are located at the Prairie Peace Park near Lincoln, NE). Martinez' statue is an 8-1/2 foot globe of the earth made up of bronze flowers and animals for the continents. Children regularly visit the statue and hang strings of folded paper cranes on it to constantly commemorate Sadako Sasaki. A small *statue of Sadako* stands at the entrance of the Plaza Resolana. The Children's Peace Statue was originally intended to stand in Los Alamos, but that city's council rejected it as critical of the creation of the atomic bomb there. Annually on August 6, Peace Day, a procession of children carrying garlands of paper cranes walk from March Field to the Children's Peace Statue at Plaza Resolana.

619. **Earth Journey, Inc.* (org).

HC 81, Box 618, Questa 87556;
(505) 586-1123.

Lama Chodruk, a student of Kalu Rinpoche

in the Kagyu lineage, leads daily practice. A 35-foot tall concrete stupa with a meditation room decorated with paintings by Cynthia Moku of Naropa Institute was completed in 1996.

620. **Kagyu Shenpen Kunchab (KSK)* Buddhist Center (1975) (org, mem).

751 Airport Rd, Santa Fe 87505;
(505) 471-1152.

Supports a continuous program of Vajrayana Buddhist teachings and meditation, following the teachings of Kalu Rinpoche in the Kagyu lineage, with facilities to which visiting lamas can be invited. A sixty-foot Bodhi Stupa and temple at the center (1986) is a place of pilgrimage to Buddhists. A bookstore offers an extensive selection of dharma literature. Contact Christina Stephenson, Manager, Noble Truth Bookstore (505-471-5336).

Coleman, Graham, ed. *A Handbook of Tibetan Culture.* Boston: Shambala, 1994.

621. **NetWorks Productions, Inc.* (1992) (org).

941 Rio Vista, Apt. A, Santa Fe 87501;
(505) 989-4482;
networks@networkearth.org;
www.networkearth.org

"We produce and disseminate media designed to inspire and educate about regenerating the Earth and caring for humanity." Projects: The Los Alamos Peace Project would transform the Los Alamos National Laboratory from manufacturing weapons of mass destruction into an "educational institution engaged in life affirming research and development." Cranes for Peace educates children around Los Alamos concerning the effects of nuclear warfare and strives to bring the Children's Peace Statue to Los Alamos. Shannyn Sollitt, Dir.

622. **Upaya Peace Institute* (1990) (org).

1404 Cerro Gordo Rd., Santa Fe 87501;
(505) 986-8518;
www.peacemakercommunity.org/Upaya

A center for reflection and learning about Buddhism. Roshi Joan Jiko Halifax, founder, and a founding teacher of the Zen Peacemaker Order (see: Village Zendo in NYC). She is the author of *A Buddhist Life in America* and other books.

— *New York State* —

32 Sister Cities. / 391 Peace Poles (includes NYC).

623. **Indian Peacemaker Museums*

Iroquois Indian Museum, PO Box 7, Caverns Rd., Howes Cave, 12092; Ganondagan State Historic Site, 1488 Victor-Holcomb Rd., Victor, 14564; Six Nations Museum, HCR 1, Box 10, Onchiota, 12989; Cayuga Museum, 203 Genesee St., Auburn, 13021; Akwesasne Museum, Akwesasne Cultural Center, RR 1, Box 14-C Route 37, Hogansburg, 13655; Seneca-Iroquois National museum, 794-814 Broad St., Salamanca, 14779

Although these museums are not dedicated to nonviolence, their historical roots can be traced to the Peacemaker. See *Manual for the Peacemaker* by Jean Houston.

ALBANY, NY

624. *Martin Luther King, Jr., Monument* (1993) (mem).

In Lincoln Park on a block of South Swan St. that has been renamed Martin Luther King, Jr., Boulevard, Albany.

An 8-foot statue of King standing before a separate, bas-relief sculpture of a crowd of his supporters. The statue uniquely depicts King "speaking with both arms outstretched and pivoting at the waist in the midst of a long stride, almost as if he were shouting directions while running." Sculptor: Eileen Barry. (See: Austin, TX).

Ringwald, Christopher. "King Memorial Dedicated in Albany."

Martin Luther King, Jr., Monument by Eileen Barry, Albany. Photograph courtesy Virginia Bowers, Historian, City of Albany.

625. **Peace & Change* (1975) (jour).

Dr. Donald Birn, Co-Exec. Ed.,
History, SUNY, Albany 12222-0001;
dbirn@csc.albany.edu;
Linda Forcey, Co-Exec. Ed.,
3041-3 Matecumbe Key Rd.,
Punta Gorda, FL 33955;
lforcey@binghamton.edu

Scholarly and interpretive articles "related to the creation of a peaceful, just, and humane society" by "building bridges between peace research, education, and activism."

AMENIA, NY

626. **The World Peace Prayer Society/ World Peace Sanctuary* (1991) (org).

26 Benton Rd., Wassaic 12592;
Rural community of Amenia,
two hours north of NYC;
(845) 877-6093;
sanctuary@worldpeace.org;
www.worldpeace.org;
www.theworldpeacesanctuary.org

Site of World Peace Prayer Ceremonies, the World Peace Festival, and Peace Pals activities. The Ninth Annual Amenia World Peace Festival occurred August 21, 1999. The flag of every nation was raised and the prayer "May Peace Prevail on Earth" was webcast on the Internet around the world. Established by the World Peace Prayer Society. The Sanctuary is also the home of the Peace Day Committee (1977) that celebrates the United Nations International Day of Peace. Vince Guerrero, Dir.

AMHERST, NY

627. **American Humanist Association* (1941) (org).

7 Harwood Drive, PO Box 1188,
Amherst 14226-7188; (800) 743-6646;
humanism@juno.com;
www.humanist.net

Advocates "a rational philosophy informed by science, inspired by art, and motivated by compassion." Has some 60 chapters. Pub. *The Humanist* magazine, ed. by Fred Edwords (Nov.-Dec. 1999 number includes articles on children's TV, discrimination in the Boy Scouts, atheism, belief in God, a vision of the year 2050).

BRONX, NY

628. *"Pacem in Terris"* (1983) (mem).

Manhattan College, Riverdale,
the Bronx.

A Japanese cherry tree and a plaque at the student center commemorates Pope John XXIII's 1963 letter "Pacem in Terris."

629. **Peace and Justice* (1988) (col).

Graduate School of Religion and
Religious Education, Fordham Univ.,
Bronx 10458; (212) 636-6424;
jelias@erols.com;
www.fordham.edu/gsre/Programs.html

MA in Church and Society/Peace and Justice Education. Contact John Elias.

630. **Peace and Justice Studies Program* (1989) (col).

Communication Dept, Fordham
University, Bronx 10458; (718) 817-4998;
andersen@fordham.edu;
www.fordham.edu/fcrh

An undergraduate certificate based on a core course and four related courses in a Jesuit Catholic context. Contact Robin Andersen.

631. **Peace Studies Program* (1971) (col).

Manhattan College, Riverdale,
the Bronx 10471; (718) 862-7943;
mgroarke@manhattan.edu;
www.manhattan.edu

Undergraduate program studies both negative and positive peace in areas of arms races, wars, economic-philosophical-social justice, conflict management, nonviolent philosophies, strategies of resistance, and world government. Peace Week Across the Curriculum in April 1999 engaged the faculty in speaking on peace and justice issues along with invited guests (Hugh Thompson, the helicopter pilot who stopped the My Lai massacre, John Grady, one of the Camden 28, and others). Margaret Groarke, Dir. (Joseph Fahey, first director).

BROOKLYN, NY

632. **United Nations Program* (1972) (col).

Long Island University, Brooklyn 11201; (718) 488-1041; *lester.wilson@liu.edu; www.liu.edu/un*

Certificate of 8 courses with MA and MS gives advanced training in the U.N. system. Lester Wilson, Dir.

BUFFALO, NY

633. **Buffalo Human Rights Center* (1985) (col).

School of Law, University of New York-Buffalo, Buffalo 14260-1600; (716) 645-6184; *hr-center@acsu.buffalo.edu; wings.buffalo.edu/soc-sci/pol-sci/hr*

Began as Graduate Group in Human Rights Law and Policy. Offers research and practice, direction and vision, in the study of international human rights law. Makau Mutua and Claude Welch. Jr., Directors.

634. **Buffalo WAND* (1980) (org).

88 Northledge Dr., Snyder 14226; (716)839-1917; 78 Brandy Wine Dr., Buffalo 14221; (716) 688-2608.

Chapter of Women's Action for New Directions. Affil. with Western New York Peace Center. Contact Judy Metzger.

635. **Western New York Peace Center* (1967) (org).

2123 Bailey Ave., Buffalo 14211; (716) 894-2123; *wnypeace@buffnet.net; www.wnypeace.org*

Originally established as a chapter of Clergy and Laity Concerned about Vietnam, WNYPC has opposed wars, Central American dictatorships, nuclear weapons, and militarism, and has taught nonviolent conflict resolution in schools, prisons, and elsewhere. Pub. bi-monthly newsletter *The Peace Center Report.* James Mang, Dir.

EAST MEADOW, NY

636. **Pax Christi Long Island* (1981) (org).

354 Cayuga Ave., E. Meadow 11554; (516) 579-2698; *msheridan2@compuserve.com*

Twice a year retreats; monthly protests at Nassau County Jail over prisoner abuse, and other demonstrations; study groups. Includes four chapters, Nassau Pax Christi (1998), etc. (Sr. Mary Fritz, Coord. 1991-99). Contact Veronica "Ronnie" Fellarath.

ELKA PARK, NY

637. **Catskill Bruderhof* (1985) (org).
Platte Clove Rd., HCR1 Box 24, Elka Park 12427; (518) 589-5103. (See Rifton, NY).

FT. TILDEN, NY

638. **EnviroVideo* (1988) (org).
PO Box 311, Ft. Tilden 11695; Free catalogue: (800) ECO-TV46; *www.envirovideo.com; http://home. earthlink.net/~envirovideo/*

Over 175 films, on such subjects as solar electricity, Three Mile Island, nuclear weapons in space. Its Enviro Close-Up TV Interview Show Series offers weekly half-hour interviews between Karl Grossman and environment, peace, and justice advocates.

GENESEO, NY

639. **Conflict Studies* (1994) (col).
Department of Psychology, SUNY, Geneseo 14454; (716) 245-5205; *duffy@geneseo.edu; www.geneseo. edu/~bulletin/academic_minors*

This minor of 27 semester hours increases understanding of the causes and management of conflict through core courses and concentration on one of 4 tracks. Karen Duffy, Coord.

HAMILTON, NY

640. **Peace Studies* (1969) (col).
Colgate University, Hamilton 13346; (315) 228-7806; *peace@mail.colgate.edu; www.departments.colgate.edu/peacestudies*

Undergraduate major (10 classes) and minor

(6 classes). Students are encouraged to participate in Colgate's Northern European study
abroad and to live at least one semester on campus at the Bunche House, where peace, justice,
and cooperative living are emphasized. Film and
lecture series also. Nigel Young, Dir.

HEMPSTEAD, NY

641. *Institute for the Study of Conflict
Transformation (ISCT)* (1999) (col).

School of Law, Hofstra University,
Hempstead 11549; (516) 463-5877;
lawgpm@Hofstra.edu;
www.Hofstra.edu/Law/isct/mission.html

Focusing on the concept of human connection, ISCT conducts research, develops and disseminates educational materials, presents training programs, organizes conferences, develops
publications, and other activities. Contact Robert Bush.

ITHACA, NY

642. *National War Tax Resistance
Coordinating Committee
(NWTRCC)* (1982) (org).

PO Box 6512, Ithaca 14851;
(800) 269-7464; (607) 277-0593;
nwtrcc@lightlink.com;
www.nonviolence.org/wtr

Coalition of war tax resistance groups. "We
oppose militarism and war and refuse to com-
plicitly participate in the tax system which supports such violence." "Through the redirection
of our tax dollars NWTRCC members contribute directly to the struggle for peace and justice for all." Specifically, the org. advocates the
U.S. Peace Tax Fund Bill. Provides pamphlets
and national contacts and counselors list. Pub.
newsletter, *More Than a Paycheck.* Founded and
directed by Karen Marysdaughter, 1991-99
(Monroe, ME). Mary Loehr, Coord.

643. *Peace Studies Program* (1970)
(org).

Cornell University, 130 Uris Hall,
Ithaca 14853-7601; (607) 255-6484;
eds3@cornell.edu;
www.einaudi.cornell.edu/PeaceProgram

An interdisciplinary program for research and
teaching on the problems of war and peace, arms
control and disarmament, and in general collective violence. Other concerns: global environmental change, social justice, ethnicity and international conflict, and women in the military.
Sponsors speakers from around the world, weekly
seminars, monthly dinner research seminars. Research supported by university and grants; for example, chemical weapons disposal, race relations
and U.S. foreign policy, regional cooperation in
eastern Europe. Charter member of the Cornell
Conflict Resolution Network (1998). Offers the
Marion and Frank Long Endowment Fund
stipend to support graduate training in peace
studies, and the Harrop and Ruth Freeman Prize
for a graduating senior who has demonstrated a
commitment to working for world peace. Pubs.:
numerous books and articles by faculty and graduate students. Elaine Scott, Dir.

LOUDONVILLE, NY

644. *Peace Studies Program* (1985) (col).

Siena College, Loudonville 12211;
(518) 783-4190; *mcglynn@siena.edu;*
*www.siena.edu/catalog/peace_studies_*
program.html

An undergraduate certificate of 24 credit
hours in a Catholic context. Contact Edward
McGlynn.

MECHANICVILLE, NY

645. *Alternatives to Violence Project*
(1975) (org).

44 N. Main St., Apt. 3, Mechanicville
12118; (518) 664-7198; *janetlugo@aol.com*

AVP started in Greenhaven Prison, Pough-
keepsie, NY, for nonviolence training in prisons. Today it conducts workshops and training
for a nonviolent life in all areas of society. Contact Janet Lugo. (See: #666).

NEW ROCHELLE, NY

646. *Peace and Justice Studies* (1977)
(col).

Center for Campus Ministries,
Iona College, New Rochelle 10801;

Fellowship of Reconciliation, Nyack. Photograph courtesy Lise St. Amant.

(914) 633-2630; *mhovey@iona.edu;*
www.iona.edu/stu_life/ministry/peace.htm

Established at the invitation of the Association of Catholic Colleges and Universities to create one of seven pilot programs in peace and justice education at Catholic institutions in the U.S. The minor program includes the Introduction to Peace Studies and related courses, and offers a summer Peace Institute in Ireland. Michael Hovey, Dir.

• NEW YORK CITY *see* entries 676–760

NYACK, NY

647. **Fellowship of Reconciliation* (International FOR 1914, U.S. FOR 1915) (org).

521 N. Broadway, PO Box 271, Nyack, 10960; (914) 358-4601; *fornatl@igc.apc.org;* *www.nonviolence.org*/for

Composed of people who explore the power of love, truth, justice, nonviolence, and reconciliation in resolving human conflict. Carries out campaigns advocating demilitarization, nuclear disarmament, racial and economic justice, and the peaceful resolution of conflict. Its Peacemaker Training Institute trains youth in nonviolence. Organized a 40-days People's Campaign for Nonviolence in Washington, DC, July 1– Aug. 9, 2000, to demand racial, social, and economic justice and demilitarization. Offers Peace Internships in communications, organizing, the international program, and the youth program. Pub. a bi-monthly magazine, *Fellowship.* Has some 50 local groups and affiliates. John Dear, Exec. Dir.

648. **Jewish Peace Fellowship* (1941) (org).

Box 271, Nyack 10960-0271; (914) 358-4601, ext. 39; *jpf@forusa.org;* *www.jewishpeacefellowship.org*

Founded by Rabbi Abraham Cronbach, Jane Evans, and Rabbi Isidor Hoffman to provide counseling for Jewish conscientious objectors to war. "We share a belief that all conflict can and should be replaced with nonviolent means of conflict resolution....We are against the continuing spending on wars past, present, and future, which takes away from human needs." JPF also opposes the death penalty and supports nuclear disarmament and social justice. Gives the Abraham Joshua Heschel Award to honor those who work to promote nonviolence in the Jewish community. Pub.: literature on nonviolence in the Jewish tradition; quarterly *Shalom: The Jewish Peace Letter*. Affil. With Fellowship of Reconciliation. Rabbi Philip Bentley, Hon. Pres.; Carol Toll Oppenheim and Murray Polner, Co-chairs; Joyce Bressler, Admin. Dir.

649. **Muslim Peace Fellowship/Ansar as-Salam* (1994–gradually) (org).

PO Box 271, Nyack 10960;
(914) 358-4601; *mpf@forusa.org*;
www.nonviolence.org/mpf

For "peace and justice-oriented Muslims of all backgrounds," teaching "integrity and kindness," "benevolence and compassion." Current projects: ending Iraqi sanctions, Progressive Muslim Women's Working Group, SeedHouse, Families Against Violence, Interfaith Pilgrimage, and others. Affil with Fellowship of Reconciliation. Pub.: newsletter *As-Salamu 'Alaykum*. Rabia Terri Harris, Coordinator.

650. **People's Campaign for Nonviolence* (1999) (org).

Box 271, Nyack 10960; (914) 358-4601;
peoplescampaign@forusa.org

For forty days in the summer of 2000, people gathered in Washington, DC, to call for an end to our culture of violence and injustice, and for the creation of a nonviolent, non-oppressive society with an economy that funds human needs and all life on the planet, and for substantial cuts in military spending, the abolition of nuclear weapons and all weapons of mass destruction, and the pursuit of a nonviolent foreign policy. Leading peace and justice groups from around the country brought thousands of people to spend one day or more in vigil and peaceful protest.

651. **United Church of Christ Fellowship of Reconciliation* (1982, 1998) (org).

UCC-FOR, PO Box 271, Nyack 10960;
uccfor@nonviolence.org; *uccfor@juno.com*;
www.nonviolence.org/uccfor

Seeks "to replace the system of violence, war, exploitation, exclusion, and injustice with Jesus'

Beloved Community of nonviolence, peace, and justice." In the summer of 1999, UCCFOR was focusing on the School of Americas, the Jubilee 2000 Project (Third World debt), and hate crimes. John Steitz, Convenor (*ucc18360@juno.com*).

PETERSBURG, NY

652. *Grafton Peace Pagoda* (1993) (org).

Petersburg, Rensselaer County. From Albany, take Rt. 787 N. to Rt. 7 East, go right on Rt. 278, take left Rt. 2 east to Grafton. Address: Nipponzan Myohoji, Grafton Peace Pagoda, RD 1, Box 308A, Petersburg, NY 12138.

Founded by American Indians and the Buddhist nun, Jun Yasuda, who is a disciple of Nichidatsu Fuji (1885–1985). Fuji traveled the world, chanting, "Na-Mu-Myo-Ho-Ren-Ge-Kyo," "One earth, one sky, entirely at peace," referring to the Lotus Sutra, which contains the Buddha's most important teachings about peace, nonviolence, and the sacredness of life. Over 80 of these pagodas (or *stupas*) have been built throughout the world. This Pagoda cost only $50,000 because so much work and materials were contributed free. The Pagoda is 165 feet high; the dome is 130 feet in diameter. The white dome is made of gunite, the concrete mixture used in swimming pools. The spire, representing Buddhism's eight states of enlightenment, is made of seven white concentric circles topped by a gold "flame" symbol. Hindu, Christian, Muslim, Jewish, Bahá'í, and Buddhist faiths were represented at the dedication.

Grondahl, Paul. "Grafton's Pagoda's a Prayer in Wood and Stone." *Times Union* (June 24, 1993), C1, C4.

Keepnews, James. "Walking the Walk." *Metroland* (July 27–Aug. 2, 1995) 13.

RIDGEWOOD, NY

653. **Earth Day* (1970) (org).

Earth Trustees, Inc., 1933 Woodbine St., Ridgewood 11385; *www.earthsite.org*;
www.earthdayone.org; *www.wowzone.com/wow-ed.htm* (sister site in Canada).

Offers 77 Theses to foster the peaceful nurture and care of the Planet Earth, and celebrates Earth Day on March 21 of each year. Pub. *The*

Grafton Peace Pagoda, Petersburg. Photograph courtesy the Rev. Thomas Kearns.

Daily Gist of environmental news from around the world (*www.gristmagazine.com/grist/gist*). Founded by John McConnell. In 1999, Earth Day/Earth Trustee and WOW (Wish Only Well) joined forces to "defeat the hate, fear, and violence that threatens civilization."

RIFTON, NY

654. **Bruderhof Video Productions* (1999) (org).

Rt. 213, PO Box 903, Rifton 12471; (914) 658-8351; *rayala@bruderhof.com*

655. **The Revolution Center* (1998) (mus, org).

In Rifton; P. O. Box 517, New Paltz, 12561.

The Center, based out of the Woodcrest Bruderhof, houses an art gallery, a museum celebrating the history of the Bruderhof movement, educational programs, and a magazine. The Bruderhof is a nonviolent communal movement guided by the life and teaching of Jesus.

656. **Woodcrest Bruderhof* (1954) (org).

Box 703, Rt. 213, Rifton 12471; (914) 658-8351; *www.bruderhof.org*

"Christ's spirit and teachings in the Sermon on the Mount...are both the goal and foundation of our communal life. We have no private property but share everything in common." Rooted in Anabaptism and the Radical Reformation of the early 1500s, in 1920, German theologian Eberhard Arnold, his wife Emmy, and others founded a rural settlement, until expelled by the Nazis in 1937. Members moved to England, Paraguay, and then to the United States, where today there are several Bruderhofs in New York, Pennsylvania, Tennessee, and Connecticut.

ROCHESTER, NY

657. **Institute for the Study of Democracy and Human Rights* (1997) (col).

St. John Fisher College, Rochester 14618; (716) 385-7311; *hillman@sjfc.edu*; *www.sjfc.edu/academ/isdhr.htm*

The Revolution Center located in Bruderhof Museum, New Paltz. Photograph courtesy Christine Keiderling.

A joint project of the College and Central Univ. of Venezuela, funded by USIA to facilitate faculty exchanges for curriculum development, research, and conferences. Richard Hillman, Dir.

658. **Rochester Catholic Worker* (1941) (org).

St. Joseph's House of Hospitality of Rochester, PO Box 1062, Rochester 14603; 402 S. Avenue, Rochester 14620; (716) 2332-3262.

Still functioning in same building bought in 1941, offering meals and shelter, and peace and justice education. Pub. a newsletter: the spring 1999 issue includes articles on the bombings of Yugoslavia and Just War Theory.

659. **Rochester WAND* (1997) (org).

166 Reeves Rd., Rochester 14467; (716) 334-0758.

Chapter of Women's Action for New Directions. Seeks conversion of war industry to domestic and world needs. Contact Julie Fausette.

ROCKVILLE, NY

660. **International Peace and Justice Studies* (1983) (col).

Philosophy Dept., Molloy College, Rockville Center 11571; (516) 678-5000 ext 307; *smayo@molloy.edu*; *www.molloy.edu*

Undergraduate major and minor in Catholic context seek to create actively nonviolent peace-making citizens. Stephen Mayo, Chair.

ST. BONAVENTURE, NY

661. **The Acorn* (1989) (jour, col)

St. Bonaventure Univ., St. Bonaventure 14778; (716) 375-2275.

A biannual journal "devoted to the examination of the theory and practice of nonviolence, especially as it relates to the philosophies of Gandhi and King"; founded by Ha Poong Kim. The Fall 1998 number contained four articles on Aung San Suu Kyi's relation to Gandhi, nonviolence and human rights, language and peace, and inner peace.

662. *Nonviolence Major and Minor/The Center for Nonviolence* (1981) (col).

St. Bonaventure University, St. Bonaventure 14778; (716) 375-2275; *bgan@sbu.edu; www.sbu.edu/nonviolence*

The Center teaches nonviolence as both a technique and a way of life, in a Franciscan Catholic affiliation but focusing on people such as Gandhi and King. Major and minor degrees in nonviolence are offered also. Barry Gan, Director.

SAUGERTIES, NY

662a. *World Pen Pals* (1950) (org).

PO Box 337, Saugerties 12477; (914) 246-7828; *www.world-pen-pals.com*

Encourages international friendship and cultural understanding.

SCHENECTADY, NY

663. *One Hundred Picture Books for Peace* (1998) (org).

Mohawk Valley library Association, 858 Duanesburg road, Schenectady 12306-1095.

A list of books for children that show a variety of situations where conflict is managed creatively and nonviolently.

SHOREHAM, NY

664. *Peace Pole* (1988) (mem).

In Shoreham.

Planted by the students of Wading River High School in honor of Global Education Day. A community dedication was later held on the International Day of Peace.

SUNNYSIDE, NY

665. *New York F.O.R.* (1998) (org).

39-30 46th St., Sunnyside 11104-1408;

(718) 786-2413 (home), (212) 833-3223 (work); *newyorkFOR@aol.com*

Meeting each month, emphasizes study of nonviolence and support of NYC peace actions, in 1999-2000 focused on Iraqi sanctions and death penalty. Contact: Kate Brennan.

SYRACUSE, NY

666. *Alternatives to Violence Project/USA* (1975) (org).

821 Euclid Ave., Syracuse 13210; (713) 747-9999; *avp@avpusa.org; http://avpusa.org; www.avpi.freeserve. co.uk/avplinks.htm* (international).

Its mission is "to empower people to lead nonviolent lives through affirmation, respect for all, community building, cooperation and trust." Begun by prison inmates and Quakers at Green Haven Prison, AVP now through local groups gives workshops all around the U.S. and in a dozen countries abroad to teach people conflict resolution skills.

667. *Program on the Analysis and Resolution of Conflicts (PARC)* (1986) (col).

Syracuse University, Maxwell School of Clitizenship & Public Affairs, 410 Maxwell Hall, Syracuse 13244; (315) 443-2367; *parc@maxwell..syr.edu; www.maxwell.syr.edu/parc/parcmain.htm*

Concentrates on theory-building and research aimed at preventing violence and transforming international conflicts into peace. Its activities also include an undergraduate minor in the Program in Nonviolent Conflict and Change, conferences, public lecture series, graduate teaching and research assistantships, Seminar on Multilateral Peacekeeping, Summer Institute on Creative Conflict Resolution, a Certificate of Achievement in the Syracuse Social Movements Initiative, Campus Mediation Center, and Conflict Resolution Training Group. Pub. include a newsletter, *Parc News*, books and articles, and a working papers series. Regional offices in New England, New York, Mid Atlantic, South East, Midwest, South Central, Rocky Mountain. Robert Rubinstein, Director.

668. *Syracuse Fellowship of Reconciliation.* (around 1920) (org).

8390 Cazenovia Rd., Malnius 13104; (315) 682-6694.

Meets several times a year for potluck and speaker, supports various local and national peace actions.

669. *Syracuse Peace Council* (1936) (org).

924 Burnet Ave., Syracuse 13203; (315) 472-5478; *pnl-spc@juno.com*

Dedicated to educate, organize, and agitate for world peace and social justice. Has speakers, annual spring dinner, demonstrations, press conferences. Pub. *Peace Newsletter.* Contact Beth Mosley or Paul Pearce.

TROY, NY

670. *FOR Troy* (reconvened 1998) (org).

PO Box 1511, Troy 12180; (518) 272-1468.

Focuses include nonviolence education, prejudice awareness, and Central America, through public actions, building a Resource Library, annual Martin Luther King, Jr. Day Dinner, and other activities. Contact Nora McDowell.

ULSTER PARK, NY

671. *Maple Ridge Bruderhof* (1985) (org).

10 Hellbrook Lane, Ulster Park 12487; (914) 339-6680. (See Rifton, NY).

WHITE PLAINS, NY

672. *East Timor Action Network* (1992) (org).

PO Box 1182, White Plains 10602; (914) 428-7299; *charlie@etan.org;* *info@etan.org; www.etan.org*

Supported the struggle by the people of East Timor for self-determination; now assisting the new country to gain genuine independence under the transitional UN administration. Pub. newsletter *Estafeta* (Portuguese for "messenger"). Offices also in Washington, DC, Chicago, and Brooklyn. Charles Scheiner, National Coordinator.

Hine, Sam. "Agony in East Timor Continues." *Active for Justice* (March 2000) 2 (excerpted from "Death Watch in East Timor," *The Plough Reader,* Spring 2000).

673. *Westchester Peoples Action Coalition* (1974).

255 Dr. Martin Luther King Jr. Blvd, White Plains 10601; (914) 682-0488; *info@wespac.org; www.wespac.org*

A peace, social justice, and environmental organization, focusing on nuclear dangers, militarism, redirecting the military budget to socially needed uses, invasions of foreign countries, death penalty, racism, sexism, and homophobia. Pub. semi-annual newsletter. "Speaks for over 5000 families." Mark Jacobs, Dir.

YONKERS, NY

674/5. *Hudson River Peacemaker Center* (1999) (org).

21 Park Ave., Yonkers 10701; *slkealy@aol.com; www.* *peacemakercommunity.org/hrpc/index.htm*

Offers "a meditation schedule with engagement in social action and interpersonal sharing in an interfaith setting." Revs. Sally Kealy and Francisco Lugoviña, Coordinators. Part of the Peacemaker Community (*www.Peacemaker Community.org*).

NEW YORK CITY

676. *A. J. Muste Memorial Institute* (1974) (org).

339 Lafayette St., 10012; tel: (212) 533-4335; web site: *www.nonviolence.org/ajmuste;* e-mail: *ajmusteinst@igc.org*

Makes small grants to groups doing nonviolent organizing for social change. Muste was an activist pacifist of the Fellowship of Reconciliation, the War Resisters League, and the Congress of Racial Equality, and a writer, theorist, and theologian of the left.

Robinson, Jo Ann. *Abraham Went Out: A Biography of A. J. Muste.*

677. *American Friends Service Committee, New York Metropolitan Region* (1948) (org).

15 Rutherford Place, New York City, 10003; (212) 598-0950; *anaples@afsc.org*

Serves 13 counties in NY State and 10 in NJ. Focuses on conflict resolution, criminal justice, and immigrant rights. (National office: Philadelphia).

678. *Amnesty International USA* (1961) (org).

322 8th Ave., 10001-4808; (212) 807-8400; *www.amnesty-usa.org*; *www.organic.com.amnesty* (also Washington, D.C.: 600 Pennsylvania Ave. SE, 20003; [202] 544-0200; and regional offices).

AI "is a worldwide voluntary movement that works to prevent some of the gravest violations by governments of people's fundamental human rights" as enshrined in the Universal Declaration of Human Rights. They would free all prisoners of conscience; ensure fair and prompt trials for political prisoners; abolish the death penalty, torture, and other cruel treatment of prisoners; and end extrajudicial executions and disappearances. AI has over one million members in over 150 countries with more than 6,000 local groups in over 70 countries. Won Nobel Peace Prize in 1997. Pub. *Amnesty Action* quarterly. Executive Dir.: William Schulz.

In 1999 AI and the Sierra Club created the Just Earth! Program for action on Human Rights and the Environment (*http://rights.amnesty.org/justearth/index.html*).

679. *Anne Frank Center USA* (1977) (org).

584 Broadway, Suite 408, between Houston and Prince Streets in SoHo; *afc@annefrank.com; www.annefrank.com*

Dedicated to preserving the legacy of Anne Frank, to educating people about the causes, instruments, and dangers of discrimination and violence through the story of Anne Frank. Since 1993 the Center has provided traveling displays. Pub. newsletter, *Legacy*, gives Spirit of Anne Frank Awards, and offers workshops and exhibits in their expanded headquarters. Joyce Apsel, Dir. of Education.

680. *Anti-Defamation League* (1913) (org).

823 United Nations Plaza, NYC 10017; (212) 490-2525 or 885-7700; *www.adl.org*

Committed to countering hatred, bigotry, and all other forms of prejudice, and to teaching the value of diversity and pluralism. One means of accomplishing this goal is their resource catalog offering videos, books, posters, curriculum materials, teachers' discussion guides, and classroom activities. Abraham Foxman, National Dir. (In the US ADL has a Washington and many regional offices, and an office in Downsview, ON.)

681. *Bayard Rustin Memorial* (1989) (mem).

Ralph Bunche Park across from the United Nations Plaza and near the sculpture of Bunche and the Isaiah Wall.

A small marble base holds a plate with this inscription: "Bayard Rustin, March 17, 1912–August 24, 1987, Human Rights Leader. 'The principal factors which influenced my life are nonviolent tactics, constitutional means, democratic procedures, respect for human personality, a belief that all people are one.'"

Anderson, Jervis. *Bayard Rustin, Troubles I've Seen: A Biography*. New York: HarperCollins, 1997.

Singer, Bennett. "American Socrates: The Life of Bayard Rustin." *Fellowship* (May-June 2000) 23.

Bayard Rustin Memorial, New York City. Photograph courtesy Walter Naegle, Exec. Dir. Bayard Rustin Fund.

682. **Business Leaders for Sensible Priorities* (1996) (org).

130 William St., Suite 700, NYC 10038; (212) 964-1109; *thefolks@businessleaders.org*

Founded by ice cream mogul Ben Cohen to advocate reducing the military budget by 15% (approx. $40 billion/year) and investing the savings in "state and local priorities that will ensure a safe, strong, and prosperous future for all of us."

Bleifuss, Joe. "Good News, for a Change." *In These Times* (July 11, 1999) 3.

683. **The Catholic Worker* (1933) (org).

St. Joseph House, 36 East 1st St., NYC 10003; (212) 254-1640; Mary House, 55 E. 3rd St. (212) 777-9617.

The NYC CW aims "to live in accordance with the justice and charity of Jesus Christ." Recent peace activities: demonstrations v. bombings of Yugoslavia, protests and street theater v. Iraqi sanctions, annual demonstrations on Hiroshima Day. Pub. *The Catholic Worker*, the organ of the Catholic Worker Movement, seven times a year, ed. by Sabra McKenzie-Hamilton, Lucia Russett, and Patrick Wynne. CW was founded by Dorothy Day and Peter Maurin.

684. **Center for the Study of Human Rights* (1978) (col).

School of International and Public Affairs, Columbia Univ., NYC 10027; (212) 854-3139; *jpm2@columbia.edu; www.columbia.edu/cu/humanrights*

Supports human rights programs, courses, and research on campus, in the nation, and overseas. Operates the Human Rights Advocates Training Program for professionals. Pub. annual newsletter and occasional volumes, including a three-volume series of human rights documents: *Twenty-Five Human Rights Documents, Women and Human Rights,* and *Religion and Human Rights.* J. Paul Martin, Exec. Dir.

685. **Center for War, Peace, and the News Media* (1985) (org).

New York University, Dept. of Journalism and Mass Communication, 418 Lafayette St., Suite 554, NYC 10003; (212) 998-7960; *war.peace.news@nyu.edu; www.nyu.edu/cwpnm.*

Dedicated to supporting journalists and news organizations to sustain an informed and engaged citizenry, with particular focus on media coverage of nuclear weapons, international security, and Russia. Developed The Press and the Arms Race graduate-level course in journalism at NYU. Co-sponsors the Olive Branch Awards for reporting on nuclear weapons issues. Also has office in Boston. Pub. *Deadline* bimonthly. Founded by Robert Karl Mannoff, Dir.

686. **Center for War/Peace Studies* (1966) (org).

180 W. 80th St., Ste. 211, NYC 10024; (212) 579-4206 (212) 475-1077; *hudson@cwps.org*

Creating structures to move the world toward cooperation under law, arms control and disarmament, and a Middle East settlement. Promulgator of the Binding Triad System for global decision-making and law by which two amendments to the United Nations Charter would greatly strengthen the General Assembly, transforming it into a limited world federal government or global parliament. Richard Hudson, Exec. Dir.

687. **Citizen Soldier* (1970) (org).

175 Fifth Ave., Ste 2135, NYC 10010; (212) 679-2250.

Works to expose and challenge the unchecked power of the Pentagon, especially by defending individual GIs who stand up against illegal or unsafe military policies. Recent projects: mandatory anthrax vaccine program, depleted uranium shells, nuclear weapons in space. Tod Ensign, Dir.

688. **Coexistence Initiative* (1997) (org).

Slifka Family Enterprises, 477 Madison Ave., 8th fl., NYC 10022; *aboldt@halcyonpartnerships.com*

Advances a vision of a world in which different kinds of people are tolerated and coexist peacefully, by helping to create public support and global institutions for conflict resolution and coexistence. Mareike Junge, Network Coordinator (mareike@worldforum.org).

689. **Committee in Solidarity with the People of El Salvador (CISPES)* (1980) (org).

PO Box 1801, NYC 10159; (212) 229-1290; *cispesnatl@igc.org; www.cispes.org/contact.html; www.cispes.org*

CISPES supports the working people of El Salvador. Pub. *El Salvador Watch* newsletter. Cherrene Horazuk, Dir.

690. **Conflict Resolution* (1986) (col).

Dept. of Organization and Leadership, Columbia Univ. Teachers College, NYC 10027; (212) 678-3289 or 3402; *pc84@columbia.edu; idm15@columbia.edu; www.tc.columbia.edu/~academic/icccr/ Gradp1.htm*

Offers a certificate with MA and Ph.D. and for non-matriculated students also. Basic Theory and Practice of 12 credits is for personal skill development; Train-the-Trainer, 6 additional credits, is for professionals. Peter Coleman, Co-Dir.

691. **Culture of Peace Project, UNESCO* (1998) (org).

www.unesco.org/cpp/uk/index.htm

UNESCO aims to promote values, attitudes, and behaviors leading to peaceful solutions to problems through innovative activities. See: *Manifesto 2000.*

692. **Disarm Education Fund* (1976) (org).

36 East 12th St., NYC 10003; (212) 475-3232; *disarm@igc.apc.org*

In 1994, Disarm launched its Cuban Medical Project, which has delivered $17,750,000 worth of medical supplies to Cuba in opposition to the U.S. embargo. Ramsey Clark, Pres.; Bob Schwartz, Exec. Dir.

693. **Dispute Resolution Consortium (DRC)* (1993) (col)

John Jay College of Criminal Justice, CUNY, 899 Tenth Ave., 5th Fl., New York 10019; (212) 237-8692; *mvolpe@jjay.cuny.edu; http://web.jjay.cuny.edu/~dispute*

The first conflict resolution coalition in NYC, DRC combines public service, curriculum development, research, theory-building, and technical assistance. Annual conference, seminars, a resource Center, database. Pub. a newsletter, a *Directory of Dispute Resolution Programs in the New York City Metropolitan Area,* and a Research Working Paper Series. Maria Volpe, Dir.

694. **Dispute Resolution Program* (1981) (col).

See preceding entry. This undergraduate Certificate includes course work and internship. Course examples: Sociology of Conflict Resolution, Drama Techniques in Crisis Intervention. Maria Volpe, Dir.

695. **Doctors Without Borders/Médecins Sans Frontières* (1971) (org).

6 East 39th St., 8th Fl, NYC 10016; (212) 679-6800; *doctors@newyork.msf.org; www.doctorswithoutborders.org*

Provides medical assistance to victims of natural disasters and wars by sending medical volunteers and supplies to counteract malnutrition and disease and to provide emergency and preventive care. In 1999 more than 2,000 volunteers representing 45 nationalities worked in over 80 countries. Awarded the Nobel Peace Prize in 1999. Joelle Tanguy, Exec. Dir.; James Orbinski, Internat. Council Pres.

696. **Economists Allied for Arms Reduction* (1989) (org).

211 East 43rd St., Rm. 1501, NYC 10017; *ecaar@igc.org; www.ecaar.org*

ECAAR focuses on two main areas: the military and political economy of the U.S. in relation to international peace and security, and relations with ECAAR-Russia. To further these enterprises, ECAAR organizes panels at the annual meetings of the American Economic Assoc. and the American Social Science Assoc., and seminars in various cities; it publishes a newsletter, *ECAAR Newsnetwork,* Kelley Bates, Ed.; it maintains a web-site with a global register of arms experts and a bibliography of current work; and it works with other national ECAAR orgs. Lucy Webster, Exec. Dir.

697. **Educators for Social Responsibility Metropolitan Area* (1998) (org).

475 Riverside Drive, Rm 554, NYC 10115; (212) 870-3318, ext. 2; *esrmetro@igc.org*

Advocates the education of young people about the danger of nuclear weapons and supports the movement for nuclear abolition. Sponsors talks and conferences. Pub. monthly newsletter, *Action News.* Tom Roderick, Exec. Dir.

698. *Environmental Defense (E)* (1967) (org).

257 Park Avenue South,
NYC 10010; (212) 505-2100;
www.environmentaldefense.org

Was Environmental Defense Fund (EDF). Concentrates on four areas: biodiversity, climate, health, and oceans. Claims 300,000 members and income of $31.4 million. Offices also in DC, CA, CO, NC, and TX. Pub. *Environmental Defense Newsletter* bimonthly report to members (8pp. April 2000); longtime former editor: Norma Watson; present editor: Peter Klebnikov (pklebnikov@environmentaldefense.org). Fred Krupp, Exec. Dir.

699. *Fund for New Priorities in America* (1969) (org).

171 Madison Ave., R 1006, NYC 10016;
(212) 685-8848.

Promotes a more just, open, peaceful, and humane society, and the reduction of the military budget, through education, participatory democracy, and networking. Supports the Campaign for Youth Against Violence, Abolition 2000, Military Waste Reduction Project, and other programs. Has sponsored many conferences. Pub. *New Priorities Report* (Feb. 1998 issue includes notes on DOE fuel conversion project, U.S. controlled media, police brutality, and housing). Stanley Weithorn, Pres.; Craig Butler, Exec. Dir. (DC office: 122 Maryland Ave., NE DC 20002; 202-543-1231).

700. *Fund for Peace* (org).

In addition to other projects, FFP supports a Human Rights Program (1990) to prevent human rights abuses by strengthening local human rights organizations worldwide through training and handbooks. Mona Chun, Dir. This office ceased functioning in March 2000. See its DC office: www.fundforpeace.org

701. *Gandhi Sculpture* (1986) (mem).

Union Square Park, southwest pedestrian triangle, 14th St. at Broadway, NYC.

A slightly over life-size (7 foot) statue of Gandhi (1869–1948) wearing sandals, a Hindu dhoti, and wire glasses. He leans forward as if he is taking a step forward. The technique is re-alistic, with wrinkles and veins showing. Sculpted by Kantilal B. Patel (India).

702. *Global Education Associates* (1973) (org).

475 Riverside Dr.,Suite1848, NYC 10115;
(212) 870-3290; *globaleduc@earthlink.net;*
www.globaleduc.org

"Hopes to change international competition over weapons, money, and scarce natural resources to international cooperation through education." Project Global 2000 for rethinking national security and sovereignty; Earth Covenant: citizens' treaty for enhancement of environment; organizes conferences; Religious Orders Partnerships with over 100 Catholic orders; offers consulting services to educational institutions and churches; offers a reference library; gives the annual Jerry Mische Global Service Award. Pub. *Breakthrough News* three times a year; *Global Education Resource Guide; Star Wars and the State of Our Souls;* etc. Patricia Mische, Pres.; Sharon Fritsch, Admin.

703. *Global Resource Action Center for the Environment (GRACE)* (1996) (org).

15 E. 26th St., Rm. 915, NYC 10010;
(212) 726-9161; *grace@gracelinks.org;*
aslater@igc.apc.org; www.gracelinks.org

"Committed to forming new links between those engaged in research, policy, and grassroots community work in order to promote solutions" to planetary problems, by promoting "a global corporate ethic of responsibility and public accountability," the elimination of nuclear weapons, and solutions to toxic contamination of the environment. GRACE works "to ban the bomb and address the toxic legacy of the nuclear age." It is a founder of Abolition 2000, a global network seeking a treaty to eliminate nuclear weapons. Pub. *Gracenotes*, occasional papers. Alice Slater, President.

704. *Hague Appeal for Peace* (1996) (org).

C/o IWTC, 777 UN Plaza, NYC 10017;
(212) 687-2623 (offices also in The
Hague and in Zurich); *hap99@igc.org;*
hap@haguepeace.org; www.haguepeace.org

Mobilized citizens, organizations, and governments to participate in the Civil Society Conference in May, 1999 at the Hague to find ways to abolish war in the twenty-first century. "The

Hague Agenda for Peace and Justice for the 21st Century" contains 50 proposals for the four strands of the Appeal: Root Causes of War/Culture of Peace; International Humanitarian and Human Rights Law and Institutions; Prevention, Resolution and Transformation of Violent Conflict; Disarmament and Human Security. Highlights of the conference in the special edition of the conference newsletter *Peace Matters*, includes ideas on how to get involved in follow-up activities. *Peace Matters* 3.1 (Jan. 2000) includes articles on the First Hague Appeal for Peace Prize, peace education, the Hague Appeal in Seattle/WTO, and a special section on humanitarian intervention; 3.2 (May 2000) includes articles on Youth Against War Treaty, nuclear weapons, the World Court, Nuclear Free Zones, Global University/Peace Boat, peace education, calendar. Video *Time to Abolish War* available. Cora Weiss, Pres. Gouri Sadhwani, Dir. (*gourihap99@igc.org*); Karina Wood (*kwood@igc.org*).

Hope: Raoul Wallenberg Monument by Gustav Kraitz, New York City. Photograph courtesy City of New York Parks & Recreation.

705. *Hope: Raoul Wallenberg Monument* (1998) (mem).

Raoul Wallenberg Walk, First Ave. & East 47th St., NYC across from the United Nations.

Wallenberg led a rescue operation to save Hungarian Jews from Nazi persecution 1944-45, saving nearly 100,000 before his disappearance in 1945.

Five black columns hewn from black Swedish bedrock suggest the ruins of a devastated city. One column is capped by a blue ceramic sphere symbolizing Hope. Wallenberg's attache case rests amid the columns, crafted by Ull Kraitz, wife of Gustav. The area surrounding the pillars is comprised of granite paving blocks which once covered the streets of the Jewish ghetto in Budapest, a gift of the city of Budapest. Sculpted by Hungarian-born Swedish sculptor Gustav Kraitz. The work is a gift to the City of New York from the family of Hilel Storch of Stockholm, Sweden.

706. **Human Rights and Humanitarian Affairs* (1978) (col).

School of International and Public Affairs (SIPA), Columbia Univ., 2960 Broad, NY, NY 10027; (212) 854-3193; *jpm2@columbia.edu*; *www.columbia.edu/cu/sipa/MIA/hrha.html*

Offers a two-year MA degree in International Affairs with a concentration in Human Rights and Humanitarian Affairs. J. Paul Martin, Dir. (See above: Center for the Study of Human Rights).

707. **Human Rights Liberal Studies* (1988) (col).

Graduate School of Arts and Sciences, Columbia Univ., NYC 10027; *liberalstudiesma@columbia.edu*; *cev26@columbia.edu*; *www.columbia.edu/cu/gsas/liberalstudies/rights.html*

A MA of 30 credits and a thesis. Contact Cynthia van Ginkle, Dir.

708. **Human Rights Watch* (1978) (org).
350 5th Ave. Fl 34, NYC 10117-3501; *www.hrw.org*

Reports on human rights abuses, exposing torture and arbitrary detention, pressing for international war crimes tribunals, and a leading advocate for the establishment of the International Criminal Court. Their "blueprint for action" is the Universal Declaration of Human Rights, adopted by the U.N. General Assembly in 1948. HRW helped lead the Nobel Prize-winning campaign for a treaty to ban antipersonnel landmines; it sent investigators to document Kosovo war crimes; it prepared a book documenting the 1994 genocide in Rwanda; and many similar actions. Robert Bernstein, Founding Chair; Kenneth Roth, Exec. Director.

708a. *Institute of International Education* (1919) (org).

809 UN Plaza, NYC 10017-3580; (212) 883-8200; *www.iie.org*

To develop better understanding between people of the US and the world through higher educational exchanges. Pub. *Academic Year Abroad* annual, a guide to over 2000 overseas study programs offered by US colleges; *English Language and Orientation Programs in the U.S.*; and other resources.

709. *Institute of War and Peace Studies* (1951) (col).

School of International and Public Affairs (SIPA), Columbia Univ., NYC 10027; (212) 854-4616; *rkb4@columbia.edu*; *www.columbia.edu/cu/sipa/MIA/iwps.html*

Conducts research and publishes books, articles, and periodically an online newsletter (*www.columbia.edu/cu/iwps*), and sponsors lectures and events. Richard Betts, Dir.

710. *Interfaith Center on Corporate Responsibility* (1971) (org).

475 Riverside Dr., Rm 550, 10115; (212) 870-2295; *info@iccr.org*

Works directly to change corporate behavior by introducing resolutions at corporate annual meetings. Global warming and carbon dioxide emissions have been chief issues during the past five years, especially tackling recalcitrant Texaco. Timothy Smith, Exec. Dir.

711. *International Action Center* (1992) (org).

39 W. 14th St. Rm. 206, 10011; (212) 633-6646; *iacenter@iacenter.org*; *www.iacenter.org*

Opposes U.S. militarism and organizes opposition to U.S. interventions abroad. Founded by former U.S. Attorney General Ramsey Clark. Pub.: Ramsey Clark, *The Fire This Time: U.S. War Crimes in the Gulf* (New York: Thunder's Mouth, 1992).

712. *International Center for Cooperation and Conflict Resolution* (1986) (col).

Dept. of Organization and Leadership, Columbia Univ. Teachers College, NYC 10027; (212) 678-3112; *pc84@columbia.edu*; *www.tc.columbia.edu/~academic.icccr*

Helps schools, communities, businesses, governments, and other groups cope with conflict, through research, courses, and workshops. Peter Coleman, Co-Dir.

713. *International Conflict Resolution Program* (1997) (col).

School of International and Public Affairs, 420 West 118th St., Mail Code 3369, Columbia Univ., NYC 10027; (212) 854-5623; *ICRP@columbia.edu*; *http://sipa.columbia.edu/ICRP/index.html*

ICRP offers courses, research projects, seminars, conferences, and training sessions. Andrea Bartoli., Founder and Dir. (212-854-4449, *ab203@columbia.edu*); Erin DeOrnellas, Prog. Coord. (ed166@columbia.edu)

714. *International Organization for the Study of Group Tensions* (1970) (org).

240 E. 76th St., Apt. 1-B, NYC 10021-2958; (212) 628-1797.

Behavioral scientists and scholars seeking to increase understanding of and solutions to conflicts and to replace violence with tolerance. Pub. *International Journal of Group Tensions* quarterly and studies of conflict, violence, terrorism, war, etc. Benjamin Wolman, Pres.

715. *International Peace Academy* (1970) (porg).

777 UN Plaza, 4th fl., NYC 10017-3521; (212) 687-4300; *ipa@ipacademy.org*; *www.ipacademy.org*

Private postgraduate educational institution for professional training in conflict management skills, invitation only. Also conducts research on peacekeeping, mediation, negotiation, etc. Seminars, annual dinner. Pub. *International Peace-keeping* quarterly, *Peacekeepers Handbook*. Clara Otunnu, Pres.

716. *International Planned Parenthood Federation, Western Hemisphere Region/Federación Internacional de Planificación de la Familia, Región del Hemisferio Occidental* (1954) (org).

120 Wall St., 9th Floor, NYC 10005-3902; (212) 248-6400; *info@ippfwhr.org; www.ippfwhr.org*

As of Oct. 1999 more than 6 billion people were living on our planet, and 800 million of them were chronically malnourished, while the population grows at a rate of one billion people every 11 years. IPPF promotes the recognition of family planning as a basic human right, seeks to give women the opportunity to delay mother-hood, have smaller families, and reduce their poverty and its consequences. Pub. *Forum* magazine. Hernan Sanhueza, M.D., Regional Dir.; Zhenja La Rosa, Comm.Manager/Senior Ed. (*zlarosa@ippfwhr.org*).

717. *International Rescue Committee* (1933) (org).

122 E. 42nd, 10168-1289.

"Taking effective action to help refugees is the *sole mission*" of the IRC. Founded by Albert Einstein. Reynold Levy, President.

718. *Isaiah Wall* (1975) (mem).

East 43rd Street and 1st Avenue opposite the United Nations Plaza, and near the Ralph Bunche statue.

Inscribed on the retaining wall above the stairsteps are the words from Isaiah 2:4: "They shall beat their swords into plowshares, and their spears into pruning hooks: nation shall not lift up sword against nation, neither shall they learn war any more.

719. *Jane Addams Peace Association, Inc.* (1948) (org).

777 United Nations Plaza, 6th Fl., 10017-3521; (212) 682-8830; (831) 338-4233; *japa@igc.apc.org*; *lindabel@cruzio.com*

Isaiah Wall, New York City opposite United Nations Plaza. Photograph courtesy Art Commission City of New York.

The Women's International League for Peace and Freedom Educational Fund (see Philadelphia) (WILPF's 501c3). Jane Addams (1860–1935) founded WILPF in 1915 and won the Nobel Peace Prize in 1931. JAPA was founded by WILPF women in Chicago to honor Addams by concentrating on educational programs, including the Children's Book Award, the Living Memorial Fund, the Peace Education Committee, the Jones Children's Peace Education Fund, the Freeman Intern Fund for young women, and the quarterly newsletter, *Building Peace*. JAPA houses the WILPF UN Office in NYC and owns the Jane Addams House in Philadelphia, which serves as the headquarters for the US Section of WILPF. Linda Wasserman, President.

720. *Lawyers Committee on Nuclear Policy* (1981) (org).

211 E. 43rd St., NYC 10012; (212) 818-1861; *lcnp@lcnp.com; www.lcnp.org*

Affil. of the International Association of Lawyers Against Nuclear Arms. LCNP uses national and international law to promote peace and disarmament, provides legal resources to assist people using law for peace, and works through international bodies—the United Nations, the International Court of Justice, and others—to advance peace. LCNP is a co-founder of Abolition 2000; it seeks the implementation of the ruling from the International Court of Justice that the threat or use of nuclear weapons is generally illegal; and it is disseminating its Model Nuclear Weapons Convention for destroying all nuclear weapons. Pub. *Bombs Away* newsletter once or twice a year; the Fall 1999 number includes articles on the illegality of the bombings of Yugoslavia, the Hague Appeal, Chinese nuclear threats, citizen weapons inspections. Also pub. books, articles, and papers. John Burroughs, Dir.

721. *Leonard Rieser Research Fellowship* (1999) (org).

c/o Betsy Fader, Doris Duke Charitable Foundation, 650 5th Ave., 19th Fl., NYC 10019; *www.thebulletin.org/fellowship*

Established by the Educational Foundation for Nuclear Science, publisher of *The Bulletin of the Atomic Scientists*, to honor Mr. Rieser (1922–1998), who championed young people's efforts to build a more peaceful world. The Fellowship provides one-time awards of $2,500 to three to five undergraduate students "seeking to explore issues at the intersection of science, public policy, and global security."

722. *Madre* (1983) (org).

121 W. 27th St., Rm 301, NYC 10001; (212) 627-0444; *madre@igc.apc.org; www.madre.org*

Madre began following a trip by activists to Central America to observe the consequences of the U.S. sponsored Contra invasion of Nicaragua—schools destroyed, civilians killed. This experience led to the creation of this women-led organization "dedicated to informing people in the U.S. about the effects of U.S. policies." A second goal became the support of health and educational programs of sister organizations—begun in 1984 with baby cereal and powdered milk to Nicaragua. Since then, Madre has arranged for millions of dollars in aid to women and children in war-ravaged areas.

723. *Manifesto 2000* (1999) (org).

UNESCO, 2 United Nations Plaza, NYC 10017; *www2.unesco.org/manifesto2000*

Drafted by 24 Nobel Peace Prize laureates to advocate the transformation of the culture of war and violence into a culture of peace and nonviolence. The 6 pledges: respect all life, reject violence, share with others, listen to understand, preserve the planet, and rediscover solidarity. All people are urged to sign it.

724. *National Coalition Against Censorship* (1974) (org).

275 7th Ave., NYC 10001; (212) 807-6222; *ncac@ncac.org; www.ncac.org*

Provides information, advice, and direct assistance to teachers, librarians, and citizens in their struggles against censorship. Joan Bertin, Exec. Dir.

725. *Natural Resources Defense Council* (1970) (org).

40 W. 20th St., 10011; (212) 727-2700; *nrdcinfo@nrdc.org*

Uses law, science, and its large membership "to protect the planet's wildlife and wild places and to ensure a safe and healthy environment for all living things." Regional offices in Washington, DC, San Francisco, and Los Angeles.

726. **Pastors for Peace/Interreligious Foundation for Community Organization (IFCO)* (1987) (org).

402 W. 145th St., 10031; tel: (212) 926-5757; *ifco@igc.apc.org; www.ifconews.org*

Pastors for Peace defends the world's poor by caravans with food and medicines to victim countries—Nicaragua, Cuba, El Salvador, Guatemala, and Mexico (Chiapas). IFCO sponsors projects around the U.S. in support of refugees, political prisoners, people with HIV and AIDS, etc. Pub. *IFCO News* quarterly. Recipient of the Aachen Peace Prize 1998. Directed by Rev. Lucius Walker.

727. **Pax Christi Metro New York* (1983) (org).

135 W. 4th St., NYC 10012; (212) 420-0250; *nypaxchristi@igc.apc.org*

Founded upon Jesus's Gospel of Nonviolence and Catholic Social Teaching. Its peace work includes the Good Friday Peace Walk, an annual retreat, an annual awards dinner for a national and a local peacemaker, and an annual Fall Assembly. A major program is a conflict resolution program for adults, one for high school students, and study guides to field trip sites in NYC for school groups. Rachel Keeler, Coordinator and Regional Rep.

728. **Peace and Global Policy Studies* (1980) (col).

History Dept., New York Univ., NYC 10012; (212) 998-8623 (w), 982-3141 (h), 998-8600 (dept.); *www.nyu.edu./cas*

Undergraduate minor explores the complex issues of war and peace. Contact Michael Lutzker.

729. **Peace Day Committee* (1997) (org).

c/o WPPS, 800 Third Ave., 37th Fl., NYC 10022; (212) 755-4755; *peacepal@worldpeace.org; www.worldpeace.org/peaceday*

Supports the International Day of Peace, September 14, the opening day of the UN General Assembly, when people the world over are asked to dedicate themselves to peace by a minute of silence at 12:00 noon, and to ring a bell or light a candle—in any way to distinguish the day. Contact Deborah Moldow. See entry 626.

730. **Peace Education* (1982) (col).

Dept. of International and Transcultural Studies, Columbia University Teachers College, NYC 10027; (212) 678-3947; *bar19@columbia.edu; www.tc.columbia.edu/~academic/intl-transcultural/cie&ied.htm#Peace*

A concentration with MA/Ed.M and Ed.D. in cooperation with Columbia Univ., Union Theological Seminary, and Jewish Theological Seminary. Founded by Betty Reardon (who has left to work for the Hague Appeal).

731. *Peace Form One* (1980) (mem).

Opposite the United Nations Plaza at 1st Avenue and East 43rd St., adjacent to the "Isaiah Wall," NYC.

Peace Form One, Ralph Bunche Memorial, by Daniel La Rue Johnson. Photograph by Steven Jonas, M.D., courtesy Art Commission of the City of New York.

A sculpture honoring Ralph J. Bunche, a 50 foot stainless steel rectangular shaft tapering wedge-like toward the top, mounted on a pentagonal bronze base approximately 20 feet in width. The sculptor was Daniel La Rue Johnson.

Henry, Charles. *Ralph Bunche: Model Negro or American Other?* New York: NYUP, 1998.

Urquhart, Brian. *Ralph Bunche: an American Life. New York: Norton, 1993.*

732. *Peace Fountain* (1985) (mem).

1047 Amsterdam at 112th St., 10025, Cathedral Church of St. John the Divine; (212) 662-4479.

The complex bronze sculpture, rising 40 feet, is an allegory of peace with Michael the Archangel casting out Satan at the top, a smiling sun and moon, giraffe, lion and lamb, and other figures around the middle, and a DNA-like double helix for the base. Surrounding the sculpture are over 100 bronze reliefs and sculptures of animals that were designed by children. Sculptor: Greg Wyatt. A brochure is available.

"Children's Sculpture Garden," *New York Times* (August 9, 1991); *New York Tribune* (Oct. 16, 1984).

733. **Program on Negotiation and Conflict Resolution* (1995) (col).

Wagner Graduate School of Public Service, New York Univ., NYC 10012; (212) 998-7410; *howard.newman@wagner.nyu.edu; www.nyu.edu/wagner/conflict*

Seeks to help managers and administrators of the future to deal effectively with conflict, through courses and programs within NYU and around NYC and the world. Supported by the Hewlett Foundation. Contact Howard Newman.

734. **Quaker United Nations Office* (1947) (org).

777 UN Plaza, NYC 10017; *qunony@pipeline.com; www.quno.org*

"Seeks to manifest traditional Quaker concerns for equality, justice, and peace" at the UN. Its Quaker House (purchased in 1953), near the UN, brings people together for negotiation and mediation, conferences and seminars. QUNO also offers internships. Focuses on peacebuilding, development, human rights, disarmament. Pub. newsletter *In & Around.* National office in Philadelphia (afscinfo@afsc. org).

Peace Fountain Monument by Greg Wyatt, Cathedral Church of St. John the Divine, New York City. Courtesy Greg Wyatt.

735. **Unitarian Universalist United Nations Office* (1949) (org).

777 UN Plaza, Suite CC, NYC 10017; (212) 986-5165; *uuuno2@aol.com*

Supports the UN in its search for peace and informs UU members of UN activities. Rev. Ben Bortin, Pres. Richard Kopp, Exec. Sec't.

• **UNITED NATIONS** *see* **entries 744–760**

736. **United Nations Association of the U.S.A. (UNA-USA)* (1943) (org).

801 Second Ave., NYC 10017-4706; (212) 907-1341; *unahq@unausa.org; www.unausa.org*

Begun by Eleanor Roosevelt as the American Association for the United Nations, which in 1964 merged with the U.S. Committee for the United Nations to form the UNA of today. Works to educate and mobilize citizens to support the work of the U.N in preventing and resolving conflicts, promoting human rights, raising the standard of living for all, and protecting the environment. UNA-USA has some 25,000 members and over 175 Chapters. More than 100 national organizations (education, religion, labor, environmental, etc.) have enlisted in UNA's Council of Organizations. One focus is the annual U.N. Day (October 24) each year. A new Adopt-a-Minefield Campaign uses the internet to educate the public and raise funds. Leadership is based both in New York and D.C. Pub.: *The InterDependent*, ed. by John Tessitore, man. ed. Susan Woolfson; *A Global Agenda: Issues Before the 54th General Assembly of the United Nations* (1999-2000 issue of annual edition, an indispensable guide to the workings of the UN). The Summer 1999 issue of *The Interdependent* contains articles on such subjects as Congress and U.N. funding, minefields, child labor, The Hague Conference, Model U.N., the Better World Campaign. President: William Luers; Jeffrey Brennan, Director of Information Systems (*jbrennan@unausa.org*).

737. **United Nations Children's Fund/Fonds des Nations Unies pour l'enfance (UNICEF)* (1946) (org).

3 UN Plaza, NYC 10017; (212) 326-7000; *netmaster@unicef.org*; *www.unicefusa.org*

The UN's advocate for children's rights and needs, especially for the victims of war, disasters, poverty, illness, violence, and exploitation, guided by the Convention on the Rights of the Child. Raises funds through sales of UNICEF greeting cards, notes, calendars, etc. Charles Lyons, Pres.; Carol Bellamy, Exec. Dir.

738. **United States Servas, Inc.* (1949) (org).

11 John St., Suite 407, NYC 10038-4009; *usServas@Servas.org*; *servas-info@servas. org*; *www.servas.org/welcome.htm*

An "international network of hosts and travelers building peace and understanding by providing opportunities for personal contact between people of diverse cultures." (Servas means "We serve" in Esperanto.). Servas began in Denmark, held its first international conference in 1952 in Germany, and in 1973 became a U.N. non-governmental organization. Based in Switzerland, Servas now works in over 100 countries.

739. **War Resisters League* (1923) (org).

339 Lafayette St., NYC 10012; (212) 228-0450; *wrl@igc.apc.org*; *www.nonviolence.org/wrl/nva.htm*

The only national secular pacifist organization in the U.S., founded by Jessie W. Hughan with Albert Einstein, Honorary Chair. 1998 was its 75th Anniversary. Its activities include: A Day Without the Pentagon campaign against militarism, educating "Where Your Income Tax Money Goes," YouthPeace against the militarization of young people, resources for high school students to counter military recruiting, opposition to nuclear weapons and U.S. interventions abroad, annual military budget analysis, war tax resistance, annual Peace Calendar, and a magazine, *The Nonviolent Activist* (the Sept.-Oct. 1999 issue includes articles on Mumia Abu-Jamal, NASA's plutonium Cassini space mission, orphans of war, International Youth-Peace Week, book reviews).

740. **War Tax Resistance/WRL* (1969) (org).

339 Lafayette St., 10012; (212) 228-0450; *gunorlictn@aol.com*

Steve Gulick, Coordinator

741. **World Conference on Religion and Peace (WCRP) International* (1970) (org).

777 United Nations Plaza, NYC 10017; *info@wcrp.org*; *www.wcrp.org*

Strives for conflict reconciliation, human rights and responsibilities, child and family development, sustainable ecology, disarmament, and peace education. Pubs. include: *Children and Violent Conflict, Ending Poverty, Disarmament and WCRP*. William Vendley, Sec't. General.

742. **World Conference on Religion and Peace USA* (1970) (org).

Same address as in preceding entry; *tkireopoulos@wcrp.org*

Antonios Kireopoulos, Sec't. General.

743. **YouthPeace Program* (1994) (Now "Roots") (org).

339 Lafayette St., NYC 10012; (212) 228-0450;

*youthpeace@imaginemail.com,
www.nonviolence.org/wrl*

A national network of youths who seek to manifest the pacifist principles of the War Resisters League and to protest the sources of violence in the world. Among other activities: organizes the annual International YouthPeace Week. Contact Asif Ullah.

UNITED NATIONS (1945)

744. *United Nations Headquarters* (1946) (org).

Eighteen acres on East Side of Manhattan.

The land was purchased by John D. Rockefeller, Jr., and the City of New York. The Headquarters is comprised of several connected buildings: the Secretariat Building, the Conference Building, the General Assembly Building. The U.N. has six main bodies: General Assembly, Security Council, Secretariat, Economic and Social Council (alternating between New York and Geneva), Trusteeship Council, and International Court of Justice (at The Hague, Netherlands). Some subsidiary organs created by the General Assembly: U.N. Children's Fund (UNICEF, 1946), Office of the U.N. High Commissioner for Refugees (1949), U.N. Conference on Trade and Development (1964), U.N. Development Program (1965), Office of the U.N. Disaster Relief Coordinator (1971), U.N. Environment Program (1972), U.N. Center for Human Settlements (1977). October 24 is United Nations Day.

Boutros-Ghali, Boutros. *Unvanquished: A U.S.-U.N. Saga.* New York: Random House, 1999.

Burns, Arthur, and Nina Heathcote. *Peacekeeping by U.N. Forces, from Suez to the Congo.* New York: Princeton Center of International Studies/Praeger, 1963.

Humphrey, John. *Human Rights & the United Nations: A Great Adventure.* Dobbs Ferry, NY: Transnational, 1984.

United Nations Conference on the Committee on Disarmament. *Comprehensive Study of the Question of Nuclear-Weapon-Free Zones in All Its Aspects; Special Report.* New York: 1976.

United Nations Headquarters Building. Photograph courtesy Pamela Zapata, Public Inquiries Unit, United Nations.

745. *United Nations Headquarters Building* (1951) (org).

The Headquarters Building, thirty-nine stories high and costing $20 million, was designed by a team of world architects headed by Wallace K. Harrison. The Secretariat services the organs of the UN and administers its programs. The Secretariat is headed by the Secretary-General, who is appointed by the General Assembly for a five-year term. There have been seven Secretaries-General: Trygve Lie (Norway) 1946–1952; Dag Hammarskjöld (Sweden) 1953–1961; U Thant (Burma, now Myanmar) 1961–1971; Kurt Waldheim (Austria) 1972–1981; Javier Pérez de Cuéllar (Peru) 1982–1991; and Kofi Annan (Ghana) 1997–.

746. *United Nations Environment Program* (UNEP) (1973) (org).

2 UN Plaza, Rm. DC2-0803, United Nations, NYC 10017 (regional office for North America); (212) 963-8210; *info@rona.unep.org*

Seeks to develop a sustainable environment. One project is the annual photo contest, to raise global environmental awareness (888-272-3836; www.unep-photo.com).

MEMORIALS AT THE UN

747. *Children's Fountain* (1952) (mem).

In front of the Secretariat Building.

Paid for through contributions of children from the U.S.A., Puerto Rico, and the Virgin Islands in a campaign sponsored by the A.A.U.N. The floor of the Fountain is decorated with white and black pebbles, the black pebbles, some 45 tons, gathered from the island of Rhodes by the wives of local fishermen, a gift of the Greek government.

748. *Count Folke Bernadotte Memorial* (1998) (mem).

In the General Assembly Lobby near the Meditation Room.

Bernadotte was the first U.N. mediator and the first to die in the cause of peace (assassinated in Jerusalem in 1948). Also see the plaque to Bernadotte near the entrance to the Meditation Room.

749. *Dove of Peace* (1979) (mem).

General Assembly lobby.

A reproduction of a mosaic in the Constantinian Basilica of St. Peter. Presented by Pope John Paul II.

750. *The Golden Rule* (1985) (mem).

Third floor of the Conference Building next to the Economic and Social Council Chamber.

A mosaic designed by Norman Rockwell (USA) depicting people of different nationali-

The Golden Rule **by Norman Rockwell, Conference Building. Photograph courtesy Pamela Zapata, Public Inquiries Unit, United Nations.**

ties, recalling the U.N.'s Charter's injunction "to practice tolerance and live together in peace."

751. *Kente* (1995) (mem).

Second floor of the General Assembly Building.

This Ashanti style double-weave *kente*, a hand-woven cloth in the design of "Adwene Asa," signifies "a consensus has been reached." Gift from Ghana.

752. *Let Us Beat Swords into Ploughshares* (1959) (mem).

The north garden area at UN Headquarters.

The 9-feet tall bronze statue of a man with a raised hammer in his right hand in the process of shaping a sword held by his left hand into a plow-share, symbolizing human desire to convert the means of destruction into creative tools for the benefit of humankind. Created by Evgeniy Vuchetich, a gift of the Soviet Union.

Non-Violence by Karl Reutersward, apron of General Assembly. Photograph courtesy Pamela Zapata, Public Inquiries Unit, United Nations.

753. *Non-Violence* (1988) (mem).

Apron of the General Assembly Building facing First Avenue at 45th Street.

This sculpture of a large replica in bronze of a .45 –calibre revolver with its barrel tied into a knot was created by Swedish artist Karl Fredrik Reutersward and given to the UN by Luxembourg.

754. *Peace and Freedom Tapestry* (1952) (mem).

Security Council Chamber (known as the Norwegian Room) covering most of the east wall.

By Per Krohg of Norway, symbolizes the promise of future peace and individual freedom.

755. *Peace and Human Happiness* (1964) (mem).

West side of the General Assembly lobby.

A stained-glass free-standing panel 15 feet wide by 12 feet high designed by Marc Chagall (France) depicting themes of peace and human happiness and in memory of the late Secretary-General, Dag Hammarskjöld.

756. *Peace Bell* (1954) (mem).

The West Court Garden of the Secretariat Building.

The base and pavilion are a gift from the Israeli government, the bell from the Japanese

Let Us Beat Swords into Ploughshares by Evgeniy Vuchetich, north garden. Photograph courtesy Pamela Zapata, Public Inquiries Unit, United Nations.

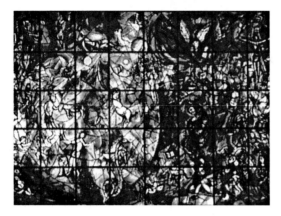

Peace and Human Happiness by Marc Chagall, General Assembly Lobby Building. Photograph courtesy Pamela Zapata, Public Inquiries Unit, United Nations.

Association for the UN. Cast from coins from over 60 countries, the Bell weighs 993 pounds. Inscribed on one side of the bell, in Japanese, are the words, "Long live absolute world peace."

Peace Bell, West Court Garden Secretariat Building. Photograph courtesy Pamela Zapata, Public Inquiries Unit, United Nations.

757. *Single Form* (1964) (mem).

Circle in front of the Secretariat Building.

The 21-feet tall, 5½ ton bronze abstraction carries out the wish of Dag Hammarskjöld, the second UN Secretary-General, that the circle in front of the Secretariat building be adorned with an appropriate sculpture.

Mr. Hammarskjöld was killed in a plane accident in Northern Rhodesia (now Zambia) while attempting to negotiate peace in the Congo. The statue was created by Barbara Hepworth (UK), who interpreted her work as symbolizing the idealism and singleness of purpose of the Secretary-General's quest for peace.

758. *Struggle for Peace Mural* (1953) (mem).

Third floor of the Conference building.

60 feet long and 10 feet high, the mural depicts the eternal struggle for lasting peace, beginning with the destruction of a family, the agony of modern war (concentration camps, bombings, hunger), the planting of the UN emblem, and finally the restoration of human rights, peace, and the family. Painted by José Vela Zanetti; gift from the John Simon Guggenheim Memorial Foundation.

759. *Triumph of Peace Tapestry* (1954) (mem).

Near the stairway to the General Assembly Chamber.

Mural tapestry made of 94,000 miles of yarn, 42 by 28 feet, designed by Belgian artist Peter Colfs.

760. *Woman and Bird Statue* (1953) (mem).

Left wall of the Trusteeship Chamber (known as the Danish Room) facing the podium.

Nine-foot teak wood statue of a woman with arms upraised to a blue bird with wings outstretched, designed by Henrick Starcke (Denmark).

Woman and Bird Statue by Henrick Starcke, Trusteeship Chamber. Courtesy Pamela Zapata, Public Inquiries Unit, United Nations.

— *North Carolina* —
(NC)

19 Sister Cities. / 42 Peace Poles.

ASHEVILLE, NC

761. Canceled.

762. *Episcopal Peace Fellowship, Asheville Area* (1998) (org).

374 Genesis Circle, Black Mountain 28711; (828) 669-9051; *dmycoff@owl.warren-wilson.edu*

Occasional newsletter. Contact David Mycoff.

BURNSVILLE, NC

763. *Rural Southern Voice for Peace* (1981) (org).

1898 Hannah Branch Rd., Burnsville 28714; (828) 675-5933; *rsvp028714@yahoo.com*

Affil. with Fellowship of Reconciliation (1984). Provides organizing assistance for nonviolent social change particularly through the Listening Project. Contact Aaron Thompson.

CHAPEL HILL, NC

764. *Curriculum in Peace, War and Defense* (1970) (col).

College of Arts and Sciences, CB#3200, 401 Hamilton Hall, University of North Carolina, Chapel Hill 27599-3200; (919) 962-3093 or 8601; *pumphrey@email.unc.edu* or *jackie@unc.edu; www.unc.edu/depts/pwad/*

Strives to instruct undergraduates on issues of human conflict and its resolution, national and global security and defense. ("Closest equivalent is the War Studies Dept. at Kings College, University of London"). Jackie Gorman, Programs Admin.

765. *International Development and Social Change* (1993) (col).

University Center for International Studies, Univ. of North Carolina, Chapel Hill 27599; *nsteiner@unc.edu; www.unc.edu/depts/ucis/academics/graduate1.htm*

A graduate certificate open to graduate students in all departments. Core course, seminar, and thesis. Contact Niklaus Steiner.

766. *Orange County Peace Action* (1989) (org).

PO Box 2822, Chapel Hill 27515; (919) 942-8245; *bridgetteburge@hotmail.com*

Local Chapter of Peace Action: speakers, booths at street fairs, march in Holiday Parade, advocate peaceful toys, observe MLK Day, respond to current issues, such as Kosovo and Iraq, with demonstrations and member alerts through tel. and e-mail network. Had a giant peace dove puppet made for use in parades and demonstrations. Contact Lorna Chafe (*lchafe@duke.edu*).

767. *Physicians for Social Responsibility, North Carolina Triangle Chapter* (1981) (org).

PO Box 3218, Chapel Hill 27515; (919) 942-9365; N_A_Coulter@med.unc.edu

PSR, the U.S. affiliate of International Physicians for Prevention of Nuclear War (Nobel Peace Prize 1985) has its national office in Washington, DC. PSR is composed of "health professionals and concerned citizens committed to preventing nuclear war, regional and community violence, and environmental degradation." The Triangle Chapter has organized symposia, hosted visits by Soviet physicians, sponsored a Concert for Peace, arranged a conference on prevention of violence, and sponsors an annual contest on peace and nonviolence for middle school students, and other projects. It focuses now on reducing military spending, canceling nuclear weapons, and cleaning up toxic and radioactive wastes. Pub. quarterly newsletter, *Vital Signs*.

768. *Synergetic Society* (1959) (org).

1825 N. Lakeshore Drive, Chapel Hill, 27514; (919) 942-2994.

Promotes synergy, peace, and fairness on our planet, using a new heuristic science of human development called Synergetics. Publishes a journal, *Change*, the basic purpose of which is to abolish war through a synergic cultural evolution of the human "heartmind" and society. Books: *Synergetics: An Experiment in Human Development* (1955); *Synergetics: An Adventure in Human Development* (1976). Founding president, Bill Sell; Arthur Coulter, M. D., President.

769. *Triangle Institute for Security Studies* (1958) (col).

Univ. of North Carolina, Chapel Hill, 27599; (919) 962-8601; pumphrey@ email.unc.edu; www.unc.edu/depts/tiss

A consortium sponsored by three Carolina research universities concerned with the safety of people and nations. Carolyn Pumphrey, Coord., Peter Feaver (Duke Univ.), Dir.

CHARLOTTE, NC

770. *Baptist Peace Fellowship of North America* (1984) (org).

4800 Wedgewood Dr., Charlotte 28210-2909; (704) 521-6051; bpfna@bpfna.org

Arose out of the Baptist Peace Fellowship (1940). BPFNA seeks "to unite and enable Baptist Christians to make peace in our warring world." It seeks reconciliation among people and the healing of the nations, believing that peacemaking is an issue of spirituality, justice, and love through Jesus Christ, that peace is the will of God (that one day lion and lamb will lie together), and that peace is actively waged. Some 1998 activities: mediation assistance to Naga people of India, dialog between Protestants and Roman Catholics in Chiapas, a sponsor of 4th international Baptist peace conference in Australia in 2000, distributed 8,000 copies of "The Family Covenant of Nonviolence" at the Baptist World Youth Congress, Friendship Tour to migrant worker camps. Pubs. *Baptist Peacemaker* quarterly journal and *PeaceWork* bi-monthly newsletter. *Baptist Peacemaker* (Spring 1999) includes articles on Thomas Merton, the KKK, military chaplains, and BPFNA work with the Nagas in India. *PeaceWork* (No. 3, 1999) includes notes on Jubilee 2000 and a Family Covenant of Nonviolence. Also pub. *Best of Baptist Peacemaker*, a book collecting the best articles over 2 decades. Ken Sehested, Exec. Dir.; Rev. LeDayne McLeese Polaski, Managing Dir. (ledayne@bpfna.org).

771. *Concerned Philosophers for Peace* (1981) (org).

Dept. of Philosophy, U. of North Carolina at Charlotte, 9201 University City Blvd., Charlotte, 28223-0001; (704) 547-2266; wcgay@email.uncc.edu; www.cpp-phil.org

Encourages philosophers to study and to write about issues of violence, war, militarism, disarmament, and peace, and to support appropriate political actions. Pub. a newsletter, *Concerned Philosophers for Peace*, ed. By William C. Gay, and since 1989 several books on war and peace. Executive Dir.: William C. Gay (to 1999), then Larry Bove (1pbove@sssnet.com). A parallel organization, IPPNO in Virginia, offers a more international orientation for philosophers, but many of their members also belong to CPP.

GREENSBORO, NC

772. *Peace and Conflict Studies* (1981) (col).

Guilford College, 5800 West Friendly Ave., Greensboro 27410; (336) 316-2224; jgroves@guilford.edu; www.guilford.edu/ pages/modules/10000/15x/15190_ac.cfm

A major and concentration infused with the College's Quaker values—committed to nonviolent, practical problem solving. Internship required. The program enjoys support from the Julian Price Peace Studies Reading Room, the Conflict Resolution Resource Center, and the AFSC/Steinfeldt Scholarships in Peace Studies. Joseph Groves, Dir.

773. *International Civil Rights Center & Museum* (under development).

Downtown Greensboro, c/o Sit-In Movement, Inc., 134 S. Elm St., Greensboro 27401; (910) 274-9199.

With the (to be restored) F. W. Woolworth store as its core, where on February 1, 1960, four black students demanded service at its segregated lunch counter and began a national sit-in movement, Sit-In Movement, Inc. hopes to develop a civil rights museum and library, classrooms, and bookstore. Project leaders: Melvin "Skip" Alston and Earl F. Jones.

GREENVILLE, NC

774. *Greenville Peace Committee* (1968) (org).

610 Elm St., Greenville 27858; (252) 758-4906; *mawebber@eastnet.educ.ecu.edu*

Affil. of Peace Action rep. 1st and 3rd congressional district. Relays action alerts to local activists. Contact Caroll Webber.

775. *Peace Oak Trees* (1986) (org).

Two live oak trees were planted to celebrate peace ceremonies on the Greenville Town Common.

776. *Robert Lee Humber's Grave* (1970) (mem).

Cemetery on 2nd St., near Pitt St., Greenville.

World Federation leader Humber (1898–1970) is buried in Greenville, with an epitaph celebrating world unity on his marble tombstone, a tall obelisk. The long inscription includes these sentences: "Man is my brother," "The world is my country," and "all men are citizens of this world community." Humber's house is across the street from City Hall, downtown.

RALEIGH, NC

777. *North Carolina Peace Action* (1986?) (org).

PO Box 10384, Raleigh 27605; (919) 942-8245; *bridgetteburge@hotmail.com*

A Peace Action Chapter. Does statewide political action via e-mail/phone network, education through conferences, State Fair booth, working on a statewide phone and e-mail network. With Wake County affiliate pub. a quarterly newsletter *Peace Talk.* Lorna Chafe (*lchafe@duke.edu*) and Joe Burton, Co-chairs.

778. *Wake County Peace Action* (1985?) (org).

703 Greenwood Circle, Cary 27511; (919) 469-0831; *billtowepa@juno.com*

Active for the Comprehensive Test Ban Treaty and the Arms Transfer Code of Conduct, and against the Iraqi sanctions. Contact Bill Towe.

SWANNANOA, NC

779. *Peace Studies Program* (1985) (col).

Warren Wilson College, Swannanoa 28778; (828) 298-3325 ext. 372; *dbartlet@warren-wilson.edu; www.warren-wilson.edu/*

Besides coursework, the undergraduate concentration includes campus involvement and community outreach. Many graduates have entered the Peace Corps. Presbyterian affil. Contact Douglas Bartlett.

—— *North Dakota* ——

2 Sister Cities. / 22 Peace Poles.

BISMARCK, ND

780. *North Dakota Peace Coalition* (early 1982) (org).

PO Box 2547, Bismarck 58502; (701) 258-2554 or 224-9407; *brian@abolitionjournal.org; www.abolitionjournal.org.*

"…committed to working for peace, human dignity, economic and social justice, and a responsible relationship with the environment." Special emphasis on ICBMs in ND, economic conversion, and human rights. Sponsors the annual Fall Peace Congress, a forum for national speakers, workshops, etc.; the Prairie Peacemaker Award to a North Dakota peacemaker; quarterly educational events across the state. Pub.: newsletter, *Abolition Journal*, ed. Stanley Dienst (editor@abolitionjournal.org). Brian Palecek, founder.

781. *North Dakota Progressive Coalition* (1992) (org).

PO Box 482, 704 N. Mandan St., Bismarck 58501; (701) 224-8090; *nodakpc@aol.com*

Brings important issues into public debate, sometimes on peace issues, and gives a voice to ordinary people.

DUNSEITH, ND

782. *Annual Festival for Peace, June 25–27* (1983) (org).

Dunseith is north of Rugby on US #5 and south of the International Peace Garden.

The 1999 17th Festival's theme is "A Safe World: Growing Peace from Home to Ozone." One of the many annual events and displays at the *International Peace Garden* located on the border between North Dakota and the U.S., which include more than 150,000 flowers planted each summer, the Peace Chapel straddling the border and replete with quotations from people of peace etched into the walls, and an international music camp.

GRAND FORKS, ND

783. *Conflict Resolution Center* (1988) (org).

University of North Dakota, Box 8009, Grand Forks 58202; (701) 777-3664; *udcrc@badlands.nodak.edu*; *www.und.nodak.edu/dept/crc*

Offers one- to five-day seminars on all aspects of mediation for individuals, families, and businesses.

784. *Peace Studies Program* (1994) (col).

University of North Dakota, University Station, Grand Forks 58202; (701) 777-4414; *jamoen@badlands.nodak.edu; www.und.edu/dept/AdmisInfo.Ugdept/depts/ps.html*

Undergraduate major of 32 credits, including five core courses, an internship, and a senior seminar. Contact Janet Moen.

MINOT, ND

785. *Peace Tree* (1999) (mem).

Minot State U, west side of MSU administration building.

A Natural Scotch pine tree accompanied by a granite marker reading: "Make Us Instruments of Peace."

—— Ohio (OH) ——

50 Sister Cities. / 1087 Peace Poles.

AKRON, OH

(In *Peace Within Our Grasp*, the author, Crandall Kline, refers to Akron as "The Peace City" and lists some of its peace achievements.)

786. *Center for Conflict Management/Resolution* (1999) (col).

University of Akron, Akron 44325; (330) 972-7008; *conmang@uakron.edu; GoZips.uakron.edu./~conmang*

Formerly Center for Peace Studies (1972, founded by Warren Kuehl), CCM sponsors workshops for teachers, campus programs, and research projects. A certificate in CM/R is offered, requiring 21 semester hours. Scholarships available. James Stanley, Dir.

787. *House of Peace Catholic Worker Community* (1998) (org).

838 Princeton St., Akron 44311; (330) 384-1112.

Offers hospitality to the homeless, often from Latin America, in an inner-city integrated neighborhood. Also home to a *Pax Christi* group, through which is expressed opposition to the death penalty and support for Colombian communities threatened by paramilitary violence. Pub. a newsletter.

ATHENS, OH

788. *Article 9 Society* (1991) (org).

7815 Angel Ridge road, Athens, 45701; (740) 593-5759; *overby@bobcat.ent.ohiou.edu*

Dedicated to the preservation of the Japanese Constitution's Article 9, which "forever renounces war," and to the adoption of Article 9's principles by all nations. Charles and Ruth Overby, Dirs. (In 2000 Japan was considering abolishing the Article, since the U.S. and other nations want it to "assume its international responsibilities," and Japan already has one of the world's largest "Self-Defense Forces").

Overby, Charles. *A Call for Peace: The Implications of Japan's War-Renouncing Constitution.* Trans. M. Kunihiro (a bilingual book). Tokyo: Kodansha International, 1997; New York: Kodansha America, 1998.

789. *Contemporary History Institute* (1987) (col).

Brown House, 2 University Terrace, Ohio University, Athens 45701; (740) 593-4362; *conhist@ohiou.edu; www.cats.ohiou.edu/~conhist*

The study of history is grounded in a "commitment to peace, believing that the most crucial lesson to be learned in this 'treacherous no-man's land' of contemporary history is how to defuse mechanisms of war while fostering opportunities for peace in the post–Cold War period." Joan Hoff, Dir.

BLUFFTON, OH

790. *Lion and Lamb Peace Arts Center* (1987) (col).

Bluffton College, 280 W. College Ave., Bluffton 45817; (419) 358-3207; *lionlamb@bluffton.edu*

"Tucked away in a beautiful wooded setting on the campus," the Center promotes peace for children through the arts and literature: training in ways of peace and conflict resolution; a Caldecott Read-In; story and song festival; etc. Affil. with General Conference Mennonite Church. Pub. *The Lion and the Lamb Peace Arts Center Newsletter:* the Winter/Spring 1999 issue includes several book reviews and articles on the Sudan, South Africa, and Bosnia-Herzegovina.

791. *Northwest Ohio Fellowship of Reconciliation (after WWII)* (org).

c/o Elaine Sommers Rich, 112 S. Spring St., Bluffton, OH 45817; (419) 358-1515.

Meets monthly Sept.–May with programs on Christian Peacemaker Teams, international conflicts, etc. Activities include helping international students, sponsoring a peace booth for children at a local fair, letter-writing on peace and justice issues, etc. Also contact: Wendy Chappell Dick, 139 N. Spring St., Bluffton 45817; Olwen Pritchard/James Satterwhite (*satterwhitej@bluffton.edu*).

792. *Peace and Conflict Studies* (col).

History Dept., Bluffton College, Bluffton 45817; (419) 358-3280; *johnsl@bluffton.edu; www.bluffton.edu/dept/history/pcs.htm*

In addition to course work, the PCS program includes an elective one-semester academic semester in Northern Ireland. Works closely with the Lion and Lamb Peace Arts Center. Loren Johns, Dir.

793. *Peace Wall and Gate* (1997) (mem).

Near the Lion and Lamb Center and the Library, Bluffton College Campus, Bluffton 45817.

The Wall and Gate anchor a sculpture garden and sections of the wall contain the names of world peacemakers from throughout the ages and names of political prisoners, and one section is composed of graffiti tiles to suggest the Berlin Wall. Passing through the Gate symbolizes the refusal to allow walls to separate people. The memorial was designed by Jon Barlow Hudson.

CINCINNATI, OH

794. *Center for Peace Education* (1979) (org).

103 William Howard Taft Rd., Cincinnati 45219; (513) 221-4863.

Peace Wall and Gate, Bluffton College, Bluffton. Photograph courtesy Lion and Lamb Peace Arts Center and Libby Hostetler.

Advocates policies for peace and social justice and provides educational programs to promote these policies: creative response to conflict, peer mediation, cooperative discipline, bias awareness, and related methods. Two national conferences were held on racism in conflict management and meetings on the subject continue. Pub.: quarterly newsletter *Peace Connections*; a lesson plan manual, *A Year of Students' Creative Response to Conflict*; and a student handbook, *Peer Mediator's Guide*.

795. *The New School* (1994) (mem).

3 Burton Woods Lane, Cincinnati 45229; (513) 281-7971.

In 1999 celebrated their 30th anniversary with a rededication of their *Peace Pole* and of their "The Ripple Effect" quilt in tribute to their peace education curriculum. The peace core is based on the words of Lao Tzu in the Tao Te Ching: "Your behavior influences others through a ripple effect." The Peace Pole is a 6' tall hexagonal inscribed with "May Peace Prevail on Earth"

in five languages and animal pawprints signifying commitment to saving animals. Located near the front entrance of the school and surrounded by seasonal flowers, the Pole has been the locus of many special events. "The Peace Commitment" was written for the dedication; it reads in part: "We promise to be peacemakers. We will treat each person with respect and kindness." Contact Shawn Dougherty (*skdoughrty@ aol.com*).

796. *One Percent, Connecting the Community* (org).

3590 Roundbottom Rd. #246352, Cincinnati 45244; (617)557-3036.

Aims to reduce violence and suffering in our dislocated society by bringing one percent of the caring population to talk and share with each other and to celebrate life. The founder of One Percent, Jack Winn/Jack Francis walks the world distributing his booklet *1%, Connecting the Community*. (See: Peace Pilgrim).

797. *Peace and Justice Programs Center* (1981) (col).

Dorothy Day House, Xavier University, 3800 Victory Parkway, Cincinnati, 45209-2910; (513) 745-3046; *www.xu.edu/spiritual/peacejus.htm*; *www.xu.edu/peace/ben.htm* ("Xavier Self-Study").

Activities: off-campus study in Nicaragua and urban studies; diverse community outreach, including a weekly radio program, "Faith and Justice Forum." Houses seven student peace and justice organizations. Peace Studies Minor integrates perspectives of various disciplines in search of a just and peaceful world by studying the causes and consequences of war and social conflict, the ethical implications of violence and peace, strategies for conflict resolution, and the relationship between peace, justice, and ecological sustainability. Visiting lecturers and practicums supplement regular course work. Benjamin Urmston, S. J., Director.

798. *Thousand Years of Peace Project* (1999) (org).

1615 Republic St., Cincinnati 45210; (513) 241-5615; *www.americancatholic.org/Features/Peace*; *St.Anthony@AmericanCatholic.org*

The Catholic Sisters of Sisters United News, Greater Cincinnati Region, and St. Anthony Messenger Press have issued an invitation to people who want to build world peace. Their goal is to encourage 1000 years of peacemaking activities by the end of the year 2000 by persuading people to pledge a certain number of hours to peacemaking during 2000.

799. *Urban Center for Peace Research Implementation, Development, and Education (UCPRIDE)* (1990) (col).

College of Education, U of Cincinnati, Cincinnati 45221; (513) 556-3608; *ucpride@uc.educ*; *marvin.berlowitz@uc.edu*; *www.oz.uc.edu/~berlowmj/UCPRIDE.html*

Administers the Certificate in Peace Education and conducts workshops, seminars, conferences, research, and internships in pursuit of peace education. The Certificate requires 21 credit hours of courses on conflict resolution, diversity, human rights, peace theory and history, structural violence, and related courses. Also has produced a film, "Reflections of Peace and Justice Leaders," about 7 leaders of the movement aged 70 and older, accompanied by a study guide for grades 7-college. Marvin Berlowitz, Dir.

CLEVELAND, OH

800. *Cleveland Peace Action* (1981) (org).

Peace House, 10916 Magnolia Drive, Cleveland 44106; (216) 231-4245; *chiapski@aol.com*

Originally the Greater Cleveland Nuclear Weapons Freeze Campaign, now an affil. of Peace Action (1993). Activities: speakers, legislative alerts, vigils, demonstrations. Pub. a newsletter 3–4 times a year (Fall 1999: CTBT rejection, analysis of Pentagon budget FY 2000, militarization of space, etc.). Marji Edguer, Pres., or contact Francis Chiappa, Vice Pres.

801. *Global Issues Resource Center* (1985) (org).

4250 Richmond Rd., Eastern Campus— East 1, Cuyahoga Community College, Cleveland 44122; (216) 987-2224; *peggy.wertheim@tri-c.cc.oh.us*; *GIRCADM@library.cpl.org*; *www.tri-c.cc.oh.us/east/docs/girc.htm*

Seeks to educate teachers and the public about the sources and management of conflict, nuclear weapons, arms control, environmental endangerment, and related issues. The Center offers educational programming, custom designed skills training, an award winning multimedia library collection available on-line, public lectures, seminars, and diverse other resources for peace. Contact Peggy Wertheim.

802. *Peace Pole* (1998) (mem).

At the United Methodist Church, Cleveland.

Dedicated at the Spring District Conference with a ceremony which included "May Peace Prevail on Earth" in many languages. Initiated by Don Swartz.

COLUMBUS, OH

803. *Columbus Campaign for Arms Control* (1979) (org).

1101 Brydon Rd., Columbus 43205; (614) 252-9255(w); *walk@igc.org*

Originally organized as a chapter of the United Nations Assoc. in the 1970s, and then 1979 connected with the nuclear freeze movement. Works to counter violence, racism, and sexism. Activities: nuclear disarmament, human rights, women, youth, native rights, bread v. guns, Middle East peace, Central America, annual Hiroshima-Nagasaki commemoration, and more. Has pub. *Voice for Justice and Peace* newsletter but now uses a web site. Mark Stansbery, Pres.

804. *Mershon Center* (1962) (col).

Ohio State University, Columbus 43210; (614) 292-1981; *lebow.1@osu.edu;* *www.mershon.ohio-state.edu*

Research on national security, including democratization, post-Cold War relations, economic development, the Middle East, and conflict prevention and resolution. Emphasizes collaboration with other institutions. Research grants available for faculty and graduate students. Also supports undergraduate studies in diverse ways. Ned Lebow, Dir.

805. *Peace Studies* (late 1980s) (col).

Dept. of International Studies, Ohio State University, Columbus 43210; (614) 292-9657; *IntStds@osu.edu;* *http://psweb.sbs.ohio-state.edu/* *international/PeaceStudies.htm*

Offers a major, minor, and certificate on the history, theory, and application of peacemaking. Internships, field studies, and international exchanges encouraged. Active student International Studies Club. Contact Tony Mughan.

DAYTON, OH

806. *Dayton Peace Action* (1990) (org).

1060 Salem Ave., Dayton 45406; (937) 233-3425; *lucas@dayton.net;* *www.cyberfaith.org/dpeaceact.htm;* *www.dayton.net/~lucas*

Originally Dayton Citizens for Arms Race Reduction (1979), then *Dayton Citizens for Global Security* (1990), now a Peace Action affil. DPA concentrates on eliminating forces that threaten global future: militarism, weapons of mass destruction, regional and ethnic conflicts, and promotes peaceful resolution of global social and economic conflicts and injustices. Contact Jim Lucas.

807. *Peace Studies* (1988) (col).

Dept. of Political Science, Wright State University, Dayton 45435-0001; (937) 873-2904; *d.schlagheck@wright.edu;* *www.wright.edu/Dept/pls/pls.html*

A specializing track in the international studies BA program. Students participate in the annual peace studies conference held by the city and the university. Contact Donna Schlagheck.

GROVEPORT, OH

808. *Lion and Lamb Project* (1999) (porg).

6200 Commerce Dr., Groveport 43125; 877-WOW-KIDS; *promotions@ZanyBrainy.com;* *TradeAToy@zanybrainy.com;* *www.zanybrainy.com/stc/promo/lionlamb/* *intro.jsp?sid=2128219*

Offered a toy trade-in program (until Dec. 24, 1999) for exchanging war toys for peaceful and educational toys, sponsored by Zany Brainy stores and ZanyBrainy.com, which sell nonviolent toys. This project was launched in conjunction with The Lion & Lamb Project, a "Parent Action Kit" to provide information about the effects of violent entertainment, toys, and games on children's behavior.

KENT, OH

809. *Center for Applied Conflict Management* (1994) (col).

Kent State U.; *cacm@kent.edu;* *www.kent.edu/cacm/*

Created as a living memorial to May 4, 1970, when four war protesters were killed and others wounded on campus by the National Guard. Formerly known as the *Center for Peaceful Change* (1971), it was initially an independent unit that housed the school's peace studies program, which included study, research, public service, an annual candlelight vigil, as well as other May 4 activities. The Center houses the conflict studies program attached to the department of political science.

http://www.library.kent.edu/exhibits/4may95/ *48.html*

Gordon, William. *The Fourth of May: Killings*

and Coverups at Kent State. Buffalo, NY: Prometheus, 1990.

Hensley, Thomas. *The Kent State Incident: Impact of Judicial Process on Public Attitudes.* Westport, CT: Greenwood, 1981.

Kelner, Joseph and James Munves. *The Kent State Coverup.* New York: Harper & Row, 1980.

United States. President's Commission on Campus Unrest. *The Kent State Tragedy: Special Report.* Washington, D.C.: U.S. Government Printing Office, 1970.

810. **Institute for the Study and Prevention of Violence (ISPV)* (1998) (col).

191 Gym Annex, ISPV/RAGS, Kent State U, Kent 44240; (330) 672-7917 or 672-2775; *dflanne1@kent.edu;* *www.kent.edu/violence*

Promotes interdisciplinary research into the causes and prevention of violence, designs and implements community-based programs for violence prevention, and trains teachers, law enforcement personnel, and other professionals on the principles and practices of violence prevention. Current (1999-) projects include: Peacebuilders (study of elementary school violence prevention project) and Children Who Witness Violence (pilot program of mental health services to children who have witnessed domestic violence).

811. **May 4 Collection* (1970) (lib).

Department of Special Collections and Archives, Kent State U., *www.library.kent.edu/exhibits/4may95/may4cont.html*

Over 160 cubic feet of materials documenting the events of May 1970. Flyers, newspaper articles, songs, poems, lectures, correspondence, etc.

812. *May 4 Memorial* (1990) (mem).

A 2½ acre wooded site overlooking Kent State University's commons.

A plaza 70 feet wide, extending 22 feet onto the hill and bound by a granite walkway, commemorates the events of May 4, 1970, when four students were killed and nine were wounded by National Guard troops during an anti-war protest on the campus. (The Memorial is some distance from the actual site of the shootings.) A

sculpture constructed of carnelian granite and surrounded by 58,175 daffodils, the number of the country's deaths in the Vietnam War, compose the heart of the Memorial. Engraved in the plaza's stone threshold are the words "Inquire, Learn, Reflect." A progression of four black granite disks embedded in the earth lead from the plaza to four free-standing pylons on the hill. A fifth disk to the south acknowledges the many victims of the events. A 48-foot bench along the granite walkway provides visitors a place to rest and to view the memorial. The Memorial was designed by Bruno Ast. The Memorial to the slain students continues to grow. In June, 1998, Kent State agreed to make a memorial out of parking spaces where the four students were killed by the Guardsmen by erecting markers in the spaces.

813. *May 4 Memorial Windows* (1973) (mem).

Kent State U., May 4 Memorial room in the University Library.

Four stained glass windows created by Kent State graduate Theodore Abel, a gift from the artist.

http://www.library.kent.edu/exhibits/4may95/exhibit/memorials/window.html

Kidron, OH

814. **Mennonite Central Committee/ Great Lakes* (1980) (org).

13363 Jericho Rd., Box 82, Kidron 44636; (330) 857-7721; *bglick@mcc.org; mccgl@mcc.org*

Carries out the mission of MCC in the Great Lakes area. Pub. quarterly newsletter. Bruce and Helen Glick, Co-Directors.

North Canton, OH

815. *Brother Francis Blouin Peace Park* (1993) (mem).

Outside Farrell Hall, administration building, Walsh Univ., N. Canton

Triangular-shaped Park includes: Garden, Peace Pole, explanatory Stones commemorating the visit of six Nobel Peace prize winners, Shalom Pavilion (gazebo-like structure with circular seating for up to 30, gift of Jewish community), a relief-statue of man beating sword into plowshare, armillary sphere with words from "God has willed that all people should constitute one family," a circular sidewalk seating, a statue of St. Francis, an Earth flag and a UN flag flanking the US flag with explanatory stones, and a brochure-holder with brochures explaining the elements of the Park. Joseph Torma and committee, designers.

816. *Institute for Justice and Peace* (1985) (col).

Walsh University, North Canton 44720; (330) 490-7199 or 490-7052; *torma@alex.walsh.edu; www.walsh.edu*

Promotes the social justice teachings of the Catholic Church, through lectures, a play, concerts, summer workshops, video series, and more. Joseph Torma, Dir. (author of *Principles of Justice and Peace: An Introduction to Catholic Social Thought*, Walsh, 1990).

OBERLIN, OH

817. *Episcopal Peace Fellowship, Diocese of Ohio* (1980?) (org).

94 S. Cedar St., Oberlin 44074; (440) 774-1169; *deano@apk.net*

Some years ago this EPF engaged in dialog with the Soviet Union, sending two delegations there. More recently it sent a delegation to Cuba. It has supported Pastors for Peace, offers an annual award for a person outstanding in work for peace and justice, offered a two-year program on Dietrich Bonhoeffer, and in September of 2000 organized Peace Week with workshops on alternatives to violence. Meets monthly. Dean Wolfe, Co-Convenor.

SOUTH BASS ISLAND, OH

818. *Perry's Victory and International Peace Memorial* (1913) (mem).

South Bass Island in Lake Erie about 3 miles from the mainland.

This is a war monument and part of the history of U.S. imperialism, but the Treaty of Ghent led to lasting peace between the United States and Great Britain, leading to the Rush-

Bagot Agreement two years later, which limited the number of warships on Lake Erie, and to the permanent disarmament of the 4,000-mile border between the U.S. and Canada in 1871. The Memorial thus honors not only a battle but the principle of settling differences between nations by negotiation. Designated a national monument in 1936, the Memorial rises 352 feet above the lake (78 courses of pink Massachusetts granite topped by an eleven-ton bronze urn). It was designed by Joseph Freedlander. A distinctive feature of the Memorial, extremely rare in war memorials and another reason for considering it a peace memorial, is the reinterment in 1913 of not only the three U.S. officers killed in the battle but of the three British officers as well, an act which anticipates the great World War II cenotaph on Okinawa, in which all of the killed soldiers on both sides (and all civilians) are listed on the stone walls.

TOLEDO, OH

819. *Greater Toledo Fellowship of Reconciliation* (1978) (org).

7815 Hedingham Rd., Sylvania 43560; (419) 882-2480; *75041.2670@compuserve.com*

An FOR group existed in the area as early as 1950s. Participates in the Interfaith Justice & Peace Center and its newsletter *Linkages*. Supports national FOR projects.

WILMINGTON, OH

820. *Peace Resource Center & Hiroshima/Nagasaki Collection* (1975/1992)

251 Ludovic St., Wilmington College, Pyle Center Box 1183, Wilmington 45177; (937) 382-6661, ext. 371; *jim_boland@wilmington.edu; prc@wilmington.edu; www.wilmington.edu*

Housed in the family home of Elsie McCoy, who bequeathed the property to the College, the Center began in 1975 with the acquisition of the Hiroshima/Nagasaki memorial Collection from Barbara Reynolds, Quaker peace activist, who had acquired the materials relating to the 1945 bombings while living in Hiroshima. The Center, rededicated in 1992, provides a circulating library and other educational materials and activities on nonviolence, conflict resolution, the peace movement, environmental issues, and disarmament. Pub.: newsletter, *News from Peace House* (Fall 1999 includes a notice on a peace symposium and an annot. list of new books and films for rental). Dr. Jim Boland, Director; Jean True, Coordinator. Affil. With the Religious Society of Friends (Quakers).

821. *Peace Studies and Applied Peace Studies* (1970) (col).

Dept of Religion and Philosophy, Wilmington College, Wilmington 45177; (937) 382-6661 ext. 210; *ron_rembert@ wilmington.edu; www.wchome.wilmington.edu; www.wilmington.edu/relphil.htm*

Two minor degrees: PS of 24 semester hours, APS 30 hours, in a Quaker context. Contact Ronald Rembert.

YELLOW SPRINGS, OH

822. *Peace Studies* (1991) (col).

Cultural and Interdisciplinary Studies, Antioch College, Yellow Springs 45387; (937) 767-6444; *pmicshe@antioch-college.edu; www.antioch-college.edu/ Catalog/html/ peace%20studies.html*

In this concentration, besides course work, students must be involved with two peace and conflict co-ops, a student organization, and a civic group or community organization. Contact Patricia Mische (pronounced Mishee), Lloyd Professor of Peace Studies and World Law.

YOUNGSTOWN, OH

823. *Peace Action Youngstown* (1981) (org).

204 Broadway, Youngstown 44504; (330) 747-5404; *peaceactyo@cboss.com*

Supports national PA agenda; pub. monthly newsletter. Therese Joseph, Devel. Dir. Francie Kerpsack and Rick Judy, Co-chairs.

824. *Peace & Conflict Studies Program* (1988) (col).

429 DeBartolo Hall, Youngstown State Univ., Youngstown 44455; (330) 742-

3437; *kjlepak@cc.ysu.edu; www.as.ysu.edu/~polisci/global.htm*

An interdisciplinary minor program in the College of Arts and Sciences offering studies of human conflict and its management. Works with the Global Studies Program to bring speakers to campus and provide internships. Keith Lepak, Coord.

— Oklahoma (OK) —

11 Sister Cities. / 29 Peace Poles.

OKLAHOMA CITY, OK

825. *The Peace House* (1981) (org).

2912 N. Robinson, Oklahoma City 73103; (405) 524-5577; *opsnews@aol.com*

State Office of Peace Action. Does education and advocacy on many justice and compassion issues: organizes public events like the annual Fall Peace Festival, brings in speakers, like Alan Nairn on East Timor, provides information, editorials, and alerts to oppose military spending and capital punishment and to encourage the building of a nonviolent, democratic, tolerant, just, and sustainable world. Members seek to practice the nonviolence of Jesus. Pub. *Oklahoma Peace Strategy News*, 16 pp. Nathaniel Batchelder, Dir.

—— Oregon (OR) ——

35 Sister Cities. / 68 Peace Poles.

ALBANY, OR

826. *Linn-Benton PeaceWorks* (1986) (org).

3440 NW Eagle View Drive, Albany 97321; (541) 926-7070; *hemmi@juno.com*

Chapter of Oregon PeaceWorks. (Originally a chapter of Citizen Action for Lasting Security [1982]). April 15 distributes flyers on military budget at post offices, participates in antiwar demonstrations, supports Pastors for peace visits, etc. Contact Ed and June Hemmingson.

ASHLAND, OR

827. **International Peace Studies* (1985) (col).

Interdisciplinary Programs,
Southern Oregon University,
Ashland 97520; (541) 552-6131;
Rhoades@sou.edu;
www.sou.edu/catalog/99-00/Interdis/
PEACE.htm

Undergraduate minor of core and elective courses. Don Rhoades, Coord.

828. **Peace House* (1982) (org).

PO Box 524, Ashland 97520;
(541) 482-9625;
peacehse@mind.net

Affil with Fellowship of Reconciliation in 1983. Priorities 1999: cultural violence, militarism, Earth Day focus on nuclear waste, Watershed Stewardship Alliance, mentoring youth activism, free weekly community meal for homeless and low income, Ceasefire Oregon, Rogue Institute for Economy and Ecology. Offers a resource library, monthly meetings, and other projects. Ruth Coulthard, Coordinator.

CORVALLIS, OR

829. **Federalist Caucus* (1976) (org).

1544 NW Dixon St.,
Corvallis 97330-4651;
(541) 752-4067.

Advocates system of global law and justice to reduce conflict between nations and to move beyond the war system. Kermit Rhode, Pres.

830. **Linus Pauling Institute* (1973) (org).

Oregon State University, Corvallis.

Pauling (1901–1994), a graduate of OSU, received the 1962 Nobel Peace Prize. His Institute, originally in Palo Alto, CA, is now at OSU, and the Ava Helen and Linus Pauling Papers are at OSU's Valley Library. "Our loyalty now should be to the whole of humanity. The time

Linus Pauling protesting nuclear tests in front of White House, April 1962. Photograph from Linus Pauling memorial booklet.

has come when we can make the world a great place for all human beings, everywhere, through the use of the resources of the world and the discoveries made by scientists for the benefit of humanity, and not for war, death, and destruction." 1967 lecture on "The Challenge of Scientific Discovery."

Goertzel, Ted, and Ben Goertzel. *Linus Pauling: A Life in Science and Politics.* New York: Basic Books, 1995.

Hager, Thomas. *Force of Nature: the Life of Linus Pauling.* New York: Simon and Schuster, 1995.

Linus Pauling, In Memoriam, 1901–1994. Palo Alto, CA: Linus Pauling Institute of Science and Medicine, n.d.

Marinacci, Barbara, ed. *Linus Pauling in His Own Words: Selected Writings, Speeches, and Interviews.* New York: Simon and Schuster, 1995.

831. **Peace Studies* (1986) (col).

Dept. of Speech Communications,
Oregon State University;
Corvallis 97331; (541) 737-2461;
walkerg@cla.orst.edu; www.orst.edu/dept/
*gencat/coldep/libarts/peace/pe*ace.htm

Undergraduate certificate of core courses and electives. Contact Gregg Walker.

EUGENE, OR

831a. *Eugene PeaceWorks* (1979) (org).

454 Willamette, Eugene 97401;
(541) 343-8548; *eugpeace@efn.org;*
www.efn.org/~eugpeace

Chapter of War Resisters League. Provides office space and organizing resources for peace-making/opposition to militarism, nuclear weapons, media control by the military-industrial complex, Copwatch, and other programs, through nonviolent direct action and weekly video presentation.

832. *Eugene-Springfield Fellowship of Reconciliation* (1979) (org).

1910 Monroe St. Eugene 97405;
(541) 683-2332.

Orig. New Call to Peacemaking, affil. with Fellowship of Reconciliation in 1988. Sponsors the Pacifica Forum organized by Orval Etter. Contact Melena Thompson.

833. *Lane County WAND* (1997) (org).

1527 West 25th Ave., Eugene 97405;
(541) 342-5325

Branch of Women's Action for New Directions. Actively supports national WAND campaigns for the CTBT and conversion from military to civilian economy and against landmines. Locally it supports women political candidates (see WAND's WiLL project) and coalition with other peace groups. Contact Leslie Brockelbank.

834. *Peace Studies* (1986) (col).

University of Oregon, Eugene 97403;
(541) 346-4198; *dfrank@oregon.uoregon.edu;*
http://darkwing.uoregon.edu/~uopubs/
bulletin/cas/peace_studies.html#top

The undergraduate minor of core and elective courses examines the causes and alternatives to violence. Contact David Frank.

835. *Skipping Stones* (1991) (jour).

PO Box 3939, Eugene 97403;
(541) 342-4956; *skipping@efn.org;*
www.nonviolence.org/skipping

A nonprofit multicultural children's magazine that encourages cooperation, creativity, and celebration of cultural and environmental richness. Winner of several awards.

FOREST GROVE, OR

836. *Peace and Conflict Studies* (1984) (col).

Pacific University, Forest Grove 97116;
(503) 359-2150; *boersema@pacificu.edu;*
nellie.pacificu.edu/provost/catalog/archive/
97_98/13.html#PACS

Undergraduate minor focuses on violence—in self, society, and nations—and alternatives. The Pacific Humanitarian Center (1992) (*www. pacificu.edu,* catalog link) assists in placing students in public service positions for academic credit. Contact David Boersema.

LAFAYETTE, OR

837. *Northeast Oregon Peace Network* (1982, 1987) (org).

60366 Marvin Road, La Grande 97850;
(541) 962-8877; *Maray@worc.org* or
fkreider@chdinc.org

Formerly, La Grande Peace Advocates. Works for peace and safe transportation and clean-up of nuclear waste at Hanford and DOE complex. Contact Fuji Kreider.

837a. *PeaceBike Team* (1999) (org).

PO Box 761, Lafayette 97127;
info@peacebike.org; www.peacebike.org

Tad Beckwith and Frank Pollari (Ontario, Can) are biking around the world to advocate friendship and cooperation, building "peace one friendship at a time." Part of their plan is to create pen pals through their web site.

MARYLHURST, OR

838. *Conflict and Culture* (1998) (col).

Communications Studies, Marylhurst University, Marylhurst 97036;
(503) 699-6269; *jsweeney@marylhurst.edu;*
www.marylhurst.edu

Undergraduate concentration is for students interested in techniques of dispute resolution, negotiation, mediation, and intercultural communication. Jeff Sweeney, Dir.

NEWBERG, OR

839. *Center for Peace Learning* (1984) (col).

George Fox University, Newberg 97132; (503) 554-2680; *rmock@georgefox.edu; http://cis.georgefox.edu/cpl/*

CPL performs research, teaching, and resources for peacemaking in a Quaker Christian setting. It also coordinates the undergraduate minor and certificate academic program. Ron Mock, Dir.

PORTLAND, OR

840. *Conflict Resolution* (1996) (col).

Philosophy Dept., Portland State University, Portland 97207; (503) 752-3502; *d8rg@odin.cc.pdx.edu; www.conflictresolution.pdx.edu/*

MS/MA program includes a thesis and practicum on community projects; internships available. Robert Gould, Dir.

841. *International Peace Garden* (1977) (mem).

University of Portland, center of campus, about 500 yards inside main entrance, between the Student Center and Buckley Center Auditorium.

The garden is 15 feet by 20 feet, inside an uneven stone wall, filled with plants from every continent, with a dedication stone in the center with the words: "In this small patch of earth, plants from every continent live in peace and harmony. You who pass by, pray God that the same may one day be said for the whole human race."

842. *Oregon Committee for War Tax Resistance/WRL* (1991) (org).

2000 NE 42nd Ave., Suite 224, Portland 97213; (503) 233-1545.

A branch of the War Resisters League.

843. *Peace and Conflict Studies (PACS)* (1990-1996) (col).

Social and Behavioral Sciences, Sylvania Campus, Portland Community College, Portland 97280; (503) 977-4289; *msonnlei@pcc.edu; www.pcc.edu*

Major, minor, and certificate offered from core and elective courses. Contact Michael Sonnleitner.

844. *Peace Studies* (1975) (col).

Depts. Of History, Political Science, & Theology, University of Portland, Portland 97203; (503) 943-7541; *pomer@up.edu; www.up.edu/default.lasso*

The undergraduate Peace Studies Certificate and minor were founded by Joseph Powers, and now a major is offered. The campus has a *peace garden.* Claude Pomerlean, Dir.

845. *Portland Peace and Justice Works* (1986) (org).

PO Box 42456, Portland 97242; (503) 236-3065; *pjw@agora.rdrop.com; www.rdrop.cim/~pjw/index.html*

Formerly Portland Peaceworks. An umbrella organization that seeks to "educate the general public on important issues" including "peace, justice, the environment, and human rights," by working through project or affinity groups. Present groups are: Portland Copwatch, Iraq Affinity Group, Aid to Former Yugoslavia, and Pentagon Porkbusters. PJW's largest activity has been the Peace and Justice Fair on Memorial Day "to remember those who gave their lives in war by working toward a world without war." Contact Dan Handleman.

SALEM, OR

846. *Oregon Fellowship of Reconciliation* (1930s, 1967) (org).

490 19th St., NE, Lower Level, PO Box 222, Salem 97308-0222; (503) 391-5933; *frazierd@efn.org*

Priorities: support FOR groups in Oregon, educational projects, coalition action projects. Organizes annual statewide meeting and annual fall retreat, helps to plan regional Seabeck retreat, annual Hiroshima Day, annual Martin Luther King Jr. event, weekly peace vigils,

Peace Plaza, Salem; artists Larry Watson and Peggy O'Neal. Photograph courtesy Mike Swaim, Mayor; Marlene McMahon, Community Services Dept.

educating and actions for nuclear disarmament, many other activities. Donna Frazier, State Staff.

847. *Oregon PeaceWorks* (1986) (org).

333 State St., Salem 97301;
(503) 585-2767; *opw@teleport.com;*
www.teleport.com/~opw

Pub. *Oregon PeaceWorker* newspaper, Peter Bergel, ed. (503-371-8002). The March 2000 number of 23pp. included articles about the globalization of capital, money's control of politics, the death penalty, review of Winona LaDuke's book on Native American dispossession, the killings of civilians in Guatemala, Congressman Kucinich's intention to introduce legislation for a Department of Peace, harm done to Africa by U.S. "help," animal liberation. Michael Carrigan, Dir. of OPW.

848. *Peace Plaza* (1988) (mem).

Salem, Oregon, between City Hall and the City Library.

Banners with the word "Peace" in diverse languages, a Peace Wall containing 106 peace quotation plaques, glass artwork, again with "Peace" in many languages, by Elizabeth Mapelli, and a 36-by-12-foot mural showing the likenesses of about 20 Salem residents from different ethnic groups by the artists Larry Watson and Peggy O'Neal. Each banner visually interprets one element of an ancient Chinese proverb: "If there is compassion in the heart, there will be love in the home. If there is love in the home, there will be wholeness in the community. If there is wholeness in the community, there will be harmony in the nation. And if there is harmony in the nation, there will be peace in the world." From a brochure: The Peace Plaza is Salem's "opportunity to express our commitment to promote peace." The Dedication included an address by the noted peace advocate William Sloan Coffin.

849. *Salem Fellowship of Reconciliation* (1945) (org).

490 19th St. NE, Lower Level,
PO Box 222, Salem 97308-0222;
(503) 566-7190.

Networks with other Salem peace and justice groups, monthly program, fall retreat with OR FOR, opposes JROTC and death penalty, tabling at various events. Pub. *Salem Area Fellowship of Reconciliation* monthly newsletter. Contact Rosemary Cooperrider.

Peace Plaza, Peace Wall, Peace Plaza, Inc., Salem. Photograph courtesy Mike Swaim, Mayor; Marlene McMahon, Community Services Dept.

— *Pennsylvania (PA)* —

29 Sister Cities. / 189 Peace Poles.

AKRON, PA

850. **Mennonite Central Committee (MCC)* (1920) (org).

21 S. 12th St., PO Box 500, Akron 17501-0500; (717) 859-1151or 859-3889; *mailbox@mcc.org; jzh@mcc.org; www.mcc.org/; www.mennonitecc.ca/mcc/*

A relief, service, community development, and peace agency of the North American Mennonite and Brethren in Christ churches. As part of its mission, MCC "strives for peace, justice, and dignity of all people by sharing our experiences, resources, and faith in Jesus Christ." Mennonites are rooted in the radical wing of the 16th-century reformation that called itself Anabaptist. Their core beliefs include: stewardship and simplicity in lifestyle; love and compassion as the central values, including concern for human needs and the enemy; and rejection of violence, military service, and war. One of the three historic peace churches in North America, along with the Church of the Brethren and the Quakers. Mennonite conscientious objectors were drafted and punished during WWI; in WWII and the Korean and Vietnam Wars they did alternative service; and nonregistration for the draft is sanctioned. Gradually, Mennonite opposition to war has come to include attention to all forms of violence and peacemaking. MCC has three departments that focus primarily on peace and peace education: the international MCC Peace Office, MCC Canada Peace Ministries, and MCC U.S. Peace and Justice Ministries. *Peace Office Newsletter* quarterly. Nine regional offices in Canada and the U.S. disseminate Mennonite values and services. *MCC East Coast* is located at this address.

851. **New Call to Peacemaking* (1976) (org).

PO Box 500, Akron 17501; (717) 859-1958; *jkstoner@ptd.net*

Sponsored by the Mennonites, Brethren, and Friends, NCP nurtures nonviolence by identifying the kinds of violence in our culture of violence, by promoting conscientious objection to war, and by inspiring peacemaking within faith groups and local congregations. Pubs.: *Call to Peacemaking* newsletter; *Called to Be Peacemakers* (guidebook of ten chapters); *New Call for Peacemakers*. John Stoner, Coordinator.

BIRDSBORO, PA

852. **Circles for Peace/Peace Action Network* (1998) (org).

c/o Mrs. Deni Gross, Birdsboro 19508; *cfpeace@hotmail.com; www.theoservice.org*

Circles for Peace focuses on daily meditation and prayer for personal and planetary peace; Peace Action Network works on world issues. Both are activities of the *Theosophical Order of Service Peace Department*, which publishes the magazine *For the Love of Life*, which has articles on such subjects as the global sale and transfer of arms, the worldwide military recruitment of child soldiers, the elimination of nuclear weapons, the remembrance of Hiroshima and Nagasaki, and violent, racist, and sexist toys; and which offers a number of action resources. The Peace Department of TOS has also inaugurated "Gardeners for Peace." See entry 1073.

BRYN MAWR, PA

853. **Conflict Resolution* (1997) (col).

Graduate School of Social Work, Bryn Mawr College, Bryn Mawr 19010; (610) 520-2601; *www.brynmawr.edu/gsswsr/conflict.html*

A graduate-level certificate for practitioners to deepen understanding and techniques. (Searching for new coord. Spring 2000).

854. **Peace and Conflict Studies* (1985) (col).

Dept of Political Science, Bryn Mawr College, Bryn Mawr 19010; (610) 526-5326; *mross@brynmawr.edu; www. brynmawr.edu/Adm/academic/peace.html*

This undergraduate Concentration is a joint

venture with Haverford College (Bryn Mawr-Haverford Peace and Conflict Studies), a six-course cluster, including Managing Conflicts in Nations and Organizations, and The League of Nations and the World. Marc Ross, Coord.

CHAMBERSBURG, PA

855. **Peace Studies Program* (1998) (col).

Dept of Behavioral Sciences, Wilson College, Chambersburg 17201; (717) 264-4141 ext3281; *lwoehrle@wilson.edu; www.wilson.edu/ Academics/aca3intstud.htm*

Undergraduate minor of four courses in a Christian affiliation.

CHESTER, PA

856. *Martin Luther King, Jr., Historical Markers* (mem).

At Crozer-Chester Medical Center, Upland (1992), and Calvary Baptist Church, Chester (1984).

Nobel Peace Prize laureate, 1964. King earned his Bachelor of Divinity at Crozer Theological Seminary and later ministered at this church. (See Tennessee).

CRESCO, PA

857. *Peace Pole* (1998) (mem).

In front of the Paradise Township Municipal Building in Cresco.

Planted by the Scranton Pocono Girl Scout Junior Troop #364.

ELIZABETHTOWN, PA

858. **Peace and Conflict Studies* (1989) (col).

Dept of Religious Studies, Elizabethtown College, Elizabethtown 17022; (717) 361-1240; *marshalle@etown.edu; www.etown.edu/web/religion.html*

This Church of the Brethren school offers an undergraduate minor of core, electives, and capstone seminar. Elizabethtown College is a sister school with Juniata and Manchester colleges. Contact Ellen Marshall.

ELKINS PARK, PA

859. *Lucretia C. Mott Historical Marker* (1974) (mem).

PA 611 N of Cheltenham Ave.,
Elkins Park.

Mott (1795–1880) ardently opposed slavery and advocated peace, women's rights, and temperance.

ERIE, PA

860. *Pax Christi USA* (1972) (org).

532 W. 8th St., Erie, 16502-1343; (814) 453-4955; *info@paxchristiusa.org; www.nonviolence.org/pcusa/*

Composed of some 550 Roman Catholic religious communities committed to nonviolence, PCUSA works for disarmament and demilitarization, economic and interracial justice, human rights, and education for peace. "Pax Christi USA rejects war, preparations for war, and every form of violence and domination." Sample activities: denounced renewed bombing of Iraq, air strikes in Afghanistan and Sudan, death penalty, violence against gays and lesbians, U.S. nuclear deterrence policy, Indian nuclear testing and hypocrisy of other nuclear states. Gives the Paul VI Award and the Pax Christi Book Award. Pub. *Catholic Peace Voice.* Nancy Small, Nat. Coordinator; Phyllis Jepson, Local/Regional Coord. (paxwpb@gate.net). Affil. With Pax Christi International, the Catholic peace movement (1945), headquartered in Brussels.

FARMINGTON, PA

861. *Plough Publishing House* (1920) (org).

Rt. 381 North, Farmington 15437-9506; (800) 521-8011; *jca@plough.com; www.plough.com* (The Bruderhof web page is *www.bruderhof.org).*

The publishing arm of the Bruderhof communities. Pub. books by Johann Christoph Arnold, the founder of Bruderhof, Philip Berri-

gan, Archbishop Romero, Dan Halleck, and others.

862. *Spring Valley Bruderhof* (1990) (org).

PO Box 260, Rt. 381 North, Farmington 15437; (724) 329-1100.
See Rifton, NY.

GETTYSBURG, PA

863. *Conflict Resolution and Global Interdependence (CRAGI)* (1993) (col).

Community College, Gettysburg 17325; (717) 337-6790; *ppitney@gettysburg.edu; www.gettysburg.edu/~jpowers/cragi.html*

Works to introduce the International Curricular Peace Thread in schools globally, to teach skills of conflict resolution, prejudice reduction, and peaceful co-existence. The Thread is designed to be taught in any culture from preschool through college. CRAGI also acts locally to reduce conflict in schools and community settings. Contacts with UNICEF, UNESCO, the Carter Center, and IPRA reflect CRAGI's strategy of international education for peace. Tricia Pitney, Dir. (717-677-8784).

864. In 2000 "peace-loving citizens of Adams County" planned to erect a *Peace Pole* with 8 languages.

Contact Tricia Pitney (ppitney@popserver. facmail.gettysburg.edu).

GLENSIDE, PA

865. *International Peace and Conflict Resolution Program* (1998) (col).

Beaver College, 450 S. Easton Rd, Glenside 19038-3295; (215) 572-2900; *mazzucelli@beaver.edu; www.beaver.edu*

The MA degree enables students to concentrate in the discipline, make international contacts, and gain practical field experience. The program builds on a long tradition of international study at Beaver, including the Center for Education Abroad (1965–). And its innovations include a partnership with the USIP in the first on-line seminar in the field using Real Audio, Fall 1999. Colette Mazzucelli, Dir.

HARRISBURG, PA

866. *Peace Garden* (1990) (mem).

Riverfront Park on the Susquehanna River, along a footpath parallel to a highly traveled street, Emerald to Maclay Street, Harrisburg.

Flowers, trees, a *peace pole* saying "May Peace Prevail on Earth" in four languages, and stone and bronze inscriptions by Gandhi, Martin Luther King, Jr., Dwight Eisenhower, Pope Paul VI, and others "are intended to stimulate reflection and promote harmony over hostility and violence." Three sculptures by Dr. Frederick Franck emphasize this affirmation of life. One, entitled "Seven Generations," depicts the great Iroquois law that "we must be mindful of the impact of our decisions on the seven generations to follow ours." Another, "Hiroshima— the Unkillable Human," evokes the shadow of a fellow human burned into a concrete wall at the moment the bomb struck and that human rising like a phoenix from the ashes. The Garden was inspired by a challenge given by Dr. Bernard Lown to create parks to affirm life's fragility and the human spirit's resilience. Dr. Lown accepted the Nobel Peace Prize on behalf of the International Physicians for the Prevention of Nuclear War. The Garden was placed in Riverfront Park by Physicians for Social Responsibility and the City of Harrisburg.

HAVERFORD, PA

867. *Peace and Conflict Studies* (1985) (col).

Haverford College, Haverford 19041; (610) 896-1055; *hglickma@haverford.edu; www.haverford.edu/pols/hcpeace/hcpeace.html*

Undergraduate concentration is in cooperation with Bryn Mawr. Harvey Glickman, Coord. at Haverford.

HUNTINGDON, PA

868. *Baker Institute of Peace and Conflict Studies* (1971) (col).

Juniata College, Huntingdon 16652-2119;

Peace Garden, Riverfront Park, Harrisburg. Photograph courtesy Physicians for Social Responsibility, James Jones, M.D., and Mary Herzel.

(814) 641-3464 or 643-6211; *cookhu@juniata.edu; www.juniata.edu; www.juniata.edu/pacs*

The Institute celebrates the vision of peace of Elizabeth Evans Baker and John Calhoun Baker. Juniata offers a full major in peace and conflict studies, supported by a library collection of over four thousand volumes related to war, peace, and conflict resolution, a collection of the best journals in the field, an excellent audio visual collection, and student field trips and conferences. For example, it sponsored a conference Fall 1999 on "Women and Peace." The College includes the *Elizabeth Baker Peace Chapel*. Andy Murray, Dir.; Celia Cook-Huffman, Assoc. Dir.

869. *Elizabeth Evans Baker Peace Chapel* (1989) (org).

Just east of the Juniata College campus, off Warm Springs Ave., Huntingdon.

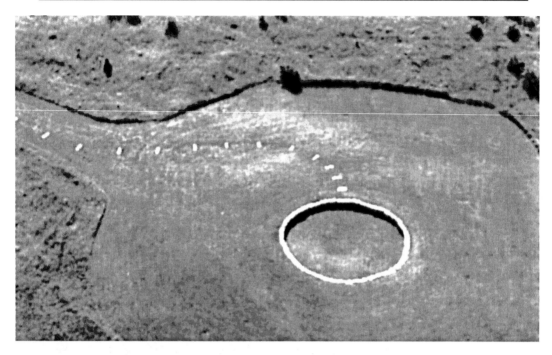

Elizabeth Baker Peace Chapel by Maya Lin, Juniata College, Huntington. Photograph courtesy Baker Institute, Celia Cook-Huffman and Marta Daniels.

Consists of two main sites. A series of 24 granite steps rise up an incline to a 40-foot circle composed of 53 rough-cut blocks of granite in an open field. Nearby in a grove of trees on a higher knoll rests a single smooth granite disc, four feet in diameter, situated for individual, private meditation. The Chapel occupies 14 acres in all and is part of the 170-acre Baker-Henry Nature Preserve. Peace studies classes, Earth Day celebrations, poetry readings, and diverse peace events are held at the Chapel. Designed by Maya Lin, designer of the Vietnam Veterans Memorial in Washington, DC, and the Civil Rights Memorial in Montgomery, AL.

JENKINTOWN, PA

870. *American Anti-Vivisection Society (AAVS)* (1883) (org).

801 Old York Rd. #204, Jenkintown 19046-1685; (215) 887-0816; *aavsonline@aol.com; www.aavs.org*

Works to end the use of animals in biomedical research, dissection, testing, and education. Founded by Caroline Earl-White. Tina Nelson, Exec. Dir.

LANCASTER, PA

871. *Women in Black—Lancaster* (1993) (org).

730 Hamilton St., Lancaster 17602; (717) 394-9110; *ajgoeke@igc.org*

Chapter of the international Women in Black organization (*wib@matriz.net*) founded to protest the atrocities of war especially in the Balkans, to pay homage to all victims of war and express solidarity with all those who oppose war and militarism. The Lancaster group has performed many public vigils, spoken in class rooms, participated in coalition peace events, and have raised funds for the Belgrade Women in Black. Anne de la Bouillerie Goeke and June Lang, Founders/Coordinators; Janice Lion and Luz Meck, Coords.

LANGHORNE, PA

872. *Bucks County Peace Center* (1982) (org).

102 W. Maple Ave., Langhorne 19047-2820; (215) 750-7220; *peace@comcat.com*

Dedicated to the nonviolent resolution of conflict in community and world. Offers a library and resources center, networks with Bucks County Anti-Violence Coalition, Adopt-a-Minefield Project, and other groups. Brian Conklin, Exec. Dir.

NEWTOWN, PA

873. *Edward Hicks* (1997) (mem).

122 Penn St., Newtown.

Hicks (1780-1849), primitive artist, painted more than 50 versions of "The Peaceable Kingdom," based on a prophecy of Isaiah.

(Pennsylvania has about a dozen historical markers commemorating peace and peacemakers in cast-aluminum mounted on posts, most of them dedicated during the past decade.)

PENNSBURG, PA

874. *Frank N. D. Buchman Historical Marker* (1991) (mem).

772 Main St., Pennsburg.

World peace advocate, Buchman (1878–1961) founded Moral Rearmament in 1938, twice nominated for the Nobel Peace Prize.

PHILADELPHIA, PA

875. **American Friends Service Committee* (1917) (org).

1501 Cherry St., Philadelphia, 19102-1479; (215) 241-7000; *afscinfo@afsc.org; www.afsc.org*

An independent Quaker organization founded to provide conscientious objectors with an opportunity to aid civilian victims during WWI. Today it carries on programs of service, social justice, and peace education in 22 foreign countries and many places in the U.S. AFSC supports the rights of immigrants, undocumented workers, small farmers, farmworkers, and refugees. It advocates on behalf of people who are hungry, poorly housed, homeless, or unemployed. It has programs on Indian reservations, in high schools, in rural areas such as Appalachia and northern New Mexico, in crowded cities, in prisons, and in factories along the Mexico–U.S. border. Its Help Increase Peace program promotes nonviolent conflict resolution and trust in schools and communities. Opposes military presence in schools. And it has many programs abroad. Its Peace Education Division resists war policies around the world and publishes the AFSC Peace Education Division Bulletin. In 1947, the AFSC and Friends Service of Britain together received the Nobel Peace Prize. Regional offices in Baltimore, Cambridge, MA, Chicago, Des Moines, New York, Pasadena, San Francisco, and Seattle.

876. **Conflict Studies* (col).

Communication Sciences, Temple University, Philadelphia 19122; (215) 204-1890; *folger@vm.temple.edu; www.temple.edu/commsci/maapp.htm*

Offers the MA in Applied Communication in Conflict Processes (1985). Doctoral students can choose an emphasis in this area (1992). Contact Joseph Folger.

877. **Delaware Valley Fellowship of Reconciliation* (1997) (org).

753 N. 24th St., Phila. 19130-2540; (215) 763-2701 (h); *hbldridi@msn.com*

Monthly meetings, education in tolerance. Dr. Barbara Lakeberg Dridi, convenor.

878. *Dorothy Day Sculpture* (1996) (mem).

LaSalle University Art Museum, 1900 W. Olney Ave., Philadelphia, PA 19141.

Relief sculpture in red oak by Charles Wells, given by Dennis and Judy O'Brien.

878a. **Faith-Justice Institute* (1977) (col).

Saint Joseph's University, 5600 City Ave., Philadelphia 19131; (610) 660-1765; *fhort@sju.edu; www.sju.edu/cos/faith-justice*

Offers an undergraduate certificate on Jesuit oriented social justice issues. Frances Hart, S.S.J., Dir.

879. **Friends Meeting House* (1856) (org).

1501 Cherry Street, Philadelphia; *www.afsc.org/qic.htm*

A three-building complex housing nine Quaker (Religious Society of Friends, 1600s–) organizations. Quakers reject war and creeds and

Friends Center and National Headquarters of AFSC Philadelphia. Photograph courtesy Quaker Information Center, Peggy Morscheck; AFSC, Terry Foss.

stress peace education, humanitarian activism, and inward spiritual experience. Their national headquarters is a hub of peace activities, where numerous local groups also initiate peace programs and actions; for example, the Cambridge, MA, and the Seaville, NJ, Friends organized Hiroshima Day commemorative events.

A plaque outside the Meeting House entitled *Civilian Public Service* (1996) recognizes some 12,000 conscientious objectors' service in the WWII Civilian Public Service camps.

880. **House of Grace Catholic Worker* (1994) (org).

1826 E. Lehigh, Philadelphia 19125; (215) 426-0364.

Active against blockade of Iraq, death penalty, SOA, militarism through education and demonstrations. Pub.: *Gift of Grace* newsletter.

881. *Immigrants and Migrants Mural* (1996) (mem).

Philadelphia at the corner of Brown & N. 7th Streets.

Celebrates Quaker assistance to immigrants and migrants in Philadelphia.

882. **Nonviolence Web* (1995) (org).

PO Box 30947, Phila. 19104; (215) 724-4633; *nvweb@nonviolence.org; www.nonviolence.org/*

Provides a continued (award-winning) outlet for the nonviolence movement through free typesetting, on-line space, and marketing for about two dozen U.S.-based peace groups, as well as a twice-monthly on-line magazine, an active Discussion Board, and an Action Alert posting system. Groups served by the Web include: the Fellowship of Reconciliation, the War Resisters League, the National Campaign for a Peace Tax Fund, and the Stop Cassini Earth Flyby Campaign. Founded by Martin Kelley (editorial co-manager of New Society Publishers).

883. *Penn Treaty Park* (1976) (mem).

On Delaware Ave., foot of Cecil B. Moore Ave., Philadelphia.

Commemorates Penn's peaceful relations with the Indians. William Penn (1644-1718) founded Pennsylvania and made several treaties with the Indians (1682–84) which they considered so just that they never attacked the colony.

Dunn, Mary. *William Penn, Politics and Conscience.* Princeton, NJ: Princeton UP, 1967.

Endy, Melvin. *William Penn and Early Quakerism.* Princeton, NJ: Princeton UP, 1973.

884. **Project on Justice and Society* (1980) (col).

1900 W. Olney Ave., La Salle University, Philadelphia 19141; *www.lasalle.edu*

Undergraduate minor, the college affiliated with the Christian Brothers, an order committed to social justice. Charles Echelmeier (215-951-1048; *echelmei@lasalle.edu*) and Laura Otten, FSC (215-951-1118; otten@lasalle.edu) Directors.

885. *Quaker Contributions to Civil Rights* (1997) (mem).

Mural on the 2900-block of Germantown Avenue, Philadelphia.

Trueblood, D. Elton. *The People Called Quakers.* New York: Harper and Row, 1966.

886. **Student Environmental Action Coalition (SEAC)* (1989) (org).

PO Box 31909, Phila. 19104-1909; (215) 222-4711; *seac@seac.org; webteam@seac.org; www.seac.org*

"Dedicated to building power among high school and college students involved in environmental and social justice action." Pub.: *Threshold* newsletter.

887. **Training for Change* (1991) (porg).

4719 Springfield Ave., Philadelphia 19143-3514; (215) 729-7458; *peacelearn@igc.apc.org*

(Formerly: Training Center Workshops). "Assists groups to stand up more effectively for justice, peace, and environmental harmony and to train more people to be able to give such assistance."

887a. **Violence Against Women* (1994) (jour).

Dept. of Sociology, Saint Joseph's Univ., Phila. 19131.

Pub. by Sage. Ed. by Claire Renzetti, ed. also of the Sage Series on Violence Against Women.

888. *Violet Oakley Historical Marker* (1998) (mem).

627 St. Georges Rd., off McCallum St.

Oakley (1874–1961) is famous for her murals in Pennsylvania's State Capitol reflecting Penn's ideas for justice and peace.

889. **Women's International League for Peace and Freedom (WILPF)* (1915) (org).

1213 Race St., Philadelphia, 19107-1691; (215) 563-5527; *wilpfnatl@igc.apc.org; www.wilpf.org*

Founded by Jane Addams, WILPF is one of the world's oldest continuously-active peace organizations. WILPF has offices in Geneva and sections in 42 countries, of which this is one, with 100 local branches. From World War I to the present, WILPF has opposed wars and the root causes of wars, and has promoted peace, social justice, racial equality, and women's empowerment, believing that peace flourishes only when it is planted in non-violence, justice, freedom, opportunity, and equality for all. Its members have included five Nobel Peace Prize laureates: Jane Addams, Emily Greene Balch, Linus Pauling, Alva Myrdal, and Dr. Martin Luther King, Jr. U.S. WILPF's program has four main priorities: disarmament, ending U.S. global intervention, racial justice, and women's rights. Publishes the magazine *Peace and Freedom*, which in its Sept.-Oct. 1999 number included several articles on refugees and human rights, an article on the bombings of Yugoslavia, and an article on The Hague Appeal. Contact Kathryn Kasper (*kkasper@wilpf.org*). Phyllis Yingling, Pres. Mary Day Kent, Exec. Dir. See: Jane Addams Peace Assoc. (JAPA).

PITTSBURGH, PA

890. **Conflict Resolution and Peace Studies* (1988) (col).

Graduate Center for Social and Public Policy, Duquesne Univ, Pittsburgh 15282; (412) 396-5179, 396-6485; *stoddard@ duq2.cc.duq.edu; socialpolicy@duq.edu; www.duq.edu/liberalarts/gradsocial/*

*conflictres.html; www.duq.edu/liberalsarts/
gradsocial/policy.html*

The Center offers a graduate certificate which
can be earned in one summer or through evening courses; and a concentration in the MA in
Social and Public Policy. The Center itself, a
collaboration of the Political Science and Sociology departments, performs research, service,
and training in the Pittsburgh area. G. Evan
Stoddard, Director.

891. *National Consortium on Violence
Research (NCOVR)* (1995) (org).

Carnegie Mellon U, The Heinz School,
5000 Forbes Ave., Pittsburgh 15213;
(412) 268-8311; *www.ncovr.heinz.cmu.edu*

Researchers from different disciplines at over
20 institutions in the U.S. and abroad maintain
a Data Center and disseminate its findings.
Contact Jerry Halloran.

892. *Pax Christi OH-PENN Heart*
(1996) (org).

1100 Princeton Rd., Pittsburgh 15205;
(412) 761-4319; *b.a.finch@worldnet.att.net*

Special attention on the death penalty (in
early 2000). Contact Jack McFadden. Barbara
Finch, CSJ, Coordinator and Regional Rep.
(b.a.finch@worldnet.att.net).

893. *Peace Pole* (mem).

Carnegie Mellon University, between
Hunt Library and the School of
Industrial Administration.

The Pole is located in a garden created to
memorialize a notable faculty member, but because of the Pole, the garden is now known as
the Peace Garden. The Pole has the words "May
Peace Prevail on Earth" in English, Chinese,
Spanish, and Arabic.

894. *Pittsburgh North People for Peace*
(1982) (org).

PO Box 183, Wexford 15090; (570)
367-0383; *jsheehan@compuserve.com*

Affil. with Fellowship of Reconciliation and
Thomas Merton Center. Meets twice a month,
education in peace and justice issues, for example Guatemala, annual High School Essay Contest, annual Peace Festival in June, participates
in anti-racism coalition, and more. Contact Mary
Sheehan.

895. *Thomas Merton Center* (1973)
(org).

5125 Penn Ave., Pittsburgh 15224;
(412) 361-3022; *mertonctr@aol.com*;
www.realpittsburgh.com

Works to "instill a consciousness of values"
involved "in the issues of war, poverty, racism,
and oppression," currently focusing on racism
and economic inequality. Pub. *The New People*
monthly newsletter, ed. Sydney Cumbest. The
20-page July/August 1999 issue includes articles
on funding the UN, nonviolent protest, death
penalty, nuclear abolition, Vets for Peace, and
two pages of "Social Action Calendar." Contact: Molly Rush.

896. *US-CUBA Sister Cities Association*
(1999) (org).

320 Lowenhill St., Pittsburgh 15216;
(412) 563-1519; *uscsca@aol.com*

A development from the Mobile-Havana
Sister Cities project. Other partnerships: Madison, WI-Camaguey and Pittsburgh, PA-Matan-
zas, and several others are being created. These
municipal friendships are the product of the
U.S. government's intolerant, outdated persecution of Cuba. "USCSCA believes the people of
Cuba are part of our shared world and should
not be isolated or exempted from the global
community or refused the mutual benefits of sister city programs on the basis of political con-
siderations or agendas." Founded by Lisa Valenti
(*LisaCuba@aol.com*).

SCRANTON, PA

897. *Peace and Justice Studies* (1990)
(col).

Dept of Religious Studies, University
of Scranton, Scranton 18510; (570)
941-6309; *freinb1@uofs.edu*;
http://academic.uofs.edu/department

Undergraduate concentration with Jesuit
affiliation. Brigid Frein, Chair.

898. *Scranton Fellowship of Reconciliation*
(1979) (org).

PO Box 42, Scranton 18501; (570)
961-2021.

Fellowship of Reconciliation local group.
Meets monthly, celebrates Martin Luther King

Day and Hiroshima Day, etc. Pub. *Foresight* monthly. Contact Susan Hanley.

SWARTHMORE, PA

899. **Brandywine Peace Community* (1977) (org).

PO Box 81, Swarthmore 19081; (610) 544-1818; *brandywine@juno.com; www.nonviolence.org/nsef/brandyw*

A "faith-based nonviolent activist group committed to peacemaking and a spiritual discipline of nonviolence," "working for economic conversion of weapons-producing corporations to non-military, jobs producing, and environmentally safe utilities." Affil. with the New Society Educational Foundation. For nearly 15 years BPC campaigned against GE's weapons facilities in Valley Forge, Phila., and elsewhere. (In 1993, GE sold its Aerospace weapons division to Martin Marietta, which then merged with Lockheed to become Lockheed Martin, the world's largest weapons corporation and the U.S.'s number one arms trade and nuclear bomb contractor.) BPC organized several Hiroshima Day 1999 events.

900. **Men's International Peace Exchange (MIPE)* (1992) (org).

PO Box 36, Swarthmore 19081-0036; (610) 872-8178; *mipe00@aol.com; www.PeaceExchange.org*

Seeks to motivate men to solve problems through cooperation, collaboration, and sharing, to recognize similarities among peoples and to celebrate differences, and to perceive others as potential allies. Works through education, networking, annual conference, and community building. Pub. quarterly newsletter, *The Peace Exchange.* Mordecai Jackson, Dir.

901. **Peace Studies Program* (1989) (col).

Swarthmore College, Swarthmore 19081; (610) 328-8499; *jfrost1@swarthmore.edu; www.swarthmore.edu/Home/Academic/ catalog/dept/peace.html*

Students submit their own plan to their advisor, with six courses required, field studies, and a research thesis; internship encouraged, all in cooperation with Haverford College and Bryn Mawr. The program is supported by the largest archive on peace in the western world (see next entry). J. William Frost, Chair.

902. **Swarthmore College Peace Collection* (1930) (col, lib).

Swarthmore 19081; (610) 328-8557; *wchmiell@swarthmore.edu; www.swarthmore.edu/Library/peace*

Significant archive of peace materials. Pub.: *Guide to the Swarthmore College Peace Collection, 1981* (2nd ed.), *The Guide to Sources on Women in the Swarthmore College Peace Collection* (1988), ed. Wendy Chmielewski. Wendy Chmielewski, Director.

UNIONTOWN, PA

903. *George C. Marshall Historical Marker* (1981) (mem).

142 W. Main St. (Bus. US 40), Uniontown.

Author of the Marshal Plan for European recovery, awarded the Nobel Peace Prize.

UNIVERSITY PARK, PA

904. **Center for Research in Conflict and Negotiations (CRCN)* (1988) (col).

Penn State University, 313 Beam, University Park 16802; (814) 865-3822 or 865-0197; *lws3@email.psu.edu; b9g@psu.edu; www.smeal.psu.edu/crcn/index.html*

Established with a grant from the Hewlett Foundation, the CRCN provides research (bargaining, environmental disputes, international joint ventures, etc.) and a forum. Pubs. include: Barbara Gray, *Collaborating: Finding Common Ground for Multiparty Problems.* San Francisco: Josey-Bass, 1989. Contact Barbara Gray.

905. **Peace and Conflict Studies* (1995) (col).

STS Program Office, Penn State University, University Park 16802; (814) 865-9951; *cka1@psu.edu; www.engr.psu.edu/sts/about/programs*

An undergraduate minor for students in any major. Clemente Abrokwaa, Coord.

906. *Peace Garden* (proposed).

Pennsylvania State U, University Park, 16802, the garden will be between the north end of Henderson building and nearby McAllister Building, just to the west of the Hetzel Union Building lawn.

A gift from Penn State's Class of 1997, construction on hold in 2000 while the expansion of a neighboring building is under way.

Intercom (October 24, 1996) (Penn State's faculty-staff newspaper).

907. **Peace Science Society* (1963) (col).

Dept. of Political Science, 107 Burrowes Bldg., Pennsylvania State U, University Park 16802

Orig. the Peace Research Society (International) convened in Sweden. It became PSS in 1973 and held its first conference in Chicago. In 1997 its headquarters were lodged in Penn State. "A scientific association of individuals developing theory and methods for the study of peace," with a primary concern the improvement of social science theory as it relates to international relations. Annual conferences at major universities; international conferences held periodically. Pubs.: *Conflict Management and Peace Science*, twice a year; *Journal of Conflict Resolution*, quarterly; and a newsletter three times a year.

VILLANOVA, PA

908. **Center for Peace & Justice Education* (1985) (col).

800 Lancaster Ave., Sullivan Hall, Villanova U, Villanova 19085-1699; (610) 519-4499; *wwerpeho@email.vill.edu*; *www.peaceandjustice.villanova.edu/ index.html*

Supports the University mission statement "by focusing on the search for world peace and social justice through education rooted in the Jewish and Christian traditions generally, and Catholic Social Teaching in particular." Provides a Peace and Justice Minor and a concentration. Sponsors conferences (e.g., The Nuclear Arms Race and Strategies for Peace), luncheons to share research and ideas, a lecture series, a Career Fair, and three awards (an outstanding person or group, a graduating senior, and an undergraduate research paper or project). Pub. *Journal for Peace and Justice Studies* (1989). William Werpehowski, Dir.

909. *Peace Garden and Pole* (1993, rededicated 1999) (mem).

Outside the Center for Peace & Justice Education, Villanova U.

Peace Pole inscribed with "May Peace Prevail on Earth" in four languages and surrounded by a garden of flowers. At the Pole's base is this message from Micah 6.8: "This is what Yahweh asks of you, only this: to act justly, to love tenderly, and to walk humbly with your God."

WEST CHESTER, PA

910. *Bayard Rustin Historical Marker* (mem).

At the Henderson High School, Lincoln and Montgomery Aves., West Chester (his birthplace).

Civil rights leader and pacifist, Rustin (1910–1987) organized the 1963 March on Washington. (See NYC).

911. **Peace and Conflict Studies* (1982) (col).

West Chester University of Pennsylvania, West Chester 19383; (610) 436-2754; *fstruckmeyer@wcupa.edu; www.wcupa.edu/ _ACADEMICS/sch_cas/peac_stu/*

Undergraduate minor based upon conviction that conflict can be managed. Fred Struckmeyer, Coord.

— *Puerto Rico (PR)* —

2 Peace Poles.

MANATI, PR

912. **Committee Against Environmental Experimentation/Comité Contra las Experimentaciones Ambientales* (1998) (org).

Urb. San Fernando #18, PO Box 152, Manati 00674; (787) 854-4546; *vicrod@prtc.net; www.geocities.com/ SunsetStrip/Villa/1482*

An affiliate of Global Network (#216). Founded to protest NASA experiments in our atmosphere (releasing dangerous chemicals in violation of the Montréal Protocol). CCEA seeks to educate people about the importance of protecting our environment and especially the ozone layer. The org. is also supporting the people of Vieques against U.S. Navy bombing training there. Contact Victor Rodriguez.

SAN JUAN, PR

913. *Caribbean Project for Justice and Peace/Proyecto Caribeño de Justicia y Paz* (1973) (org).

PO Box 13241, San Juan 00908-3241; (787) 722-1640; *wandac@coqui.net*

A pacifist group which originated in the Youth Exchange Program, sponsored by the Quakers, and now focuses also on education and documentation in the areas of militarism, human rights, and peace education, and which works in coalition with diverse peace groups, including the Comité Contra las Experimentaciones Ambientales. Its Peace Education Program on the effects of violence on children, which includes concern for toys of war and violence, is sponsored by the National Council of Churches. Its Documentation Center provides information for many kinds of consultation and orientation against war and other types of violence. CPJP also promotes exchanges, conferences, and lectures throughout the Caribbean, Central and South America, and elsewhere, for the self-determination of peoples, demilitarization and base conversion, and respect for cultural and ethnic identities. Wanda Colón Cortez, Director.

914. *Puerto Rican Alliance for the Environment/Alianza Ambiental Puertorriqueña* (1998) (org).

497 Ave. E. Pol, Box 94, San Juan 00926-5636; (787) 755-0410; *eco-isla@earthsystems.org; rioss@coqui.net; enlacepr@caribe.net; www.earthsystems.org/eco-isla*

Sponsor of Eco-Isla/Auspiciador de Eco-Isla Auspicia, a communication network that serves as a forum for organizations and individuals who are concerned for the environment in Puerto Rico and the planet. Abel Vale, Moderator (*enlacepr@caribe.net*).

—— *Rhode Island* ——

6 Sister Cities. / 7 Peace Poles.

FOSTER, RI

915. *St. Joseph the Worker House and Family* (1997) (org).

122 Johnson Rd., Foster 02825; (401) 392-1358.

The Lund-Molfese family-based Catholic Worker House on a 5-acre farm helps the poor and works for national and international peace.

PAWTUCKET, RI

916. *Sri Chinmoy Peace Bridge* (1990) (mem).

Main St., over the Blackstone River (City of Pawtucket, 137 Roosevelt Ave., 02860).

The plaque on the bridge calls Chinmoy the "first global man of the 20th century." See entry 1066.

Madhuri. *The Life of Sri Chinmoy.* Jamaica, NY: Agni, 1972.

PROVIDENCE, RI

917. *Rhode Island Mobilization for Peace and Justice* (1995) (org).

134 Mathewson St., POB 23157, Providence 02903-4102; (401) 273-4650.

Formed by the merger of two RI activist groups: R.I. Mobilization for Survival (1973–1995) and Women for a Non-Nuclear Future (1979–1995). RIMPJ promotes policies for human and environmental needs, to eliminate nuclear arsenals and nuclear energy production, to maintain human rights, and for a more equitable distribution of natural and economic resources. Activities include: Phone Tree, Peace Festival 2000 (near the Newport War College), Campaign of Conscience for the Iraqi people, vigils at Newport War College in Providence and the Undersea Warfare Center in Middletown. Pub. *Peace Talks* bimonthly (legislative updates, a calendar of events, and articles; in the

Sept.-Oct. 1999 number: Peace Festival 2000, Third Annual A Day Without the Pentagon, Global Network Against Weapons and Nuclear Power in Space). Contact Phil Edmonds.

918. *Rhode Island Peace Action* (1989?) (org).

c/o Karina Wood, 85 John St., Providence 02906; (401) 276-0377; *kwood@igc.org*

A chapter of Peace Action. Discussion meetings, demonstrations (weekly vigils during the bombings of Iraq and Yugoslavia), lobbying members of Congress. Paul McNeil, Dir. Karina Wood, Field Coordinator of Project Abolition and U.S. Outreach Coordinator, Hague Appeal for Peace.

— South Carolina — *(SC)*

7 Sister Cities. / 22 Peace Poles.

CHARLESTON, SC

919. *Holocaust Memorial* (1999) (mem).

In the city's historic district, in the central park at the old Citadel, Charleston.

The 7,000 square foot memorial honors Nazi Holocaust victims and survivors who settled in South Carolina. It consists of a two-story-high screen of stainless steel, with a 16-foot bronze

Holocaust Memorial by Jonathan Levi, at Old Citadel, Charleston. Photograph courtesy of the Charleston Information Bureau.

sculpture at its center depicting a twisted piece of cloth intended to provoke thought and empathy. The memorial also includes a public assembly area, a wall inscribed with a list of names of local survivors and their descendants, and an explanation of the monument's mission. Architect: Jonathan Levi.

COLUMBIA, SC

920. *Carolina Peace Resource Center* (1981) (org).

PO Box 7933, Columbia 79202; 305 S. Saluda Ave., Columbia 29205-3926; (803) 252-2221; *cprcrogers@mindspring.com*

Affil. with Fellowship of Reconciliation in 1998. Offers conflict resolution training, education on nonviolence, public accountability of DOE and Savannah River Site, demonstrations, participation in Stop the Hate Campaign. Contact Rebecca Burgess-Rogers and Harry Rogers Jr.

921. *Conflict Resolution* (1997) (col).

Columbia College of South Carolina, Columbia 29203; (803) 786-3181; *madugan@colacoll.edu;* *www.colacoll.edu/conflres/conres.htm*

The MA of 45 semester hours and the Cer-

tificate of Advanced Graduate Studies in Conflict Resolution are intended especially for working professionals, offering distance, weekend, limited-residency, and on-line arrangements. Maire Dugan, Program Chair.

JOHNS ISLAND, SC

922. *Esau Jenkins Gravesite* (1972) (mem).

Wesley United Methodist Church, 2726 River Road, Johns Island.

Local supporter of citizenship schools and other rights activities. His headstone reads: "Love is Progress. Hate is Expensive."

ORANGEBURG, SC

923. *Orangeburg Massacre Memorial* (1969) (mem).

On campus of South Carolina State College (now University), 300 College St., Orangeburg.

Three students were killed and twenty-eight more wounded in a police riot, February 8, 1968, during a protest against segregation. A granite marker encircled with flowers, near the site of the incident, commemorates the tragedy.

Orangeburg Massacre Memorial, South Carolina State College, Orangeburg. Photograph courtesy South Carolina Archives and History Center.

The Smith-Hammond-Middleton Memorial Center, Orangeburg. Photograph courtesy of South Carolina Archives and History Center.

924. *The Smith-Hammond-Middleton Memorial Center* (mem).

Honors the slain students Henry Smith, Samuel Hammond, and Delano Middleton.

Bass, Jack, and Jack Nelson. *The Orangeburg Massacre.* Macon, GA: Mercer UP, 1984.

Williams, Cecil. *Freedom & Justice: Four Decades of the Civil Rights Struggle as Seen by a Black Photographer of the Deep South.* Macon, GA: Mercer UP, 1995.

— *South Dakota (SD)* —

4 Sister Cities. / 10 Peace Poles.

ABERDEEN, SD

925. *Peace Pole* (1991) (mem).

Sisters of the Presentation of the Blessed Virgin Mary, Presentation Heights, 1500 North Second St., Aberdeen 57401-1238; (605) 225-0420.

A metal Pole on the front lawn and a wooden one in the hall near the front entrance reflect the Presentation Sisters' decision to promote alternative actions for peace. "May Peace Prevail on Earth" is written in Lakota, Spanish, Chinese, and English, the four cultures to which the Sisters have reached out in their ministry.

"Presentation Sisters' Gathering Features Powwow." *Aberdeen American News* (July 12–13, 1991).

BROOKINGS, SD

926. **Nonviolent Alternatives* (1991) (org).

825 Fourth St., Brookings 57006; (605) 692-3680 or (605) 692-8465; *carlek56@hotmail.com*

Sponsored the summer 2000 program "Explore Alternatives to Violence in Lakota/Dakota Communities or India" and provides resources for schools. Pub. a newsletter, *One Step* (from Newman's hymn, "Lead Kindly Light," "one step enough for me," which Gandhi liked), which

Peace Pole, Aberdeen. Photograph courtesy Presentation Sisters.

in recent issues includes articles about Gandhi, environmentalists in India, and their study programs at home and abroad. Contact Carl Kline.

MOBRIDGE, SD

927. *Fool Soldier Band* (mem).

A stone monument (1909) and a bronze marker (1973) commemorate a youthful group of Santee Sioux (possibly Hunkpapa Dakota) who rescued white hostages captured by other Sioux Dakota in 1862.

WATERTOWN, SD

928. **South Dakota Peace and Justice Center* (1979) (org).

PO Box 405, Watertown 57201;
(605) 882-2822; *sdpjc@dailypost.com*

An interfaith group seeking harmony between indigenous and non-indigenous citizens of SD, disarmament and economic conversion, just international relations, death penalty abolition, and other purposes. Contact Mitakue Oyasin; Jeanne Koester, Dir.

—— *Tennessee (TN)* ——

16 Sister Cities. / 53 Peace Poles.

See Davis, *Weary Feet, Rested Souls*, 342–380, for more Civil Rights Movement sites.

MEMPHIS, TN

929. *"I Have Been to the Mountaintop"* (1977) (mem).

Poplar Avenue and North Main Street, Memphis.

A steel tribute to King's last speech on April 3, 1968.

930. *Mid-South Peace & Justice Center* (1982) (org).

PO Box 11428, Memphis 38111, or 499 Patterson Ave., Memphis 38111; (901) 452-6997; *pax5@usit.net*

Programs: Nonviolence: Peaceful Learning and Living teaching nonviolence in two public schools and opposition to the death penalty; Militarism: protested NATO bombing of Yugoslavia, Iraqi sanctions, Tax Day, supported Test Ban Treaty, conference on landmines, Disarmament Task Force, Hiroshima/Nagasaki Commemoration; Central America: public forum, delegation to Ft. Benning vs. School of the Americas; economic justice: advocated a more progressive tax structure; Jubilee 2000; and other activities. Pub. *Just Peace* newsletter every other month. Gerry Vandeerhaar, 1999 Board Chair; Lorenzo Banks, 2000 Chair of Board. Contact Bill Akin.

931. *M.K. Gandhi Institute for Nonviolence* (1991) (col).

Christian Brothers College, Memphis 38104; (901) 452-2824; *gandhi@cbu.edu; www.cbu.edu/Gandhi*

Founded by Arun and Sunanda Gandhi to teach and promote the philosophy and practice of nonviolence. Arun is M.K. Gandhi's grandson.

932. *The National Civil Rights Museum* (1991) (org).

Lorraine Motel, 450 Mulberry St., Memphis, 38103-4214; (901) 521-9699; *www.civilrights.org*

Dr. Martin Luther King, Jr., was assassinated at the Lorraine Motel, April 3, 1968. The Museum employs 10,000 square feet of permanent exhibits, an auditorium, a courtyard, a changing gallery, a shop, and offices, to bring the Civil Rights Movement to life and place it in historical perspective. It includes a timeline of the civil rights struggle relating to African Americans in the 1950s and 1960s. The Museum gives annual national and international Freedom Awards and annually celebrates the national holiday for Dr. King's birthday in January. There are also ongoing lectures, seminars, and artistic performances.

933. *Peace Studies* (1980) (col).

Christian Brothers College, Memphis 38104; (901) 321-3359; *pgathje@cbu.edu; www.cbu.edu/arts/phil*

Undergraduate minor seeks to advance a just society for fullest individual potential. Peter Gathje, Coord.

NASHVILLE, TN

934. *Battle of Nashville* (1926) (mem).

South of Nashville on Franklin Road at junction of U.S. 31 and Thompson Lane.

There are chauvinist messages on its marble base, but the statue depicts a youth, representing unity, restraining two charging steeds representing the North and the South. The angel on top of the accompanying obelisk represents peace. The monument was designed by the Italian artist, G. Moretti.

935. *First Baptist Church Marker* (mem).

319 Eighth Avenue North, Nashville.

First Baptist was the center of Nashville's Civil Rights Movement nonviolent experiments and workshops. A historical marker stands at the old site.

Marquee announcing the grand opening of The National Civil Rights Museum. Photograph courtesy of the museum.

936. *Fisk University* (org).

1000 Seventeenth Avenue North, Nashville.

One of four black educational institutions (Meharry Medical College, American Baptist Theological Seminary, and Tennessee Agricultural and Industrial State College) that formed the basis of Nashville's Student Movement. CORE had a chapter there by 1965. Fisk Memorial Chapel was a chief meeting place for workshops and organizing.

937. *Franciscan Peace Center* (1998) (org).

2209 Buchanan St., Nashville 37228; (615) 313-3663; albertmerz@aol.com; sjpsuding@aol.com

Provides a spiritual program based upon the example of Saints Francis and Clare of Assisi, to eliminate personal violence, and for inner peace through self-examination, contemplation, retreats, study circles, workshops, etc., the final goal, the creation of peacemakers to counteract mainstream U.S. social conditioning in violence and domination. The Co-directors: Albert Merz, OFM, and Stephen Suding, OFM.

938. *Looby House, Library, and Community Center* (mem).

2012 Meharry Boulevard, Nashville.

Z. Alexander Looby was a NAACP lawyer for the Nashville Movement. His house was bombed in 1960, but he and his wife escaped and the house was rebuilt. Today a library and a community center in Nashville's Metro Center bear his name.

939. *Schweitzer and Bach Sculpture* (2000) (mem).

Vanderbilt Medical Center; www.mindspring.com/~lequire

Life-size bronze statue of the two men. Dedicated on opening day of *Symposium 2000*. Sculpted by Alan LeQuire. LeQuire is also creating the official Symposium 2000 Commemorative Coin with the image of Schweitzer on one side and that of Bach on the other.

940. *Symposium 2000* (1998) (org).

Tennessee Players, Inc., 304 West Due West Ave., Madison 37115-4511; (615)

868-3738; symposium2000@webtv.net; www.spaceformusic.com/symposium2000

A year-long celebration of Albert Schweitzer and Johann Sebastian Bach that included an original symphony, "Paths of Peace," by Michael Rose, dedicated to Schweitzer and performed by the Nashville Symphony; a life-size statue of Schweitzer and Bach by Alan LeQuire placed at the Vanderbilt Medical Center; a "Bells Ringing for Peace Around the World" ceremony; a visit of the Hiroshima Boys' Choir; a multimedia theatrical production by the Tennessee Players entitled *The Spirit of Albert Schweitzer*; and a *Commemorative Program Book*. Thurston Moore (Tennessee Players), Dir.

941. *Walgreen's* (mem).

226 Fifth Avenue North, Nashville.

The only remaining store of those where students in February 1960 initiated the Nashville Movement, the first group to test the concept of "jail, not bail" to emphasize injustice. The store today is part of a historic downtown walking tour.

NEW MARKET, TN

942. *Highlander Research and Education Center* (1932) (org).

1959 Highlander Way, New Market 37820-4939 (20 miles east of Knoxville off U.S. 25-70 onto Russell Gap Rd.); (423)933-3443; hrec@igc.apc.org

Founded by two white theology students, Myles Horton and Don West, Highlander has educated blacks and whites together in grassroots organizing. The original school was confiscated by the state on a trumped-up charge of bootlegging, but it was reestablished at another site, which became a training center for civil rights workshops all over the South during the 1960s. It finally settled at its present location in 1972 to carry out its program of assisting activists and communities that seek solutions to pressing social problems (civil rights, cultural diversity, economic democracy, environmental justice, global education, etc.). Conference facilities avail. Books, videos, tapes, and CD's for research. Bill Moyers made a two-hour PBS documentary about Highlander in 1981; in 1982 it was nominated for the Nobel Peace Prize.

OAK RIDGE, TN

943. *Oak Ridge Environmental Peace Alliance* (1988) (org).

100 Tulsa Rd., Suite 4A,
Oak Ridge 37830; (423) 483-9725;
orep@earthlink.net

Works to end production of nuclear weapons in Oak Ridge because of the environmental devastation.

——— *Texas (TX)* ———

59 Sister Cities. / 105 Peace Poles.

AMARILLO, TX

944. *The Peace Farm* (see: Panhandle).

AUSTIN, TX

945. *American Friends Service Committee (AFSC), Texas/Arkansas/Oklahoma (TAO),* (1950) (org).

1304 E. 6th St. #3, Austin 78702;
(512) 474-2399; *tao@afsc.org*;
josecast@swbell.net; www.afsc.org

Three areas of special engagement: global economy, anti-militarization, grassroots peace movement support. Josefina Castillo, Prog. Coord.

946. *Austin Peace and Justice Coalition* (1982) (org).

701 East 44th St., Austin 78751;
(512) 452-7140; *apjc@igc.org*

Resists class, racial, gender, and other forms of oppression. Founded Austin Living Wage Coalition, Austin-Tan Cerca de la Frontera. Pub. weekly APJC Community Calendar (austin_pjc@yahoo.com).

947. *Central Texas Fellowship of Reconciliation* (1990) (org).

1105 Faircrest Dr., Austin 78753;
(512) 990-1257; *charliej@tnti.com*

Fellowship of Reconciliation, local group. Works with UT Metropolitan Ministries and other peace groups in the area; responds to issues by letter writing, public actions, etc. Contact Charlie Jackson.

948. *Conflict Resolution* (1981) (col).

St. Edward's University, Austin 78704;
(512) 448-8607 *tome@admin.stedwards.edu*;
andresp@admin.stedwards.edu;
www.stedwards.edu/mahs/

This Catholic university offers a Certificate (two core courses) and a specialization with MA (the first in Texas) in Human Services (four courses). Thomas Evans, MA in Human Services; Andres Perez, Graduate Admission Coord.

949. *Human Rights Documentation Exchange* (1983) (org).

PO Box 2317, Austin 78768;
(512) 476-9841.

As a clearinghouse of information on human rights abuses and country conditions worldwide, HRDE works to prevent the return of asylum-seeking refugees into the hands of their persecutors.

950. *Martin Luther King, Jr., Statue* (1999) (mem).

University of Texas campus, East Mall
(next to the ROTC bldng.);
www.Austin360.com/news

The statue of King, dressed in doctoral robes, looks eastward with an outstretched arm. The base of the statue depicts scenes in King's life, accompanied with quotations, including: "We will meet your physical force with soul force." "Freedom is never voluntarily given by the oppressor; it must be demanded by the oppressed." Created by Jeffrey Varilla and Anna Koh-Varilla of Chicago.

Jayson, Sharon. "Tribute to King." *Austin American-Statesman* (Sept. 25, 1999) A1, A5.

951. *Nonmilitary Options for Youth* (1997) (org).

PO Box 49594, Austin 78765;
(512) 452-7140; *pmosley@eden.com*;
www.bga.com/~liana/nmofy

"Founded on the belief in the power of nonviolence," the group reaches out to youth "with information about the realities of militarism" and about "alternatives—both to enlistment and to the idea of war." Contact Susan Van Haitsma (512-467-2946). Related orgs.: Project YANO, CCCO, AFSC National Youth and Militarism Program. (This org. has been absorbed by Austin Peace and Justice Coalition, see above).

BELLAIRE, TX

952. *Houston Nonviolent Action/War Resisters League* (1981) (org).

See below under Houston.

BELLVILLE, TX

953. *Peace with Justice Program, United Methodist Church–Texas Conference* (org).

179 Camilla Circle, Bellville 77418; (409) 865-9698; *whardt@phoenix.net*

Concerns include: nuclear disarmament, reduction of military spending, Jubilee 2000 debt reduction. Contact Brenda Hardt.

CUERO, TX

954. *Peace Pole* (1998) (mem).

At Cuero High School.

Organized by Ada Kirk, English teacher at the High School, whose students created dedicatory events of music, theater, and poetry.

CYPRESS, TX

955. *Pax Christi Texas* (1997) (org).

12831 Raven South Drive, Cypress 77429; (281) 955-0342; *fjskeith@texas.net; www.flash.net/~aonstad/paxchristitx.htm*

A regional branch of Pax Christi USA, located in Erie, PA. Projects: abolishing the death penalty, Jubilee 2000, ending sanctions on Iraq, closing the School of Americas. Frank Skeith, Regional Rep.

Martin Luther King, Jr., Statue by Jeffrey Varilla and Anna Koh-Varilla, University of Texas, Austin. Photograph by Dick Bennett.

DALLAS, TX

956. *Conflict Resolution* (1995) (col).

College of Adult Education, Dallas Baptist University, Dallas 75211; (214) 333-5337; *caed@dbu.edu; www.dbu.edu/Graduate/Grcob.htm*

Concentration with MA in organizational management teaches through lectures, groups discussions, and particularly practice mediation sessions. Barbara Sleeper, Prog. Dir.

957. *Dallas Peace Center* (1981) (org).

4301 Bryan St., Suite 202, Dallas 75204; (214) 823-7793;

cliff@dallaspeacecenter.org; jansan@ airmail.net; www.dallaspeacecenter.org

Based on an ethic of reconciliation, the DPC promotes research, education, dialogue, and action for peace and justice. Six active campaigns: Arms Control and Disarmament, Nonviolent Conflict Resolution, Peace Education, Community-Building, Human Rights, and Social Justice (see web site for details). Pub. the *Dallas Peace Times* monthly newspaper; *Pax Facts*, a monthly electronic "menu" of activities in North Texas; E-mail Action List; and the web site has an area called "Peace News Now" that is regularly updated. Cliff Pearson, Interim Director, Communications Dir. Or contact Jan Sanders.

958. *Emery Reves Arch of Peace* (1991) (mem).

East entrance to the Morton H. Meyerson Symphony Center, Dallas.

Reves wrote *The Anatomy of Peace* in 1945. Translated into many languages and breaking all known records for political book sales, the book supports the creation of a World Federation governed by one international set of laws, a "one law" concept predicated on the interdependence of humankind and a concern for the common good. From Chapter 1: "Nothing can

Emery Reves. Courtesy Dallas Symphony Orchestra, Emily Nelson.

distort the true picture of conditions and events in this world more than to regard one's own country as the center of the universe.... It is inevitable that such a method of observation should create an entirely false perspective. Yet this is the only method admitted and used by the...governments of our world, by our legislators and diplomats, by our press and radio" (1). Asked for an answer to the atomic bomb, Albert Einstein urged people to read *The Anatomy of Peace*. His widow, Wendy Reves, gave $2 million to the Symphony to help pay for the new building designed by I. M. Pei, to commission a major symphonic composition based upon her husband's book, and to endow an annual weekend of classical concerts in his memory. The 6-by-9-foot limestone and concrete Arch frames the front façade of the building and represents a gateway. Pei said of the Arch: "Its form recalls a giant theater proscenium through which one views the lively activities of the building. From within as well one will be aware of its soaring presence inviting us to experience the art of the Dallas Symphony." The symphonic suite in one movement, composed by Marvin Hamlisch and entitled "Anatomy of Peace," was performed at the Symphony Center November 19, 1991.

959. *Pax Christi Dallas* (1990) (org).

3305 Princess Lane, Dallas 75229; (214) 350-2267; *kandjg@flash.net*; *www.flash.net/~aonstad/paxchristitx.htm* (Pax Christi Texas).

Monthly meetings, protest Iraqi sanctions, conference on the death penalty. Contact John and Karyl Gindling.

DENTON, TX

960. *Alternative Dispute Resolution* (1997) (col).

Institute of Applied Economics, University of North Texas, Denton 76203; (940) 565-3437; *mckee@scs.cmm.unt.edu*; *www.unt.edu/aeco/adrguide.htm*

Undergraduate minor and certificate of core courses and electives, and a practicum for the Professional Certificate in Alternative Dispute Resolution (1997). Also an internal faculty/staff/student dispute mediation program (1995) and the Denton County Dispute Resolution system (1999). William McKee, Advisor.

EL PASO, TX

961. *Tabor House* (org).

PO Box 1482, El Paso 79948.
See Mexico, entry 1378.

FORT WORTH, TX

962. *Texas Peace Action* (2000) (org).

PO Box 1561, Fort Worth 76101;
(817) 237-0111; *patexas@igc.apc.org*

Seeks to augment the nonviolent citizens' movement to reverse the world arms race, abolish nuclear weapons, and teach and practice nonviolent resolution of conflicts. State Rep. Lon Burnam, Chair. Contact Linda Foley.

FREDERICKSBURG, TX

963. *Japanese Garden of Peace* (1997) (mem).

Behind the main hotel complex, Fredericksburg; *gchs@ktc.com*

Trees, plants, pool, and brook, with walkway and benches surrounding, a gift of the people of Japan.

964. *John O. Meusebach Bust* (1936) *and Treaty Monument* (1997) (mem).

The bust is in front of the Vereins Kirche Museum on Marktplatz, Fredericksburg.

The Monument, near the water wheel in the history walk in the Marktplatz, Fredericksburg includes a life-size bronze statue of Meusebach and commemorates the peace treaty with the Comanche Indians in 1847.

HOUSTON, TX

965. *A.A. White Dispute Resolution Institute* (1988) (col).

College of Business Administration, University of Houston, Houston 77204; (713) 743-4933; *rpietsch@uh.edu; www.uh.edu/aawhite*

Established to foster public understanding of conflicts and conflict resolution and to find less

Japanese Garden of Peace, Fredericksburg. Photograph courtesy Visitor Bureau, Fran Cheek.

Holocaust Museum, Houston. Photograph courtesy of the museum, Julie Lambert.

expensive and more expeditious methods. Also provides assistance to the courts and educational institutions. Ken Rediker, Dir.; Robyn Pietsch, Prog. Manager.

966. *Casa Juan Diego/Houston Catholic Worker* (1980) (org).

PO Box 70113, Houston 77270; (713) 869-7376; *info@cjd.org; www.cjd.org.*

As a chapter of the CW movement, the CJD seeks to "do the works of mercy instead of the works of war," helping the poor, immigrants, and refugees; recently involved in WTO protests. Contact Mark and Louise Zwick.

967. *Holocaust Museum Houston* (1991) (mus, org).

5401 Caroline St., Houston, 77004; (713) 942-8000; *glendar@hmh.org; www.hmh.org*

Contains an exhibit of the history of the Jewish people in Europe; a theater for showing the film "Voices" and other activities; a gallery for art, photography, and receptions; a lending library and archive; classrooms; and a sculpture garden in memory of the perished Jewish children.

968. *Houston Fellowship of Reconciliation* (1991) (org).

1844 Kipling Rd., Houston 77098; (713) 524-2682; *leeloe@igc.org*

Chapter of the Fellowship of Reconciliation. Focuses on ending Iraq sanctions, on lowering Pentagon spending, on peace education, human rights, and racial and economic justice. Monthly meeting, Hiroshima Day, Peace Picnic. Works with many other groups. Contact Lee Loe.

969. *Houston Nonviolent Action/WRL* (1981) (org).

850 Jacquet, Bellaire 77401; (713) 661-9889; *nanedwards@aol.com*

As an affil. of the War Resisters League, HNA strives for a nonviolent and just world. Monthly meetings in Southwest Loop area. Focuses on developing an interest in peace and justice among young people, and countering military recruiting. Contact Bob Henschen (713-661-9889) or Nancy Edwards.

970. *Houston Peace Action* (c. 1986) (org).

849 Harvard St., #C, Houston 77007; (713) 861-2494 (h) or (713) 743-9022 (w); *hrothschild@uh.edu*

Activities: Peace Voter 2000; education about U.S. nuclear policies, especially deployment of Ballistic Missile Defense system; and about U.S. military support of undemocratic governments. Contact Herbert Rothschild, Jr.

971. *Houston Peace and Justice Center* (1998) (org).

3139 W. Holcombe PMB 110, Houston 77025; day (713) 743-9022 or night 861-2494; *hrothschild@uh.edu; hpjc@flash.net; www.hpjc.org*

HPJC seeks to enhance the work of organizations in the Houston area that promote non-violence, human rights, and economic, social, and environmental justice through collaboration. Contact Herb Rothschild.

972. *Houston Peace Forum* (1985) (org).

1515 Antoine St., Houston 77055;(713) 681-6267; First Unitarian Universalist Church of Houston, 5200 Fannin, Houston 77004-5899; (713) 526-5200.

Informs public on peace and justice issues to motivate people to work for peace and justice. Sponsors speakers, videos, discussions. Activities listed in the Unitarian newsletter and the *Houston Peace News*. Pat Nichols, Co-ordinator.

973. *Houston Peace News* (1983?) (jour).

PO Box 8763, Houston, 77249-8763; (713) 524-2682; *leeloe@neosoft.com; leeloe@igc.org.lee*

Alternative newspaper for Houston's peace, justice, and environmental communities. The 8-page paper prints 2,000 copies, with local, state, national, and international news and opinion. Lee Loe, Managing Editor. Ginger Hobart, Marilyn White, Jacquelyn Batisse, eds. Scott Askew, Calendar Editor. Carl Schaer, Treas.

974. *Houstonians Against U.S. Military Involvement* (1999) (org).

5212 Crawford St., Houston 77004; (281) 546-7173; *kenfree@hal-pc.org; www.hal-pc.org/~kenfree/IraqCoalition. htm; http://home.flash.net/~hpjc/ who.htm#usmil*

Developed from the Houston Coalition to End the War against Iraq in order to confront all instances of US militarism abroad. The group is dedicated to de-militarizing U.S. foreign policy and ending U.S. armed intervention abroad, through education and direct action. Current concerns: U.S. military expansion in Colombia, and Israel.

975. *Rothko Chapel* (1971) (mem, org).

1409 Sul Ross, Houston 77006; (713) 524-9839; *rothkoch@neosoft.com; www.menil.org/rothko.html*

Founded by John and Dominique de Menil as a sanctuary open to people of all beliefs and a rallying place for all people concerned with peace, freedom, and social justice throughout the world, the Chapel was inspired by the paintings of U.S. abstract expressionist, Mark Rothko. Designed by Rothko and Philip Johnson, with Howard Barnstone and Eugene Aubrey.

Rothko Chapel, Houston. Photograph courtesy Rothko Chapel.

976. **St. Joseph Catholic Church, Social Justice Group* (1995) (org).

1505 Kane St., Houston 77007; (713) 222-6193; *sjgintx@esc4.com; www.esc4.com/webs/sjgintx*

Main focus on justice as the foundation of peace. Among its several projects: opposition to the death penalty, sister community in El Salvador. Contact Allen Pape (281-837-9472).

977. **Texans Against Gun Violence, Greater Houston Chapter* (1995) (org).

13164 Memorial, Box 160, Houston 77079; (713) 827-8916; *tagvhou@insync.net; www.insync.net/~tagvhou*

Dedicated to significantly reducing gun violence in Texas through education and legislation. Current projects: working with the police to institute the "Boston Plan," making presentations in schools, promoting legislation requiring mandatory training for handgun purchasers, regulation of sales at gun shows, strengthening the law that makes adults criminally responsible for misuse of guns by minors.

978. **Texas Coalition to Abolish the Death Penalty* (1995) (org).

3400 Montrose, Suite 312, Houston 77006; (713) 529-3826 or 520-0300; *dpatwood@igc.org; www.lonestar.texas.net/~acohen/tcadp; www.smu.edu/~deathpen*

A statewide group of organizations affiliated with the National Coalition, working "to educate the public about the injustice and barbarity of the death penalty, support individuals on death row and their families, and stop executions." Focusing especially on barring the execution of the mentally ill and retarded. Has five chapters: Houston, Dallas-Ft. Worth, Austin, San Antonio, South Texas. Pub. quarterly newsletter and frequent press releases. David Atwood, Pres.; Rick Halperin, V-Pres.

979. **Tomorrow's Bread Today* (1996) (org).

301 E. 26th St., Houston 77008; (713) 516-8006; *www.tbt.org*

A Catholic Worker organization for individuals and families needing long-term help. Peace activities include protesting unpeaceful business and political leaders. Contact Don McCormick.

980. **Women's International League for Peace and Freedom, Houston Group* (1985?) (org).

5929 Queensloch #134, Houston, TX 77096; (713) 726-1266; *lfuray33@aol.com*

(Not a formal chapter of WILPF). Concerns: disarmament, ending U.S. intervention abroad, racial justice, women's rights, reducing sales of war toys. Contact Lynn Furay.

NACOGDOCHES, TX

981. **Peace History Society* (1964) (col, org).

History Dept., Stephen F. Austin State Univ., Nacogdoches 75962; (936) 468-2285; *sbills@sfasu.edu; www.swarthmore.edu/library/peace/Peace*

Originally the Conference on Peace Research in History, then the Council on Peace Research in History (1986), and finally PHS (1994). Sponsors annual conference: in 2000 on "The Politics of Peace Movements," co-chaired by Mike Foley (msfoley@earthlink.net) and Wendy Chmielewski (w_chmiel@swarthmore.edu). Co-operates with COPRED in the pub. of *Peace and Change: A Journal of Peace Research* quarterly (*www.albany.edu/PeaceAndChange*). Scott Bills, Pres., Stephen F. Austin; Linda Schott, Vice-Pres, U of Texas San Antonio.

PANHANDLE, TX

982. *Madre del Mundo* (mem).

Peace Farm, HC 2, Box 25, Panhandle 79068; (806) 335-1715; *peacefarm@earthlink.net*

One of four identical sculptures (another at the Nevada Test Site) of a female holding a globe of the earth in her lap, with the inscription: "Save the Mother/Save the Land/Honor All Treaty Rights/Stop Nuclear Testing/ On Our Sacred Earth." Artist: Marsha Gomez (deceased).

983. **The Peace Farm* (1986) (org).

HC 2, Box 25, Panhandle 79068 (located

on 20 acres south of U.S. 60, about halfway between FM 1912 and FM 2373, about 16 miles east of Amarillo); (806) 335-1715; *peacefarm@earthlink.net*

Formed to raise awareness of the role of Pantex in U.S. nuclear weapons production and of the risk it poses to the health and safety of workers, the public, and the environment of the Texas Panhandle. Member of the Alliance for Nuclear Accountability, Texas Peace Action, and STAR (a coalition of groups opposed to expanded nuclear weapons missions for Pantex), and cooperates with the Red River Peace Network, the War Resisters League, and the Fellowship of Reconciliation. Monthly public programs, annual peace camp, speaker bureau, nonviolence training. Mavis Belisle, Dir.

984. *Red River Peace Network (FOR/WRL)* (1982) (org).

C/o Peace Farm, HCR 2, Box 25, Panhandle 79068-9603; (806) 335-1715; *peacefarm@earthlink.net*

Affil. with Fellowship of Reconciliation and War Resisters League in 1983. Composed of OK, NM, and TX groups acting nonviolently for peace and justice. Works closely with Peace Farm, across from Pantex, a nuclear weapons disassembly point and plutonium storage area. Annual Peace Camp at Peace Farm; annual Hiroshima/Nagasaki Commemoration; regional actions.

SAN ANTONIO, TX

985. *Benedictine Resource Center* (1985) (org).

530 Bandera Rd., San Antonio, 78228; (210) 735-4988.

BRC offers a variety of ministries to assist workers, the poor, children, and Hispanics. It has a Retreat Center in Boerne. Its P.E.A.C.E. Initiative (1990) is a coalition of more than 40 public and private organizations that work to end family violence.

986. *Esperanza Peace and Justice Center* (1987) (org).

922 San Pedro, San Antonio, 78212; (210) 228-0201.

Grassroots organization dedicated to creating a better world through the arts, dialogue, and action, especially for Chicanos and all people of color, women, lesbians and gay men, and the working class and poor. Graciela Sanchez, executive director.

González, Bárbara. "Remember the Alamo Part II." *Z Magazine* (April 1999) 13–16.

987. *Institute for International Human Rights* (col).

School of Law, St. Mary's University, San Antonio 78228; (210) 436-3424; *admiss@law.stmarytx.edu; www.stmarytx.edu*

Offers a summer study abroad (previously to El Salvador and Guatemala) to study international treaties and human rights law. Contact Monica Schurtman and Larry Hufford. Roman Catholic affil.

988. *Miguel Hidalgo y Costilla* (1941) (mem).

On the main walkway of Hemisfair Park, next to the Mexican Cultural Institute, San Antonio.

The bronze statue of the "Father of Mexican Freedom" was given to the U.S. by President Manuel Avila Camacho of Mexico. In presenting the monument, President Camacho's representative declared all old differences were over, and the people of Mexico desired to be "united fraternally" with the peoples of the continent.

989. *Peace and Justice Studies* (1986) (col).

Dept of Religious Studies, University of the Incarnate Word, San Antonio 78209; (210) 829-3887; *Lozada@universe.uiwtx.edu; www.uiw.edu*

Graduate certificate, minor, and MA for study of social justice, the MA requiring 30 hours of course work and a six-hour internship. Roman Catholic affiliation. Contact Francisco Lozada, Jr. or Sr. Martha Kirk (*kirk@universe.uiwtx.edu*).

990. *President's Peace Commission* (1984) (org).

St. Mary's University, San Antonio 78228-8572; *diane@stmarytx.edu; engric@stmarytx.edu*

Fosters ethical commitment to create world peace and to the Roman Catholic perspective as a foundation. Puts on three-day teach-ins on peace and human rights each semester, and an annual spring President's Peace Concert. Diane Deusterhoeft, Faculty Coordinator.

991. *San Antonio Fellowship of Reconciliation* (1978, 1982) (org).

1202 Tampico Rd., San Antonio 78207; (210) 225-6913.

Presentations at colleges and churches on nonviolence, organized a Children's Creative Response to Conflict chapter, annual nonviolent toys event, and other activities. Contact Rod and Patti Radle.

SHERMAN, TX

992. *Center for Nonviolent Communication* (1966) (org).

PO Box 2662, Sherman 75091-2662; (903) 893-3886; *cnvc@compuserve.com; www.cnvc.org*

Founded by Marshall Rosenberg, the Center teaches groups how to resolve conflicts and build harmony by using language that creates good will. In 1990 the Center extended its programs to war-torn areas to assist peacemaking. CNVC coordinators and trainers are worldwide. Gary Baran, Exec. Dir. Pub. N*onviolent Communication: A Language of Compassion* by Marshall Rosenberg (1999) (*www.keepcomingback.com*), and other books and pamphlets on nonviolent communication; newsletter *Network News*.

993. *Contemporary Policy Studies Program* (1972) (col).

Austin College, 900 N. Grand Ave., Sherman 75090-4440; (903) 813-2218; *gmiddents@austinc.edu*

Inter-disciplinary studies of social policy issues after which students create alternative solutions.

Middents, Gerald. "Public Education and Public Accountability." *The Canadian Health Care System: Lessons for the United States.* Eds. Eve, Havens, and Ingram (North Texas UP, 1994).

TYLER, TX

994. *Tyler Interfaith Peace Fellowship* (1981) (org).

10547 State Highway 110 N., Tyler 75704-3731; (903) 592-4263.

Affil. with Fellowship of Reconciliation in 1983. Occasional activities: Hiroshima commemoration, letters to editor, etc. Contact Elihu Edelson.

—— *Utah (UT)* ——

5 Sister Cities. / 26 Peace Poles.

SALT LAKE CITY, UT

995. *Conflict Resolution Program* (col).

Department of Communications, University of Utah, Salt Lake City 84112; (801) 581-9662; *welch@admin.comm.utah.edu; hawes@admin.comm.utah.edu; www.hum.utah.edu/communication/certif/crcert/index.html*

Graduate certificate emphasizing mediation skills for working professionals, using research projects, simulations, demonstrations, and role playing. Leonard Hawes, Dir.

996. *International Peace Gardens* (1940, 1952) (mem).

Jordan Park, 1000 S. 900 West, at Ninth West and Tenth South, Salt Lake City, about one mile west of Interstate 15.

The twenty-four gardens covering 8.25 acres were initiated by Mrs. O. A. Wiesley of the Salt Lake Council of Women in 1940, developed by local ethnic and national groups, dedicated in 1952, and now maintained by the City's Public Services Department. The gardens honor diverse national heritages and provide a "lesson in peace and understanding between nations." Nations represented: USA (1948), Japan (1950), Sweden (1953), Denmark (1955), China (1955), Finland (1961), Brazil (1963), India (1965), Canada (1971), Wales (1971), Norway (1972), Africa (1976), Korea (1985), Soviet Union/Russia

International Peace Gardens, Jordan Park, Salt Lake City. Photographs courtesy of International Peace Gardens, Mary Anne Siegendorf.

(1987), Italy (1965, 1989), Vietnam (1989), England (no official dedication of this or the following gardens), the Netherlands, Germany, Ireland, Lebanon, Mexico, Philippines, and Switzerland. Each garden flies its national flag (Ethiopia for Africa), but otherwise each is unique. The African Garden flower bed is shaped in the form of Africa; the Canadian Garden has pine trees and log-lined pathways; the Danish Garden displays a replica of a Viking burial mound, a Beech tree flag pole, a replica of the mermaid statue of Anderson's "Little Princess of the Deep"; the Indian Display offers a bronze Buddha and a statue of Mahatma Gandhi; and so on. See entry 1318.

997. *Jacob Hamblin* (1933) (mem).

Hwy. 89 south across from 4 Seasons Motel, in Davis County.

Plaque and monument of Mormon frontiersman and Indian missionary who negotiated peace with the Indians.

998. *Peace Child of Hiroshima* (1991) (mem).

South of Eccles Business College, University of Utah, Salt Lake City.

Bronze statue of Sadako Sasaki by Seattle sculptor Darrell Smith, inspired by the statue that stands in the Hiroshima Peace Park (see Nebraska). A plaque below the statue tells the Japanese girl's story. Sadako acquired leukemia from the fallout at Hiroshima. A friend told her that if she folded a thousand cranes (the Japanese symbol of hope and longevity), she would recover. She had completed more than 600 when she died at age 12.

—— *Vermont (VT)* ——

BELMONT, VT

999. *Volunteers for Peace International Workcamps* (1982) (org).

1034 Tiffany Road, Belmont 05730; (802) 259-2759; *vfp@vfp.org;* *www.vfp.org*

A program of international service and an inexpensive way to travel and live abroad. Pub. the

International Volunteer newsletter and the annual *International Workcamp Directory* containing "over 1500" programs. "In 1998 we exchanged over 1,300 volunteers with our partners in seventy countries." Recipient of a "Peace Cereal" grant. Assoc. with the Coordinating Committee for International Voluntary Service (CCIVS) at UNESCO, the International Youth Action for Peace (YAP), and the Alliance of European Voluntary Service Organizations. Peter Coldwell, Dir.

BRATTLEBORO, VT

1000. *Campaign for Equity and Restorative Justice* (1997) (org).

217 High St., Brattleboro 05301-3018; (802) 254-2826; *info@cerj.org*

Works for alternatives to the criminal injustice and prison-industrial system. John Wilmerding, General Secretary.

1001. *Center for Social Policy and Institutional Development (CSPID)* (1995) (porg).

Kipling Road, PO Box 676, Brattleboro 05302-0676; (802) 258-3339 or 3334; *cspid@sit.edu; john.ungerleider@sit.edu;* *www.sit.edu/ictp*

CSPID researches issues facing NGOs, civil society, government, and business, and offers short courses and technical assistance. Its 1999 Summer Institute explored the theme of "Intercultural Conflict Transformation and Peacebuilding." CSPID is part of the School for International Training (SIT) (1964), which is the accredited college of World Learning. Roberto Mugnani, Director.

1002. *School for International Training* (1964) (col).

Kipling Road, PO Box 676, Brattleboro 05302; (802) 258-3339; *cspid@sit.edu;* *www.sit.edu/conflict/index.html*

SIT offers courses in mediation and conflict transformation as part of its Master's Program in Intercultural Management and operates the Center for Social Policy. Summer 2000 courses: International Policy Advocacy, Conflict Transformation Across Cultures,. Roberto Mugnani, Coord. Program Development (roberto.mugnani@sit.edu).

CHESTER, VT

1003. *United Nations Association/ Vermont Chapter* (1992) (org).

PO Box 58, Chester 05143; (802) 875-3617.

Arose out of the Southern Vermont Peace Coalition. Supports UN goals and funding; supports the Model UN Program in schools. Observed (with AFSC, local World Federalists, and local WILPF) the 54th anniversary of the founding of the UN with an address by Senator Jim Jeffords. Pub. newsletter biannually, *The Spark*. Contact David Edelman.

MONTPELIER, VT

1004. *Certificate Program in Mediation/ Conflict Management* (1984) (col).

Continuing Education, Woodbury College, Montpelier 05602; (802) 223-2926; *nealr@woodbury-college.edu; www.woodbury-college.edu/public/ Academics/mcm.html*

Offers a certificate in mediation that includes internship in the community (courts, nonprofits, etc.). Woodbury also operates the Woodbury Dispute Resolution Center to serve Vermont citizens. Lee Bryan, Dir.

1005. *Peace Park* (1998) (mem).

Along the Winooski River in Montpelier.

Memorializes people who have worked for peace and social justice. Created by the local Women's International League for Peace & Freedom, the local American Friends Service Committee, and the Friends of Montpelier Parks.

Taylor, Matthew. "Capital Cultivates Peace Park." *Times Argus* (October 16, 1998).

NORTHFIELD, VT

1006. *Peace Corps and Service Leadership Program* (1987) (org).

Box 58, Harmon 223, Norwich University,

Northfield 05663; (802) 485-2648; *mitch@norwich.edu*

"To prepare students for community service in culturally diverse contexts, and to inspire a lifelong commitment to social responsibility." A 4-semester program in junior and senior years composed of academic courses and community service, leading to employment in the Peace Corps, international relief and development agencies, and other governmental, professional, and volunteer agencies. Mitchell Hall, Dir.

STOWE, VT

1007. *International Institute for Peace through Tourism/institut international pour la paix par le tourisme (IIPT)* (1986) (org)

Fox Hill 13, Cottage Club Road, Stowe, 05672; (802) 253-2658; *conference@iipt.org; www.iipt.org*

Seeks to "harness the immense power of the travel and tourism industry as the world's first 'Global Peace Industry'" for sustainable tourism. The Institute's first global conference, "Tourism: A Vital Force for Peace" was held in Vancouver in 1988. Its Third Global conference, "Building Bridges of Peace, Culture, and Prosperity through Sustainable Tourism," was in Glasgow, 1999, and "Global Summit on Peace Through Tourism" occurred in Amman, Jordan, in 2000. The Institute also encourages Peace Parks, and in 1992 it identified 381 parks in Canada dedicated to peace. Louis D'Amore, President and Founder.

—— *Virginia (VA)* ——

29 Sister Cities. / 66 Peace Poles.

ABINGDON, VA

1008. *Appalachian Peace Education Center* (1982) (org).

PO Box 2611, 236 Barter Dr., Abingdon 24212; (540) 628-9905.

Originally a coalition of regional groups concerned about nuclear war, Central America, parenting for peace and justice, etc. Now more a Washington County, VA, group working on race relations, the SOA, Jubilee 2000, and other peace issues. Pub. *APEC* newsletter (recent issues included articles on its migrant farm workers' fiesta, race relations in college, violent war toys, Amnesty International). Annually: Martin Luther King celebration, International Dinner (1990). Contact Maura Ubinger.

ARLINGTON, VA

1009. *Catholic Worker Home Page* (1994) (org).

5236 N. 5th St., Arlington 22203; *agf@cais.com. www.awadagin.com/cw/index.html*

Provides basic information about Dorothy Day and the Catholic Worker Movement, featuring biographies and writings of Dorothy Day, Peter Maurin, and Ammon Hennacy, a bibliography on the CW movement, a directory of CW houses, and links to major CW archival collections and other related Web sites. Anne Fullerton, Compiler.

BLACKSBURG, VA

1010. *Peacework Development Fund* (1989) (org).

305 Washington St., SW, Blacksburg, 24060-4745; (540) 953-1376; *sdarr@compuserve.com; www.peacework.org*

Sends volunteers to work building schools, houses, orphanages, hospitals, and other constructions around the world, managing "over $3.6 million in volunteer programs since 1989." For example, in Dec. 1998–Jan. 1999, and in Jan. 2000 PDF sent a group to build a schoolhouse in Vietnam, led by Prof. Don Voth, Univ. of Arkansas, Fayetteville.

BRIDGEWATER, VA

1011. *Peace Studies* (1987) (col).

Dept of Philosophy and Religion, Bridgewater College, Bridgewater 22812; (540) 828-5346;

wabshire@bridgewater.edu; www.bridgewater.edu/catalog/catalog97/ courses/phil_rel.html

This Church of Brethren college offers a minor in peace, justice, and conflict resolution. W. M. Abshire, Dept. Chair.

CHARLOTTESVILLE, VA

1012. *Center for the Study of Mind and Human Interaction* (1988) (col).

School of Medicine, Blue Ridge Hospital, Charlottesville 22908; (804) 982-1045; *vdv@virginia.edu; www.med.virginia.edu/medicine/interdis/ csmhi/home.html*

Promotes a method for reducing large-group tensions and building communities. Pub. quarterly journal *Mind and Human Interaction.* Vamik Volkan, M.D., Dir., Joy Boissevain, prog. Dir.

1013. *Charlottesville Center for Peace and Justice* (1982) (org).

PO Box 3381, Charlottesville 22903; (804) 961-6278; *ccpj@avenue.gen.va.us; www.avenue.gen.va.us/*

Promotes "an agenda of active nonviolence and justice in the world" particularly through networking. Recent activities include: helping the Latin-American Solidarity Committee and Hillel Center; walking to churches on Hiroshima Day to deliver "Never Again" displays; protesting French nuclear testing; sponsoring speakers on civil rights, the death penalty, and Mordechai Vanunu; opposing war in Yugoslavia. Pub.: *Peace Center Newsletter.* Contact: Katherine Chudoba (804) 982-2921; *kchudoba@virginia.edu;* (804) 971-7931; (804) 296-5105; (804) 296-4232.

1014. *Institute for Environmental Negotiation* (1981) (col.).

Univ. of Virginia, Charlottesville 22903; (804) 924-1970; *envneg@virginia.edu; www.virginia.edu/~envneg/IEN.html*

Offers mediation and consensus building services to organizations, governments, and businesses in relation to land use, and promotes sustainability. Richard Collins, Dir.

1015. *Virginians for Alternatives to the Death Penalty* (1991) (org).

PO Box 4804, Charlottesville 22905; (804) 263-8418; *mail@vadp.org; www.vadp.org*

Extensive program: action alerts, vigils, pen pals, prison inmates, death penalty schedules, etc. Henry Heller, Dir.

FAIRFAX, VA

1016. *African/African American Peace Summit* (1999) (org).

Sponsored by the Alliance of African/African American Peacemakers (AAAP) and NCPCR (see below), first Summit in Phoenix.

1017. *Consortium on Peace Research, Education, and Development (COPRED)* (1970).

The Evergreen State College, Mail Stop: Seminar 3127, Olympia, WA 98505; (360) 867-5230; *copred@evergreen.edu; www.evergreen.edu/user/copred/*

A community of educators, researchers, and activists working together for the nonviolent resolution of conflict. Provides an annual conference (Loudonville, NY, 1999; Austin, TX, 2000), a membership directory, a quarterly academic journal *Peace and Change*, a newsletter "The Peace Chronicle," a *Global Directory of Peace Studies Programs*, and a *Peace Calendar*. Recent articles in *Peace and Change* include: "Dilemmas of Humanitarian Action," "Grass-Roots Conflict Resolution Exercises," "Incarcerating Japanese Americans"; numerous book reviews. The *Global Directory* gives full identification of each peace studies program in the world. Simona Sharoni, Exec. Dir. Barbara Wien and Daniel O'Leary, recent Exec. Dir.

1018. *Institute for Conflict Analysis and Resolution (ICAR)* (1982) (col).

George Mason University, 4260 Chain Bridge Rd., Fairfax 22030-4444, 16 miles from Washington, D.C.; (703) 993-1300; *icarinfo@gmu.edu; www.gmu.edu/departments/icar*

ICAR seeks to advance understanding and resolution of protracted and deep-rooted conflicts from individuals to nations through research, teaching, and outreach. Academic programs: Ph.D. and MS in Conflict Analysis and Resolution. Internships abroad available. Affil. Orgs.: Consortium on Peace Research, Education, and Development; National Conference on Peacemaking and Conflict Resolution; Northern Virginia Mediation Service; University Dispute Resolution Project. Pubs.: *ICAR Newsletter* and many books, including *Annotated Bibliography of Conflict Analysis and Resolution* by Birkhoff et al. (1997). Sandra Cheldelin, Dir.

1019. *National Conference on Peacemaking and Conflict Resolution (NCPCR)* (1989) (org).

George Mason University, 4400 University Drive, Fairfax, 22030-4444; (703) 993-2440 or 764-6115; *ncpr@gmu.edu; www.gmu.edu/departments/NCPCR*

"Promotes the use of nonviolent approaches to the resolution of conflict and the improvement of conflict resolution theory and practice" by a biennial conference of representatives of peace and conflict fields. Some past sites: Montréal, Charlotte, Portland. 1999: Phoenix, "Weaving a New Beginning: Liberation, Healing, and Community." Sohini Sinha, Dir.

1020. *Northern Virginia Mediation Service* (1988) (org).

c/o Institute for Conflict Analysis & Resolution, George Mason U, 4260 Chain Bridge Road, Suite A-2, Fairfax 22030; (703) 993-3656; *www.gmu.edu/departments/nvms*

A regional mediation center, providing training in mediation and conflict resolution. Robert Scott, Exec. Dir.

1021. *World Summit of Youth Peacemakers* (1999) (org).

The 1st World Summit is sponsored by NCPCR (see above). (215) 382-1391 or (877) 397-3223. Sohini Sinha, Dir.

FALLS CHURCH, VA

1022. *American Red Cross* (1881) (org).

8111 Gatehouse Rd., Falls Church 22042; *www.redcross.org*

Provides relief to victims of disasters and helps prevent, prepare for, and respond to emergencies. Follows the principles of the International Red Cross and Red Crescent Movement: humanity, impartiality, neutrality, independence, voluntary service, unity, universality. Dr. Bernadine Healy, President.

Shabtai, Rosenne. *Participation in the Geneva Conventions (1864–1949) and the Additional Protocols of 1977.* Geneva: International Committee of the Red Cross; Martinus Nijhoff, 1984.

GOOCHLAND, VA

1023. *Little Flower Catholic Worker* (1996) (org).

1780 Hadensville-Fife Rd., Goochland 23063; (804) 457-2631.

Peacemaking includes vigils and civil disobedience at Yorktown Naval Weapons Station (a nuclear weapons storage facility); actions for closing the SOA; anti-war vigils at Richmond Federal Bldg.; ending sanctions against Iraq; Latin American solidarity. Contact Sue Frankel-Streit, Jeff Winder.

HARRISONBURG, VA

1024. *Center for Mediation* (1989) (col).

James Madison University, Harrisonburg 22807; (540) 568-6496; *kimseywd@jmu.edu;* *www.jmu.edu/mediation/index.html*

Supports research and services for the University and community. JMU also offers an undergraduate minor in Conflict and Mediation Studies. William Kimsey, Co-Dir.

1025. *Common Ground: A Network for Peace, Justice, and the Environment* (1984) (org).

284 E. Water St., PO Box 1385, Harrisonburg 22801; (540) 433-8212;

common-ground@juno.com; *www.homestead.com/cground*

A network of 40 organizations mainly in the Shenandoah Valley, providing support in areas of peace, justice, and the environment through education, research, and civic action. Pub. a monthly newspaper.

Ms. Dale Diaz, Director or contact John Eckman.

1026. *Conflict Transformation Program* (1994) (col).

Eastern Mennonite U, Harrisonburg 22802-2462, 25 miles from Washington, D.C. and 115 miles from Richmond, VA; (540) 432-4490 or (800) 710-7871; *ctprogram@emu.edu;* *www.emu.edu/ctp/ctp.htm*

The Program prepares "Reflective Practitioners" by "encouraging non-violent and restorative responses to conflict" and "sustaining a long-term commitment to peacebuilding and working for just social structures." The M.A. degree offers advanced preparation for persons with experience in working across cultures in conflict transformation; the Graduate Certificate Program offers an abbreviated version of the M.A. The Summer Peacebuilding Institute offers 7-day intensive training. Pubs.: *Footpaths* newsletter; cumulative Program reports.

HUDDLESTON, VA

1027. *Pax Christi Virginia* (1990) (org).

110 Lee Drive, Huddleston 24104; (540) 297-6493; *delrauth@aol.com*

Through the "spirit of gospel nonviolence," PCV seeks "to bring about systemic change in society and church as regards war, disarmament, ecology, inclusivity, oppression, capital punishment, and rights to all life." Activities: Annual peace walk from Appomattox to Yorktown (165 miles), vigils for executions at 10 locations, initiated in 1995, participates in annual Peace Summit of all peace organizations in Va. and WVa, supports Pax Christi Haiti, demonstrations at Yorktown Naval Weapons Depot, opposition to the SOA, supports Plowshares activists in prison. Pub. a newsletter. Bob and Adele DellaValle-Rauth, Co-coordinator and Regional Rep.

LYNCHBURG, VA

1028. *Lynchburg Peace Education Center* (1984) (org).

PO Box 3143, Lynchburg 24503; (804) 847-5477; *paydentravers_j@mail.lynchburg.edu*

Promotes peace and justice "in the individual human heart and mind, in the home and workplace, in places of worship, in schools, on the streets, and in the world community." Activities include: vigils, international dinners, sponsors lectures, nonviolence training, speakers bureau, displays at mall. Pub. newsletter, *Citizen's Report*, twice a year. Jack Paydon-Travers, Dir.

1029. *Virginia Peace Summit* (org).

Tabor Retreat Center, Lynchburg.

Annual meeting in June of representatives from area representatives (including Maryland and W. Virginia). Contact the Charlottesville Center for Peace and Justice, which was the year 2000 coordinator: Kathy Chudoba, PO Box 3381, Charlottesville, VA 22903; (804) 961-6278; or e-mail (ccpj@avenue.gen.va.us).

MCLEAN, VA

1030. *Institute for Victims of Trauma* (1987) (org).

6801 Market Square Dr., McLean 22101; (703) 847-8456; *ivt@microneil.com*

Focuses on "conflict transformation via understanding trauma and victimization" that arise out wars, terrorism, disasters. Related projects: Joint Program on Conflict Resolution, Building Tolerance for Diversity. Pub. packets, pamphlets, and bibliographies. Leila Dane, Exec. Dir.

NEWPORT NEWS, VA

1031. *Peninsula Peace Education Center* (1983) (org).

681 Dresden Dr., Newport News 23601; (757) 591-9596; *jurquhart@whro.net*; *www.dandelionproject.com/ppec*

Functions as a resource center for the community, develops educational programs, and fos-

ters communication on issues of world security, peace, and social justice. Pub. *The Peace Advocate*, 5–7 pages newsletter 8 times a year to approx. 500 people. Shirley McCallum, Pres. Contact John Urquhart.

NORFOLK, VA

1032. *Norfolk Catholic Worker* (1989) (org).

1321 W. 38th St., Norfolk 23508; (757) 423-5420.

A Catholic Worker House of Hospitality and Resistance in the tradition of Dorothy Day and Peter Maurin, for mercy and resisting war. Supports Plowshare movement for disarmament; involved in nonviolent civil resistance against militarism locally (Yorktown Naval Weapons Station where nuclear warheads for Atlantic Fleet Tomahawk Cruise Missiles are stored) and with Atlantic Life Community. Contact Steve Baggerly, Kim Williams.

1033. *Norfolk Quaker House* (1994) (org).

PO Box 7891, Norfolk 23509-0891; (757) 626-3304; *nqh1@nfx.net*; *www.nfx.net/~nqh1/nqh.htm*

Founded as a Christian witness for peace. Activities include counseling and legal help for people facing military service and for people needing discharge from the military for conscientious or other reasons. Also seeks to reach young people before they enlist with information about conscientious objection, military life, and alternative careers. Contact Lloyd Wilson, Coordinator; Susan Wilson, Clerk of Board of Directors.

1034. *People for the Ethical Treatment of Animals (PETA)* (1980) (org).

501 Front St., Norfolk 23510; (757) 622-7382; *peta@peta-online.org*; *www.peta-online.org/about/mission.htm*

The "largest animal rights organization in the world," PETA protects the rights of all animals: "animals are not ours to eat, wear, experiment on, or use for entertainment." The group focuses on factory farms, laboratories, the fur trade, and the entertainment industry, but its work includes numerous other harms to animals.

RADFORD, VA

1035. *International Philosophers for Peace and the Elimination of Nuclear and Other Global Threats (IPPNO)* (1983) (org).

313 Seventh Ave., Radford 24141; (540) 639-2320; *friedman@aol.com; gmartin@runet.edu; ippno@runet.edu; www.runet.edu/~gmartin/IPPNO*

Founded by John Somerville and other philosophers and concerned thinkers dedicated to peace, originally called International Philosophers for the Prevention of Nuclear Omnicide, who believe the world must be demilitarized or be "ever further degraded by hate, fear, violence, and instability." Member of the International Federation of Philosophy and as a member of the International Peace Bureau IPPNO worked to bring about the International Court of Justice ruling against nuclear weapons. Pub. *IPPNO Newsletter* and edits a series on "Ways to Peace in a Violent World." Pres. Dr. Glen Martin. Exec. Dir. Prof. Emer. Howard Friedman.

1036. *Peace and World Security Studies* (1994) (col).

Radford University, Radford 24142; (540) 728-3542; *gmartin@runet.com; www.runet.edu/Catalog/acaddept/PWSS.html*

Undergraduate minor of 18 semester hours designed by students and advising committee. Speakers, films, events sponsored by the program. Contact Glen Martin.

RICHMOND, VA

1037. *Campaign for Forgiveness Research* (1998) (org).

PO Box 842018, Richmond 23284-2018; (804) 828-1193.

Explores the role of forgiveness in healing individuals, families, communities, and nations. In 1997 the John Templeton foundation committed $5 million to launch studies of forgiveness. The Campaign was begun in 1998 to raise an additional $5.5 million. Everett Worthington, Jr. Exec. Dir.

1038. *Pax Christi Richmond* (1980) (org).

2425 Triton Dr., Richmond 23235; (804) 272-8141; *gallinjb@aol.com*

Newsletter every two months mainly listing coming events. Contact John Gallini. (Gallini compiled a directory of Virginia peace centers).

1039. *Richmond Peace Education Center* (1980) (org).

14 N. Laurel St., Richmond 23220; (804) 358-1958; *rpec@richmond.infi.net; www.rpec.org*

Promotes peace and social justice in community and around the world. Provides conflict resolution assistance in the schools. Contact Ken Willis, Jane Hare.

1040. *Richmond Peace Summit* (1985) (org).

2425 Triton Dr., Richmond 23235; (804) 272-8141; *gallinjb@aol.com*

Representatives of peace and justice organizations meet once a year to share experiences and discuss issues. Contact John Gallini.

ROANOKE, VA

1041. *Plowshares Peace & Justice Center* (1976) (org).

1402 Grandin Rd. SW, Rm. 203, PO Box 1623, Roanoke 24008; (540) 985-0808; *plowshare@plowshare.org; www.plowshare.org*

Committed to social and economic justice, respect for diversity, freedom from violence, global responsibility for the environment, universal education. Activities: Peace Wave, an annual community festival, vigils protesting executions and military actions, forums and speakers, monitoring legislation, networking. Pub. *Plowshare News* bimonthly. Manuel Dotson, Dir.

ST. PAUL, VA

1042. *Appalachian Office of Justice & Peace, Catholic Diocese of Richmond* (1972) (org).

PO Box 660, St. Paul 24283; (540) 762-5050; *aojp2@naxs.net*

Promotes the integration of Catholic social teaching into church life and communities of southwestern Virginia. Muzaffar Fazaluddin, Dir. (Sr. Clare McBrien, Ecological Educator, PO Box 882, Wytheville 23482; *aojp1@naxs. com*).

SPOTSYLVANIA, VA

1043. *Saint Francis Catholic Worker* (1979) (org).

9631 Peppertree Rd., Spotsylvania 22553; (540) 972-3218; one hour south of D.C. and one hour north of Richmond, VA.

Founded in D.C., moved to current address in 1993. Seeks to realize the nonviolent teachings of Jesus especially as expressed in the Sermon on the Mount and the call to solidarity with the poor. Offers spiritual retreats for the poor and some peace lobbying and demonstrations. Member of Pax Christi. John Mahony, Director.

VIENNA, VA

1044. *National Wildlife Federation* (1936) (org).

8925 Leesburg Pike, Vienna 22184-0001; (703) 790-4000; *www.nwf.org*

Assists individuals and organizations to conserve wildlife and other natural resources and protect the earth's environment in order to achieve a peaceful, equitable, and sustainable future. Claims more than four million members and supporters, with revenues in 1998 of $98 million. Founded by J. N. "Ding" Darling (1876-1962). Mark Van Putten, Pres.

— *Washington State — (WA)*

40 Sister Cities. / 98 Peace Poles.

CHEHALIS, WA

1045. *Bethlehem Farm Catholic Worker* (1980, 1992) (org).

508 Coal Creek Road, Chehalis 98532; (360) 748-1236; *bethfarm@localaccess.com*;

www2.localaccess.com/bethfarm/bframe. htm

Originally Jesuit, became Catholic Worker in 1992. Organizes roundtables leading to actions; e.g., the Nevada Test Site. Contact Philip Steger or Tom Bichsel (Catholic Worker in Tacoma).

FEDERAL WAY, WA

1046. *Zones of Peace International Foundation* (2000) (org).

PO Box 24803, Federal Way 98093-1803; (253) 874-2619; *wlarrimore@uswest.net*; *zopif@wolfenet.com*

Seeks to establish sites as sanctuaries of nonviolence free from weapons, violence, and environmental destruction. William Larrimore, Secretary.

HUSUM, WA

1047. *Columbia River Fellowship for Peace* (1984) (org).

PO Box 241, Husum 98623; (509) 364-3578; *crfp@hotmail.com*

Affil. with Fellowship of Reconciliation in 1991, and with Oregon Peace Works. Recent activities include sponsorship of a young person at FOR's Peacemaker Training Institute and vigils regarding Iraq and Yugoslavia. Pub. *CRFP Newsletter* once or twice a year. Contact Laurie Cross.

OLYMPIA, WA

1048. *Olympia FOR* (1976) (org).

PO Box 7273, Olympia 98507; office: 5015 15th Ave. SE, Lacey 98503-2723; (360) 491-9093; *monieram@aol.com*

Fellowship of Reconciliation local group. Contact Glen Anderson, Ramona Hinkle. See entry 1017.

POINT ROBERTS, WA

1049. *SunSweep* (1985) (mem).

Lighthouse Marine Park, Point Roberts.

One of three sculptures of Canadian black granite by David Barr, spanning 2778 miles of the US/Canadian border. Each slab has a contour of a woman's hand that evolves into a sun symbol for international friendship. In order to visit each site, the viewer must pass through both countries, due to geographical peculiarities. Because this long border lies under the path of the sun, the work is called SunSweep. The other two sculptures are at Roosevelt Campobello International Park, New Brunswick, and American Point Island, Lake-of-the-Woods, Minnesota.

POULSBO, WA

1050. *Ground Zero Center for Nonviolent Action* (1977) (org).

16159 Clear Creek Rd. NW, Poulsbo 98370 (3 acres sharing a fence with Bangor Trident Submarine Base); (360) 377-2586; *info@gzcenter.org; www.gzcenter.org*

"Committed to a world without violence and a world without nuclear weapons." Leaflets workers at Bangor Naval Station, hosts discussions and retreats, offers speakers, organizes vigils and protests at Bangor and other Kitsap County locations. Annual August 7–9 "Witnessing to Trident." Pub. the *Ground Zero* newsletter three times a year; the Summer 1999 issue was mainly about the June 1999 trial (see below); the Fall 1999 issue covers a variety of actions by the Center.

Origin of a significant court ruling in 1999: members of the Center were acquitted of civil disobedience at the Naval Submarine Base at Bangor, west of Seattle. The jury's decision was based on international treaties, which oblige the U.S. to act on nuclear disarmament. This is the first or one of the first times protesters have been vindicated under international law.

Roberts, Elizabeth. "D-5 Nine Not Guilty!" *Ground Zero* (Summer 1999) 1–5.

Shaw, Jeff. "Bangor 8 Acquitted." *Z Magazine* (September 1999) 16–17.

SEATTLE, WA

1051. *Alliance for Nuclear Accountability* (1987) (org).

1914 N. 34th St., Suite 407, Seattle 98103; (206) 547-3175.

29 organizations watching U.S. nuclear weapons sites and waste dumps and nuclear policies. In 1999 participated in "Back from the Brink," a campaign to de-alert nuclear weapons (www.dealert.org). See Washington, D.C., for list of member groups.

1052. *American Friends Service Committee, Pacific Northwest Region* (1950s) (org).

814 N.E. 40th St., Seattle, 98105; (206) 632-0500; *afscpnr@igc.apc.org*

Seattle office concentrates on youth, Indians, cross cultures, sexual discrimination; the Portland office on economic development, Latin America/Asia Pacific, education, sexual choice. Pub. a regional update three times a year. Susan Segall, Reg. Dir. (National office: Philadelphia).

1053. *The Fin Project: From Swords into Plowshares* (1998) (mem).

In Magnuson Park at Sand Point in north Seattle, on the site of the former Navy base; *jtyoung@u.washington.edu; http://weber.u.washington.edu/~jtyoung*

This 500-foot long sculpture uses 22 recycled fins from nuclear attack submarines placed at various angles and heights to resemble the dorsal fins of a large pod of orca whales or school of salmon. Each fin, painted black, weighs 10,000 pounds. John Young, Professor at the School of Art, U of Washington, Seattle 98195 (206-543-0977 or 0970), designed the sculpture; the $150,000 of private money was raised by Max Gurvich. "This artwork represents the ultimate in recycling, 'From Swords into Plowshares.'" The artist hopes that "similar 'pods' will be created around the country and the world, as symbols for peace on a global scale." He also wishes "to honor those men and women who served our country during the Cold War."

1054. *Institute for World Peace Through Prayer and Meditation* (1999) (org).

PO Box 18499, Seattle 98118; (206) 721-1800; *rschoenfeld@instituteforworldpeace.com; www.instituteforworldpeace.com*

Asks all people to pray for peace each day at noon, and sought to bring all people of the world together in prayer on New Year's Eve 2000. Robert Schoenfeld, Pres.

The Fin Project by John Young, Magnuson Park, Seattle. Photograph courtesy John Young.

1055. *International Friendship Grove* (1960) (mem).

Campus Parkway,
U of Washington, Seattle.

In commemoration of the Fifth World Forestry Congress at the U of Washington, each country is represented by a particular tree—the U.S. by a Douglas Fir, Canada by a Sugar Maple, Mexico by a Patual pine, and so on. Also known as the Peace Grove.

1056. *Lutheran Peace Fellowship* (1941) (org).

1710 11th Ave., Seattle 98122-2420;
(206) 720-0313; *lpf@ecunet.org;*
www.nonviolence.org/lpf

Offers workshops and retreats on Christian peacemaking and support for congregation, campus, and youth groups, and advocates the Nobel Laureates Decade for Peace/Nobel Peace Laureates Appeal. Pub. a newsletter about nationwide activities of LPF. Glen Gersmehl, Dir.

1057. *Mothers Against Violence in America* (1994) (org).

105 14th Ave., suite 2A, Seattle 98122;
(206) 323-2303; (800) 897-7697;
maviausa@aol.com; www.mavia.org

Dedicated to preventing violence by and against children through grassroots advocacy and student-oriented educational programs. Includes Students Against Violence Everywhere, Day of National Concern About Young People and Gun Violence, annual conference, public forums, rallies. Pamela Eakes, Exec. Dir.

1058. *Nonviolent Action Community of Cascadia (NACC)* (1979) (org).

4554 12th Ave. NE, Seattle, 98105;
(206) 547-0952; *cmtc@igc.apc.org;*
www.nonviolence.org/~nvweb/nacc

Begun as the Conscience and Military Tax Campaign by war tax resisters, NACC today acts to interrupt and transform militarism and other forms of violence, and to build a society based upon community, economic justice, environmental awareness, personal empowerment, and feminist, queer-positive, anti-racist principles, war tax resistance, and public education. It still administers the CMTC Escrow Account, one of the largest funds of resisted tax dollars in the US. Other current projects include: the Art & Revolution puppet theater and the campaign to stop resumption of nuclear weapon production at Hanford. Pub. quarterly newsletter *Nonviolent Action* (actually a rich magazine). Functions as local chapter of the War Resisters League and an affiliate of the National War Tax Resistance Coordinating Committee. Named Cascadia because Seattle is in the Cascadia bioregion.

1059. *Northwest Coalition for the Decade of Peace* (1999) (org).

1710 11th Ave., Seattle 98122;
(206) 720-0313; *lpf@ecunet.org*

Created by the major nonviolent groups in the region to expand nonviolence training. Glen Gersmehl, Coord.

1060. *Peace Action of Washington* (1977) (org).

5828 Roosevelt Way NE, Seattle 98105; (206) 527-8050;
organizer@peaceaction.gen.wa.us;
www.peaceaction.gen.wa.us

Created by the merger of Puget Sound SANE and Seattle Nuclear Weapons Freeze, PAW is affiliated with both Peace Action and Coalition to Stop Gun Violence. It works to prevent community violence, to achieve nuclear disarmament through the CNTBT and Start II Treaty, to inform voters about the positions of their representatives, to bring about an Arms Trade Code of Conduct (trade to democratic and humanitarian nations only), to reduce military spending, and to prevent the restarting of the Fast Flux Test Facility at Hanford. Scott Carpenter, Dir.

1061. *Peace & Justice Resource Center* (1975) (org).

1710 11th Ave., Seattle 98122-2420; (206) 720-0313; *lpf@ecunet.org*

Encourages discussion and action regarding peace and justice issues through their print (over 9000 books) and video library, their workshops, their assistance to schools, non-profits, and libraries in choosing peace and justice resources, and their policy analyses and resource guides. Affiliated with COPRED, Lutheran Peace Fellowship, and Western Washington FOR. Contact Glen Gersmehl. See entry 1056.

1062. *Peace and Strategic Studies Program* (1984) (col).

Psychology Dept., University of Washington, Seattle 98195; (206) 543-8784; *dpbarash@u.washington.edu; www.washington.edu/students—/gencat/academic/peace.html*

An undergraduate major particularly in the field of nuclear weapons and peace. Senior thesis. Contact David Barash. (Barash is the author of many books on war and peace; his latest: *Peace and Conflict Studies* with Charles Webel.).

1063. *Peace Park* (1990) (mem).

Ninth Ave. NE and NE 40th St., Seattle.

The creation of Floyd Schmoe to honor victims of Hiroshima atomic bombing. Contains a larger-than-life bronze statue of Sadako Sasaki on tiptoe holding aloft a paper crane. Sadako is Japanese girl who made oragami cranes in the hope of surviving the radiation exposure she suffered from the bombing of Hiroshima.
Seattle Times (Aug. 7, 1990), E3; *Seattle Post-Intelligencer* (Aug. 7, 1990), B1, B4.

1064. *Sakya Monastery of Tibetan Buddhism* (1974) (org, mem).

108 NW 83rd St., Seattle 98117; (206) 789-2573.

A center for Dharma teachings in the U.S., a shrine and library for the non-sectarian community of practitioners and visitors. The stupa commemorates the late Dezhung Rinpoche.

1064a. *Seattle/Tashkent Peace Park* (1988) (org, mem).

A one-time Tashkent /Seattle Peace Park Project to build a park in Tashkent, organized by returning Peace Corps volunteers. About $500,000 were raised and over 20,000 people contributed. A film was made of the process. Contact Arthur Rice, North Carolina SU, Raleigh, NC 27695; (919) 515-8340; *art_rice@ncsu.edu;* in Seattle: Fred Noland or Barbara Oakrock; or John MacLeod, U of Montréal (john.macleod@umontreal.ca).

1065. *Seattle Women Act for Peace* (1961) (org).

El Centro de la Raza, 2524 16th South, Seattle 98144; (206) 523-1127; *brodierose@aol.com*

Supports disarmament and economic justice, and opposes war, militarism, and oppression. SWAP writes letters, collects signatures on petitions, phones and meets with candidates and public officials, demonstrates and pickets, holds educational programs, and pub. a near-monthly newsletter (the Oct./Nov. issue included articles on WTO, militarization and global economy, CTBT, Mumia Abu-Jamal, nuclear wastes at Hanford, a cake recipe and a recipe for peace, a book review, a calendar of forthcoming events). Branch of Women Strike for Peace. Contact Rosemary Brodie.

1066. *Sri Chinmoy's Peace Relay Runs/International Peace Run* (1987) (org).

16959 26th Ave. NE, Seattle 98155; (206) 306-9991.

Brings together people across seven continents and over 120 countries to carry a torch for peace and harmony. See entry 916.

1067. **Victoria to Maui 2000 Women's Campaign* (1999) (org).

PO Box 17823, Seattle 98107; (206) 285-6768; *deb@navgates.com*; *www.navgates.com/vmcontents.html*

A women's team sailing 2308 thousand miles as "voices for Peace in the New Millenium—no war, no hate, no intolerance, no mistreatment of anyone." Deb Rigas, Exec.Dir.

1068. **Western Washington Fellowship of Reconciliation* (1966) (org).

225 N. 70th, Seattle 98103; (206) 789-5565; *wwfor@connectexpress.com*

Focuses on death penalty, economic justice, disarmament and demilitarization, racial justice, decade of nonviolence, and Iraq. Mike Yarrow, Organizer (former organizer: Nan McMurry).

SPOKANE, WA

1069. **Peace and Justice Action League of Spokane (PJALS)* (1975) (org).

224 S. Howard St., Spokane 99201; (509) 838-7870; *pjals@icehouse.net*

Some 500 members and some paid staff work on local justice and peace issues, with continuing focus on Central America and the death penalty. Close connection with the Catholic Diocese and Fellowship of Reconciliation. Contact Rusty Nelson.

1070. **Peace Studies Program* (1982) (col).

History/Political and International Studies, Whitworth College, Spokane 99251; (509) 777-4432; *johnyoder@whitworth.edu*; *www.whitworth.edu*

Presbyterian affil. Major (14 courses) and minor (5 courses), both beginning with History and Politics of Nonviolence. Internship/practicum role-playing conflict resolution classes required. John Yoder, Dir.

1071. **People to People Student Ambassador Program* (1956) (org).

Dwight D. Eisenhower Building, 110 S. Ferrall St., Spokane 99202-4800; (509) 534-0430; *info@studentambassadors.org*; *www.studentambassadors.org*

Founded by Dwight D. Eisenhower, PtP at first was administered by the U.S. State Department, but became a private, nonprofit organization in 1961. For over 40 years PtP sent some 100,000 Canadian and U.S. youths to over 25 different countries. Travel lasts 2–4 weeks in groups of approximately 30 students accompanied by adults. (See People to People in Kansas City, MO, which arranges for students abroad to come to the U.S.)

TACOMA, WA

1072. **Tacoma FOR* (1980?) (org).

3134 N. Mullen, Tacoma 98407; (253) 752-8979.

Fellowship of Reconciliation group. Monthly meetings, annual picnic, annual Seabeck Conference (WA and OR FORs). John Julius, chair.

WASHOUGAL, WA

1073. **Theosophical Order of Service* (1908) (org).

PO Box 967, Washougal 98671-0967.

Founded by Annie Besant for the more active promotion of the aims of the Theosophical Society (animal welfare, arts and music, ecology, family, healing, social service, peace). The aim of the Peace Department is to "promote the principles of goodwill, equality, compassion, tolerance, and brotherhood." See entry 852.

— Washington, D.C. —

1 Sister City. / 22 Peace Poles.

1074. **Alliance for Nuclear Accountability* (1987) (org).

1801 18th St., Suite 9-2, DC 20009; (202) 833-4668; *ananuclear@earthlink.net*; *www.ananuclear.org* (also in Seattle)

Local, regional, and national organizations working together to promote education and action regarding U.S. nuclear weapons: AFSC, Denver; Carolina Peace Resource Center; Citizen Alert; Coalition for Health Concern; Concerned Citizens for Nuclear Safety; Environmental Defense Institute; Fernald Residents for Environmental Safety and Health; Global Resource Action Center for the Environment; Government Accountability Project; Heart of America Northwest; Los Alamos Study Group; Miamisburg Environmental Safety & Health; National Environmental Coalition of Native Americans; Neighbors in Need; Oak Ridge Environmental Peace Alliance; Panhandle Area Neighbors and Landowners; Peace Action Education Fund; Nashville Peace Action; Peace Farm; Physicians for Social Responsibility; Portsmouth/Piketon Residents for Environmental Safety; Rocky Mountain Peace and Justice Center; Serious Texans Against Nuclear Dumping; Snake River Alliance; Southwest Research and Information Center; Tri-Valley CAREs; Western States Legal Foundation; Women's Action for New Directions.

1075. *Americans for Peace Now* (1981) (org).

1835 K St., NW, Suite 500, 20006; (202) 728-1893; *apndc@peacenow.org; www.peacenow.org*

Offices also in NYC and LA. Mission "to strengthen Israel's security through the peace process and to support the Israeli Peace Now movement." Raises funds for the movement. Pub. quarterly newsletter, weekly *Middle East Peace Report*. Debra DeLee, Pres. and CEO.

1076. *American University Center for Global Peace* (1996) (org).

DC, 20016-8071; (202) 895-1326 (1328); *salima@american.edu; www.american.edu/ academic.depts/acainst/cgp*

A research institute for a better understanding of the interdependent global system and working toward common security, focusing in general on the human, cultural, economic, political, and natural environments, and on eight themes: religion, human rights, arts, gender, ecology, science and technology, poverty, and culture. Organizes seminars and workshops, hosts research groups, provides assistance to universities worldwide. Offers the MA degree in International Peace and Conflict Resolution. Faculty pubs. year 2000: Aziz Said, co-ed., *Cultural Diversity and Islam*; Abu-Nimer, co-ed,

Promoting Justice and Peace Through Reconciliation and Coexistence. Dir.: Abdul Aziz Said.

1077. *Anti-Defamation League of B'nai B'rith, Washington Office* (org).

1100 Connecticut Ave., NW, Suite 1020, DC 20036; (202) 452-8320; *adlnatlgov@aol.com*

"Committed to fighting hatred, bigotry, and all other forms of prejudice for over 80 years." Pub. *Anti-Defamation League Resources for Classroom and Community*. See ADL's NYC national office.

1078. *Asia Pacific Center for Justice and Peace* (1995) (org).

110 Maryland Ave., NE (Box 70), NYC 20002; (202) 543-1094; *apcjp@igc.org; www.apcjp.org*

Brings a progressive voice to U.S. policies toward countries in Asia and the Pacific; promotes the realization of the full range of people's rights; provides channels of communication among grassroots organizations, such as the Sri Lanka Forum; organizes conferences and seminars. In 1998 sponsored conferences on the Universal Declaration of Human Rights, elections in Cambodia, and the Asian financial crisis. Pub. the *Asia Pacific Advocate* quarterly newsletter and the twice monthly *Philippine News Survey*, Exec. Dir.: Miriam Young.

1079. *Assassination Archives & Research Center* (1984) (org).

918 F St., NW, Suite 510, DC; (202) 393-1917.

Independent research of assassinations in the world especially following WWII, Kennedy and King. Pub. *AARC Quarterly*.

1080. *Cantilevers* (1993) (jour).

Provides a global forum for the development of theory and practice for the transformation of conflict and the building of peace. Its motto: "building bridges for peace." (See: Montréal, Eric Abitbol.)

1081. *Capital Area Association for Peace Studies* (1988) (org).

An informal consortium of DC area schools. Sponsors an annual student conference, workshops, and a newsletter. Contact Sr. Mary Hayes,

Trinity College in DC; Harry Yeide of George Washington Univ.; Amy Shuster, Princeton Univ.; William Barbieri, Catholic Univ. (202) 319-5700; *barbieri@cua.edu*).

1082. *Capital Punishment Program* (1976) (org).

122 Maryland Ave., NE, DC 20002; (202) 544-1681; *aclu.org@aol.com*

Anti-death penalty program of the ACLU. (See Index for other organizations, and *Fellowship*, May/June 2000, p. 21).

1083. *Carnegie Endowment for International Peace* (1910) (org).

1779 Mass. Ave., NW, DC 20036-2103.

Pub. *Foreign Policy* quarterly. Jessica Matthews, Pres.

1084. *Catholic Worker Bookstore* (1996) (org).

PO Box 3087, DC 20010; 1-800-43-PEACE or (202) 722-4783; Fortkamp Publishing/Rose Hill Books, PO Box 5198, Des Moines, IA 50306; *pmagno@pop.igc.org*

Books for peace, justice, and nonviolent resistance in the Catholic Worker tradition. Write for catalog. Contact Paul Magno.

1085. *Caux Scholars Program* (1991) (col).

1156 15th St., NW, Suite 910, DC 20005; (202)872-9077; *CauxSP@aol.com*; *http://members.aol.com/cauxsp/web/cspweb.htim*

Interfaith based courses on the moral dimensions of peacemaking, using case studies, simulations, and interactive learning as well as lectures. Naila Sherman, Prog. Dir.

1086. *Center for Defense Information* (1972) (org).

1779 Massachusetts Ave., NW; (202) 332-0600; Fax (202) 462-4559; *info@cdi.org; www.cdi.org*

CDI "opposes excessive expenditures for weapons and policies that increase the danger of war," and "believes that strong social, economic, political, and military components and a healthy environment contribute equally to the nation's security." Pub. *The Defense Monitor* reports and videos. Bruce Blair, Pres.; Eugene Carroll, Jr., Vice President.

1087. *Center for Environmental Citizenship* (1993) (org).

1611 Connecticut Ave. NW #3-B, DC 20009; (202) 234-5990; *susan@envirocitizen.org*; *www.envirocitizen.org/*

Originally Campus Green Vote, renamed CEC when CGV became a project of CEC. Encourages 18-24 year olds to be active in protecting the environment and to vote for the environment especially by involving them in Green Voter Campaigns, computer networking, and campus activism. Pub. *EarthNet News*. Susan Comfort, Exec. Dir. Rani Corey, CGV Dir. (19 Cortes St. #5, Boston, MA, 02116; 617-290-8927; *rani@envirocitizen.org*). (Seattle, WA, office: Doug Israel, *cecnw@envirocitizen.org*). (Denver office, Phil Winters, cecwest@envirocitizen.org).

1088. *Center for Global Peace* (1996) (col).

American Univ., 4400 Massachusetts Ave. NW, Washington, DC 20016; (202) 895-1326; *salima@american.edu*; *www.american.edu/academic.depts/acainst/cgp*

Organizes seminars and workshops; coordinates research groups; provides assistance to universities worldwide. Pub. books and the *Journal of Peacebuilding and Development*, the January 2001 issue on "Developing Peace In Africa." Abdul Aziz Said, Dir.; Betty Sitka, Assoc. Dir.

1089. *Center to Prevent Handgun Violence* (1983) (org).

1225 Eye St., NW, Suite 1100, DC 20005; (202) 289-7319; *www.cphv.org*

The legal, research, and education affiliate of Handgun Control, Inc., a lobbying organization. The Center builds bridges among diverse groups in search of solutions to gun violence. The Legal Action Project helps gun victims have their day in court. The Law Enforcement Relations department works directly with police. The Research department provides data. Project Lifeline is the Center's national education program.

1090. **Coalition to Reduce Nuclear Dangers* (1996) (org).

110 Maryland Ave., NE, Suite 505, DC 20002; (202) 546-0795; *coalition@clw.org; jsmith@clw.org; www.crnd.org; www.clw.org/pub/clw/coalition*

Especially concentrates on eliminating nuclear testing (CTBT) as a way of reducing and eventually ending nuclear arsenals. Pub. pamphlet "For a Safer America: The Case for a Comprehensive Test Ban Treaty," and distributes other CTBT materials; for example, the Center for Defense Information's video, "Test Anxiety—Should the United States Ratify the CTBT?" The Coalition is hosted by The Council for a Livable World Education Fund (1980) and is affiliated with the Disarmament Clearinghouse (*disarmament@igc.org*), 20/20 Vision (*ctbt@2020vision.org*), FCNL (*rachel@fcnl.org*), Peace Action (*bhall@peaceaction.org*), and other nuclear arms control groups. Daryl Kimball, Exec. Dir.; Stephen Young, Dep. Dir.

1091. **Coalition to Stop Gun Violence* (1974) (org).

1000 16th St. NW, Suite 603, DC 20036; (202) 530-0340; *noguns@aol.com; www.gunfree*.org

Seeks ban on private sale and possession of handguns in U.S. Comprised of 46 national organizations and over 100,000 members. Activities: grassroots organizing, education, youth organizing, lobbying legislators. Its sister organization is the *Educational Fund to End Handgun Violence* (1978), for public education, litigation, and grassroots development. One of its programs is Hands Without Guns for young people; another is the Firearms Litigation Clearinghouse, which provides assistance to victims and attorneys seeking to hold the gun industry accountable. Pub. *Stop Gun Violence News* newsletter and *Register Citizen Opinion*, a Congressional voting directory. Michael Beard, Pres.

1092. **Conflict Resolution Education Network (CREnet)* (1994) (org).

1527 New Hampshire Avenue, NW, DC 20036; (202) 667-9700; *nidr@crenet.org; www.crenet.org*

Successor to the National Association for Mediation in Education and the National Institute for Dispute Resolution (NIDR). Membership organization advocating the effectiveness of conflict management skills and processes in schools and communities. Sponsors the MTV Conflict Resolution Affiliates program, the Youth Vision awards program, and standards for school-based peer mediation programs. Pubs.: *Fourth R* newsletter and *Forum* journal.

1093. **Conflict Resolution Skills Institutes* (1995) (org).

American University, (see: International Peace and Conflict Resolution Program), 4400 Massachusetts Ave., NW, DC 20016-8071; (202) 885-1622; *peace@american.edu; www.american.edu/ academic.depts/sis/peace*

Practical training in methods offered fall and spring semesters over a single weekend for college credit to American U. and Washington Consortium students.

1094. **Council for a Livable World* (1962) (org).

110 Maryland Ave., NE, Rm 409, DC 20002.

One of the oldest arms control organizations, CLW fought for the ban of above-ground nuclear explosions in 1963 and today works for the approval of the Comprehensive Test Ban Treaty and the defeat of the Senators who voted against it.

1095. **Crisis Corps* (1999) (org).

Peace Corps, 1111 20th St. NW, DC 20526; (800) 424-8580, ext. 2250; *crisiscorps@peacecorps.gov/www.peacecorps. gov/crisiscorps/index.html*

A new program for returned Peace Corps Volunteers to provide short-term assistance to countries that have experienced disasters.

1096. **Department of Peace* (proposal) (2000) (org).

Office of Rep. Dennis J. Kucinich, Congressional Office Bldng., DC 20510; (202) 225-5871; *www.house.gov/kucinich/action/peace.htm*

Rep. Kucinich announced in Jan. 2000 his plan to draft a bill in Congress to create a Department of Peace.

1097. *Disarmament Clearinghouse* (1994) (org).

1101 14th St. NW #700, DC 20005; (800) 4-denuke; (202) 898-0150 x232; *disarmament@igc.org*; *www.disarmament.org*; *www.house.gov/kucinich*

A project of: Friends Committee on National Legislation, Peace Action, Physicians for Social Responsibility, 20/20 Vision, and Women's Action for New Directions. Promotes passage of the Comprehensive Test Ban Treaty (CTBT) to ban all nuclear explosions and which President Clinton signed but the Senate rejected in the fall of 1999. The Treaty would curb the spread of nuclear weapons, help guard against the renewal of the nuclear arms race, and establish a global monitoring system. DC urges all to contact their Senators (Capitol switchboard: (202) 224-3121) to continue the struggle. DC also works on missile defense, de-alerting, nuclear weapons proliferation and abolition, and more. In April 2000 DC organized "house parties" nationally for viewing George Clooney's live remake of the 1964 nuclear war film *Fail Safe*. Joan Wade, Coordinator.

1098. *Dorothy Day Catholic Worker* (1981) (org).

503 Rock Creek Church Rd. NW, DC 20010; (202) 882-9649.

Follows the principles of Catholic Worker co-founder pacifist Dorothy Day. Among its many peace activities, DDCW holds regular vigils against militarism and war at the Pentagon and the White House and for Mordechai Vanunu at the Israeli Embassy. Three times a year it joins Jonah House (in Baltimore) for a "Faith and Resistance" Retreat. Pub. newspaper, *The Little Way*; the Summer 1999 number contains seven articles, half of them wholly or partly about resistance to wars and violence, and two pages of "Resistance Update."

1099. *Educational Fund to End Handgun Violence* (1978) (org).

1000 16th St., NW, Suite 603, DC 20036; (202) 530-5888; *edfund@aol.com*; *www.gunfree.org*

Provides public education on handgun violence in the U.S., particularly as it affects children. The sister organization of Coalition to Stop Gun Violence.

1100. *Episcopal Peace Fellowship* (1939) (org).

PO Box 28156, DC, 20038; (202) 783-3380; *epf@peacenet.org*; *www.nonviolence.org/epf/*

Encourages all Episcopalians to strive for justice and peace among all people and to bear nonviolent witness to Christ's call to peace, justice, reconciliation, and nonviolence, including "a commitment to renounce, so far as possible, participation in war and other forms of violence." Supports Episcopalian conscientious objectors, war tax resistance, peace conferences, local chapters. Pub. *EPF Newsletter* and many pamphlets, including "Working for Peace in the Parish" and "The Cross Before the Flag; Episcopal Statements on War and Peace." Affil. with the Fellowship of Reconciliation. Has some 10 local chapters, many of which are included in this Directory. Mary Miller, Exec. Secretary; John Sophos, Newsletter Ed.; Rev. David Selzer, Chair of National Exec. Council.

Pierce, Nathaniel, and Paul Ward. *The Voice of Conscience: A Loud and Unusual Noise: the Episcopal Peace Fellowship 1939–1989*. Episcopal Peace Fellowship, 1989.

1101. *Evolving Peace Site* (mem proposed).

The creator of the Developing Peace Site in Sonoma County planned to create a similar memorial on the Mall at the Jefferson Stone in the year 2000.

1102. *Freeman Fellowship* (2000) (org).

Peace Action Education Fund, Attn: Freeman Fellowship, 1819 H. St., NW, Suite 425, DC 20006-3603; (202) 862-9740, ext. 3004.

The Ruth S. and Harrop A. Freeman Fellowship offers a monthly stipend of $1,000 for one year to people in college or recent graduates "interested in promoting campus activism for peace, disarmament, and economic justice." The Freeman Fellow coordinates the Student Peace Action Network (SPAN).

1103. *Friends Committee on National Legislation* (1943) (org).

245 Second St., NE, 20002-5795; (202) 547-6000; *fcnl@fcnl.org*; *www.fcnl.org*

FCNL has lobbied for peace, justice, and earth care for sixty years. Quaker political action arm includes alternatives to violence and war, seeking peace through peaceful means. The FCNL lobbies for freezing and reducing military spending, strengthening the United Nations, budgets that address the root causes of war, halting the expansion of NATO and other military alliances, civil organizations which strengthen democracies, and a Code of Conduct on arms transfers, and other alternatives to militarism. For example, it sent a letter to Pres. Clinton prior to the bombing of Yugoslavia on March 24 presenting peace-building steps the U.S. could follow instead of violence. Pub. *FCNL Washington Newsletter* (Nov. 1999 no. includes articles on the Senate rejection of CTBT, military spending,, budget priorities, GOP tax cut policy). Joe Volk, Exec. Secretary.

1104. **Friends of the Earth* (1969) (org).

1025 Vermont Ave., NW, 3rd Fl, DC 20005; (202) 783-7400, ext. 113; *foe@foe.org; lspeckhardt@foe.org; www.foe.org/about.html*

Dedicated to preserving the health and diversity of the planet for future generations, with affiliates in 63 countries. Focuses on three programs: economics for the earth, international development for people, and empowering citizens for the struggle. Founded by David Brower.

1105. **Fulbright Association* (1977) (org).

1130 17th St., NW, Suite 310, DC 20036; (202) 331-1590; *fulbright@fulbright.org; www.fulbright.org*

Membership of alumni and friends of the Fulbright International Exchange Program. Many chapters worldwide. Gives the J. William Fulbright Prize for International Understanding. Pub. *Fulbright Association Newsletter*.

1106. **Fulbright Exchange Scholarships* (1946) (org).

See: Institute of International Education below.

Originated by the Fulbright Act of 1946, named for its sponsor, Senator J. William Fulbright of Arkansas, the program seeks to promote better understanding between the peoples of the U.S. and other countries through annual awards for U.S. citizens to study or work in other lands and enables persons of other countries to study or work in the U.S.

1107. *Gandhi Statue*, gift of government of India (in preparation).

1108. **Global Green USA* (1994) (org).

1025 Vermont Ave., NW, Suite 300, DC 20005-6303; (202) 879-3181; *pwalker@globalgreen.org; www.globalgreen.org*

The U.S. affiliate of Green Cross International founded by Mikhail Gorbachev (1992). Committed to a sustainable world, focusing on weapons demilitarization in both Russia and the U.S.

1109. **Global Peace Services USA* (1997) (org).

PO Box 27922, DC 20038-7922; (202) 216-9886; *www.globalpeaceservices.org*

GPS, in development, is "a movement to create a professional peace service by promoting education and skills-training for men and women based on a philosophy of active nonviolence." In 1999 it was forming several Working Groups; for example to develop educational peace service curricula at all academic levels. Pub. newsletter *Global Peace Services USA*. John Eriksson, Pres. (*johnrerik@cs.com*).

1110. **Greenpeace* (1971) (org).

1436 U St., NW, 20009; 1-800-326-0959; *www.greenpeaceusa.org*

A leading opponent of the war by vested interests against the Earth. Because verbal protests are inadequate, GP actively but nonviolently aids endangered species and monitors conditions of the environment—greenhouse affect, radioactive and toxic wastes, CTBT, media campaigns. Projects include the Global Ancient Forests Campaign. Pub. *Greenpeace Magazine* (Fall 1999 issue includes articles on renewable energy, resistance to toxic pollution in Louisiana, the destruction of the Great Bear Rainforest, and book and web site reviews). Exec. Dir. Kristen Engberg.

1111. *Guns to Plowshares* (1997) (mem).

Across from the Judiciary Square Metro stop.

Given to the District of Columbia "as a symbol of the hope that this city will share with the

Guns to Plowshares Sculpture by Esther and Michael Augsburger, Washington, D.C. Photograph courtesy Esther and Michael Augsburger.

world a quest for peace," the sculpture is a 20-foot high steel plowshare with 3,000 handguns welded onto it (mostly donated by the D.C. police). The sculpture was designed and constructed by artists Esther Augsburger and her son Michael Augsburger, members of the Mennonite faith tradition. The project was a partnership between the Metropolitan Police Dept. and InterChurch, which supports artists throughout the world for the cause of peace and justice. The name of the sculpture is a reference to Isaiah 2:4: "They shall beat their swords into plowshares."

1112. *Handgun Control* (1974) (org).

1225 Eye St., NW, Rm 1100, DC 20005-3991; *www.handguncontrol.org*

1999 marked the 25th year HC has struggled for gun control laws against the National Rifle Association, its first big success being the Brady Bill (1993). Its programs today include licensing and registration of guns, child access prevention laws, gun industry responsibility laws. Sarah Brady, Chair.

1113. *Herbert Scoville Jr. Peace Fellowship* (1987) (org).

110 Maryland Ave., NE, Suite 409, DC 20002; (202) 543-4100; *www.clw.org/scoville/*

Enables college graduates to spend six months in Washington as full-time assistants at the participating organization of their choice. While a member of the Arms Control and Disarmament Agency, Scoville advocated the limited Test Ban Treaty, the Non-Proliferation Treaty, and the Strategic Arms Limitation Talks. Later he spearheaded opposition to the MX missile, MIRVed warheads, and the Star Wars program. He was the author of *Towards a Strategic Arms Limitation Agreement, Missile Madness,* and *MX: Prescription for Disaster.*

1114. *Canceled*

1115. *Interfaith Alliance* (1994) (org).

1012 14th St., NW, Suite 700, 20005; (202) 639-6370; *tia@tialliance.org; www.tialliance.org*

Mainstream, faith-based group opposing the extreme religious right, claiming over 100,000 members from over fifty faith traditions.

1116. *International Peace and Conflict Resolution Division* (1995) (col).

School of International Service, American Univ., DC 20016; (202) 885-1632; *peace@american.edu; www.american.edu/academic.depts/sis/peace*

Undergraduate minor or interdisciplinary BA that includes IPCR courses. Also the Washington Semester and World Capitals program offers internships and travel. Graduate MA (1995), which can also become a dual degree in MA in Theology, MA in Teaching, MA/JD; internships available. Abdul Aziz Said, Dir.

1117. *Jeannette Rankin Statue* (1985) (mem).

Statuary Hall, U.S. Capitol.

A duplicate of the statue in Helena, Montana (see #576-7).

1118. *Jennings Randolph Program for International Peace* (1987) (org).

United States Institute of Peace, Jennings Randolph Program, 1200 17th St. NW, Suite 200, DC 20036-3011; (202) 457-1700; *www.usip.org/fellows.html*

Supports research by scholars, policymakers, journalists, and other professionals on "the nature of interstate or civil conflict and peaceful ways to manage and resolve it." Named for the former U.S. Senator from West Virginia.

1119. *Jubilee 2000/USA* (1998) (org).

222 E. Capitol St., NE, DC 20003-1036; (202) 783-3566; *coord@j2000usa.org; www.j2000usa.org*

Part of a worldwide movement to cancel the debt of impoverished countries.
Brecher, Jeremy. *Global Village or Global Pillage.*
Smiley, Robert. *Life in All Its Fullness.*

1120. *Kate Sherman Peace and Environmental Fellowship* (1999) (org).

20/20 Vision, 1828 Jefferson Place, NW, DC 20036.

A one year fellowship for college graduates providing a stipend of $1,000 a month to learn the workings of a non-profit organization devoted to peace and the environment. In honor of the founder of 20/20 Vision (see).

1121. *Martin Luther King, Jr., Memorial* (to be built).

Four-acre site not far from the Lincoln memorial, where King delivered his "I have a dream" speech in 1963, halfway between the Lincoln and the Jefferson memorials. The new memorial to Franklin Roosevelt is just to the south. The memorial will cost "tens of millions of dollars," according to the project chairman, John Carter.

1122. *Lawyers Alliance for World Security (LAWS)* (1980) (org).

1901 Pennsylvania Ave., NW, Suite 201, DC 20006; (202) 745-2450; *disarmament@lawscns.org; www.lawscns.org*

Works to educate the public about the dangers of nuclear weapons and other weapons of mass destruction by arms control measures and the rule of law. Chapters operate in three other cities in the U.S. (Boston, Phila., Chicago). The Committee for National Security (CNS), a subsidiary of LAWS, focuses primarily on building a public constituency in support of arms control and non-proliferation. In the fall of 1999 LAWS was actively urging NATO to support a no-first-use policy for nuclear weapons. Pub. *Lawyers' Alliance for World Security Newsletter* quarterly; has available speeches and articles by staff. Thomas Graham, Jr., Pres; Alex Slesar, Dir. of Administration.

1123. *Methodists United for Peace with Justice* (1981) (org).

1500 16th St. NW, DC 20036; (301) 896-0013; *mupj@igc.org*

Composed of lay and clerical members, not affiliated with any Methodist denomination. Pub. *Peace Leaf* quarterly. Howard Hallman, Chair.

1124. *Mexico Solidarity Network* (1998) (org).

1247 E St., SE, DC 20003; (202) 544-9355; *www.mexicosolidarity.org*

Strives to form grassroots alliances between Mexico and the U.S. and to expose the ruthlessness of elites on both sides and of capital-centered globalization. National Coordinator: Tom Hansen.

1125. *National Association for Community Mediation (NAFCM)* (1993) (org).

1527 New Hampshire Ave., NW, DC 20036.

A membership organization of community mediation programs which provides technical assistance to its membership, policy development, and a full-service clearinghouse.

1126. *National Campaign for a Peace Tax Fund* (1972) (org).

2121 Decatur Place, NW, DC 20008-1923; 1(888) PEACETAX; *peacetaxfund@igc.org*; *www.nonviolence.org/peacetax/*

Advocates for legislation enabling conscientious objectors to war to have the military portion of their federal income taxes directed to a special fund for projects that enhance peace. The Peace Tax Fund Bill, first introduced in Congress in 1972, has the endorsement of over 150 organizations, and in the last Congress two dozen Representatives cosponsored the Bill, led by Rep. John Lewis and Rep. Jim Leach, and Sen. Tom Harkin. Its Peace Tax Foundation informs Congress and the public about alternative tax payment programs that are based on moral, religious, and ethical opposition to participation in war. The International Conference on War Tax Resistance and Peace Tax Campaigns has met in Europe or Asia in the past, but in 2000 it met in Washington, DC. Pub. a newsletter. Founded by Dr. David Bassett, among others. Exec. Dir.: Marian Franz. Member of Conscience and Peace Tax International.

1127. *National Coalition to Abolish the Death Penalty* (1976) (org).

1436 U St., NW, Suite 104, DC 20009; (202) 387-3890; *ncadp1@nicom.com*; *www.ncadp.org/ncadp*

Formerly the National Coalition Against the Death Penalty. Pub.: *The Abolitionist's Directory, Lifelines/Execution Alert* monthly newspaper (executions also on web site). Steven Hawkins, Exec. Dir.

1128. *National Interreligious Service Board for Conscientious Objectors* (1940) (org).

1830 Connecticut Ave. NW, 20009-5732; (202) 483-2220; *nisbco@igc.apc.org*; *www.nonviolence.org/nisbco/*

Originally the National Service Board for Religious Objectors, NISBCO is committed to helping all who conscientiously question participation in war, by counseling and legal support, public education, and advocating legislation. Sponsored by an association of religious bodies who join to protect the rights of conscientious objectors. Publications include: "Basic Draft Information" and "Advice to Conscientious Objectors Facing Draft Registration," and a quarterly newsletter, *The Reporter for Conscience's Sake.*

1129. *National Peace Corps Association* (1979) (org).

1900 L St., NW, Suite 205, DC 20036; (202)293-7728; *npca@rpcv.org*

Supports the Peace Corps through public education (e.g., information fairs, speakers' bureau) and informing returned volunteers about employment opportunities. Maintains a network of affiliates and chapters. Gives the Ruppe Award and the Sargent Shriver Award. Pub. *WorldView*, a quarterly; *The Advocate* newsletter; and an annual calendar. Dane Smith, Pres.

1130. *National Peace Foundation* (1982) (org).

1835 K St. NW, Suite 610, DC 20006; 1-800-237-3223; *www.nationalpeace.org*

Concerned with the development and implementation of conflict resolution education and training, and with peacebuilding and democracy-building internationally. Publishes the *Peace Reporter*, and gives Peacemakers/Peacebuilders awards (in 1997: Archbishop Tutu and Attorney General Reno; James Mang, Barbara Simmons, Barbara Wiedner).

1131. *National Peace Garden* (mem proposed).

One Grumman Hill Road, Wilton, CT 06897; (877) 467-3223; *pgarden@celebrate.org*; *www.celebratepeace.org*

To be set on ten acres at the southern tip of the peninsula where the Potomac, Washington Channel, and Anacostia River converge, one of the last major sites in the monumental core of Washington, D.C.

The only monument in the U.S. capital to celebrate peacemakers and peace initiatives will be paid for by private funds, to cost an estimated $13.2 million and become a part of the National Park Service. Robert Royston designed the Monument. Terry Ferrari, Dir.

Hesburgh, Theodore. "What Washington Needs Now." *Christian Science Monitor* (November 20, 1996).

1132. **Network of East-West Women* (1990) (org).

1601 Connecticut Ave., NW, #603, DC 20009; (202) 265-3585; *eastwest@neww.org; www.neww.org*

Links women across national boundaries to share resources, knowledge, and skills, to promote tolerance, democracy, non-violence, health, and respect. NEWW especially supports the formation of independent women's movements in order for women to intervene effectively on policy regarding women's lives. Current projects include NEWW On-Line linking women's NGOs, the Legal Fellowship Program providing recently graduated women lawyers with four month placements with human rights organizations, and the Book and Journal Project of gifts of books and magazines to women's centers in Central and Eastern Europe and the newly independent states. To contribute or request books or journals contact Ann Snitow (*newwny@ igc.apc.org*).

1133. **New Voices* (1999) (org).

1825 Connecticut Ave. NW, DC 20009; (202)884-8051; *newvoice@aed.org*

A national fellowship program to help non-profit organizations bring innovative new talent to human rights groups and organizations of international cooperation.

1134. **Nicaragua Network Education Fund* (1979) (org).

1247 E. St. SE, DC 20003; (202) 544-9355.

Organizations united in opposition to U.S. intervention in the Central American/Caribbean region; facilitates establishment of sister-city relationships between U.S. and Nicaraguan cities; raises funds for Nicaraguan projects.

1135. **Nonviolence International* (1988) (org).

4545 42nd St., NW, DC 20016; (202) 244-0951; *nonviolence@igc.apc.org; www.igc.org/nonviolence/*

Founded by Dr. Mubarak Awad; grew out of the Palestinian Center for the Study of Nonviolence established in Jerusalem before Awad's expulsion. Assists nonviolent change through training and education. Pub. *Frontline* newsletter and booklets on organizing.

1136. **Nuclear Information and Resource Service (NIRS)* (1978) (org).

1424 16th St. NW, No. 404, DC 20036; (202) 328-0002; *nirsnet@nirs.org; www.nirs.org*

Information and networking center helping communities defend their rights to environmental justice—prevention of nuclear contamination, radioactive waste, senseless nuclear transportation, radiation—and for sustainable energy. Campaigns include resistance to deregulation and to recycling of atomic waste into the marketplace, and watchdogging nuclear sites. Michael Mariotte, Dir.; contact Diane d'Arrigo.

1137. **Parents, Families, and Friends of Lesbians and Gays (PFLAG)* (org).

1101 14th St. NW, Suite 1030, DC 20005; (202) 638-4200, ext. 212; *eferraro@pflag.org*

Strives to reduce bigotry and violence against gays and lesbians. Rev. Paul Beeman, Pres.; Kirsten Kingdon, Exec. Dir.

1138. **Partners for Peace* (1989) (org).

1250 4th St. SW, Suite WG-1, DC 20024-2903; (202)863-2951; *bird@pfp.org; www.partnersforpeace.org*

Seeks peace and justice between Israel and Palestine through public education and networking. Projects: Jerusalem Women Speak tours, media training for local activities, seminars for leaders in Washington area, maintaining Directory of Middle East organizations, human rights advocacy. Jerri Bird, Pres.

1139. *Pax Christi Metro DC* (1991) (org).

3047 4th St., NE, DC 20017;
(202) 635-0441; *eirik@igc.apc.org*

Eirik Harteis, Coordinator and Regional Rep.

1140. *Peace Action* (1957) (org).

1819 H St. NW, Suite 420, 20006-3603;
(202) 862-9740; *pamembers@igc.apc.org*;
www.peace-action.org

Formerly SANE/FREEZE, this large membership organization with affiliates and chapters in several states works to reduce arms sales, to bring about a comprehensive nuclear test ban treaty, to abolish nuclear weapons and U.S. interventions abroad, to challenge waste and fraud in the military budget, and to shift U.S. priorities from military to human needs. PA worked for the 1963 treaty to ban above ground nuclear testing, for the 1996 signing of the Comprehensive Test Ban Treaty, for ending the war in Vietnam, and blocking weapons sales abroad, among other activities. In the summer of 1999 it organized the rally in Albuquerque to commemorate the atomic bombings of Hiroshima and Nagasaki, to call for the abolition of nuclear weapons, and to protest at Los Alamos. Pub. *Grassroots Organizer* newsletter and *Action Report* quarterly. The June 1999 number of *AR* included articles on the upcoming demonstration in New Mexico, military spending, nuclear weapons abolition, weapons trafficking, and Yugoslavia. Gordon Clark, Exec. Dir.

1141. *Peace Action Education Fund Freeman Fellowship* (see: Freeman Fellowship (1999) (org).

1819 H. St., NW, Suite 425,
DC 20006-3603.

The Freeman Fellow coordinates the Student Peace Action Network (SPAN). $1000 monthly stipend plus health insurance.

1142. *Peace Action International* (1987) (org).

866 UN Plaza, room 4053, NYC
10017-1822; (212) 750-5795;
paintl@igc.apc.org; www.webcom.com/peaceact; www.peace-action.org

An organization of Peace Action. Serves as a liaison to peace organizations abroad and monitors and participates in U.N. forums concerning disarmament and economic justice. Coordinates the Peace Caucus of non-governmental organizations, and supports Abolition 2000, the Hague Appeal for Peace, and the Women's Peace Petition. A Project of Peace Action Education Fund. Contact Tracy Moavero.

1143. *Peace and Justice Studies* (1983) (col).

School of Religious Studies,
Catholic Univ. of America,
620 Michigan Ave. NE, DC 20064;
(202) 319-5700; *barbieri@cua.edu;*
http://religiousstudies.cua.edu

A minor requires six courses, core and elective, internships encouraged. Moral, theological, and philosophical focus. William Barbieri, Prog. Dir.

1144. *Peace and World Order Studies* (1982) (org).

School of Religious Studies, Catholic University of America, DC 20064;
(202) 319-5700; *barbieri@cua.edu*

Offers an interdisciplinary minor of six courses plus a thesis and internship opportunities, intended to provide students with training for peace and justice and conflict resolution within the university's Catholic identity and social mission. William Barbieri, Dir.

1145. *Peace Corps of the United States* (1961) (org).

1990 K St., NW, DC 20526;
(202) 606-3970; *www.peacecorps.gov*

Founded by President Kennedy, the PC organizes two-year volunteers for humanitarian work in remote places around the world for little money and long hours. By 1999, 152,000 U.S. citizens had volunteered. 6,700 were abroad in 1999, and the number is increasing. Also sponsors Peace Corps Partnership Programs, financial support to selected programs; World Wise Schools, linking US classrooms and overseas volunteers; and Fellows/USA, returning former volunteers to high-need US communities. Pub. *Peace Corps Times* bimonthly. Mark Gearan, Dir.

1146. *Peace Corps Partnership Program* (1964) (org).

1990 K. St. NW, DC 20526;
800-424-8580, ext. 2170; *www.peacecorps.gov/contribute/partnership.html*

Links U.S. contributors and requests for project assistance abroad, facilitating participation in the development process and fostering cross-cultural exchange. In 1997 over 400 U.S. Partner groups assisted small-scale projects throughout the world. See the web site for projects in need of assistance.

1147. *Peace Education Commission (PEC)* (org).

c/o Peace Studies Certificate Program, Enderis Hall, PO Box 413, Univ. of Wisconsin, Milwaukee 53201.

A commission of the International Peace Research Assoc. (IPRA), PEC facilitates international exchanges about peace education and research. Twice a year pub. newsletter, *Peacebuilding*, available in cyberspace (*www.uwm.edu/ Dept/Peace/pecnews.pdf*) and mailed to members, contributions sought. Contact Ian Harris.

1148. *Peace Links* (1985) (org).

666 11th St., NW, suite 202; DC 20001; (202) 783-7030; *peacelinks@peacelinksusa.org; www.PeaceLinksUSA.org*

An international network of women that brings people together to look for alternatives to violence locally and globally. Activities: initiates citizen diplomacy around the world; sends and hosts delegations from other nations—Russia, Japan, Cuba; a Pen Pals for Peace program between U.S. and Soviet/Russian citizens; participated in The Hague Appeal for Peace conference; works to abolish nuclear weapons; a middle school program on violence, "Youth Links." Pub. *Connection* newsletter, which in its Spring 1999 number included notes on the US/Cuba women's exchange, the Youth Links project, the Pen Pals program, and The Hague Appeal for peace. Has chapters. Betty Bumpers, Founder and Pres. Deedie Runkel, Dir.

1149. *Peace Psychology Division of American Psychology Association* (1990) (org).

Division 48: Peace Psychology, Administrative Office, 750 First St. NE, DC 20002-4242; (202) 336-5500, (516) 447-6700; *peacewk@laker.net; http://moon.pepperdine.edu/~mstimac/ Peace-Psychology. html*

PPD would develop "sustainable societies through the prevention of destructive conflict and violence, the amelioration of its consequences, the empowerment of individuals, and the building of cultures of peace and global community." Activities: working groups on children, families, and war; ethnicity and peace; feminism and peace, militarism, disarmament, and conversion; and more. Pub. *Peace and Conflict: Journal of Peace Psychology* quarterly, ed. by Milton Schwebel, Rugers U.; and *Peace Psychology Newsletter* (3 issues a year), ed. by Eileen Borris and Christine Montiel. Ervin Staub, President (Dept. of Psychology, U of Mass., Amherst, MA 01003). Contact Paul Donnelly, APA Division Services (*pdonnelly@apa.org*).

1150. *Peace Sculpture* (2000) (mem).

Capital Children's Museum

A child-sized house, the bottom layers filled with violent toys (plastic guns, video games, etc.), higher layers rising into recycled peaceful toys. Sponsored and organized by the Lion & Lamb Project (Bethesda, MD), toys collected in 32 different states around the U.S. Designed by six students from the Massachusetts College of Art. A traveling sculpture; see website for present location: *www.lionlamb.org/sculpture.html*

1151. *Peace Studies* (1992) (col).

Dept. of Religion, Building O, George Washington Univ., DC 20052; *yeide@gwu.edu; www.gwu.edu/~bulletin/ugrad/pstd.html*

A minor of studies of peace as a human value, in national/international systems, and in interpersonal relations. Contact Harry Yeide, Jr.

1152. *Peacebuilders Partnership* (1999) (org).

1819 H St. NW, Suite 1200, DC 20006.

PP is the merger of the Institute for Multi-Track Diplomacy and the National Peace Foundation. IMID's mission is to promote a systems approach to peacebuilding for the transformation of deep-rooted social conflict (202) 466-4605; *www.imtd.org*). NPF's mission is to promote the implementation of conflict resolution education in the U.S. and peacebuilding and democracy-building internationally (202) 223-1770; *www.nationalpeace.org*). The magazine *Peacebuilder* is the first joint project of this new partnership.

1153. **PeacePAC* (1982) (org).

110 Maryland Ave., NE, 20002;
(202) 543-4100; *skerr@clw.org;*
www.clw.org/pub/clw/welcome.html

A political action committee that supports candidates for the U.S. House of Representatives who are committed to nuclear arms control, nuclear disarmament, the prevention of nuclear war, and significant reduction in military spending. An affiliate of the Council for a Livable World (1962). Provides the Arms Control Voting Index, a record of votes by representatives on nuclear arms issues, and a Nuclear Arms Control Hotline (202-543-0006).

1154. **Physicians Committee for Responsible Medicine* (1985) (org).

5100 Wisconsin Ave., NW, Suite 404, 20016; (202) 686-2210; *pcrm@pcrm.org;*
www.pcrm.org

Promotes preventive medicine through innovative programs and broader access to medical services. Campaigns against cruel treatment of animals in experiments and education. Pub. *Good Medicine* quarterly. Neal Barnard, M.D., Pres.

1155. **Physicians for Social Responsibility* (1961) (org).

1101 14th St., 7th Fl., Suite 700, DC 20005; (202) 898-0150;
psrnatl@psr.org; www.psr.org.

Formed by a group of physicians, dentists, and medical students troubled by the dangers of nuclear weapons testing in the atmosphere and by lack of data on the medical and environmental consequences of nuclear war. A leader in educating officials and the public about the devastating capabilities of thermonuclear weapons, and supports the Comprehensive Test Ban Treaty (CTBT). In 1999 PSR inaugurated its campaign against gun violence, considering it a public health epidemic. Its 2000 national conference in Arlington, VA included Ted Turner, Deb Callahan, Sen. Douglas Roche, Peter Wilk, Jonathan Schell, and many others. Pub. *PSR Reports* quarterly: the Winter 2000 issue included articles on the missile defense system failures, climate change campaign in New Hampshire, handgun licensing and registration, drinking water safety. Affiliated with International Physicians for the Prevention of Nuclear War, which won the Nobel Peace Prize for 1985. Amy C. Sisley, M.D., Dir.; Robert Musil, CEO.

1156. **Program on Justice and Peace* (1993, 1995) (col).

English Dept., Box 571131, Georgetown Univ., DC 20057; (202) 687-7647;
schwarh1@gusun.georgetown.edu;
www.georgetown.edu/departments/pjp/

Undergraduate minor in College of Arts and Sciences and Certificate, School of Foreign Service- 18 hours each, reflecting the Jesuit mission of solving world problems by understanding their structural origins. Active in the annual DC Capital Area Association of Peace Studies Programs (CAAPS) student conference. Contact Henry Schwarz.

1157. **Proposition One Committee* (1981) (org).

Lafayette Park (Peace Park), 1601 Penn. Ave., in front of the White House;
PO Box 27217, 20038; (202) 462-0757;
prop1@prop1.org; http://prop1.org

A 24-hour-a-day anti-nuclear vigil and grassroots movement for conversion of the arms industries to human and environmental needs. An expression of their advocacy is DC Initiative 37 in 1993, which inspired Rep. Eleanor Holmes Norton to introduce House Bill, "The Nuclear Disarmament and Economic Conversion Act" in 1994, 1995-6, and 1997-8 sessions. Perhaps the longest continuous vigil in history.

1158. **Psychologists for Social Responsibility (PsySR)* (1982) (org).

2604 Connecticut Ave. NW, DC, 20008;
(202) 745-7084; *psysrusa@compuserve.com;*
www.rmc.edu/psyer

Some 3000 psychologists around the world dedicated to using psychological knowledge to build a peaceful world. Its first mission was to reduce the threat of nuclear war, toward which end it pub. *Dismantling the Mask of Enmity: An Educational Resource Manual on the Psychology of Enemy Images.* Now in addition it focuses on reducing tensions that can lead to war by the use of nonviolent conflict management, on reducing nuclear weapons, military spending, and conventional arms sales, and for support of the UN. Pub. *War Trauma and Recovery* (1993) in response to the war in the former Yugoslavia. In 1998 PsySR adopted the theme, "Building Cultures of Peace" for the next several years, in coordination with the UN Declaration of the year

The third room of the Franklin Delano Roosevelt Memorial, West Potomac Park, Washington, D.C. Photograph by Chuck Wasson.

2000 as the Year for a Culture of Peace. To further this work, PSR has established the Culture of Peace News Network (CPNN) (*psysripn@ aol.com*, David Adams). PsySR and the Society for the Study of Peace, Conflict, and Violence: Peace Psychology Division of the American Psychological Association, have established the International Peace Practitioners' Network to stimulate cooperation for peace among psychologists, a project supported by a grant from the Joe F. Wall Service Award from Grinnell College. George Albee, Pres. (1999-2000); Daniel Christie (2000-20001). National Coordinator: Anne Anderson.

1159. *Results* (1980) (org).

440 First Street NW, Suite 450, 20001; (202) 783-7100; *results@action.org; http://results.action.org*

Grassroots political action organization dedicated to alleviating hunger and poverty. Achievements include: individual savings accounts for the poor; Congressional bill requiring half of 1999 microcredit foreign aid funds be devoted to very poor people by small loans. Pub. newsletter *Entry Point*. Exec. Dir.: Lynn McMullen.

1160. *Roosevelt Memorial* (1997) (mem).

West Potomac Park, between the Tidal Basin and the Potomac River and between the Jefferson and Lincoln memorials.

The 71/2 acres are composed of four outdoor galleries or "rooms" for each of FDR's terms in office, with walls of red South Dakota granite, paintings, quotations carved into the granite, water cascades, and quiet pools throughout. In one room is inscribed: "I have seen war. I hate war." During its first year, 3 million people visited the memorial. The memorial was designed by Lawrence Halprin; stone carving by John Benson; many prominent U.S. artists are represented. It is a part of the National Park Service.

1161. *(Eleanor) Roosevelt Statue* (1997) (mem).

Fourth room of the Franklin Delano Roosevelt Memorial, in West Potomac Park, between the Tidal Basin and the Potomac River.

The statue of Eleanor Roosevelt (1884–1962) in the fourth "room" or outdoor gallery, commemorates her role as First Lady and her work

Eleanor Roosevelt, Franklin Delano Roosevelt Memorial, West Potomac Park, Washington, D.C. Photograph courtesy Bettie Lu Lancaster.

as our first United Nations delegate and champion for human rights. Next to her statue are inscribed these words: "The structure of world peace cannot be the work of one man, or one party, or one nation.... It must be a peace which rests on the cooperative effort of the whole world."

Berger, Jason. *A New Deal for the World: Eleanor Roosevelt and American Foreign Policy.* New York: Social Science Monographs/Columbia UP, 1981.

Hareven, Tamara. *Eleanor Roosevelt: An American Conscience.* Chicago: Quadrangle, 1968.

Kearney, James. *Anna Eleanor Roosevelt: The Evolution of a Reformer.* Boston: Houghton Mifflin, 1968.

Roosevelt, Eleanor. *This I Remember.* New York: Harper, 1949.

1162. *Rush-Bagot Memorial Tablet* (1935) (mem).

On the grounds of the Columbia Hospital, D.C.

Here the agreement was signed in 1817 which brought about the removal of armed vessels from the Great Lakes. Erected by Kiwanis International.

1163. **Seeds of Peace International Summer Camp* (1993) (org).

1321 Wisconsin Ave., NW, DC 20007; (202) 337-5530.

Brings together teenagers from regions of conflict and war to its month-long summer camp in Maine. Seeds of Peace was awarded the UNESCO Peace Prize. Founded by John Wallach. Contact Bobbie Gottschalk (or Marieke van Woerkom, 370 Lexington Ave., Suite 1409, NYC 10017).

1164. **Sister Cities International* (1956/1967) (org).

1300 Pennsylvania Ave., NW, Suite 250, DC 20004-3002; (202) 312-1200; *info@sister-cities.org; www.sister-cities.org*

Administers the Eisenhower International Scholarship Fund which provides scholarships for international students to attend U.S. postsecondary educational institutions. Pubs.: *1998 Sister Cities International Directory, Sister City News* quarterly, and *Inside SCI* bimonthly. The annual conference was held in Little Rock, AR, July 1999, and in Denver in 2000.

1165. **SOA Watch* (1990) (org).

PO Box 4566, 20017; 1719 Irving St., NW, DC 20010; (202) 234-3440; *soawatch@knight-hub.com; www.derechos.org/soaw; www.soaw.org*

Dedicated to the elimination of the School of the Americas at Fort Benning, GA, where Latin America's repressive military elites have been trained to murder dissidents. Typical actions: Nov. 22, 1998, 2,319 demonstrators led by actor Martin Sheen entered Ft. Benning. In 1999 Sheen again led demonstrators into the base, this time double the numbers of the previous year. Father Roy Bourgeois was one of the founders and has sustained the protest at the School. May 1–4, 1999, "Close the School of the Americas" demonstrations at the White House, Capitol, and Pentagon. SOA also has an office in Columbus, GA.

Altenberg, Patricia. "Crossing the Line." *The Nonviolent Activist* (Jan.-Feb. 1999) 12–13.

Nelson-Palmeyer, Jack. *School of the Assassins.* 1997.

1166. **Society of Professionals in Dispute Resolution Council* (1972) (org).

815 15th St., NW, Suite 530, DC 20005-2201; (202) 783-7277; *spidr@spidr.org; www.spidr.org*

Composed of arbitrators, mediators, hearing examiners, and fact finders, who promote negotiation, collective bargaining, the role of neutrals in dispute resolution, and training in mediation. Pub. *Annual Conference Proceedings.*

1167. **Student Peace Action Network (SPAN)* (1995) (org).

1819 H St., NW, Suite 425, DC 20006; (202) 862-9740, ext. 3051; *span@peace-action.org; www.peace-action.org/span.html*

An organization within Peace Action. Strives to coordinate and focus peace and justice concerns among youth, especially regarding the connections between corporate power and the decay of democracy and peace. SPAN is supported by Peace Action Education Fund (*www.peace-action.org/paef.html).*

1168. **20/20 Vision* (1986) (org).

1828 Jefferson Pl., NW, DC 20036; (202) 833-2020; *ctbt@2020vision.org; natalie@2020vision.org; www.2020vision.org/ctbt.html*

Endorses democratic political campaigns not bought by big money, reduction of military spending, the Comprehensive Test Ban Treaty, and protection of the environment (safe water), ending sale of weapons to dictators, by sending a monthly postcard recommending a strategic 20 minute action, writing a letter that might help determine a vote, or making a phone call to affect an outcome. Every six months 20/20 sends a report on the results of the efforts. Founded by Lois Barber and Jeremy Sherman in Amherst, MA, following a peace march. Contact Marie Rietmann.

1169. **United States Institute of Peace (USIP)* (1984) (org).

1200 17th St., NW, Suite 200, 20036-3011; (202) 457-1700, 429-3828; *wopperer@usip.org; usip_requests@usip.org; www.usip.org*

Established by Congress to promote peaceful resolution of international conflict. Provides grants to nonprofit organizations, public institutions, and individuals; fellowships to study violent international conflicts and ways of resolving them under the Jennings Randolph Program for International Peace; the Jeannette Rankin Library Program on peace and conflict management; various public outreach programs including the annual National Peace Essay Contest for high school students. Offers scholarships to high school students who have successfully competed in USIP's annual Essay Contest. Graduate students in the Washington area are eligible for Research Assistantships. Peace Scholar Ph.D. Dissertation Fellowships are also available, and approximately 15 Senior Fellowships per year. Also designs and performs research. And many more programs. Pubs. include the bimonthly *PeaceWatch; Special Reports*, which reports on USIP work; *PeaceWorks*, which is more comprehensive; and many books (800) 868-8064; (703) 661-1166. Spring 1999 books: *Chinese Negotiating Behavior, Ukraine and Russia, Hydropolitics in the Third World, Jordanians, Palestinians, and the Hashemite Kingdom.* Chester Crocker, Chairman; Richard Solomon, President.

1170. **Veterans for Peace, Inc.* (1985) (org).

733 15th St. NW, Suite 928, DC 20005; (202) 347-6780; *vfp@igc.org; www.veteransforpeace.org*

Program: to increase awareness of the costs of war, to restrain the government from intervening militarily in the internal affairs of other nations, to reduce and eventually eliminate nuclear weapons and other weapons of mass destruction, to oppose war as an instrument of international policy. Members pledge to use nonviolent and democratic means to attain these ends. VFP has responded to a wide range of issues, such as closing the School of the Americas, reconciliation with Vietnam, and delegations to Central America, Bosnia, Chiapas, Iraq, and other counties. Organizes an annual convention in August—in 1999 in Philadelphia, in 2000 in D.C. Lee Vander Laan, Exec. Dir.

1171. *Violence Policy Center* (1988) (org).

1140 19th St., NW, Suite 600, DC 20036; (202) 822-8200; mail@vpc.org; www.vpc.org

Formerly: New Right Watch. Does research and publishes reports and books on reducing firearms violence in U.S. Pubs. include: *Cease Fire: A Comprehensive Strategy to Reduce Firearms Violence.* Josh Sugarmann, Exec. Dir.

1172. *Washington Peace Center* (1963) (org).

1801 Columbia Road NW, Suite 104, DC 20009; (202) 234-2000; wpc@igc.org; www.washingtonpeacecenter.org

A multi-issue peace and justice, anti-racist group committed to nonviolent social change, serving as a clearinghouse and resource center to the DC metropolitan progressive community. Pub. monthly *Washington Peace Letter* and weekly Activist Alert (by email). Maria Ramos, Coord.

1173. *Witness for Peace* (1983) (org).

1229 15th St. NW, 20005; (202) 588-1471; witness@witness4peace.org; www.witness4peace.org/wfp

Mission statement (1998): "We are people committed to nonviolence and led by faith and conscience. Our mission is to support peace, justice, and sustainable economies in the Americas by changing US policies and corporate practices

which contribute to poverty and oppression in Latin America and the Caribbean." Engages in direct action by sending observers to Latin America. Pub. the *WFP Newsletter.* Contact: Sarah DeBolt.

1174. *Women for Women International* (1993) (org).

1725 K St., NW #611, DC 20006; (202) 822-1391; www.womenforwomen.org

Inaugurated to help women in Bosnia-Herzogovina: found sponsors and micro-credit loans in the U.S. for distressed women there. In 1999 focused on women returnees in Kosova through the Solidarity Project to bring aid to returned refugees and to foster links among women throughout the region who are survivors of political violence.

1175. *Women Strike for Peace* (1961) (org).

110 Maryland Ave., NE, #102, DC 20002; (202) 543-2660.

WSP began with a one-day strike by 100,000 women to protest the arms race and atmospheric testing of nuclear weapons. With the help of SANE and Linus Pauling, the U.S. soon signed the Limited Test Ban Treaty of 1963. WSP's campaigns include support for HR82 to begin the writing of a treaty to abolish nuclear weapons; support for HR732 to close the School of the Americas; opposition to the National Missile Defense Act of 1999 (HR4 & S251); and support for the Cuba Humanitarian Trade Act (HR 230 & S327). Its Lobby-by-Proxy program educates legislators about peace. Pub. *Legislative Alert* newsletter.

Amy Swerdlow, *Women Strike for Peace.* Chicago: U of Chicago P, 1993.

1176. *Worldwatch Institute* (1974) (org).

1776 Massachusetts Ave., NW, DC 20036; (202) 296-7365; worldwatch@worldwatch.org; www.worldwatch.org

Dedicated to fostering the evolution of an environmentally sustainable society through inter-disciplinary non-partisan research on climate change, depletion of the stratospheric ozone layer, the loss of biological diversity, violent conflicts, and other global issues. Pubs.: *World Watch Magazine, State of the World* (annual collection of summative essays), Worldwatch books and papers, database disk subscription. Founder and president: Lester R. Brown.

1177. *Youth M-Power* (1999) (org).

1527 New Hampshire Ave., NW, 3rd Fl., DC 20036; (202) 667-9700, x201; *hrobert@spidr.org; www.youthm-power.org*

Youth Making Peaceful Options with Effective Results seeks to empower youth to develop a culture of respect, constructive conflict resolution, and peace. Funded by the Surdna Foundation, M-Power is a collaborative initiative of four dispute resolution organizations. Heather Robert, Program Coord.

1178. *Zero Population Growth (ZPG)* (1968) (org).

1400 Sixteenth St., NW, Suite 320, DC 20036 (3 blocks down P St. from Dupont Circle); (800) POP-1956; *info@zpg.org; www.zpg.org*

Advocates increased family planning to reduce population growth (in the U.S. by 2.6 million every year, in the world to double within the next 45 years to 12 billion people) and lobbies U.S. Congress, which cut funds in 1996, to support family planning in the U.S. and abroad. Pub. the magazine *ZPG Reporter.*

– West Virginia (WV) –

4 Sister Cities. / 13 Peace Poles.

GERRARDSTOWN, WV

1179. *Panhandle Peace and Justice Coalition* (1991) (org).

PO Box 81, Gerrardstown 25420; (304) 229-9569; writeforpub@aol.com

PP&J originated in opposition to the Gulf War. Since then it has participated in various justice and peace events in Jefferson, Morgan, and Berkeley counties, and some members have represented PP&JC at the annual Virginia Peace Summit. Contact Bob Naylor.

—— Wisconsin (WI) ——

36 Sister Cities. / 52 Peace Poles.

APPLETON, WI

1180. *Fox Valley FOR* (1991) (org).
1906 East Lourdes Drive, Appleton 54915; (920) 735-9198.

Fellowship of Reconciliation local group meets monthly, annually sponsors an August 6 Peace Lantern Float, participates annually in the October 7th Stop the Hate Campaign and the annual protest of the School of the Americas at Fort Benning, GA, and other activities. Often collaborates with other groups, especially Toward Community and the Unitarian Universalist Social Action Committee. Pub. *Peace News* four times a year. Contact Donna Van Grinsven.

ASHLAND, WI

1181. *Conflict and Peacemaking Program* (1985) (col).

Northland College, 1411 Ellis Ave., Ashland 54806; (715) 682-1232; *thastings@northland.edu; ssandstrom@northland.edu; www.northland.edu*

Wisconsin's first and still largest peace studies program, with a nonviolent focus, major and minor programs. Internships required. United Church of Christ affil. Founded by Kent Shifferd. Tom Howard-Hastings, Coord.

DODGEVILLE, WI

1182. *Iowa County Fellowship of Reconciliation* (1985) (org).

3817 Evans Quarry Rd., Rock Ridge Community, Dodgeville 53533; (608) 935-3007; *kavalosk@edgewood.edu*

A rural network offering speakers, remembrance of Hiroshima and Nagasaki by floating lanterns in the Wisconsin River, and currently a special concern over U.S. military expansion in Colombia. Contact Vince and Jane Hammatt Kavaloski.

EAU CLAIRE, WI

1183. *Political Science Program* (early 1970s) (col).

Political Science Dept.,
University of Wisconsin,
Eau Claire 4004; (715) 836-2092;
gambrell@cns.uwec.edu;
www.uwec.edu/Academic/PolSci/

Courses on war and peace in the department; for example, Dilemmas of War and Peace. Contact Leonard Gambrell.

KENOSHA, WI

1184. *Conflict Analysis and Resolution* (1996) (col).

Communication Department,
University of Wisconsin-Parkside,
Kenosha 53141;
(262) 595-2218;
jonathan.shailor@uwp.edu;
www.uwp.edu/catalog/arts.
sciences/communication.html

This undergraduate certificate consists of core and elective courses and an internship. Contact Jonathan Shailor.

LA CROSSE, WI

1185. *Anidonts* (1983) (mem).

Myrick Park, 9th and
Mississippi, La Crosse.

A two-piece aluminum ensemble of a man and a dog, one 13 feet high, the other 42 inches high and 8 feet 7 inches long, suggesting adult and animal love of children. Arata specified that it be located in a public park in which children play. Created by Luis Arata as a gift to La Crosse children and as a contribution to peace and liberty, for the artist was a refugee from the Argentine regime of Juan Peron.

"Shaping the Way for Peace and Children." *Good News* (12-1982).

LUCK, WI

1186. *Anathoth Community* (1987) (org).

740 Round lake Rd., Luck 54853;
(715) 472-8721; *anathoth@win.bright.net*

"We practice nonviolence and sustainable living as a way of life" and engage in peacework by opposing US warmaking in general, specifically at present Project ELF, the sanctions against Iraq, and war taxes. Contact Mike Miles.

1187. *Coalition to Stop Project ELF* (1990) (org).

See Nukewatch; *nukewtch@win.bright.ne*

Organized by Nukewatch, Laurentian Shield, and Anathoth Community, with several dozen organizations supporting. The Navy's Extremely Low Frequency communication system enables Trident nuclear submarines to make a preemptive first-strike, which violates the principle of deterrence. Also, the International Court of Justice has ruled that the threat to use nuclear weapons is a violation of binding international law. John LaForge and Bonnie Urfer.

Anidonts Sculpture by Luis Arata, Myrick Park, La Crosse. Photograph courtesy City of La Crosse Park and Recreation Department, Robert Berg, Matt Jurvelin.

1188. **Nukewatch* (1979) (org).

PO Box 649, Luck, 54853; (715) 472-4185; *nukewtch@win.bright.net*

Challenges nuclear weapons and the politics that protect them by imaginative nonviolent protests: the H-bomb Truck Watch, the Missile Silo Mapping Project, the Military Radioactive Waste Train Watch, Stop Project ELF!, the Missouri and North Dakota Missile Silo Peace Camps, etc. The summer of 1999 saw the third "Tromp Trident Trek" to Project Elf and the Great Lakes Action Camp (training for shutting down nuclear reactors). Nukewatch calls for an environment free of the nuclear industry, nuclear weapons, and radioactive waste. Publishes the *Pathfinder*; the Summer 1999 number contains a page of "Nuclear Shorts" (selections from world media) and three articles on the protest march from the Hague to NATO headquarters in Brussels, the continuing protest against ELF, and the transportation of radioactive nuclear waste across the country; the Spring 2000 number includes articles on NATO's war against Yugoslavia, NATO war crimes, the U.S. Air Force's Law of War, ELF, Martin Luther King, Jr.'s opposition to the Vietnam War, missile silos at Minot, and many more. Co-directed by Bonnie Urfer and John LaForge.

MADISON, WI

1189. *Elizabeth Link Peace Park* (1984) (mem).

452 State St., Madison.

Ms. Link had a lifelong commitment to world peace and social justice, especially expressed through her long local leadership in the Women's International League for Peace and Freedom (WILPF). A plaque reads: "To Elizabeth Link, Madison Branch of Women's International League of Peace and Freedom, Whose Courage, Vitality and Devotion To World Justice, Peace, and Freedom Inspire Our Own. Dedicated On Memorial Day 1984."

1190. **Independent Studies in Peace* (col).

Edgewood College, Madison 53711; (608) 663-2242; *kavalosk@edgewood.edu; www.edgewood.edu*

BA, courses and internship in peace groups around Madison. Travel seminar to the United Nations annually and essay contest sponsored by Philosophy dept. Member of Wisconsin Institute for the Study of Peace and Conflict and the Wisconsin Consortium of Peace and Justice. Roman Catholic affil. Contact Vince Kavaloski.

Elizabeth Link Peace Park, Madison. Photograph courtesy Katherine Rankin, Preservation Planner.

1191. **U.S. Campaign to Free Mordechai Vanunu* (1992) (org).

PO Box 43384
Tucson, AZ 85733

Seeks to secure the release of Vanunu, imprisoned in Israel since 1986 for telling a British newspaper about his government's secret nuclear weapons program, and works for a nuclear-free Israel and world. Felice Cohen-Joppa, Coord.

1192. **Wisconsin Coordinating Council on Nicaragua* (1984) (org).

PO Box 1534, Madison 53701;
(608) 257-7230; *wccn@execpc.com;*
www.execpc.com/~wccn

For the advancement of peace and justice in Nicaragua and against military and economic coercion by the U.S. Two main projects: U.S.-Nicaragua Women's Empowerment Project exchanges and Nicaraguan Credit Alternatives Fund. Pub. *Nicaraguan Developments* newsletter and *Friends in Deed: The Story of US-Nicaragua Sister Cities* by Liz Chilsen and Sheldon Rampton (1988). Also facilitates the sister city relationship between Madison and Managua.

MANITOWOC, WI

1193. **Lakeshore Peacemakers* (1980?) (org).

3805 S. 26th St., Manitowoc 54220;
(920) 683-3979; *jtrader@lakefield.net*

Monthly meetings to keep people informed and to find ways of reducing violence. Pub. a newsletter. Bob Kaeiser, Coord. Contact Janet Trader (920-686-1053).

MAPLE, WI

1194. **Laurentian Shield Resources for Nonviolence* (1997) (org).

12833E Hwy 13, Maple 54854;
(715) 364-8533; *laurentn@cpinternet.com;*
www.serve.com/gvaughn/laurentian

Seeks "to support the use of nonviolence to manage conflict from the interpersonal to the international." Special attention to imprisoned resisters to war. Speaking, teaching, nonviolence training, organizing. Newsletter: *Long Sentences: Nonviolent Incites* ten times a year. Donna and Tom Howard-Hastings.

MILWAUKEE, WI

1195. **Casa Maria Catholic Worker House of Hospitality* (1966) (org).

1131 N. 21st St., PO Box 05206,
Milwaukee 53205; (414) 344-5745.

Started by Annette and Michael Cullen, Casa Maria gives hospitality to the homeless and advocates for peace: war tax resistance, anti-gun vigils, anti-ROTC vigils, work with other groups. Pub. *Casa Cry* newsletter.

1196. **Center for Dispute Resolution Education* (1993) (col).

Marquette University, Milwaukee 53201;
(414) 288-5535; *eva.soeka@marquette.edu;*
www.marquette.edu/disputeres

Research for better programs for resolving disputes, including a design for a mediation system for the state. Marquette also has a Graduate Program in Dispute Resolution (1995). Pub. newsletter, *Caucus* two or three times a year. Roman Catholic foundations. Eva Soeka, Prog. Dir.

1197. **Dorothy Day–Catholic Worker Collection* (lib).

Special Collections and University Archives, Memorial Library, 1415 W. Wisconsin Ave., PO Box 3141, Marquette U, Milwaukee 53201-3141; (414) 288-7256; *runkelp@vms.csd.mu.edu*

More than 150 cubic feet of the records of the Catholic Worker movement and Dorothy Day Papers.

1198. **Peace Education Commission* (1986) (org).

Dept. of Educational Policy and Community Studies, Enderis 553, Univ. of Wisconsin-Milwaukee, PO Box 413, Milwaukee, WI 53201; (414) 229-2326; *imh@uwm.edu;*
www.uwm.edu/~imh

PEC is an agency of the International Peace Research Association (IPRA), which facilitates international exchanges about peace education and research. Pub. a newsletter, *Peacebuilding*, available in cyberspace; articles, reviews, reports welcome. Contact Ian Harris (*imh@csd.uwm.edu*).

1199. **Peace Studies* (1990) (col).

University of Wisconsin, Milwaukee 53201; (414) 229-6943; *lakshmi@csd.uwm.edu*; *www.uwm.edu/Dept/Peace*

An undergraduate certificate in courses and fieldwork. Sponsors peace events on campus. Affil. with The Wisconsin Institute for Peace and Conflict Studies. Contact Lakshmi Bharadwa.

OREGON, WI

1200. **Deer Park Buddhist Center* (1975) (org, mem).

4548 Schneider Dr., Oregon 53575; (608) 835-5572.

A teaching center dedicated to enhancing Buddhist practice. Regular classes during the week, several retreats a year. The temple was built in 1981.

PLATTEVILLE, WI

1201. **Wisconsin Institute for Peace and Conflict Studies* (1985) (col).

University of Wisconsin, Platteville. See below.

Comprising 20 member institutions, WIPCS seeks to encourage and legitimize teaching and research on the roots of violence, national and global security issues (including ecological), and on all factors necessary for a just global peace. Some of the 1999-2000 programs: student conference, speakers program, the *Journal for the Study of Peace and Conflict*, the "Dilemmas of War and Peace" curriculum, distinguished faculty and student awards, student internships, and other activities.

STEVENS POINT, WI

1202. **Peace Studies* (2000) (col).

College of Letters and Sciences, Univ. of Wisconsin, Stevens Point 54481;

(715) 346-3429; *eyonke@uwsp.edu*; *www.uwsp.edu/acad/hist/pax.htm*

A variety of peace-related courses led to the new undergraduate minor. Eric Yonke, Coordinator.

1203. **Wisconsin Institute for Peace and Conflict Studies* (1985) (col).

UWSP LRC/900 Reserve St.; Stevens Point 54481; (715) 346-3383; *wiinst@uwsp.edu*; *www.uwm.edu/~imh/wiscinst.htm*

Seeks to encourage teaching and research "on the roots of violence, on national and global security issues (including ecological security) and on all factors necessary for a just global peace." Offers an essay contest, annual conference, annual student conference, and a speaker's bureau. Pubs.: *Bulletin of the WIPCS* and *The Journal for the Study of Peace and Conflict* (annual, articles for '98-'99 include topics of International Criminal Court, Working Women, Persian Gulf War, Military in Turkey). Gary Boelhower, Editor. Kent Shifferd (1989-99), Northland College, WIPCS past Exec. Dir.; Martin Farrell, Ripon College, current Exec. Dir. Contact Sharon Roberts (*sroberts@uwsp.edu*).

TURTLE LAKE, WI

1204. **Dorea Peace Community* (1980) (org).

1645 60th St., Turtle Lake 54889; (715) 268-8925; *tkessler@win.bright.net*

Affil. with Fellowship of Reconciliation (1982). Participates in Project ELF against nuclear war. Contact Tom Kessler.

—— *Wyoming (WY)* ——

2 Sister Cities. / 24 Peace Poles.

CHEYENNE, WY

1204a. *Martin Luther King, Jr., Park* (1991) (mem).

Corner of Lincoln Way and Missile Drive, 9½ acres.

Both a sports and nature park, with plaza and creek with bridge. On August 1, 2000, a bust of King was dedicated, created by Guadelupé Barajas. The park was the idea of former State Senator Liz Byrd. Contact: Rick Parish (307-637-6423), Ann Redman (307-632-4667).

DANIEL, WY

1205. *De Smet Monument* (1925).

Between Pinedale and Daniel; 3.8 miles south of Daniel turn off Hwy 189 and follow gravel road 2.4 miles. (A historical marker is located on Rt. 189, 1.4 miles west of Daniel).

The monument is a small church building open on one side. Father Jean Pierre De Smet labored his lifetime for the welfare of Indians especially in the Flathead country on the Bitterroot River of present day Montana. He established 16 treaties during his lifetime, crossed the ocean 19 times, and traveled 180,000 miles for the Indians.

Laveille, E., S. J. *The Life of Father DeSmet, S.J.*

LARAMIE, WY

1206. *Peace Poles* (mem).

At least three Poles: St. Paul's United Church of Christ, 602 E. Garfield; Washington Park, Sheridan St.; and 70 Harmony Lane, the home of Becki Burman.

Canada and United States Border

1207. *Kiwanis International* (1934–).

During the 1930s–1950s, Kiwanis erected 31 plaques and tablets all along the border and elsewhere to celebrate the lasting peace between the two countries. The markers typically feature two female figures holding wreaths that surround the seals of the two nations. The U.S. figure also carries a cornucopia and the Canadian figure a sheaf of wheat, representing bounty. One tablet says: "This unfortified boundary line between the Dominion of Canada and the United States of America should quicken the remembrance of the more than a century-old friendship between these countries—a lesson of peace to all nations." Locations of some of the markers (east to west):

St. Croix Bridge, connecting Calais, Maine, and St. Stephen, New Brunswick, 1935.

International Friendship Grove and Garden, Pawtucket, Rhode Island, 1934.

Roosevelt Bridge, Cornwall, Ontario, Across St. Lawrence River from Hyando, New York, 1936.

Ambassador Bridge connecting Detroit, Michigan, and Windsor, Ontario, 1935.

Trout River, New York, 1937.

Lacolle, Québec, 1937.

Cornwall, Ontario, 1936.

Port Huron, Michigan, on St. Clair River, across from Sarnia, Ontario, 1935.

Sault Sainte Marie, on St. Mary's River, 1936.

Emerson, Manitoba, near northwest corner of Minnesota, 1936.

Fort Frances, Ontario, Across Rainy River, from international Falls, Minnesota, 1936.

International Peace Garden, between North Dakota and Manitoba, 1937.

Blaine, Washington, between United States and Canada Custom Houses, 1936.

International Peace Bridge, Niagara River at Buffalo and Fort Erie. Photograph courtesy Anthony Masiello, Mayor, City of Buffalo.

ONTARIO AND NEW YORK STATE

1208. *International Peace Bridge* (1927).

Crosses the Niagara River to connect the State of New York at Buffalo with Fort Erie, Ontario.

Commemorates 100 years (from 1814 to 1914) of peace between the two countries, "That all may learn that war must cease/When nations yearn and plan for Peace" (from a poem written for the dedication). The bridge is the property of the Dominion of Canada and the State of New York.

1208a. *A Pilgrimage of Friendship Plaque* (1936).

Located on the Canadian side of the International Peace Bridge.

Marks the crossing from the United States to Canada of a delegation from the Associated Country Women of the World and is dedicated to the rural women of the North American continent.

MANITOBA AND NORTH DAKOTA

1209. **International Peace Garden* (1932) (mem).

On top of Turtle Mountains between Dunseith, North Dakota, and Boissevain, Manitoba; (701) 795-5193 in North Dakota, (204) 956-7959 in Canada.

Composed of 2,339 acres (9.3 km), 900 in North Dakota, 1,451 in Manitoba, the Garden originated with Dr. Henry J. Moore of Islington, Ontario, at a meeting of the Association of Gardeners from the U.S. and Canada in Toronto in 1929, to "commemorate the 115 years of peace" between the two countries. At the top of one of the mountains this message is inscribed on a bronze plate: "To God in His glory we two nations pledge ourselves that as long as men shall live we will not take up arms against one another." A new *Interpretive Center* was opened in May 1998 to assist visitors in understanding the history of the park and in appreciating the lakes, buildings, greenhouses, and botanical gardens. Several components of the Garden signify peace also; for example, the Peace Tower has four columns representing people from the four corners of the world coming together to form two

similar but distinct nations with a common base. Ms. Keiko Anabuki gave seven Peace Poles to the Garden in 1998, which stand at the border.

Bird, Brad. "A Year of Challenge and Change." *Deloraine Times & Star* (September 16, 1998) 2, 9.

Storman, John. "A History of the International Peace Garden" (rev. 1981 by Tom Wilkins).

ALBERTA AND MONTANA

1210. *Waterton-Glacier International Peace Park* (1932) (mem).

Composed of the contiguous parks Glacier Park, Montana, and Waterton Lakes Park, Alberta.

Probably the first proponents of an international park for the two parks were George Brown and Henry Reynolds in the early twentieth century. Alberta and Montana Rotarians adopted a resolution in 1931 calling for an International Peace Park, and by the following year both countries had passed the idea into law.

Top and above right: International Peace Garden, Manitoba and North Dakota. Photographs courtesy Historic Resources Branch, Manitoba Culture, Heritage and Citizenship, Bruce Donaldson.

Waterton-Glacier International Peace Park, Alberta and Montana. Photographs courtesy Glacier National Park, Mary Cornell, Larry Frederick.

The U. S. dedication was held in 1932, the Canadian in 1936. The Park now contains 1720 square miles (4450 km), 1,122,481 acres, three score glaciers, three hundred lakes, five hundred waterfalls. But each nation retains administrative control of its area. In addition to the plaques at East Glacier and Prince of Wales placed during the dedication ceremonies, the following plaques and monuments exist: 2 International Cairns at Chief Mountain; 2 plaques in memory of Tom J. Davis (East Glacier and Prince of Wales); 2 plaques honoring Canon Middleton (same location); 1 monument to Kootenai Brown (Waterton Townsite); 1 IPP sign at Waterton Information Centre; 1 memorial plaque for Harry R. Hutchings (Information Center); 1 memorial plaque for Harvey S. Greenway (Information Centre). A bronze tablet unveiled at the U. S. dedication reads: "Permanently commemorating the long existing relationship of peace and good will between the peoples of Canada and the United States." Gradually the united parks have also come to represent the commitment to cooperation and stewardship in a world of shared resources. It was designated a Biosphere Reserve by UNESCO, and in 1996, UNESCO designated the Park as a World Heritage Site. In 1997 an international conference in South Africa produced the "Cape Town Declaration on Parks for Peace" for the establishment of transfrontier conservation areas, based upon the model of the Glacier-Waterton Park.

MacDonald, Graham. "Where the Mountains Meet the Prairies: A History of Waterton Lakes National Park." 128–138.

Scace, Robert. *Waterton-Glacier International Peace Park: Interpretive Management Unit, Story Line Document.* Calgary, Alberta, 1978 (a proposal to erect a Park Exhibit in Waterton Townsite to give the history of the Park, prepared for Parks Canada, Western Region).

"Waterton/Glacier International Peace Park." Canadian Park Service and U.S. National Park Service, 1997 (the Park brochure and map).

International Peace Arch, Blaine, Washington. Photograph courtesy George Muldrow.

Built by the International Peace Memorial Association of British Columbia and a cooperating United States committee to celebrate over 100 years of peace. On the United States side is the inscription: "Children of a Common Mother" (England), and on the Canadian side: "Brethren Dwelling together in Unity." On the west side is a picture of the Mayflower and a relic of the ship in a vault; on the east side is a picture of the Beaver, one of the first ships of the Hudson Bay Company, with its relic. Parks beautify both sides of the border.

BRITISH COLUMBIA AND WASHINGTON STATE

1211. *International Peace Arch* (1921) (mem).

About five blocks from the center of Blaine, Washington, overlooking the Strait of Georgia, an arm of the Pacific Ocean.

YUKON TERRITORY AND ALASKA

1212. *Wrangell-St. Elias National Park and Preserve* (Alaska, 1978) and *Kluane National Park* (Yukon, 1972).

To Wrangell-St. Elias: Hdqts. In Copper Center, 210 miles east of Anchorage via Glenn Highway (Alaska 1); PO Box 439,

Copper Center, AK 99573; (907) 822-5235; *www.nps.gov/wrst* Kluane: Haines Junction, YT YOB ILO (403-634-2251).

The combined parks encompass the largest parkland in North America (Wrangell-St. Elias: 13.2 million acres; Kluane: 5,440,000 acres/8500 sq. mi./2,201,000 hectares/22010 sq. km.), and, along with Glacier Bay National Park and the

Tatshenshini-Alsek Park in British Columbia, have been designated a World Heritage Site. Although neither park is designated a peace park, they express the peacemaking effect of all adjacent border parks—cooperating and interchanging staffs in order to preserve a mutual natural heritage in peace. And any World Heritage designation indicates a peaceful intent.

Canada

According to The World Peace Prayer Society, as of October 29, 1998, Canada had 55 Peace Poles; and the *1998 Sister Cities International Directory* lists 49 Sister Cities.

— *Alberta (AB)* —

5 Peace Poles.

ALBERTA

1213. *Peace River* (named 1782?).

A major stream, flowing NE from eastern British Columbia through Alberta to the Slave River, 1050 miles (1690 km) long.

Named for the peace made between the Knisteneaux (Cree) and the Beaver Indians at Peace Point near Lake Athabasca in 1782. Different Indian groups have other names for the river (translated as Large River, Beautiful River, etc.).

CALGARY, AB

1214. **Certificate in Conflict Resolution* (col).

Faculty of Continuing Education and Extension, Lincoln Park Campus, Mount

Royal College, Calgary, AB T3E 6K6; (403) 240-6867; *www.mtroyal.ab.ca/ programs/conted/courseidx.htm*

Designed for professionals for settling disputes in the family, school, community, and other areas. Core and elective courses and a final mediation assessment. Contact Martha McManus.

1215. **Conflict Management* (col).

Faculty of Continuing Education, Univ. of Calgary, Calgary, AB T2N 1N4; (403) 220-2877; *www.ucalgary.ca; www.ucalgary.ca/UofC/faculties/CTED/ home/conflicrestt.html*

A certificate for professionals consisting of core and elective courses.

1216. **Lawyers for Social Responsibility/ Avocats en Faveur d'une Conscience Sociale* (1984) (org).

5120 Camey Rd. NW, Calgary, AB T2L 1G2; (403) 282-8260; *delong@nucleus.com*

LSR seeks to obtain the signing of a convention setting out a binding timetable for the elimination of nuclear weapons worldwide; to encourage the ratification of the new Ottawa Treaty on Landmines; to encourage the establishment of an International Criminal Court; to encourage the use of law to build international peace. The organization has cosponsored with the Canadian Bar Assoc. the first international conference on law and nuclear weapons; provided legal, lobbying, and administrative support for the work of Mines Action Canada in its successful call for a ban on landmines; organized educational meetings on legal aspects of the arms race; published regular newsletters on legal issues concerning peace and war. Contact Beverley Delong.

1217. *Mennonite Central Committee, Alberta* (1964) (org).

76 Skyline Crescent NE,
Calgary, AB T2K 5X7;
(403) 275-6935;
mccab@cadvision.com; www.mcc.org

Branch of the North American Mennonite and Brethren in Christ Churches, dedicated to peace, justice, and the dignity of all people in Jesus Christ.

1218. *Peace Grove* (1992) (mem).

Calgary, AB.

A plaque fastened to a large boulder says in English and French: "PEACE GROVE. This peace grove of twelve elm trees has been dedicated in celebration of Canada's 125th birthday in recognition of Canada's international peacekeeping role." Contact Beverley Delong (*delong@nucleus.com*).

1219. *Project Ploughshares Calgary* (1982) (org).

2919-8 Ave., NW, Calgary,
AB T2N 1C8; (403) 270-7366.

National Ploughshares and PPC beliefs include: nuclear warfare and poverty are the common enemies of all people; international peace rests on a common commitment to global peace and justice; global security must include the security of people and the planet as well as the security of states; non-violent conflict resolution can be taught. Supports the national Ploughshares (Waterloo, ON) through education, research, dialogue; monthly meetings, an office and resource center; briefings for government, schools, and media; workshops. Pub. a monthly newsletter.

Peace Grove and Plaque, Calgary. Photograph courtesy Beverley Delong, Canadian Network to Abolish Nuclear Weapons.

Toil and Peaceful Life Markers for Doukhobors, Cowley. Photographs courtesy Chris Robinson.

COWLEY, AB

1220. *Toil and Peaceful Life* (1995) (mem).

Both sides of Highway 3, 1 km west of Cowley, AB.

The identical markers commemorate the June 29, 1995 centennial of the destruction of weapons by Doukhobors in Transcaucasia. They decided that "Thou shalt not kill" were words to live by, and in 1895 they burned their weapons. As a result, they suffered the persecutions of starvation, exile, beatings, and family separation. See Saskatchewan.

EDMONTON, AB

1221. *Servas Canada* (1960) (org).

6707 108 Ave.,
Edmonton, AB T6A 1P7;
chesley@netcom.ca; oneworld@sympatico.ca

An exchange program of hosts and travelers now operating in over 100 countries to build peace, goodwill, and understanding between people of different backgrounds and cultures. Gerry Staring, Dir.

HOBBEMA/WETASKIWIN, AB

1222. *Hills of Peace Cairn* (1927, 1959, 1976) (mem).

East side Highway 2A at Hobbema, AB, 1 km north of Highway 611, near the city of Wetaskiwin (meaning Peace Hills).

Made of field stones, many of which were transported by schoolchildren, the Cairn commemorates the peace negotiated by the Woods Cree Chief, Maskepetoon, between the Blackfeet and the Cree Indians in 1867. Originally (1927) two tomahawks crowned the Cairn, but they have disappeared. Legend says that during a fierce battle between the Cree and Blackfoot

Hills of Peace Cairn, Hobbema near Wetaskiwin. Photograph courtesy Carolyn Hill, Wetaskiwin Archivist.

Nations, two braves, engaged in single combat, became weary and stopped to rest. They shared a pipe, symbolic of peace, and, as a result, the battle came to an end, and the area was named Wee-Tas-Ki-Win-Spatinow, "The Place Where Peace Was Made." The Cairn commemorates this event.

OKOTOKS, AB

1223. *Canadian Centres for Teaching Peace* (1997) (org).

PO Box 70, Okotoks, AB T0L 1T0; (403) 938-5335; *stewartr@peace.ca; www.peace.ca*

Mainly an electronic virtual peace center: web site and PeaceBuilders email list server (see web site). Also works with the Canadian Commission for UNESCO to develop a National Culture of Peace Program for Canada (1999-2000).

RED DEER, AB

1224. *Bahá'í Council of Alberta* (1997) (org).

128 Norby Cresc., Red Dear, AB T4P 2C6; (403) 343-1214; *bca@cadvision.com*

Bahá'í works for world peace, sustainable and equitable development, human solidarity, equality of women and men, dialogue between science and religion, and sound world governance. The first local Bahá'í community in Alberta was formed in Edmonton in 1943. There are now 34 local Spiritual Assemblies in the province plus 24 Bahá'í groups. They support ongoing training institutes and annually celebrate Unity in Diversity Week the second week of November, The Day for the Elimination of Racial Discrimination on March 21, and The Day of the Covenant on Nov. 26. Pub. *Alberta Action* and the *Eagle* (First Nations) newsletters. Judie Bopp, Secretary.

— *British Columbia —* *(BC)*

BC is a nuclear free province.
7 Peace Poles

ABBOTSFORD, BC

1225. *Mennonite Central Committee, BC* (1963) (org).

Box 2038, Abbotsford, BC V2T 3T8; (604) 850-6639; *mccbcadm@rapidnet.net; www.mcc.org/; www.prairienet. org/community/religion/mennonite*

Branch of the Mennonite and Brethren in Christ churches. Activities include support of refugees, aboriginal neighbors, and peace and justice education in schools. Edward Janzen, Exec. Dir.

BOWEN ISLAND, BC

1226. *Muriel Neilson Memorial Peace Garden* (1992) (mem).

Bowen Island Community School,

Mahatma Gandhi Bust by Wagh Brothers, Simon Fraser University, Burnaby, British Columbia. Photograph courtesy Public Relations Office, Gloria Asmundson.

Bowen Island, BC V0N 1GO; (604) 947-9337; *www.sd45.bc.ca*

The Garden commemorates Muriel Neilson, teacher and peace activist, who bequeathed a trust fund for the cultural enrichment of local schoolchildren. Contact Principal Glenn Rose.

BURNABY, BC

1227. *Mahatma Gandhi Bust* (1969) (mem).

Simon Fraser University, BC, Science Mall in Peace Square in the Academic Quadrangle.

One and one-half times life size (3 ft. high) bronze bust dedicated during Gandhi Year, 1969 being his birth centenary year. The bust is a replica of the one at Howard University in Washington, D.C. A gift of the East Indian Community of British Columbia. Artist: Wagh Brothers Studios in Bombay.

CASTLEGAR, BC

1228. *Brilliant Cultural Centre* (1977) (org).

PO Box 3024, Castlegar, BC V1N 3H4 (near the Village Museum across the Kootenay River); (250) 365-3613.

Doukhobor Cultural Center, Castlegar. Photograph courtesy Michael M. Verigin.

Doukhobor Historical Village and Tolstoy Statue, Castlegar. Photograph courtesy Koozma J. Tarasoff.

Contains a stage and large auditorium and banquet facilities. Operated by the Union of Spiritual Communities of Christ, one of the two main Doukhobor groups (the other the Doukhobor Society of Canada), which subscribes to the historic peace mission of the Doukhobors to rid the world of war and violence. A second USCC center is at Grand Forks.

1229. *Doukhobor Historical Village Museum and Leo Tolstoy Statue* (1987) (mus, mem).

R.R. 1, Site 2, Comp. B4, Castlegar, BC V1N 3H7; (250) 365-5327; *cds@kootcom.kootenay.net*

The Doukhobor Village Museum, or Castlegar Doukhobor Museum, Ooteshenie, is across from the Castlegar Airport; Castlegar is located at the confluence of the Kootenay and Columbia Rivers between Trail and Creston.

The statue stands in front of a double story home used as a residence for community Doukhobors from 1913 to 1940s. Tolstoy played a very important role in the migration of 7500 Russian Doukhobors to Canada in 1899, after the Doukhobors had burned their weapons and declared their pacifist commitment, by raising money from the proceeds of his novel *Resurrection* to send them on their journey.

1230. *Spirit Wrestlers Associates* (1993) (org).

Inaugurated to create inexpensive popular publications on the people called Spirit Wrestlers, Doukhobor nonviolent activists who emigrated from Russia. Founders: Larry Ewashen (RR 11, Site 2, Comp. B-4, Castlegar, *cds@koot com.kootenay.net*) and Koozma Tarasoff (882 Walkley Rd., Ottawa, ON K1V 6R5, tarasov@ igs.net).

1231. *Yasnaya Polyana Bakery/Café Project* (1999) (org).

c/o Alex Jmaeff, Site 23, C-18, RR2, Castlegar, BC V1N 3L4; (250) 359-7253; *tolstoy@wkpowerlink.com; www.tolstoy.bc.ca*

A joint project by Canadian Doukhobors, the people of the village of Yasnaya Polyana, and the great-great-grandson of Lev N. Tolstoy at Yasnaya Polyana, Tolstoy's estate, where he is buried, near Tula, Russia, 200 km south of Moscow.

Cumberland Peace Park, Cumberland. Photograph courtesy Ramona Boyle and John MacLeod.

CUMBERLAND, BC

1232. *Cumberland Peace Park* (1993) (mem).

Box 615, Cumberland, BC V0R 1S0; (250) 336-8442; *rboyle@comox.island.net*

Located at the entrance to this small village of about 2000 people. Created through the efforts of the Bahá'í member, Elizabeth Austin, and maintained by that group, which also paid for a yellow cedar sign inscribed: "Cumberland Peace Park." Contact Ramona Boyle.

DUNCAN, BC

1233. **Bahá'í Council of British Columbia and the Yukon* (1997) (org).

2174 Diedre Road, Duncan, BC V9L 6M2; (250) 701-0060; *lynsmith@island.net*

The first Local Spiritual Assembly in BC was formed in 1927 in Vancouver. Active in engaging First Nations linguistically, socially, and spiritually, based upon Bahá'í commitment to building relationships between diverse peoples. Lynn Smith, Secretary.

GABRIOLA ISLAND, BC

1234. **New Society Publishers Canada* (1980) (porg).

PO Box 189, Gabriola Island, BC V0R 1X0; (250) 247-9737; *info@newsociety.com; www.newsociety.com*

NSP began in Philadelphia and became solely Canadian in 1995. This company publishes books that build an ecologically sustainable, just, and nonviolent society. Offers over 75 titles on environment and justice, resistance, ecological design, feminism, progressive leadership, accountable economics, education, parenting, and related subjects. New Fall 1999 books on genetically altered foods, harms of economic development, straw bale building, raising boys with values of peace and justice, home schooling, and more. Contact Christopher Plant or Will Dubroy.

GRAND FORKS, BC

1235. **USCC (Doukhobor) Community Centre* (1943) (org).

Known as Community Doukhobors, the USCC is the main organized Canadian Doukhobor organization today, possessing the largest cultural resources, including two major community centers in Grand Forks and Brilliant, BC. Promotes peace and disarmament events, including annual youth festivals. Publishes the monthly journal *Iskra*, the official publication of the Union of Spiritual Communities of Christ, one of the two main Doukhobor groups.

NAKUSP, BC

1236. **Whatshan Retreat Centre* (1999) (org).

In the wilderness near Nakusp, BC, famous for its hot springs.

A new Doukhobor institution, part of their Spirit Wrestlers movement, which includes a pacifist nonviolent ethic, opposing killing because a human is an abode of God and all are global citizens in a brother-sister relationship in one universe. Contact Elmer Verigin, P.O. Box 192, Genelle, BC VOG 1GO; (250) 693-2240; *everigin@vader.kootenay.net*

NORTH VANCOUVER, BC

1237. **20/20 Vision* (1990) (org).

103-209 Westview Drive,
North Vancouver, BC V7N 4N2;
(604) 983-2525;
smacdonald@nvsd44.bc.ca;
www.2020vision.bc.ca

Seeks to enable concerned individuals to influence policymakers to protect our environment and enhance peace. Each month 20/20 Vision polls peace and environmental organizations regarding the urgent issues and selects one for a monthly action postcard mailed to members. Members are committed to spending 20 minutes a month writing a letter or making a call to the person(s) recommended in the action alert. Contact Pru Moore (604) 926-3417. U.S. office Washington, DC.

VANCOUVER, BC

1238. **Amnesty International, Pacific Regional Office, Canadian Section (English Speaking)* (1984) (org).

#4–3664 E. Hastings St.,
Vancouver, BC V5K 2A9;
(604) 294-5160 or 294-9450
(Refugee Coord.); *pro@amnesty.ca*;
info@amnesty.bc.ca; www.amnesty.bc.ca

AI takes action to free all prisoners of conscience, ensure fair and prompt trials for political prisoners, abolish the death penalty, torture, and other cruel treatment of prisoners, and end extrajudicial executions, political killings, and disappearances. Vancouver has had members ever since the beginning of AI in 1961. In Sept. 1999 all branches of AI in Canada focused wholly upon the East Timor crisis. Shannon Colby, Office Coordinator. AI national headquarters in Vanier, ON; also a Toronto office.

1239. **Committee for a Nuclear Free Nanoose* (1999) (org).

2150 Maple St., Vancouver, BC V6J 3T3.

Opposes the federal government's attempt to expropriate Nanoose Bay for U.S. nuclear submarines and weapons. Composed of several peace groups, including WILPF-BC and BC Teachers for Peace & Global Education.

1240. **End the Arms Race* (1982) (org).

825 Granville St., No.405,
Vancouver, BC V6Z 1K9;
(604) 687-3223; *info@peacewire.org*;
www.peacewire.org

Promotes two objectives: "Ending the arms race, through disarmament and demilitarization; diverting money from military spending to the funding of human needs." Works closely with Public Education for Peace Society, which shares the web site, Peacewire. Peter Coombes, Canadian Organizer. Contact Jillian Skeet.

1241. *Harding International Good Will Memorial* (1925) (mem).

The east side of the open area between the Pavilion and the Malkin Bowl, Stanley Park, Vancouver, BC.

The Memorial was dedicated by Kiwanis International to commemorate the visit in 1923 of

Harding International Good Will Memorial designed by Charles Marega, Stanley Park, Vancouver. Photograph courtesy Carol Haber, Archivist.

Warren G. Harding, the first U.S. President to visit foreign soil during his term of office, and to affirm the spirit of understanding and good will between the two nations. The inscription from an address made by President Harding during a visit to Canada says in part: "What an object lesson of peace is shown today by our two great countries to all the world." The Memorial is composed of wide granite steps leading to two women facing each other at the center. To the right is Britannia, with her left hand resting on a carved Canadian ensign, her right on a laurel wreath nearly touching the fingers of her companion to the left, "Liberty," who occupies a similar position with her hand resting on the Stars and Stripes. At each end are large bronze eagles also facing each other. An interesting feature of the Memorial is the carved lion's head fountain at the rear of the monument, only visible to someone approaching from behind. Charles Marega designed the Memorial.

1242–1245. Entries deleted.

1246. *Peace and Conflict Studies* (1989) (col).

100 West 49th Ave., Langara College, Vancouver, BC V5Y 2Z6;

(604) 323-5360; *mgoldie@langara.bc.ca; www.surf.langara.bc.ca/progcours/ programs/AS_Peace.html*

Undergraduate concentration in the two-year Associate of Arts degree. Mary Goldie, Program Coordinator.

1247. *Peace Fountain* (1987) (mem).

Seaforth Park, south end of the Burrard Bridge near downtown Vancouver, BC.

Simple square pool, in the middle of which a granite boulder rests upon a bronze pyramid; upon the boulder rests another stone from which an eternal flame burns; water flows from the base of the flame. The Fountain is surrounded by trees dedicated to world peace, planted by various associations and international conferences. A rallying point for peace marches in the eighties.

1248. *Public Education for Peace Society* (1984) (org).

825 Granville St., # 405, Vancouver, BC V6Z 1K9; (604) 687-3292; *info@peacewire.org; www.peacewire.org*

Conducts peace education campaigns and provides resources for educators. Katherine Odgers, Pres. Peter Coombes, Staff.

Seaforth Peace Park and Peace Fountain, Vancouver. Photograph courtesy Vancouver Park Board, Terri Clark, John MacLeod.

1249. *Society Promoting Environmental Conservation* (1969) (org).

2150 Maple St., Vancouver BC V6J 3T3; (604) 736-7732; *enviro@spec.bc.ca*; www.spec.bc.ca

Environmental advocacy and education. Current projects include: ending logging in Greater Vancouver's watersheds and opposing Ottawa's expropriation of provincial land at the Nanoose Bay submarine weapons test range. Pub. *Spectrum* newsletter (Winter 1999-2000 issue included articles on transportation in Vancouver, genetically modified foods, Congo rain forests, and recycling). David Cadman, Pres.

1250. *Women's International League for Peace and Freedom—British Columbia* (1960) (org).

PO Box 365, 916 W. Broadway, Vancouver, BC V5Z 1K7; (604) 298-3571; *ckline@unixg.ubc.ca*; *dmorgan@web.net*; *www.grannyg.bc.ca/wilpf.html*

WILPF would abolish wars by strengthening the UN and international laws, the environment, and equality by establishing an international economic order "founded on meeting the needs of all peoples and not on profit and privilege." Seminars, workshops, vigils; sent its Pres. to Iraq. Linda Morgan, Pres. Contact Eve Eriksen (1276 Whitsell Ave., Burnaby, BC V5C 5E4)

VICTORIA, BC

1251. *Conscience Canada* (1982) (org).

PO Box 8601, Victoria Centre PO, Victoria, BC V8W 3S2; (250) 384-5532; *peacetax@islandnet.com*

Strives to establish the legal right of conscientious objectors to refuse paying that portion of their taxes that goes to the military. Through lobbying, networking, the efforts of MP Sven Robinson and his Bill C-399, and the Peace Tax Trust Fund, CC hopes to create new laws for COs. Pub. a newsletter 3 times a year. Coordinators: K. Mansfield and C. Fox.

1252. *Institute for Dispute Resolution* (1989) (col).

University of Victoria, PO Box 1700 STN CSC, Victoria, BC V8W 2Y2; (250) 721-8777; *uvicidr@uvic.ca; www.dispute.resolution.uvic.ca*

Founded for research and dissemination of knowledge through conferences, professional training, and education for public and private organizations. Pubs. on diverse subjects. The Institute has also developed a MA on public sector DR, consisting of core and elective courses and a project or thesis. Contact David Turner.

1253. *Peace, Earth, & Justice Lists* (1996) (org).

Victoria Peace Centre. peace@islandnet.com and *www.islandnet.com/~emerald/ peace.htm; earth@islandnet.com; www. islandnet.com/~emerald/earth.htm; justice@islandnet.com* and *www.islandnet.com/~emerald/justice.htm*

A free email news service provides daily news and opinion on peace, environment (earth), and justice issues. The editors say "no junk" but edited, worthwhile pieces. "Postings that demonstrate the linkages between peace, earth, and justice issues are given prominence." Al Rycroft, Founding Editor.

1254. *Teachers for Peace and Global Education* (1985) (org).

6703 Medd Rd., Nanaimo, BC V9V 1A1; *jbrayden@nanaimo.ark.com*

A Provincial Specialist Association of the British Columbia Teachers Federation which seeks global peace, social and economic equality, democracy in the classrooms and world, environmental balance of humans and other living creatures, and respect for all life. Each year TPGE sponsors a conference. In August 2000, TPGE, the UN Victoria Assoc., and the Univ. of Victoria sponsored the conference "Valuing the Culture of Peace," which explored ways to implement a peace curriculum in the learning environment of the classroom. Contact *Kathryn_Godfrey@sd63.bc.ca*; Judy Brayden, Pres.

1255. *Victoria Anti-War Coalition* (1999) (org).

c/o Vancouver Island Public Interest Research Group, PO Box 3035 Stn CSC,

Victoria, BC V8V 3P3; (250) 472-4558; *vipirg@uvic.ca*

Active against NATO's war against Yugoslavia. Contact Stacy Chappel.

1256. *Victoria Peace Centre* (1983) (org).

PO Box 8307, Victoria V8W 3R9; (250) 595-7955; *peace@islandnet.com; www.IslandNet.com/~emerald/peace.htm*

A focus on common security leads VPC to advocate reduced military budgets to free money to reduce pollution, population, hunger, disease, and ignorance. VPC also seeks the abolition of nuclear weapons, the expansion of nuclear free zones, increased support for the United Nations, an end of Canadian arms trade, and similar purposes. VPC arose from the Victoria Coalition for Disarmament of the 1970s and the Greater Victoria Disarmament Group of 1982, which pushed a local referendum for nuclear weapons free zones. The annual Earth Walk is another activity, as well as educational meetings, speakers, and cooperation with other groups. Supports a Resource Centre, located in the United Nations Assoc. office, containing a large library of books, videos, and audio tapes. And offers an email news service with daily news and opinion on peace, environment, and justice issues. In the summer of 1999 it was engaged in opposition to the Nanoose Bay Weapons Testing Range. Pub. the *Peace Update* (on-line and newsprint). Contact Al Rycroft & Kealey Pringle (250-653-9973; *emerald@saltspring.com*).

— *Manitoba (MB)* —

NEEPAWA, MB

1257. *Dove Peace Flag* (1997) and *Margaret Laurence Home* (1987) (mem & mus).

At the Margaret Laurence Home (museum) in Neepawa, Highway 16, 312 First Ave., corner of First Ave. and Brydon St.; Box 786, Neepawa R0J 1H0; (204) 476-3612; *mlhome@login.mb.sympatico.ca*

Laurence (1926-1987) won many awards for her novels. "The last decade of her life focused

Margaret Laurence Home and Dove Peace Flag, Neepawa. Photograph courtesy Dorothy Henderson, Director.

on promoting causes she passionately supported—peace, social justice, the equality of women, environmental protection…. The last lines of the 'Prayer for Passover and Easter' are a timeless plea for peace, tolerance, and the unity of all peoples." Dorothy Henderson, Dir.

WINNIPEG, MB

1258. *Building Peace Through Play* (1984) (org).

745 Westminster Ave., Winnipeg, MB R3G 1A5; (204) 775-6579; *projectp@escape.ca*

Strives to educate especially parents, teachers, and caregivers about the detrimental effects of violent toys and entertainment and to present nonviolent alternatives to the sexist and commercialized toys and videogames being marketed to children. Annual Peaceful Play Festival, speakers, pamphlets. Jennifer Wushke, Dir.; Ruth Taronno (204-775-6579).

1259. *Conflict Resolution Studies* (1989) (col).

Univ. of Winnipeg, Menno Simons College, 380 Spence St., Winnipeg, MB R3B 2E9; *david.falk@uwinnipeg.ca; www.uwinnipeg.ca/~msc/crsprog.htm*

Undergraduate major in the Anabaptist Mennonite tradition of peace and service, consisting of core and elective courses. The CRS program offers a BA involving public dispute resolution, communication theory, mediation and law, human rights, conflict transformation, aboriginal issues, and related issues (some 30 courses). Six full-time faculty, twelve part-time instructors. Classes are interdisciplinary, problem-based, and small. Menno Simons with Mennonite Bible College and Concord College form the Mennonite College Federation (www.mcfed.mb.ca), in which the CRS courses are mutually available. David Falk, Director. Paul Redekop, Prog. Coord. (*p.redekop@uwinnipeg.ca*).

1260. *Mennonite Central Committee, Canada* (1963) (org).

134 Plaza Drive, Winnipeg, MB R31 5K9; (204) 261-6381 or (888) 622-6337.

One of the three pacifist churches, with the Quakers and the Brethren (to which should be added the Bahá'í, and in Canada the Doukhobors), opposing war and the military. MCC is the peace, relief, and service agency of Canadian Mennonites and Brethren in Christ, with sub-agencies in several provinces. Its Peace and Social Concerns Committee (1964) raises awareness and takes action on peace and current social issues: working with the Intercollegiate Peace Fellowship, consulting editors for the *MCC Peace Section Newsletter*, cooperating with MCC and provincial MCCC peace committees, counseling alternatives to military service. An Ottawa office (1974) facilitates relations with government. A victim-offender ministry offers mediation as an alternative to the secular justice system. By 1990 MCCC had grown to a staff of 50 and budget of $17 million. (U.S. MCC in Akron, PA).

Frank Epp, ed. *Partners in Service: The Story of Mennonite Central Committee Canada*. Winnipeg: Mennonite Central Committee Canada, 1983.

Friesen, Bert. *Where We Stand.*

MCC Canada Report, 1986; *Responses to Militarism.*

1261. *Victims of War Memorial* (1985) (mem).

At the Manitoba Legislative building in Winnipeg.

Marking the 40th anniversary of the atomic bombing of Hiroshima, a plaque rests on a boulder in a gravel garden with trees and shrubs. The plaque contains the Manitoba crest and reads: "Dedicated to the memory of all victims of war: 'There is no way to peace, peace is the way.' The people of Manitoba, August 6, 1985." (Other memorials to victims: Santa Cruz, CA, and Sherborn, MA, USA).

— *New Brunswick* — *(NB)*

FREDERICTON, NB

1262. *Center for Conflict Studies* (1980) (col).

Univ. of New Brunswick, Faculty of Fine Arts, Fredericton, NB E3B 5A3; (506) 453-4587; *conflict@unb.ca*; *www.unb.ca/arts/CCS*

Established for research and publishing in the field of low-intensity conflict (LIC)—political

Victims of War Memorial, Winnipeg. Photograph courtesy Travel Manitoba, Colette Delaurace.

terrorism, propaganda, special operations, etc. David Charters, Dir.

1263. **Human Rights Program* (1998) (col).

Saint Thomas University,
Fredericton, NB E3B 5G3;
(506) 452-0640;
pmalcolm@stthomasu.ca; www.stthomasu.ca/academics/depts/humnriin.htm

A major in the basic instruments, institutions, and ideas of human rights. Draws on the resources of the Atlantic Human Rights Centre on campus. Patrick Malcolmson, Dir.

WELSHPOOL, NB

1264. *Roosevelt Campobello International Park* (1964) (mem).

PO Box 9, Welshpool, Campobello Island, NB, E0G 3H0, off Route 774; PO Box 97, Lubec, ME, 04652. From Boston take I-95 north to Bangor, ME; continue east on Route 1A to Ellsworth and then east on Route 1 to Whiting Village. Take Route 189 to Lubec and cross the International Bridge to Campobello Island.

The 2800 acre park signifies the close relationship between Canada and the U.S. Here are the cottage, the grounds, and the waters where President Franklin D. Roosevelt vacationed. The Park was established under an agreement signed by President Lyndon Johnson and Prime Minister Lester Pearson on January 22, 1964 and officially opened on August 20, 1964. The Park is administered by a joint U.S./Canadian Commission, funded equally by the two countries.

1265. *SunSweep* (1985) (mem).

Roosevelt Campobello International Park, NB.

A slab of Canadian black granite laser etched with a line of a woman's hand with circles symbolizing the sun radiating outward, one of three similar sculptures along the U.S./Canadian border, the others at Point Roberts, Washington, and American Point Island, Lake-of-the-Woods, Minnesota, an international art project spanning 2778 miles. All three were carved from one slab of Canadian black granite. In order to experience each site, the viewer must pass through both countries, to dramatize the friendship of the two countries. A gift of the artist David Barr. Explanatory pamphlet available from the Park Commission.

—— *Newfoundland* —— *(NF)*

MOUNT PEARL, NF

1266. *Mount Pearl Bahá'í Peace Garden* (1981, rededicated 1988) (mem).

P.O. Box 781, Mount Pearl,
NF A1N 2Y2; (709) 747-1263;
jeanine.hayes@excite.com

Located near a soccer/tennis complex. In 1988 the Bahá'ís expanded the garden to 14 feet by 6 feet and dedicated it to world peace, as stated on the accompanying plaque. The City now assists in the cost of plantings and maintenance. Contact Jeannine Hayes.

ST. JOHN'S, NF

1267. **Newfoundland and Labrador Human Rights Association* (1968) (org).

155 Water St., Suite 206;
PO Box 6203, St. John's A1C 6J9;
(709) 754-0690; (709) 754-0690;
nlhra@nf.sympatico.ca;
http://calvin.stemnet.nf.ca/nlhra/po.htm

NLHRA promotes "respect for and observance of Human Rights as indicated in the Universal Declaration of Human Rights; the Constitution and Charter of Rights and Freedoms; the Canadian Human Rights Act; and the Newfoundland Human Rights Code" and in related conventions and covenants. Develops educational programs and activities to expand awareness of human rights, monitors legislation, provides training, and similar activities. Jerry Vink, Exec. Dir.

——— *Northwest* ———
Territories (NT)

KEELE RIVER, NT

1268. *Call to the Mountain Dene* (1990) (mem).

Near the head of the Keele River, five miles downriver from the junction of the Keele and the Natla Rivers, inaccessible by road. The closest community is Deline (formerly Fort Norman), which is 200 kilometers away as the crow flies.

This plaque gives an account of the negotiation of Treaty 11 in 1921 on behalf of the native people who traded at Fort Norman, Chief Albert Wright's long journey up the Keele river to notify the Mountain Dene to meet at Fort Norman for the treaty, and their subsequent residence east of the continental divide.

— *Nova Scotia (NS)* —

BEDFORD, NS

1269. **Bahá'í Council of the Atlantic Provinces* (1997) (org).

PO Box 48135, Bedford NS B4A 3Z2; (902) 857-2067; *scallion@fox.nstn.ca*

First formation of a Spiritual Assembly in the Atlantic provinces was in Moncton, NB, in 1938. The Council operates workshops and youth projects, and sends travelers throughout the region. Lena Scallion, Secretary.

CLEMENTSPORT, NS

1270. **Pearson Peacekeeping Centre* (1994) (org).

Cornwallis Park, PO Box 100, Clementsport, NS B0S 1E0; (212) 460-1500; *registrar@ppc.cdnpeacekeeping.ns.ca; www.cdnpeacekeeping.ns.ca*

The PPC supports and enhances Canada's contribution to international peace, security, and stability by teaching the concepts of "the New Peacekeeping Partnership." The Center was named in honor of Lester B. Pearson, former Prime Minister of Canada who invented peacekeeping at the time of the 1956 Suez Crisis, for which he was awarded the 1957 Nobel Peace Prize. The Center offers a wide range of peacekeeping programs; its library facilitates studies on all aspects of the New Peacekeeping partnership. Memorial Hall is dedicated to all Canadian peacekeepers who have died in that service, and a plaque lists their names. Pub. *Peacekeeping and International Relations* bimonthly (its Jan.-Feb. number included articles on interventions, Angola, Haiti, Cambodia, Kosovo, book reviews, and a map of UN peacekeeping operations). Alex Morrison, Pres. (902-638-8040; *president@ppc.cdnpeacekeeping.ns.ca)*.

DARTMOUTH, NS

1271. *World Peace Pavilion* (1995) (mem, mus).

Dartmouth (across the harbor from Halifax), at the Ferry Terminal Park; (902) 435-9221; *alva@dbis.ns.ca*

The concept of a testament to peace began in 1989 when a group of youth, the Metro Youth for Global Unity, held a Unity Conference. They decided to write the countries of the world requesting a symbolic rock, to represent the Earth we all share, and a brick, to represent our efforts to shape our future. The Local Council donated land and money, and the G7 Summit was chosen as the time to build the facility. A design contest was held, and the winner was based on a pyramid: the equilateral triangle base is a symbol of equality and unity. The Pavilion is constructed of the rocks and bricks sent by most of the world's countries (including a chunk of the Great Wall of China, some remains of the Berlin Wall, gems from Uruguay, a plate from Ecuador, and a plaque from Slovakia specially commissioned). The top was left open to the stars. The exhibits, ordered geographically starting with Canada, are placed in a unifying ribbon of Nova Scotia sand facing towards the harbor. Within the facility is an amphitheater for individual reflection or educational purposes. Over the exhibits are the words: "Let Your Vision Be World-Embracing," from Bahá'í writings. The

World Peace Pavilion, Dartmouth. Photograph courtesy Sandra Taylor.

Pavilion is now under the stewardship of the Dartmouth Bahá'í Community. Above all, the Pavilion is an example of what children and youth can do for world peace. Contact Ms. Alva Robinson, World Peace Pavilion Stewardship Committee Chair.

HALIFAX, NS

1272. *Negotiation and Conflict Management Programme* (1996) (col).

Henson College, Dalhousie Univ., Halifax, NS B3H 3J5; (902) 494-1683; *conflict.management@dal.ca; www.dal.ca/~henson/ncmp.htm*

A certificate for professionals requiring 90 hours of training. NCMP also provides special training, workshops, and consultancy. Lloyd Fraser, Dir.; Grant MacDonald, Acting Dir. 1999-2000.

1273. *Peace and Conflict Studies (PAX)* (1996) (col).

Mount Saint Vincent Univ., Halifax, NS B3M 2J6; *sue.mcgregor@msvu.can; www.msvu.ca/pax*

Offers an undergraduate major and minor of core and elective courses. Affil with The Sisters of Charity. Sue McGregor, Coord.

—— *Ontario (ON)* ——

38 Peace Poles.

CHATHAM, ON

1274. *St. Agnes School Peace Garden* (1996) (mem).

55 Croydon St., Chatham, N7L 1L5; (519) 354-0530; *kearnsla@kentrc.on.ca;*

larrkear@enoreo.on.ca;
www.kentrc.on.ca/st.agnes2

Part of the school yard is a garden, wildlife habitat, land lab for active learning about the environment, a stage for performance by musicians and storytellers, for friends, group work, breaks, classes, and a link to other peace gardens to encourage peace in Canada and abroad. "School Peace Gardens invite young people to dedicate, maintain, and nurture the peace garden as a symbol of hope for the future." Packet of information available from Larry Kearns, including his essay, "Nurturing the Growth of Peace."

This garden is part of the International School Peace Gardens program sponsored by the International Holistic Tourism Education Centre, *www.geocities.com/rainforest/vines/6016;* also see the Ontario Parks Association's website: *www.opassoc.on.ca*

DUNDAS, ON

1275. **Mundialized Cities* (1967) (org).

Peace Research Institute (see next entry).

A municipal initiative transforming provincial towns and cities into international/United Nations cities ("mundus" meaning "world") interdependent with other cities around the world. It resembles the Sister Cities program, but whereas an SC is twinned only, the Mundialized city is twinned and flies the United Nations flag. Several Ontario towns are committed to Mundialized principles (Dundas and Hamilton, 1967 and 1968, were the first), and a few in Alberta, BC, and in Japan and France. There is no overall organization, but a conference is held every other year.

1276. **Peace Research Institute—Dundas (PRI-D)* (1976) (org).

25 Dundana Ave., Dundas, ON L9H 4E5; (905) 628-1830; *info@prid.on.ca*

Publishes the *Peace Research Reviews Journal,* 100-page monographs on literature surveys and reports and collections of essays; such as: "Alternatives to War in Sri Lanka," "Aboriginal Dispute Resolution," "Peace Research Since 1984," and "The Spirit of Cooperation." PRI-D also publishes the *Peace Research Abstracts Journal* (1960s-), now a bi-monthly journal of abstracts of articles and books. And it has published a series of books on voting in the UN

General Assembly. Research at the Institute has included the Inter-Nation Tensiometer for the Prevention of War, and a series on the National Patterns in the U.N. Much of the research is published in journals other than their own. Abstracts are invited. The Institute founded the Canadian Peace Research and Education Association. Founded by Dr. Alan Newcombe and Dr. Hanna Newcombe; Hanna Newcombe, Dir. Hanna Newcombe co-edited *United Nations Reform* with Eric Fawcett (1995) and edited the essays, *Hopes and Fears: The Human Future, Science for Peace* and wrote the book *Design for a Better World* (1983). PRI-D has also published four volumes of *Interethnic Conflict and Political Change in the Former USSR* in collaboration with Dr. Airat Aklaev and his colleagues in Moscow.

GEORGINA, ON

1277. *Georgina Peace Garden* (1998) (mem).

26557 Civic Centre road, Keswick, ON L4P 3G1; (905) 476-6167; *lsmith@interhop.net*

In 1997, teacher Shaeron Aldridge started a Peacemakers club for children at the elementary school, with the motto: "World peace begins with me." A local horticulturist, David Hoar, assisted in bringing together the children, Bahá'ís, the local Horticultural Society, and others to create a peace garden. The Town of Georgina joined in by allocating a space in front of the Civic Centre. Local citizens contributed and planted flowers and shrubs. Activities include celebrating the International Day of Peace and Earth Day. Contact David Hoar.

GLOUCESTER, ON

1278. *Gloucester Peace Park* (1989) (mem).

Spiritual Assembly of the Bahá'í is of Gloucester (L'Assemblée spirituelle des Bahá'ís de Gloucester), Box CP 556, Orléans, ON K1C 1S9; *nhansen@magi.com*

A small green space between the sports arena and the police station. Calls attention to the need for unity in the world, in support of World Religion Day, World Day of Peace, and similar events.

Georgina Peace Garden, Keswick. Photograph courtesy David Hoar, John MacLeod.

GUELPH, ON

1279. *Dispute Resolution Program* (1998) (col).

Office of Open Learning, University of Guelph, Guelph, ON N1G 2W1; (519) 824-4120, ext. 4737; *dcastle@open.uoguelph.ca; http://dallas.open.uoguelph.ca/offerings/ offeringstemplate.cfm?courseid=268*

A certificate composed of three courses and an optional internship. David Castle, Prof. Manager.

HAMILTON, ON

1280. *Centre for Peace Studies* (1989) (org).

McMaster University, 1280 Main St. West, Hamilton, ON L8S 4K1; (905) 525-9140, ext. 24729; *peace@mcmaster.ca; www.mcmaster.ca/peace*

Offers an undergraduate Minor as well as an informal area of concentration at the graduate level. Aims and activities: research in peace and conflict, graduate and undergraduate courses, resource centre, worldwide partnerships, policy recommendations to governmental and non-governmental groups, community initiates and practical involvement in peace-making. Sponsors annual lectureships as well as interdisciplinary research and conferences. Two annual lecture series: The Bertrand Russell Peace Lectures focus on the maintenance of peace based on respect for human rights, democracy, and justice; and The Mahatma Gandhi Lectures on Nonviolence focus on the problems of violence at the local, national, and global level, and on the strategies and values associated with nonviolence. The annual Alan G. Newcombe Prize is awarded to a student who combines high academic achievement in Peace Studies with leadership in extracurricular endeavors. Mark Vorobej, Dir.

1281. *Father's Day Coalition for Peace* (1999) (org).

Ontario Public Interest Research Group (OPIRG), Box 1013, McMaster University,

1280 Main St. West,
Hamilton, ON L8S 1C0;
(905) 627-2696; *grassroots@hwcn.org*

A group of people from the area active in opposing violence to solve human problems, as in
the Gulf conflicts and in Yugoslavia. The name
of the group derived from an air show that emphasized military hardware and advertised as a
Father's Day celebration, which the group opposed, and several members arrested. Contact
Murray Lumley (905) 648-1507 or Randy Kay
(phone and email above).

Behrens, Matthew. "Ontario Activists Champion Homes Not Bombs." *The Nuclear Resister*
(Jan. 11, 2000) 8.

1282. **Hamilton Mundialization
Program* (1968) (org).

c/o Mayor's Office, 71 Main St. W,
Hamilton, ON L8N 3T4;
(416) 546-2700.

The City Council of Hamilton resolved to
foster awareness of the increasing interdependence of all municipalities, peoples, and countries, to encourage and expand twinning and
cultural exchange programs with other cities in
the world, to further the work of the United Nations, and to encourage the development of international law. The city sponsors exchanges of
many kinds (college, musical, hospital, industry);
twinnings with schools, towns, hospitals, businesses; and numerous educational activities promoting international
understanding. The
word "mundialization"
is derived from the
Latin word "mundus"
meaning "world." It is
a symbolic act whereby
the City Council de-
clares its city to be a
"world city" linked to
cities with different
ideologies and cul-
tures, "with the idea
that future peace and
progress are dependent
on cooperation, good-
will, and understand-
ing." The concept was
introduced by Dr. Alan
Newcombe and Dr.
Hanna Newcombe.

KING, ON

1283. **Bahá'í Council of Ontario* (1996)
(org).

PO Box 98, King, ON L7B 1A4;
(905) 833-0894;
wilson-wynen@sympatico.ca

Collaborates with 114 local Spiritual Assemblies in Ontario, works with Bahá'í youth and
children, trains teachers of children's classes,
summer camps. Ann Wilson-Wynen, Secretary.

LONDON, ON

1284. *London Peace Garden* (1987)
(mem).

Intersection of York and Thames streets;
(519) 661-2111, ext. 88567;
pmarcotte@jullian.uw.ca

Dedicated to the principles of freedom, justice, truth, and love, which are represented by
different elements and areas of the garden. It was
built by a large group of volunteer landscapers
and masons. Various activities related to the
UN, human rights, and peace have been held in
the garden ever since its creation. Contact Paula
Marcotte.

London Peace Garden, London. Photograph courtesy John MacLeod.

Spirit of the Earth Centre, London. Photograph courtesy Walter Kacera.

1285. *Spirit of the Earth Centre & Collective Community* (1983) (porg).

5871 Bells Rd., London, ON N6P 1P3; (519) 652-0230.

Offers a full year schedule of courses, meetings, and retreats. A *Peace Pole* is in the center of their Peace Garden. Walter Kacera, Director.

MERRICKVILLE, ON

1286. *Sustainability Project* (1985) (org).

PO Box 374, Merrickville, ON K0G 1NO; (613) 269-3500; *sustain@web.net; www.cyberus.ca/choose.sustain*

Teaches ways to develop a society harmonious in itself and with the Earth. Originally the Institute for the Study of Cultural Evolution (1971). Two main programs: "Question of Direction" economic expansion vs. sustainability) and "Measuring Well-Being" (qualitative measures in contrast to the GDP). Diverse pubs.: *Change the World I Want to Stay On* (1977), *Planning for Seven Generations* (1993), pamphlets (see

web page), discussion kit and guide. Mike Nickerson, Exec. Dir.

MISSISSAUGA, ON

1287. *International Holistic Tourism Education Centre (IHTEC)* (1994) (org).

3343 Masthead Crescent, Mississauga, ON L5L 1G9; (905) 820-5067; *julia@ihtec.on.ca; www.ihtec.on.ca*

Dedicated "to developing programs that educate young people through tourism as a force for peace." Sponsors several programs—Watershed Peace Pathways, for example—and the main one: the International School Peace Gardens (next entry). Recent IHTEC activities: accentuating September 14, the UN International Day of Peace; a brochure for the UN International Year for the Culture of Peace; dedication of Bedford Parkette Peace Garden at OISE/UT in Toronto; coordinating school twinning between schools in Canada and several African nations; attending UNESCO Culture of Peace

Committee in Toronto; many more. Julia Morton-Marr, founder and president.

1288. *International School Peace Gardens (ISPG)* (1994) (org).

International Holistic Tourism Education Centre (IHTEC), 3343 Masthead Crescent, Mississauga, ON L5L 1G9; (905) 820-5067; *www.pathcom.com/~ihtec/ispgfaqabout.htm*

ISPG "develops peace building curriculum and educational programs using Peace Parks and Gardens as strategies" to invoke thoughts and actions of peace and a sustainable planet. The concept of a Peace Garden derived from ancient traditions of resolving conflicts in a Peace Grove, a "Bosco Sacro." In 1992 Louis D'Amore, founder of the International Institute for Peace Through Tourism, launched "Peace Parks Across Canada," resulting in over 400 peace parks. Out of D'Amore's initiative arose the ISPG, its first garden at West Humber Collegiate Institute in Etobicoke, ON, in 1993; since then many gardens and parks have been dedicated. Founder and President: Julia Morton-Marr. (See St. Agnes Peace Garden, Chatham, ON).

1289. *Peace Grove* (1995) (mem).

Erindal Park, Mississauga.

As part of the UN's 50th Anniversary, young people of many associations and faiths held a "Spirit of the Earth Peace Grove Dedication" ceremony. Trees were donated by the city.

NEWMARKET, ON

1290. *Newmarket Peace Grove* (1992) (mem).

North end of Cane Parkway, south end of Fairy Lake, Newmarket; (905) 830-1585; *lsanewmarket@home.com*

A circle of 12 trees with a bench and flagpole in the center. A plaque reads: "We believe that World Peace is inevitable," and lists the names of the donors. Originated by the Bahá'ís, with contributions from the public, and the city contributed the land, machinery, and labor. Each year on the United Nations Day of Peace (3rd Tuesday in September) the public gathers for prayers. Contact Carol Plummer.

OTTAWA, ON

1291. *Campaign for Nuclear Phaseout/Campagne contre l'expansion du nucléaire* (1989) (org).

1 Nicholas St., Suite 412, Ottawa, ON K1N 7B7; (613) 789-3634; *cnp@web.net; www.cnp.ca*

Seeks to educate the public and decision-makers about issues relating to nuclear power and uranium mining. Pubs. include: *Atomic Atlas: Map and Overview* and *Nuclear Sunset: The Economic Costs of the Canadian Nuclear Industry.*

1292. *Canadian Institute for Conflict Resolution* (1988) (col).

223 Main St., St. Paul Univ., Ottawa, ON K1S 1C4; (613) 235-5800; *cicr@ustpaul.uottawa.ca*

Dedicated to fostering the resolution process through "common sense, compassion, and spirituality," within the field of Community-Based Conflict Resolution with its Third Party Neutral training. Offers a Certification Program for nonviolent, third-party conflict management. More advanced training available. Robert Birt, Founder and past Pres.; Vern Redekop, Pres.

1293. *Canadian International Institute of Applied Negotiation/L'Institut International Canadien de la Négociation Pratique* (1992) (org).

Suite 701, 200 Elgin St., Ottawa, K2P 1L5; (613) 237-9050; *conciian@intranet.ca; www.canadr.com*

CIIAN is dedicated to professional training in negotiation, dispute resolution, and consensus building and to developing Canadian capability in conflict resolution internationally. Grants a Program Certificate in Alternative Dispute Resolution. Pub. *CIIAN News* newsletter.

1294. *Canadian Network to Abolish Nuclear Weapons* (1996) (org).

c/o Physicians for Global Survival, 145 Spruce St., Suite 208, Ottawa K1R 6P1; (613) 233-1982; *http://watserv1.uwaterloo.ca/~plough/cnanw/cnanw.html*

Established to coordinate Canadian efforts to abolish nuclear weapons in cooperation with the global Abolition 2000 campaign. The CNANW functions as a forum for information-sharing and cooperation among groups and individuals working for abolition, and not as a separate organization itself. The activities of the network are coordinated by the Contact Group, composed of approximately a dozen Canadian peace groups. Any organization or individual who agrees to support an international agreement to establish a timetable for the abolition of nuclear weapons can become a member of the Network. Anyone may subscribe to the network's discussion list by sending e-mail to *majordomo@wat serv1.uwaterloo.ca* with only the message "subscribe abolition <subscriber's e-mail address>" in the body of the text.

1295. *Canadian Peacebuilding Coordinating Committee/Comité Coordonnateur Canadien pour la Consolidation de la Paix* (1994) (org).

1, rue Nicholas St., #510, Ottawa, ON K1N 7B7; (613) 241-3446; *cpcc@web.net; www.cpcc.ottawa.on.ca*

Formerly the Ad Hoc Working Group on NGOs and Peacebuilding, CPCC is a network of Canadian NGOs, NGIs, academics, and other individuals striving to develop national policies toward cooperative solutions to conflicts for a future global community. Among its present focuses: children and armed conflict, gender and peacemaking, small arms.

1296. *Coalition to Oppose the Arms Trade* (1989) (org).

541 McLeod St., Ottawa, ON K1R 5R2; (613) 231-3076); *ad207@ncf.ca; www.ncf.ca/coat*

Pub. *Press for Conversion* quarterly, ed. by Richard Sanders (the Sept. 1999 number include articles on Yugoslavia—U.S war budget increase, etc., Iraq—depleted uranium, etc., Indonesia, and Canada) Offers a video documentary, "Mothers' Day at the War Show," about U.S. air shows, militarism, violence, and bombing Iraq.

1297. *CUSO* (1961) (org).

400-2255 Carling Ave., Ottawa, ON K2B 1A6; *renee.sylvester@cuso.ca*

Assists people in working in the developing world for self-determination, gender and racial

equality, and cultural survival, by sharing information, providing resources, and promoting policies advantageous to global sustainability. Supported by the Canadian International Development Agency and private donations. Exec. Dir.: Melanie Macdonald.

1298. *Friends of the Earth/Les Ami(e)s de la Terre* (1978) (org).

260 St. Patrick St., Suite 206, Ottawa, ON K1N 5K5; (613) 241-0085; *foe@intranet.ca; www.foecanada.org*

A voice for the environment, nationally and internationally, to inspire renewal of communities and the earth, through research, education, and advocacy. Current campaigns include: clean air, climate change, green electricity, and ozone. Beatrice Olivastri, Chief. Exec. Officer.

1299. *Human Rights Research and Education Centre* (1981) (col).

University of Ottawa, 57 Louis-Pasteur St., Ottawa, ON K1N 6N5; (613) 562-5775/5800; *hrrec@uottawa.ca; www.uottawa.ca/hrrec/index.html*

A research and educational institution for the promotion of human rights and social justice, providing a documentation center with large bilingual database. "The first university-based human rights center of its kind in Canada." Pub. *Human Rights Research and Education Bulletin* and other writings. Contact Errel Mendes.

1300. *The Mediation Centre* (1992) (col).

Room A824, Loeb Bldng., Carleton University, Ottawa, ON K15 5B6; *rramkay@ccs.carleton.ca; www.ncf. carleton.ca/freenet/rootdir/menus/prof.assoc/ mediation/about.txt*

Offers mediation services, public education, consultation, training, and research for the university and community. Rena Ramkay, Coord.

1301. *Mines Action Canada* (1995) (org).

1210-1 Nicholas St., Ottawa, ON K1N 7B7; (613) 241-3777; *macelina@web.net; www.minesactioncanada.com*

A coalition of 45+ Canadian NGOs working to ban anti-personnel landmines.

National Peacekeeping Monument, Ottawa. Photograph courtesy Gallery 101.

1302. *National Peacekeeping Monument* (1992) (mem).

In the Capital Core Area and the ceremonial route known as Confederation Boulevard, Ottawa; occupying a traffic island west of Sussex Drive, between St. Patrick and Murray Streets and between the new U.S. Embassy and the National Gallery of Canada.

The Monument is composed of a circle and a triangle. The circular part, called the Peace Grove, consists of a mound of grass-covered earth surrounded by twelve oak trees and a curved wall of piled stones. An inscription inside the wall reads: "Their name liveth for evermore," designating a memorial or cenotaph. Where the two converging, twenty-feet high walls of the triangle or vectoral section meet rise three ten-feet high bronze statues of peacekeepers on guard duty. In the back section of the vector lie an area of rubble suggesting a war-torn landscape. On the outer northern wall are one hundred plaques that declare past UN assignments. The impetus for its construction came from the awarding of the 1988 Nobel peace prize to the United Nations for its forty-year record of international peacekeeping. Having participated in virtually all UN peacekeeping missions, Canada was made the official recipient. The monument also honors Lester B. Pearson, who received the same prize in 1957 for proposing peacekeeping forces to the UN. The Monument was designed by Cornelia Oberlander (landscape architect), Jack Harman (sculptor), and Richard Henriquez (urban designer and architect).

Léger, Marc James. "Touring the Ideological Landscape: Ottawa's Peacekeeping Monument." *Driving the Ceremonial Landscape.* Ottawa: Gallery 101, 1996.

1303. **Norman Paterson School of International Affairs* (1965) (org).

Carleton University, 1125 Colonel By Drive, Ottawa, ON K1S 5B6; (613) 520-2600, ext. 6667; *vivian_cummins@carleton.ca*

The graduate M.A. program includes a course of studies on conflict analysis.

1304. **Peace and Environment Resource Centre* (1982) (org).

174 First Ave. (corner of Bank), PO Box 4075, Station E, Ottawa, ON K1S 5B1;

(613) 230-4590; *perc@flora.org;*
www.perc.flora.org;
www.waste-line.flora.org

Organizes environmental and peace workshops, referral and resources services. Pub. *Peace
and Environment News* (*pen-editor@perc.flora.
org*). Contact Mike Kaulbars (dq430@freenet.
carleton.ca).

1305. **Peacefund Canada/Fond Canadien
Pour La Paix* (1985) (org).

145 Spruce, Suite 206, Ottawa, ON K1R
6P1; (613) 230-0860; *pfcan@web.apc.org;*
www.web.net/~pfcan

Works through adult education and supporting adult peace educators to build a more humane, nonviolent and de-militarized world. Al-
locates the majority of its funds in project grants
to initiatives for peace, more than half of which
in 1997 were made to people seeking to de-mil-
itarize the communities and regions in which
they live. Publishes an annual report and newsletter; gives annual Honour Awards to individuals and organizations for advancing peace and
social justice. In the fall of 1999 Peacefund initiated a Program on Nonviolence to promote
the Hague Agenda for Peace, in particular Article 9 on nonviolence, to participate in the
global movement to abolish nuclear weapons,
and to encourage long term alternative, nonviolent security systems to replace the current mil-
itary-based systems. Founded by Murray Thompson. Sponsored by the International Council for
Adult Education

1306. **Physicians for Global Survival
Canada/Médecins pour la Survie
Mondial* (1980) (org).

208-145 Spruce St., Suite 208,
Ottawa, ON K1R 6P1; (613) 233-1982;
pgs@web.net; www.pgs.ca

Originally Physicians for Social Responsibility, then Canadian Physicians for Prevention of
Nuclear War, and now PGS (1994). PGS strives
to abolish nuclear weapons, prevent wars, and
promote nonviolence and social justice in a sustainable world. Supports Abolition 2000, and
worked for the decision by the International
Court of Justice that nuclear weapons are illegal under international law; seeks the elimination of landmines; opposes the arms trades.
Turning Point magazine. Debbie Grisdale, Exec.
Dir. Dr. Barbara Birkett, Pres.

1307. **United Nations Association in
Canada* (1946) (org).

900-130 Slater St.,
Ottawa, ON K1P 6E2; (613) 233-1982;
info@unac.org; www.unac.org

Emerging out of a similar League of Nations
Society, the UNAC has some 15 branches and
15,000 members/supporters.

1308. **Women's International League for
Peace and Freedom (WILPF),
Ottawa Branch* (1970s) (org).

PO Box 4781, Sta E, Ottawa, ON K1S
5H9; (819) 647-3920; (613) 634-3403;
mholyk@kos.net

Women in Canada working to obtain world
peace via campaigns on disarmament and human
rights. Pub. *The Canadian Women's Budget* (1993),
WILPF News irregular newsletter. Marcy Holyk,
Pres.

1309. **World Federalists of Canada/
Mouvement canadien pour une
Fédération mondiale* (1961) (org).

Suite 207, 145 Spruce St., Ottawa,
ON K1R 6P1; (613) 232-0647;
wfcnat@pop.web.net;
www.web.net/~wfcnat/WFC

Founded 1947 in Montreux, Switzerland; first
national Canadian meeting 1961; incorporated
1965. WFC seeks "to develop the democratic
world institutions of law by which the world's
people and nations can govern their relations to
assure a peaceful, just, and ecologically sustainable world community." Activities include working as convenors of two NGO networks: the
Canadian Network for an International Criminal Court and the Canadian Network for the
Hague Appeal for Peace; and monitoring a
range of UN issues. WFC is now pushing for
the ICC treaty to come into force more quickly.
Pub.: quarterly journal *Mondial* and special
Briefing Papers on a range of global governance
issues. Fergus Watt, Exec. Dir.

PERTH, ON

1310. *Family Pastimes (1972) (porg).

RR 4, Perth, ON K7H 3C6;
(613) 267-4819; *fp@superaje.com;*
www.familypastimes.com

This company makes and sells cooperative games: players help each other climb a mountain, make a community, bring in the harvest, complete a space exploration, etc.

SCARBOROUGH, ON

1311. **PeaceZine* (Sept. 1999) (org).

300 Borough Drive, PO Box 55318,
Scarborough, ON M1P 4Z7;
(416) 439-3381;
ashworth@peacezine.prg;
essays@peacezine.org;
www.peacezine.org

An on-line organization dedicated to the promotion of nonviolence and tolerance for world peace by offering an open forum for anecdotes and commentaries from around the world. Also sponsors an essay contest and "The Citizens World Peace Accord" to solicit ideas for the compilation of principles of world peace. Adam Ashworth, Publisher.

1312. *United Nations Peace Water Garden* (1996) (mem).

Adjacent to the Bladen Library,
University of Toronto at Scarborough,
greater Toronto area.

A bog and pond to teach students about the environment and responsibility for the ecosphere.

STOUFFVILLE, ON

1313. *Stouffville Peace Park* (1992) (mem).

c/o Town of Whitchurch-Stouffville,
19 Civic Ave., Box 419,
Stouffville, ON L4A 7Z6;
(514) 271-2709 or
(905) 640-1900 ext. 290;
stanphillips@
compuserve.com;
wsparks@interlogs.com

A grove of 12 Empress Queen maples representing each of Canada's provinces and territories was planted in the Peace Park, which is situated in a conservation area surrounding a

Stouffville Peace Park, Stouffville. Photograph courtesy John MacLeod.

reservoir. Created to celebrate Canada's 125th birthday and the country's Peacekeeping duties for the U.N., and to provide a place for youth and community activities. Originating the Park was Casey Van Meer and the Bahá'í Community of Stouffville and Louis D'Amore and the International Institute for Peace through Tourism. Community organizations which contributed the money became "Fellowship of the Trees." Stouffville joined 400 other communities in dedicating peace parks or plantings for the occasion. Designed by Parkland Nurseries, Casey Van Meer, and the Bahá'í Community. Contact Stan Phillips or Kelly Batte.

SUDBURY, ON

1314. **Alternative Dispute Resolution* (col).

Center for Continuing Education,
Laurentian University, Sudbury.

Undergraduate and graduate certificates in mediation, arbitration, negotiation as alternatives to litigation. Gerry Spencer, Prog. Manager.

1315. *Wanup Public School Peace Pole/Garden* (1999) (mem).

The dedication ceremony involved students, staff, and community, included addresses, a song by the Peace Choir (grades 1–8), "Song of the Earth," and all singing "Hands United in Peace."

National Center of the Bahá'í Community of Canada, Thornhill. Photograph courtesy John MacLeod.

THORNHILL, ON

1316. *National Centre of the Bahá'í Community of Canada* (1948) (org).

7200 Leslie St., Thornhill, ON L3T 6L8; (905) 889-8168; *externalaffairs@cdnbnc.org; www.ca.bahai.org*

Like all Bahá'í centers, this one is dedicated to constructive social processes leading to world harmony by providing a model of equitable and just relationships. The Bahá'í communities support social and economic programs around the world and in every province and territory in Canada. Pub. *One Country*. Judy Filson, Secretary General.

1317. *Peace Garden* (1998) (mem).

Johnsview Village Public School, 41 Porterfield Cres., Thornhill, ON L3T 5C3.

A garden of trees, flowers (mostly native perennials planted by the students), a bridge, and composters, where classes and musical presentations can be held, and a place for lunch and recess, or a Tai Chi class. Contact Principal D.

Smith (905) 881-3360 or Robyn Craig (905-881-4225; *robyncraig@home.com*).

THUNDER BAY, ON

1318. *International Friendship Garden* (1965/1993) (mem).

Victoria Ave. between Tarbutt and Waterloo Streets, Thunder Bay, ON.

Initiated by Soroptimist International of Thunder Bay and created by Canadians of varied ethnic origins as a Centennial gift to Canada and the community, the eighteen individual gardens were planned, designed, constructed, and financed by the respective groups. The gardens surround two artificial lakes. Entrance to the Garden is through archways installed by the Soroptimist International of Thunder Bay. The nations represented around Reflection Lake (Stage I of the development): Canada, Holland, Finland, Slovakia, Lithuania, Germany, Hungary, Poland, and the Ukraine; nations around Soroptimist Lake (Stage 2): Slovenia, Scotland, China, Greece, Croatia, Portugal, Philippines, India. Contact Enid Mckenzie (648 Riverview Dr., Thunder Bay, ON P7E 3M8). See entry 996.

International Friendship Garden, Soroptimist International, Thunder Bay. Photographs courtesy Enid McKenzie.

Frim, Rose. *International Friendship Garden: Centennial Project of Soroptimist International of Thunder Bay.* Ed. Gladys Neale. Thunder Bay, Ontario: Soroptimist International of Thunder Bay, 1998.

TORONTO, ON

1319. **Amnesty International, Toronto Office* (1982) (org).

56 Temperance St., 8th Fl., Toronto, ON M5S 3V5; (416) 929-9477; *toronto@amnesty.ca*

National office in Vanier, ON.

1320. **Canadian Friends Service Committee* (1931) (org).

60 Lowther Ave., Toronto, ON M5R 1C7; (416) 920-5213.

CFSC acts on the peace and social justice concerns of the Religious Society of Friends (Quakers) in Canada. For example, in WWII it organized an Ambulance Unit at the Chinese frontier; in the 1960s it provided aid to victims of both sides of the Vietnam War; in 1998 it co-sponsored a conference in Cuba on sustainable development; now it is supporting rehabilitation for landmine amputees in Cambodia; in Mexico and other countries it promotes organic agriculture. Pub.: *Quaker Concern* quarterly newsletter.

1321. **Canadian Peace Alliance/ L'Alliance canadienne pour la paix* (1985) (org).

555 Bloor St. W, Suite 5, Toronto M5S 1Y6; (416) 588-555; *cpa@web.net*; *www.acp-cpa.ca*

"Canada's largest grassroots umbrella peace organization," CPA promotes concerted action in opposing wars, cutting the military budget and redirecting moneys to social needs, commissioning public opinion polls on such issues as nuclear weapons and military spending, campaigning against a nuclear submarine program and attack helicopters, and many other issues. CPA is a member of the Canadian Network to Abolish Nuclear Weapons. Tryna Booth, coordinator.

1322. *Certificate Program in Dispute Resolution* (col).

Division of Continuing Education, York Univ., 4700 Keele St., Toronto, ON M3J 1P3; (416) 736-5616; *dce@yorku.ca; www.atkinson.yorku.ca/~dce/dispute1/ dispute2.html*

A certificate for both professionals and beginners, both courses and skill practice. Desmond Ellis, Prog. Coord.

1323. *Coalition for Gun Control* (1990) (org).

PO Box 395, Sta. D, Toronto, ON M6P 1H9; (416) 604-0209; *71417.763@compuserve.com; www.guncontrol.ca*

Founded in the wake of the Montréal massacre, CGC works to reduce gun deaths, injuries, and crime in Canada. It has been credited for the passage of two pieces of legislation (Bill C-17 in 1991 and C-68 in 1995). Pubs: several articles in journals; for example, "Firearms and Small Arms Control," *Peace Magazine* (March-April 1998). Chantale Breton, Exec. Dir.; Wendy Cukier, Pres.

1324. *Greenpeace Canada* (1971) (org).

250 Dundas St. West, Suite 605, Toronto, ON M5T 2Z5; (416) 597-8408; *greenpeace.toronto@green2.greenpeace.org; www.greenpeacecanada.org*

Greenpeace originated in Vancouver, Canada, with the intention to create a green and peaceful world, and motivated specifically by U.S., atmospheric nuclear tests on Amchitka island off the west coast of Alaska. A small group set sail from Vancouver to try to stop the tests, which were eventually halted in 1972. Amchitka is now a bird sanctuary. Today, Greenpeace has offices in over 30 countries with some three million members worldwide. The organization is best known for nonviolent direct actions which bring public opinion to bear on decision makers. But it also conducts research and lobbies for change. For example, Greenpeace took the lead in developing an ozone-safe refrigerator. It is credited with international treaties and conventions of the U.N. and other bodies on such issues as toxic waste, climate change, and endangered species. Many publications. Tracy Frauzel, Information Office, (*tracy.frauzel@dialb.greenpeace.org*)

1325. *Homes Not Bombs* (1998) (org).

509 St. Clair Ave. West, PO Box 73620, Toronto, ON M6C 1C0; (416) 651-5800; *tasc@web.net*

Calls for an end to excessive spending on the corporate greed/military budget ($11 billion) in order to build affordable homes, daycare, and other social programs. The War Department should be changed to the Housing Department. Works through education, lobbying, vigils, street theater, and civil resistance. Pub. bimonthly newsletter, *The Long Arc.*

1326. *International Association of Educators for World Peace, Canada* (1969) (org).

2 Bloor St. West, Suite 100-209, Toronto, ON M2W 3E2; (416) 924-4449; *mgold@homeplanet.org; www.homeplanet.org/*iaewp

Teachers, students, and administrators united to achieve world peace through education. Especially promotes UNESCO and seeks to implement the UN Universal Declaration of Human Rights. Also pursues the question of the qualities of an International Peace 2000 City. Contact Mitchell Gold.

1327. *International Peace City 2000 Project* (1997) (org).

2 Bloor St., West Ste 100-209, Toronto, ON M4W 3E2; *www.homeplanet.org/ events/ipcproject01.htm*

To create a vehicle of social change through the mayors' office and the International Association of Educators for World Peace. Officially launched at the United Nations Peace Day, September 16, 1997.

1328. *Peace and Conflict Studies Program* (1985) (col).

University of Toronto, Univ. College,

Toronto, ON M5S 3H7; (416) 978-8148;
pcs.program@utoronto.ca;
www.library.utoronto.ca/pcs.htm

Offers a major and a specialist concentration covering three perspectives: strategic, conflict, and peace. Thomas Homer-Dixon, Dir.

1329. **Peace Brigades International, Canada* (1981) (org).

427 Bloor St. West, Suite 201,
Toronto, ON M5S 1X7;
(416) 324-9737; *pbican@web.net;*
www.ncf.carleton.ca/pbi/

PBI sends teams by invitation into areas of political repression and conflict to provide accompaniment for human rights and democracy activists who have been threatened by political violence. In early 1999 PBI had projects in Guatemala, Colombia, Haiti, Chiapas, and the Balkans, at present also in East Timor. Pub.: *PBI Monthly Project Bulletin*, country reports. Dir.: Charles Levkoe. International Secretariat: 5 Caledonian Road, London N1 9DX, UK; (*pbiio@gn.apc.org*).

1330. *Peace Garden* (1984) (mem).

Nathan Phillips Square, facing the City Hall, Toronto.

A green island surrounded by the paving of the plaza; in its center a simple, unfinished structure with four doorways. Designed by the Urban Design Group of the City of Toronto.

Greenberg, Kenneth. "Peace Garden in City Hall Square, Toronto, Canada." *Places for Peace.* Ed. Karl Linn and Carl Anthony. Boston: IADPPNW/ADPSR, 1988.

1331. **Peace Magazine* (tabloid 1983, magazine 1985) (jour).

736 Bathurst St., Box 248, Sta. P,
Toronto, ON M5S 2R4;
(416) 533-7581(bus) or 789-2294 (ed);
mspencer@web.net; www.peacemagazine.org

On the masthead: "...favors multilateral disarmament and within that broad context takes no editorial position." Thus PM provides an open forum for discussion of issues related to peace, disarmament, and conflict resolution. The Fall 1999 issue includes articles on human

Peace Garden, City Hall, Toronto. Photograph courtesy John MacLeod.

security, democracy, and East Timor (see web site for contents of back issues—soft power, culture of peace, international justice, etc.). Metta Spencer, Editor.

1332. *Science for Peace* (1981) (org).

Rm H-02, 15 King's College Circle,
University College, Univ. of Toronto,
ON M5S 3H7; (416) 978-3606;
sfp@physics.utoronto.ca;
www.math.yorku.ca/sfp/

Organization of natural and social scientists, engineers, scholars in humanities, and lay people seeking to advance peace, justice, and an environmentally sustainable future. Recent activities: opposition to nuclear testing, proposing better ethical code for scientific research, public lectures, exhibiting *Hiroshima-Nagasaki: Fifty Years of Deceit and Self-Deception* (duplicity of Allied governments over decision to drop the atomic bomb on Hiroshima and Nagasaki). Newsletter *Science for People*, ed. Eric Fawcett (fawcett@physics.utoronto.ca). Carolyn Langdon, Exec. Dir.; Mel Watkins, Pres. (416-406-2486); Eric Fawcett, Founding President.

1333. *Shriner's Peace Memorial* (1930) (mem).

In Exposition Park, 2 Strachan Ave., west of the Better Living Centre, Toronto, facing Lake Ontario.

The bronze statue of a winged female figure, the Goddess of Peace, is 25 feet high and faces the Niagara River, which forms part of the Canada-U.S. border. She stands on the world and holds aloft an olive branch in each hand. The globe rests on two sphinxes, who in turn rest on a bronze disk. This sculpture is encircled first by shrubs and flowers and then by a large fountain and pool of water (added when rededicated in 1958), which is circled by another bed of flowers. A plaque reads: "Erected and Dedicated to the Cause of Universal Peace by the Ancient Order of the Nobles of the Mystic Shrine for North America, June 12, 1930." Behind the statue is a limestone seat which bears the inscription: "Peace be on You—On You be the Peace." In 1989 the monument was again rededicated with the addition of the Shriners' Bell directly south of the monument. The monument commemorates the over 100 years of

Shriner's Peace Memorial Statue by Charles Keck, Niagara River and Lake Ontario, Toronto. Photograph courtesy L.L. Coban, CNE Archives.

peaceful relations between Canada and the U.S. Statue designed by Charles Keck.

1334. *Voice of Women for Peace* (1960) (org).

761 Queen St., West #203,
Toronto, ON M6J 1G1;
(416) 603-7915; *vow@interlog.com;
www.interlog.com/~vow*

Offers a workshop kit for the International Year (and Decade) for the Culture of Peace which explores the dimensions of the culture of peace, our present culture of violence, the sources and hindrances to a culture of peace, how men and women and individuals and groups can promote peace. Facilitators available. Nest Pritchard, Admin. Asst.

1335. *Women's International League for Peace and Freedom (WILPF),* Toronto Branch (1996) (org).

901, 70 Mill St., Toronto, ON M5A 4R1;
(416) 535-6586; *leapfwd@idirect.com;
wilpfto@web.net*

WILPF was founded by Jane Addams to promote peace and freedom for women and children by women. The Toronto branch contributed to the World March Women 2000 in Toronto and runs an anti-violence project called the "Clothesline Project." (Bruna Nota, International President, *wilpfto@web.net;* International Secretariat in Geneva, *wilpf@iprolink.ch).*

TWEED, ON

1336. *Lester B. Pearson Peace Park* (1967) (mem).

On Trans-Canada Highway No. 7,
near Tweed, ON, 120 miles from
Toronto, 110 miles from Ottawa.

Named after Canada's Nobel Peace Prize winner, the park is "founded on the principles of peace, love, and understanding between all peoples of the world." The Park includes the International Peace Column, the Peace Pagoda Shrine, the Vietnamese Pavilion, and the Mothers' Shrine and Tower of Hope. More than a memorial park, the supporting organization, led

by founders Roy and Priscilla Cadwell, has sponsored many peace advocacy events, including an annual poetry contest.

Cadwell, Roy. *25 Years of Peace: History of the Lester B. Pearson Peace Park.* Tweed, ON: Canada Pub. Co., n.d.

UXBRIDGE, ON

1337. *Nuclear Awareness Project* (1979, 1983 current name) (org).

PO Box104, Uxbridge, ON L9P 1M6;
(905) 852-0571; *nucaware@web.net*

Dedicated to educating the public about nuclear weapons proliferation, the links between civilian and military nuclear power, and other nuclear issues. Pub. *Nuclear Awareness News.*

VANIER, ON

1338. *Amnesty International Canadian Section-English Speaking* (1973) (org).

214 Montréal Rd, Suite 401,
Vanier, ON K1L 1A4; (613) 744-7667;
*info@amnesty.ca; aiamnest@web.net;
www.amnesty.ca*

AI is a worldwide voluntary movement that works to prevent violations by governments and groups of people's fundamental civil and political rights. It tries to free all prisoners of conscience, ensure fair and prompt trials for political prisoners, abolish executions, torture, and other cruel treatment of prisoners, and to end political killings and disappearances. AI promotes universal human rights. Bob Goodfellow, Exec. Dir.; Alex Neve, Sec't. General.

WATERLOO, ON

1339. *Institute of Peace and Conflict Studies* (1997) (org).

Conrad Grebel College, Waterloo,
ON N2L 3G6; (519) 885-0220, Ext. 254
or 380; *lmewert@uwaterloo.ca;
http://watserv1.uwaterloo.ca/~congreb*

The IPACS program at Conrad Grebel in co-operation with the University of Waterloo explores the origins of conflict and violence and ways to manage and utilize them, peace, war, nonviolence, mediation, human rights, social justice and related topics. Offers internships and a Certificate in Conflict Management, which provides practical skills for dealing with day-to-day conflict. Lowell Ewert, Dir.

1340. *The Network: Interaction for Conflict Resolution* (1985) (org).

Institute of Peace and Conflict Studies,
Conrad Grebel College,
Waterloo, ON N2L 3G6;
(519) 885-0880;
nicr@nicr.ca; www.nicr.ca

An association of organizations and individuals dedicated to the development of collaborative conflict resolution throughout Canada. Provides resources for expanded applications of conflict management, educates public and officials about conflict resolution, and promotes ethical standards for conflict resolution. Affiliated with IPACS in 1991. Pub. *Interaction* quarterly and *Peacebuilder Magazine* (for youth and schools), and distributes over 150 books (e.g., *Peace: Perspectives on Peace and Conflict*, on global conflicts, militarism, teaching skills). Sponsors The Canadian Conflict Resolution Directory On-line; NICRBooks, Canada's "largest mail-order bookstore dedicated to providing conflict resolution resources"; and a national conference every two years (Vancouver, June 10-13, 2000). Jennie Kruger, Admin. Coord.

1341. *Project Ploughshares* (1976) (org).

Institute of Peace and Conflict Studies,
Conrad Grebel College,
Waterloo, ON N2L 3G6;
(519) 888-6541, ext. 259;
kepps@ploughshares.ca; www.ploughshares.ca

PP promotes the "concept of 'common security': that security is the product of mutuality, not competition; that peace must be nurtured rather than guarded; that stability requires the reduction of threat and elevation of trust; and that sustainability depends on participatory decision-making rather than on exclusion and control." To accomplish this concept, PP "promotes disarmament and demilitarization, the peaceful resolution of political conflict, and the pursuit of security based on equity, justice, and sustainable environment." PP actively engages these tasks through seminars, publications, and other methods. Pubs.: Ploughshares *Monitor, Armed Conflict Report, Working Papers,* and others. Local branches of Ploughshares all across Canada support its mission. Ken Epps, Program Coordinator.

WINDSOR, ON

1342. *Peace Park and Fountain* (1992) (mem).

Along the Detroit Riverfront between
Thompson Blvd. and Pillette Rd.,
Windsor.

The former Coventry Gardens was designated a Peace Park in celebration of Canada's commitment to world peace and environmental protection. The Park contains terraces of shrubs, trees, and flowers, and a circular patio of terraces resembling "rain drops falling into calm water," designed to harmonize with the *Charlie Brooks Memorial Peace Fountain* located in the Detroit River, which draws over 12,000 gallons of water per minute and propels it over 70 feet in the air. Brooks was a labor leader 1915–1917, and booster of riverfront development. The Fountain cost $562,000 to build, from public subscription matched by the City of Windsor. The Park won the Ontario Parks Association Award of Excellence for its design and development of riverfront parkland in 1977. Former Commissioner of Parks Harry Brumpton conceived the park's layout; Landscape Architect Steve Loader designed it. Richard Van Seters and T. W. Szalay designed the Fountain.

— *Prince Edward* — *Island (PEI)*

CHARLOTTETOWN, PEI

1343. *Peaceful Schools Summer Institute* (1999) (col).

Faculty of Education,
Univ. of Prince Edward Island,

Peace Park and Fountain, Windsor. Photograph courtesy Mayor Michael Hurst.

Charlottetown, PEI C1A, 4P3;
(902) 628-4304; *gpike@upei.ca;*
www.upei.ca/~extensio/

Teachers, administrators, consultants, community groups, and so on during 4 to 5 days explore strategies for nonviolent schools. A certificate is awarded for successful completion. Contact Graham Pike.

– Québec (QC or PQ) –

5 Peace Poles.

BEAUPORT, QC

1344. *Parc de la Paix de Beauport/*
Beauport Peace Park (1989)
(mem).

South part of Beauport between Ave. Royale and Boul. Ste-Anne; 3629 chemin royal, Beauport, QC G1E 1X3;
(418) 692-3955; *aai034@hermes.ulaval.ca*

Created and erected by the Bahá'í Community to commemorate the International Day of Peace 1989 and as a link in the worldwide chain of places dedicated to the establishment of peace. A plaque reads: "Ye are the fruits of one tree, the leaves of one branch, the flowers of one garden." "The well-being of mankind, its peace and security, are unattainable unless and until its unity is firmly established." Baha'u'llah (1817–1892). Designed by John MacLeod. Contact Monique Robert.

CHAMBLY, QC

1345. *Jardin de la paix/Peace Garden*
(1991) (mem).

By the side of the Chambly basin at the back of the public library; Bibliothèque municipale de Chambly, 1691, Bourgogne Ave., Chambly, QC J3L 1Y8.

Dedicated by the City to the peace of the world, a place with trees and shrubs for relaxation, and a natural amphitheater where the city presents open air concerts. Designed by John MacLeod in association with Fontaine Lamontagne et associés.

CHARLESBOURG, QC

1346. *Parc de la Paix de Charlesbourg/ Charlesbourg Peace Park* (1994) (mem).

Place du Foyer (on 70th St. East, near 10th Ave. East); (418) 626-3124; *montmartre@ globetrotter.net*

Dedicated to increasing public awareness of the importance of promoting sustainable, lasting world peace. The Bahá'í community proposed the idea and the City provided the land. The Bahá'ís maintain the site. Contact Raymond Labbé.

Top: **Beauport Peace Park, Beauport. Photograph courtesy Mayor Jacques Langlois, Monique Robert, John MacLeod.** *Bottom:* **Chambly Peace Garden, Chambly. Photograph courtesy Nicole Matton, John MacLeod.**

DRUMMOND-VILLE, QC

1347. *Parc de la Paix de Drummondville/ Drummondville Peace Park* (1995) (mem).

Corner of St. Joseph Blvd. and Cockburn St., 2455 Blvd. Lemire, Drummondville, QC J2B 7X9; (819) 477-1154; *serres-verrier@sympatico.ca.*

The city is gradually developing a park from the plan designed by John MacLeod, Pascal Bauer, and Alessandro Cassa as "a symbol of peace without reference to war. Peace is a noble value to be regarded on the same level as justice and liberty." Each year an element is added to the site: the Pathway, the Peace Tree, the Symbolic Orchard, the Great Spiral; in the future an obelisk sundial, a peace sculpture, the "Wall of Cultures and Nations," and plaques presenting the UN Manifesto 2000 and the UN Declaration of Human Rights. Many events have already been held in the park; for example on September 21, 1999, the International Day of Peace was celebrated with the Director of the Canadian Bureau of UNESCO, Mrs. Ndeye Fall, present. Contact Jean Verrier.

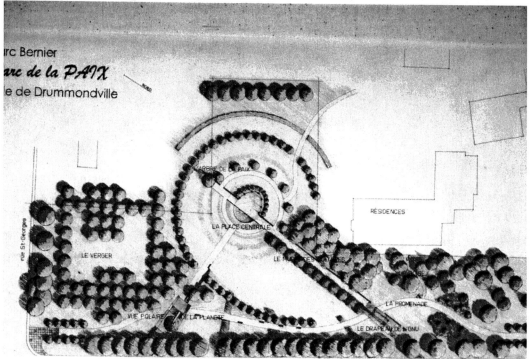

Top: Dedication of a white pine—the "Peace Tree" at Drummondville Peace Park, Drummondville. *Bottom:* Layout of Drummondville Peace Park. Photographs courtesy John MacLeod, André Montambault, Jean Verrier.

Top: Hull Peace and Remembrance Monument: War Never Again, Hull. Photograph courtesy John MacLeod. *Bottom:* Layout for Hull Peace and Remembrance Monument: War Never Again, Hull. Landscape Architect: Denis Massie.

HULL, QC

1348. **Monument à la Paix et au Souvenir à Hull: "Plus jamais la guerre"/Hull Peace and Remembrance Monument: War Never Again* (1992) (mem).

Intersection of Blvd. Saint-Joseph and Blvd. Alexandre-Taché, Hull, QC; (819) 770-5132; *d.massie@sympatico.ca*

Six wall sculptures depict the progress towards the common goal of peace, in three materials (concrete, steel, and granite) in ascending levels symbolizing hope. The monument was erected in homage to all men, women, and children of Hull and the world who have suffered in wars, and it suggests the search for harmony. The monument was a collaboration of the Royal Canadian Legion, Hull Branch, the City of Hull, and the Department of National Defense. Contact Denis Massie.

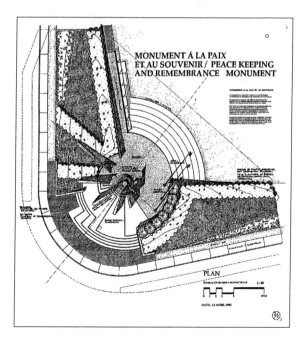

MONUMENT À LA PAIX
ET AU SOUVENIR / PEACE KEEPING
AND REMEMBRANCE MONUMENT

PLAN

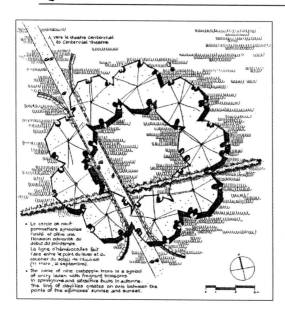

Layout for Peace Garden, Bishop's University, Lennoxville. Landscape Architect: John Mac-Leod.

LENNOXVILLE, QC

1349. *Bishop's University Peace Garden* (1989) (mem).

Conceived by members of the Bahá'í Community of Canada and dedicated to the youth of the world. Maintained by the Bahá'ís of nearby Sherbrooke (Contact Johanne Pichet, 241 Routhier, Sherbrooke, QC, J1J 2W3; 819-823-0094; *efrost@interlinx.qc.ca*) in collaboration with the university grounds department. Designed by John MacLeod.

MONTRÉAL, QC

Montréal became a nuclear weapons free city in 1986.

1350. **Action by Christians Against Torture (ACAT-Canada)* (1984) (org).

4839, rue de Bordeaux,
Montréal, QC H2H 2A2;
(514) 890-6169;
acatcan@cam.org

Strives to bring Christian churches together in solidarity with victims of injustice and tor-

ture. In 1997-98 325 interventions in favor of 1365 persons occurred and 70 groups were sent to 52 countries by the intervention committee. Its 1998 petition denouncing the enrollment of children in armed conflicts gathered more than 30,000 signatures. Nine times a year, ACAT sends a bulletin to its members proposing a letter in the interest of one or several persons. The bulletin is entitled *Le Cerf-volant*. Marie-Hélène Blanc, Dir.

1351. **Bureau international des droits des enfants/International Bureau for Children's Rights* (1994) (org).

1185, rue St. Mathieu St.,
Montréal, QC H3H 2P7;
(514) 932-7656;
tribunal@web.net;
www.web.net/~tribunal

Seeks to defend the rights and welfare of all children around the globe, based upon the United Nations Declaration on the Rights of the Child and the Convention on the Rights of the Child; to condemn all situations which cause suffering to children; and to intervene in high priority situations through the international Tribunal for Children's Rights. Andrée Ruffo, Pres.; Pierre Dionne, Dir. General.

1352. *Caesura* (1991) (mem).

Jarry Park., Montréal, QC.

Two metal walls each five meters high and eleven meters long separate the granite base in two. From the distance the walls seem impenetrable, but as one nears them one sees the opening, and sees through to another side of the world. As one sees through the walls the scene opens up to a small Japanese-inspired garden, bringing us into a new frame of reference of closeness to nature. "This dynamic of closing and opening is the central metaphor through which Caesura pays tribute to peace." Buried in cement underneath the walls are some 12,700 war toys, donated by children to protest military expenditures in a world of immense human needs. Some of the toys, cast in bronze—from swords to tanks—remain on the surface to remind us of the folly and futility of the warrior mentality and of stockpiling armaments. The creator of this monument to peace is Linda Covit, who dedicated it to Aung San Suu Kyi and "all the individuals who are engaged in the pursuit of peace."

1353. *Canadian Human Rights Foundation* (1967) (org).

1425 Boul. Rene Levesque West,
Suite 307,
Montréal, QC H3G 1T7;
(514) 954-0382

Dedicated to the defense of human rights through education in Canada and around the world, for the development of pluralistic societies. Offers training and education programs for non-governmental organizations, particularly an annual international three-week training session.

1354. *Cantilevers* (1994) (journ).

QPIRG-McGill University,
3647 University, 3rd floor,
Montréal H3A 2B3; or 4591 Ave.
du Parc, Montréal, QC H2V 4E4;
(514) 398-7432;
erica.cantilevers@sympatico.ca;
*lever@email.com; http://ssmu.mcgill.
ca/qpirg/cantilevers.html*

A magazine for "bridging people, ideas, and resources for peace," providing a global forum for theory and practice for the transformation of conflict into peace. In English and French. The Spring 1999 issue includes articles on self-determination, Northern Ireland, women in national struggles, Québec, identity politics, the Cree Nation, child soldiers. Eric Abitbol, Editor (in the U.S. Erin McCandless). (Ceased pub.)

Top and bottom: Caesura Sculpture by Linda Covit, Montréal Botanical Gardens. Photographs courtesy Parks, Gardens, and Green Spaces Service.

1355. *Centre de Ressources sur la Non-violence /Nonviolence Resources Center* (1988) (org).

6648 rue St-Denis, Montréal,
QC H2S 2R9; (514) 272-5012;
gordon@deev.com

Founded to expand the influence of nonviolence in Québec through "four main areas of intervention": to prevent violence and resolve conflicts, to support Native people, to advance disarmament and civilian-based defense, and to assist the cause of nonviolence internationally. The Center performs both research and public advocacy. To these ends, the Center provides a library and documentation service (over 4,500 books, 35 periodicals, numerous files), offers workshops and talks, an Education and Consultation Service, community and school conflict resolution programs, works directly with Aboriginal Rights groups, opposes the Canadian military establishment and arms proliferation, supports Peace Brigades and Internat. Project Accompaniment, and pub. a bulletin three times a year and has pub. a booklet on conciliation. "The priority of the Center is to promote nonviolence as a way to live and struggle." Contact Jacques Boucher or Gerry Pascal.

1356. *Coalition for Gun Control* (1990) (org).

1301 Sherbrooke St. E, Montréal
QC H2L 1M3; (514) 528-2358;
104360.1426@compuserve.com

Supports legislation for permits for all users, registration of all guns, total ban on assault weapons, control of ammunition sales, and other requirements. CGC is endorsed by over 350 organizations across Canada. See CGC's Toronto office.

Hiroshima Peace Bell by Katori Masahiko, Montréal Botanical Gardens. Photograph courtesy John MacLeod, Botanical Garden.

1357. *La Cloche de la Paix /The Peace Bell* (1998) (mem).

Jardin botanique/jardin japonais/Japanese Garden in the Montréal Botanical Gardens, 1401 Sherbrooke St. East.

A gift of the City of Hiroshima. The bell is decorated with doves of peace at the top, below which appear two constellations—the Big Dipper and the Southern Cross–representing the two hemispheres of the globe. The net that crowns the bell is an image of the universe, and the knots in the mesh are stars. Yata Garasu, the sacred crow, symbolizes the sun, while the rabbit suggests the moon's shadow. Designed by Katori Masahiko, cast by Negoro Musho, modeled on the one in Hiroshima. The Bell is a symbol of the city's treaty of friendship with Hiroshima, both nuclear free.

1358. *Commission scolaire de Montréal (CSDM)/French Montréal School Board* (1846) (org).

3737 rue Sherbrooke Est, Montréal, QC H1X 3B3; (514) 596-6112; *gagnonca@csdm.qc.ca*

On the tenth anniversary of the Polytechnic Massacre (of fourteen women), December 6, 1999, the Board gathered the employees into one place to draw attention to violence in the schools and society, for a morning of speakers and an afternoon of workshops. Contact Board member Robert Cadotte.

1359. *International Centre for Human Rights and Democratic Development* (1990) (org).

63, rue de Bresoles, Montréal, QC H2Y 1V7; (514) 283-6073; *ichrdd@ichrdd.ca; www.ichrdd.ca/adres_en.html*

Established by Act of the Parliament of Canada in 1988 with a mandate to support the development of democratic and human rights worldwide as defined in the Universal Declaration of Human Rights and its companion covenants. The Centre supports research, monitoring of events, strategic interventions, and financial assistance to key civil society actors and institutions in Canada and abroad, but most of its resources have focused in the Americas, Africa, and Asia on four themes: human rights, justice and the rule of law, women's rights, and indigenous peoples' rights. Dir.: Edward Broadbent (1989–96); Warren Allmand 1997–. Pub.: *Libertas* newsletter, a human rights essays series, a democratic development series, occasional papers, and other pubs. The Centre also maintains a Documentation Centre, which is connected to the Canada–U.S. Human Rights Information and Documentation Network.

1360. *Le Mur de Berlin/The Berlin Wall* (1994) (mem).

World Commerce Center/Centre de commerce mondial, 742 Square Victoria St., Montréal, QC.

A section of the Berlin Wall is located in the main enclosed pedestrian thoroughfare.

1361. **Pacijou* (1987) (org).

3584, Rue de Chambly, Montréal, QC H1W 3J9; (514) 524-6468.

An organization of educators, artists, scientists, and disarmament analysts desiring to contain violence and promote a culture of peace through research, teaching, and media. Pacijou participated in two large campaigns in Québec: collecting war toys (over 25,000) and a petition (over 150,00 signatures) asking the federal government to ban programming for children which used violence to solve problems and to encourage programming which asserted human rights, peace, international cooperation, and ecology. Contact Robert Cadotte.

1362. *Place de la Paix/Peace Square* (1994) (mem).

1182 Boulevard St.-Laurent (known as the Main), Montréal, QC

An urban park composed of an inner square

Top: **Berlin Wall, World Commerce Center, Montréal. Photograph by Robert Etchevery, courtesy John MacLeod.** *Bottom:* **Peace Square, Montréal. Photograph courtesy John MacLeod.**

of stones crisscrossed with grass, surrounded by trees, flowers, and benches. Robert Desjardins, landscape architect, designer.

1363. *Le Regroupement pour la surveillance du nucléaire /Canadian Coalition for Nuclear Responsibility* (1975) (org).

PO Box 236, Station Snowdon, Montréal, QC H3X 3T4; (514) 489-5118; *ccnr@web.net*; *http://ccnr.org*

CCNR began as a clearinghouse for all groups and individuals who sought to halt the proliferation of nuclear weapons and to work towards a nuclear-weapons and nuclear-power free world. It pressured the Canadian Government to hold a national inquiry into the risks and benefits of nuclear technology. And it "played a major role in bringing nuclear issues and non-nuclear alternatives to public attention in Canada," participating in government hearings "on a regular and continuing basis in every province and territory of Canada." Since 1980, CCNR became more a research and educational think-tank. Dr. Gordon Edwards, President.

1364. *La Réparation Monument À La Mémoire des Victimes des Génocides/ The Reparation Monument to the Victims of Genocide* (1998) (mem).

Parc Marcelin-Wilson, of De l'Acadie

Blvd. and Henri-Bourassa Blvd., Montréal.

White marble slab erected on the 83rd anniversary of the Armenian genocide of 1915.

QUÉBEC CITY, QC

1365. *Le Conseil Bahá'í du Québec/ Bahá'í Council of Québec* (1997) (org).

75 rue d'Auteuil, Québec, QC G1R 4C3; (418) 692-3955; *conseil_qc@compuserve.com*; *www.bcca.org/quebec*

The first local Bahá'í community in Québec was formed in Montréal in the 1940s. There are now 39 local Spiritual Assemblies across the province. In addition to the Council's basic services to families, it also celebrates the Day for the Elimination of Racial Discrimination (March 21), Unity in Diversity Week (second week of Nov.), and the Festival of the Covenant (Nov. 26), and it encourages local Bahá'í groups to establish and maintain peace parks and gardens. Monique Robert, Secretary.

Reparation Monument to the Victims of (Armenian) Genocide, Montréal. Photograph courtesy John MacLeod.

1366. *Le monument des jeunes pour la paix et le paix et le désarmement/ Youth Monument for Peace and Disarmament* (1990) (mem).

1401 Blvd. St. Joseph. Québec City, QC G1K 2L5; (418) 622-8383; *z11.region.quebec@ceq.qc.ca*

Built to contain the war toys given up by children. Each year, youths celebrate Earth Day and the Young Writers Competition under the theme "Youth's Responses to Sexism and Violence" at the monument. Contact Jacques Brodeur.

ST.-LAURENT, QC

1367. *Parc de la paix de St.-Laurent/St. Laurent Peace Park* (1992) (mem).

Intersection of Décarie Blvd. and rue du Collège; (514) 855-5710; *communication@ville.saint-laurent.qc.ca; www.ville.saint-laurent.qc.ca.*

Parc Baudet was rededicated as a peace park, and a monument was added later during one of the city's annual commemorations of the International Day of Peace. In 1999, a peace march began and ended in the park, followed by a concert featuring local musicians. Contact Roselyn Dallaire, Communications Service.

— Saskatchewan (SK) —

BLAINE LAKE, SK

1368. *Stone Cairn for Doukhobors* (1959) (mem).

Near the Petrofka Ferry on the North Saskatchewan River, some 70 kms north of Saskatoon. Blaine Lake is the nearest town.

The six-ton stone cairn and plaque was dedicated by the Saskatchewan government to honor Doukhobor settlers in the area. The Doukobors oppose militarism, weapons, and wars, and advocate pacifist nonviolence based upon Jesus' teachings of brotherly love. (See Castlegar, BC).

REGINA, SK

1369. **Human Justice Program* (mid-1970s) (col).

School of Human Justice, Univ. of Regina, Regina, SK S4S 0A2; *dan.devlieger@uregina.ca; www.uregina. ca/arts/human-justice/index.html*

The Bachelor of Human Justice incorporates human rights, civil liberties, social justice, law, violence, reconciliation, and related subjects. Course work and practicum. Dan de Vlieger, Dir.

SASKATOON, SK

1370. **Bahá'í Council of Saskatchewan, Manitoba, and Northwestern Ontario* (1997) (org).

405 Empress St., Saskatoon, SK S7K 0X9; (306) 652-0816; *snoman@sk.sympatico.ca*

The first local Spiritual Assembly in the region was established in Winnipeg, MN, in 1942. The mission of the Bahá'ís is to serve humanity. Pub. *Flashpoints*, a bi-monthly newsletter. Contact Linda McRae.

1371. **Doukhobor Society of Saskatoon Community Centre* (1955) (org).

525 Avenue I South, Saskatoon, SASK S7M 1Y6.

The major Doukhobor organization in Saskatchewan. Its members maintain a community center in the city. Annual Doukhobor Peace Day in June; annual Bread-baking in July, which supports peace-oriented activities; and many other activities. Pub. a newsletter. William Woykin, Chair (Box 110, Langham, SOK 2LO; 306-283-4770).

1372. *International Peace Plaza* (1998) (mem).

In Rotary Park on the river bank, Sasketoon.

The form of the plaza was abstracted from the Rotary wheel symbol; the floor was inlaid with engraved pavers sponsored by the public; all trees and shrubs were sponsored by the public and planted by volunteers. The focal point of

the plaza is a 12 foot tall Peace Pole on a stone base and at top an eternal flame. The pole is engraved with the message "May Peace Prevail on Earth" in English, French, Japanese, and Cree. Designed by Blair Sivertson and constructed by Doug Bentham, the Pole is original in design but was intended to connect with the international peace pole movement endorsed by the United Nations. On August 23, 1998, in a candlelight ceremony at the Pole called "Prayers for Peace" 400 people lowered their prayers into a time capsule. The park was also the site of the first annual Peace Picnic for school children in celebration of the International Day of Peace on September 15. The Park and Pole cost approximately $600,000.

VERIGIN, SK

1373. *National Doukhobor Heritage Village Museum* (1980) (mus).

Box 99, Verigin, S0A 4H0, on Highway

Top: International Peace Plaza, Rotary Park, Saskatoon. Photograph courtesy City of Saskatoon, Carol Purich. *Bottom:* National Doukhobor Heritage Museum, Verigin. Photograph courtesy Koozma Tarasoff.

5 between Canora and Kamsack, east of Saskatoon, north of Yorkton.

Originating in Russia in the eighteenth century ("Doukhobortsi" meaning "Spirit Wrestlers"), by the end of the nineteenth century the communal-living Doukhobors had rejected killing and military service. On June 29, 1895, several thousand Doukhobors destroyed their weapons to demonstrate their commitment to the Commandment "Thou shalt not kill" and their total rejection of violence. Russian response was terrible, but eventually, after the intercession of Leo Tolstoy and the Quakers, 7,500 of their group were allowed to immigrate to Canada. The Heritage Village, now a Provincial Heritage Building, contains: 1) the *Doukhobour Prayer Home* (1917), which served as the residence of the two Doukhobour leaders, Peter V. Verigin and his son Peter P. Verigin, 2) a Museum full of artifacts, 3) a statue of Tolstoy, 4) various buildings typical of a Doukhobor village in the late nineteenth and early twentieth centuries.

1374. *Leo Tolstoy Statue* (1987) (mem).

At the Doukhobor Heritage Village in Verigin, in south-eastern part of the province near the Manitoba border on No. 5 Highway.

Tolstoy helped the Doukhobors emigrate from Russia in 1899 after the Czarist government persecuted them for burning their firearms and declaring themselves pacifists. Sculptor: Yuri L. Chernov. (Identical to statue in British Columbia).

Leo Tolstoy Statue, Verigin. Photograph courtesy Koozma Tarasoff.

Mexico and United States Border

1375. *Chamizal National Memorial* (1963) (mem, mus).

Located in south-central El Paso, just north of the Rio Grande and immediately adjacent to the international boundary.

A memorial to the peaceful settlement of a long-standing dispute over the location of the

Chamizal National Memorial, between El Paso and Ciudad Juárez. Photograph courtesy Chamizal National Memorial museum.

international boundary between El Paso, Texas, and Ciudad Juárez in Chihuahua. A museum explains the history of the U.S.–Mexico border; an art gallery displays works from around the world; diverse festivals are held throughout the year; an 18-foot-high, 120-foot-long mural depicts the blending of cultures of the U.S. and Mexico; a 500-seat indoor theater performs most nights of the year (drama, dance, opera, ballet).

1376. *Friendship Monument* (1936) (mem).

On the Mexico-Laredo Highway 56 miles from Mexico City.

The monument was given to Mexico by U.S. citizens residing in Mexico as part of the open-ing of the Mexico-Laredo Highway. The inscription reads in part: "May it serve always as a path of mutual respect and as an indissoluble bond of peace between the peoples of two neighbor nations." (Baber, *Peace Symbols*).

1377. *Pan-American Friendship Symbol* (1935) (mem).

On the International Bridge over the Rio Grande connecting Laredo, Texas, with Nueva Laredo, Mexico.

In the center of the 11-foot marker is a map of North and South America with political divisions and their flags in color. An inscription reads: "One For All, All For One." (Baber, *Peace Symbols*).

Mexico

According to the World Peace Prayer Society, Mexico had 26 Peace Poles as of October 29, 1998 (Chiapas: 12; Oaxaca: 2; Chetumal: 3; Mexico City: 6; Acapulco: 1; Cancun: 3). The *1998 Sister Cities International Directory* lists 123 Sister Cities.

Servicio Paz y Justicia (SERPAJ), the leading network of peace organizations in Latin America, has chapters in 10 countries, including ones in Cuernavaca (Morelos) and Tabasco (Tabasco). These and other chapters have recently received grants from the Muste Memorial Institute.

—— *Chihuahua* ——

Ciudad Juárez

1378. *Casa Tabor/Tabor House* (1973) (org).

Fco Mena 6620, Colonia Insurgentis, Ciudad Juárez; mailing address: Tabor House, PO Box 1482, El Paso, TX 79948. Contact Betty Campbell, RSM, Peter Hende, O. Carm.

Focuses on solidarity with and education about Latin America. Opposes wars and U.S. policies which contribute to war-making. Started in Washington, DC, moved to San Antonio in 1983, and to Juarez in 1995.

—— *Federal District (Mexico, D. F., Mexico City)* ——

1379. *Acción de los Christianos para la Abolición de la Tortura/Action by*

Christians for the Abolition of Torture (ACAT) (1992) (org).

Huatusco 21-502, Roma Sur 06760, México, D.F.; (52-5) 264-6515; acat@datasys.com.mx

ACAT-Mexico is a member of International Federation of ACAT based in Paris and is part of the Mexican National Human Rights NGOs Network "Todos los derechos para todos." Juan Antonio Vega Baez, Director.

1380. *Centro de Derechos Humanos Miguel Agustin Pro Juarez, A.C./ Center for Human Rights* (org).

Serapio Rendon 57-B, Col. San Rafael, CP 06470, Mexico D.F.; (525) 566 7854, 546 8217; prodh@laneta.apc.org; http://mixcoac.uia.mx/~prodh/default.htm

Erica Schommer, Dir.

1381. *Comisión Mexicana de Defensa y Promoción de los Derechos Humanos, A. C./Mexican Commission for the Defense and Protection of Human Rights (CMDPDH)* (1989) (org).

Tehuantepec 155, Colonia Roma Sur, CP 06760 Mexico, D.F.; (525) 584-9116; cmdpdh@laneta.apc.org; www.laneta.apc.org/cmdpdh

The non-governmental Commission defends fundamental rights in Mexico and the world—to life, personal integrity, liberty, and a just legal system.

Mariclaire Acosta, President.

1382. *Médicos Mexicanos para la Prevención de la Guerra Nuclear, A.C./Mexican Physicians for the _Prevention of Nuclear War* (1981) (org).

Plaza San Pablo No. 13, Centro. 06090 México, D.F.; 542 01-52 or 542 00 77;

Instituto Nat.de Neurologia, Insurgentes Sur No. 3877, 14410 México, D.F.; Mariano Escobedo No. 353-A-601, 11570 México.

Affil. of International Physicians for the Prevention of Nuclear War (1985 Nobel Peace Prize). Cultivates respect for nature, ecology, human dignity, and the culture of Bioethics. President, Prof. Manuel Velasco-Suárez, M.D., F.A.C.S., Framboyanes #389, Col. Bosques de las Lomas, Delegaciòn Miguel Hidalgo, 11700 México, D.F.

1383. *Partido Verde Ecologista (PVEM)/ Mexican Ecological Green Party* (org).

Medicina # 74, Colonia Copilco C.P. 04360, Mexico, D.F.; 659-82-42; *pve@infosel.net.mx*; *www.pvem.org.mx*

A political organization interested in preserving nature and environment and in establishing authentic Mexican cultural values of respect for all living things—humans, animals, plants. Perceiving the environment as a whole system and adhering to a concept of solidarity with all the species that live on Earth, PVEM seeks to achieve a harmonic evolution for all living forms. "The basic principles of the PVEM are Love, Justice, and Freedom for all living beings on Earth." As a national political party, PVEM is represented in both legislative chambers, local chambers, assemblies, and municipalities. Pub. *Tucan* on the web. Lic. Jorge González Torres, Pres. (Federation of Green Parties of the Americas can be reached by this address).

1384. *Physicians Peace Park (Medicos Por La Paz)* (1991) (mem park).

Five acres in Mexico City situated in one of its most significant places—where the Treaty of Tlatelolco for the Prohibition of Nuclear Weapons in Latin America was signed in 1963. Among the gardens and corridors are an agora for meetings and expositions, *sculptures representing the five continents*, a great *arch with bell*, a *monument of eleven statues* climbing to reach a New Sun of Hope, and many *commemorative plaques* from international organizations. It was created by the Mexican affiliate of the International Physicians for the Prevention of Nuclear War (1985 Nobel Peace Prize winner). Manuel Velasco-Suárez, M.D.

Physicians Peace Park, Mexico City. Photograph courtesy Dr. Manuel Velasco-Suárez.

Physicians Peace Park, Mexico City. Photograph courtesy Dr. Manuel Velasco-Suárez.

Jalisco — *Morelos*

PUERTO VALLARTA

1385. *Plaza of Peace and Friendship/ Rotary Peace Park, with Peace Plaque and Pole* (1997) (mem).

Iturbide St., next to the main cathedral and City Hall, Puerto Vallarta.

Park, Pole, and Plaque celebrate vision of goodwill shared by Rotary Clubs and the Sister Cities Association. Puerto Vallarta is the first Rotary Peace City in Mexico. The message "Puerto Vallarta Ciudad de Paz Amistad y Buena Voluntad" (Puerto Vallarta, City of Peace, Friendship, and Goodwill) rests in front of the *Peace Pole* in a park of trees, shrubs, and flowers. Project headed by Jeffrey A. Reiss, Special Ambassador, Rotary International Peace Cities Project.

CUERNAVACA

1385a. **Servicio Paz y Justicia/ Peace and Justice Service* (1995) (org).

Apartado Postal 4-80,
CP 62431 Cuernavaca, Morelos;
(52-73) 113-640;
serpajc@cuer.laneta.apc.org.

The Cuernavaca chapter organizes the Non-violent Reflection and Action program of research, workshops, and vigils on militarism in Mexico and nonviolent response. It also was a leader in the Acteal campaign, commemorating the first anniversary of the 1997 massacre of civilian members of a nonviolent religious community in Acteal, Chiapas. Contact Pietro Ameglio Patella.

Plaza of Peace and Friendship, Rotary Peace Park, Puerto Vallarta. Photograph courtesy Jeffrey Reiss.

4679. Businessmen and university authorities are also involved. Sponsors an essay contest on peace. Two new classes promote peace—Human Rights (Derechos Humanos) and Educating for Peace (Educación para la Paz)—, part of the elective courses for 5th and 6th semesters in the high school. Contact Rodolfo Escobebo, High School Coordinator (52-8) 340-1630. Also, on its 30th birthday, September 8, 1999, the university presented a panel of Nobel Peace Prize winners. Contact: Irma Deyanira González (52-8) 338-5050 ext. 341.

—— *Nuevo León* ——

MONTERREY

1386. **Rearme Moral/Moral Rearmament* (1998) (org).

Campus Profesional, Av. Ignacio Morones Prieto 4500 Pte, 66238 San Pedro Garza Garcia, University of Monterrey/Universidad de Monterrey, NL; (52) (8) 338-5050, ext. 112; *bdiaz@udem.edu.mx*

The Center for Moral Rearmament is at the university, headed by Bertha Diaz. Students participate, contact Fernando Reiter (52-8) 303-

—— *Tabasco* ——

TABASCO

1386a. **Servicio Paz y Justicia/Peace and Justice Service* (1996) (org).

Calle 2 de Abril, No. 149, Col. Centro, Villahermosa, CP 86030 Mexico; *serpatab@laneta.apc.org*. Contact Cristina Patiño Garcia.

This chapter of SERPAJ gives workshops on civil resistance and active nonviolence, human rights, and agrarian, environmental, and indigenous rights, especially for farmers.

WORKS CITED

Andregg, Michael. *On the Causes of War.* Ground Zero MN: St. Paul, MN. 1999.

Baber, Zonia. *Peace Symbols.* N.p.: Women's International League for Peace and Freedom, 1948.

Bennett, James R. "Centers, Museums, and Public Memorials for Nonviolent Peacemaking in the US: A Visitors' Guide." *Peacework* (May 1999) 14–15.

____. *Control of Information in the United States: An Annotated Bibliography* Meckler, 1987.

____. *Control of the Media in the United States: An Annotated Bibliography.* Garland, 1992.

____. "From Patriotism to Peace: The Humanization of War Memorials." *The Humanist* (Sept./Oct. 1998) 5–9.

____. *Grassroots Militarism.* Eureka Springs, AR: Center on War & the Child, 1989.

____. "Here's To Peace and Peacemakers: Monuments and Memorials in the U.S. and Canada." *The Nonviolent Activist* 15.3 (July–August 1998), 11–13.

____. *Political Prisoners and Trials: A Worldwide Annotated Bibliography, 1900–1993.* McFarland, 1995.

Blum, Deborah. *The Monkey Wars.* New York: Oxford University Press, 1994.

Bondurant, Joan. *Conquest of Violence: The Gandhian Philosophy of Conflict.* Princeton, NJ: Princeton University Press, 1958, 1988.

Boyle, Francis. *Defending Civil Resistance Under International Law.* Dobbs Ferry, NY: International, 1988.

Brown, Michael, and Richard Rosecrance, eds.

Costs of Conflict: Prevention and Cure in the Global Arena. Lanham, MD: Rowman and Littlefield, 1999.

Chappell, David, ed. *Buddhist Peacework: Creating Cultures of Peace.* Boston: Wisdom, 1999.

Chomsky, Noam. *The New Military Humanism.* Monroe, ME: Common Courage, 1999.

____. "World Order and Its Rules." *Z Magazine* (Oct. 1999), 22–25.

Coates, Ken. "What Human Rights Really Mean." *Peace Review* 11.4 (1999) 603–07.

Dauncey, Guy. *Earthfuture: Stories from a Sustainable World.* Blaine, WA/Gabriola Island, BC: New Society, 1999.

Duffy, Terence. "Civic Zones of Peace." *Peace Review* 9.2 (1997), 199–205.

Gorsevski, Ellen. "Nonviolent Theory on Communication: The Implications for Theorizing a Nonviolent Rhetoric." *Peace and Change* 24.4 (Oct. 1999) 445–473.

Grossman, Karl. "Waging War in Space." Presentation, COPRED/PSA Conference, University of Texas, Austin, April 1, 2000.

Herr, Robert, and Judy Herr. *Transforming Violence: Linking Local and Global Peacemaking.* Scottsdale, PA: Herald, 1998.

Kaplan, Amy, and Donald Pease, eds. *Cultures of United States Imperialism.* Durham, NC: Duke University Press, 1993.

MacLeod, John. "A Short History of Places in Canada Dedicated to Peace: 1920–1995." Paper presented at the Canadian Society of Landscape Architects, March 1998. (Accessible on the internet at: *http://www.apa.*

umontreal.ca/gadrat/formcont/seminaire98/
conferences/).

Nelson-Pallmeyer, Jack. *War Against the Poor: Low Intensity Conflict and Christian Faith.* Maryknoll, NY: Orbis, 1989.

Pinches, Charles, and Jay McDaniel, eds. *Good News for Animals? Christian Approaches to Animal Well-Being.* Maryknoll, NY: Orbis, 1993.

Prados, John. *Presidents' Secret Wars: CIA and Pentagon Covert Operations from World War II Through the Persian Gulf.* Chicago: Ivan Dee, 1996.

Quinn, Daniel. *Ishmael.* New York: Bantam-Turner, 1992.

Renner, Michael. "How the Prospects for World Peace Have Grown Brighter." *World Watch* (Jan./Feb. 2000) 37–39.

Runyan, Curtis. "Action on the Front Lines." *World Watch* (Nov./Dec. 1999), 12–21.

Sharp, Gene. "198 Methods of Nonviolent Action," in *A Peace Reader*, ed. Joseph Fahey and Richard Armstrong. Mahwah, NJ: Paulist, 1972.

Tirman, John. "How We ended the Cold War." *Nation* (Nov. 1, 1999) 13–21.

Treverton, Gregory. *Covert Action: The Limits of Intervention in the Postwar World.* New York: Basic, 1987.

True, Michael. "Building a Culture of Peace One Step at a Time." *Active for Justice* 21.1 (Jan. 2000) 5.

____. "Nonviolent Action & International Law." *Fellowship* 66.3–4 (March–April) 12–13.

"The United Nations at Fifty: A Force for the Future." *The Defense Monitor* (January 1996), 8pp.

Van den Dungen, Peter. "Peace Museums." *World Encyclopedia of Peace.* Vol. 2. Ed. Ervin Laszlo and Jong Youl Yoo. Oxford/New York: Pergamon, 1986. pp. 234–243.

____. "Peaceful Future." *Museums Journal* (January 1997), 23.

____. "A Time for War, a Time for Peace." *Museums Journal* (July 1993), 20–21.

Van den Dungen, Peter, and Ursula-Maria Ruser, eds. *Peace Museums Worldwide.* Geneva: United Nations Publications on Peace, League of Nations Archives, Department of Peace Studies, University of Bradford, 1998.

Wink, Walter. *When the Powers Fall: Reconciliation in the Healing of Nations.* Minneapolis: Augsburg Fortress, 1998.

World Peace Prayer Society. *May Peace Prevail on Earth.* New York: World Peace Prayer Society, n.d.

Zinn, Howard. "The Heroes Around Us." *The Progressive* (June 2000).

INDEX

Few entries have been made for the basic categories of peace, nonviolence, justice, violence, war, etc., since all of these groups and individuals oppose war, violence, and militarism, and advocate peace and justice and, most of them, nonviolence. The exceptions are the organizations whose sole or primary function is to deal with, for example, violence. Abbreviations: U: University, SU: State University, C: College, SC: State College, CC: Community College, Sem: Seminary. Numbers refer to entries, not pages. A p. designation refers to a page number in the introductory material.